# 莊子

# CHUANG TZU

## The Complete Bilingual Edition

Traditional Chinese · English

## CHUANG TZU

*Chuang Tzu: The Complete Bilingual Edition*



This edition features:
  • Traditional Chinese text
  • English translation by Herbert Allen Giles
Original arrangement, presentation, and design by Jade Ink Press



Published by Jade Ink Press

First Edition: March 2026
Printed in the United States of America

# CONTENTS

# ABOUT THIS EDITION

Welcome to Chuang Tzu: The Complete Bilingual Edition. This book presents the complete works of Chuang Tzu (Zhuangzi) in Traditional Chinese and Herbert Allen Giles's English translation. Whether you're discovering Chuang Tzu for the first time or returning to explore Taoist philosophy more deeply, this edition lets you read and compare across languages.

The two-page spread places Traditional Chinese on the left and English on the right. Each chapter begins at the same position on both pages, making it easy to navigate between languages—though within chapters, sentences don't always line up one-to-one as meaning flows differently across Chinese and English.

Chuang Tzu (莊周) lived in the 4th century BCE, during China's Warring States period. He once served as a minor official managing a lacquer garden in Meng, but he's remembered for refusing higher office. When the King of Chu sent envoys with gifts to make him prime minister, Chuang Tzu compared the honor to a fattened ox decorated for sacrifice: impressive until the moment of slaughter. He preferred, he said, to drag his tail in the mud like a living turtle rather than have his bones venerated in a temple. He never took office again.

His writings—over 80,000 characters in the received text—are largely parables and allegories. He often mocked Confucians and Mohists, not out of spite but to shake loose rigid thinking. His philosophy traces back to Lao Tzu, but Chuang Tzu's voice is wilder, funnier, more unpredictable. Even scholars of his own time struggled to argue back. His words are playful, strange, and free-roaming, shaped to please himself rather than serve rulers or institutions.

We chose Giles's translation because it's both reliable and readable. Giles was among the first Western scholars to work seriously with Classical Chinese, and his English captures Chuang Tzu's wit and philosophical depth without flattening it into bland abstraction. Giles's original translation used the Wade-Giles romanization system with tone marks and Victorian-era ligatures; we've removed the diacritics and modernized the typography for easier reading.

This edition presents the core text without added commentary, so you can meet Chuang Tzu's butterflies, fish, and wandering sages directly. The side-by-side format lets you move between languages, notice how ideas shift in translation, and hear the rhythm of both the Chinese and the English.

We hope this bilingual edition offers clarity and delight: clarity in reading, and delight in encountering a philosophy of freedom that still feels fresh after 2,300 years.

# 莊子

## CHUANG TZU

# 逍遙遊第一

北冥有魚，其名為鯤。鯤之大，不知其幾千里也。化而為鳥，其名為鵬。鵬之背，不知其幾千里也；怒而飛，其翼若垂天之雲。是鳥也，海運則將徙於南冥。南冥者，天池也。齊諧者，志怪者也。諧之言曰：「鵬之徙於南冥也，水擊三千里，搏扶搖而上者九萬里，去以六月息者也。」野馬也，塵埃也，生物之以息相吹也。天之蒼蒼，其正色邪？其遠而無所至極邪？其視下也，亦若是則已矣。且夫水之積也不厚，則其負大舟也無力。覆杯水於坳堂之上，則芥為之舟；置杯焉則膠，水淺而舟大也。風之積也不厚，則其負大翼也無力。故九萬里，則風斯在下矣，而後乃今培風；背負青天而莫之夭閼者，而後乃今將圖南。蜩與學鳩笑之曰：「我決起而飛，槍榆枋而止，時則不至而控於地而已矣，奚以之九萬里而南為？」適莽蒼者，三餐而反，腹猶果然；適百里者，宿舂糧；適千里者，三月聚糧。之二蟲又何知！小知不及大知，小年不及大年。奚以知其然也？朝菌不知晦朔，蟪蛄不知春

# CHAPTER I

## TRANSCENDENTAL BLISS

In the northern ocean there is a fish, called the Leviathan, many thousand li in size. This leviathan changes into a bird, called the Rukh, whose back is many thousand li in breadth. With a mighty effort it rises, and its wings obscure the sky like clouds.

At the equinox, this bird prepares to start for the southern ocean, the Celestial Lake. And in the Record of Marvels we read that when the rukh flies southwards, the water is smitten for a space of three thousand li around, while the bird itself mounts upon a typhoon to a height of ninety thousand li, for a flight of six months' duration.

Just so are the motes in a sunbeam blown aloft by God. For whether the blue of the sky is its real colour, or only the result of distance without end, the effect to the bird looking down would be just the same as to the motes.

If there is not sufficient depth, water will not float large ships. Upset a cupful into a small hole, and a mustard-seed will be your boat. Try to float the cup, and it will stick, from the disproportion between water and vessel.

So with air. If there is not a sufficient depth, it cannot support large birds. And for this bird a depth of ninety thousand li is necessary; and then, with nothing save the clear sky above, and no obstacle in the way, it starts upon its journey to the south.

A cicada laughed, and said to a young dove, "Now, when I fly with all my might, 'tis as much as I can do to get from tree to tree. And sometimes I do not reach, but fall to the ground midway. What then can be the use of going up ninety thousand li in order to start for the south?"

He who goes to Mang-ts'ang, taking three meals with him, comes back with his stomach as full as when he started. But he who travels a hundred li must grind flour enough for a night's halt. And he who travels a thousand li must supply himself with provisions for three months. Those two little creatures,—what should they know? Small knowledge has not the compass of great knowledge any more than a short year has the length of a long year.

How can we tell that this is so? The mushroom of a morning knows

秋，此小年也。楚之南有冥靈者，以五百歲為春，五百歲為秋；上古有大椿者，以八千歲為春，八千歲為秋。此大年也。而彭祖乃今以久特聞，眾人匹之，不亦悲乎！湯之問棘也是已。窮髮之北有冥海者，天池也。有魚焉，其廣數千里，未有知其脩者，其名為鯤。有鳥焉，其名為鵬，背若泰山，翼若垂天之雲，摶扶搖羊角而上者九萬里，絕雲氣，負青天，然後圖南，且適南冥也。斥鴳笑之曰：「彼且奚適也？我騰躍而上，不過數仞而下，翱翔蓬蒿之間，此亦飛之至也，而彼且奚適也？」此小大之辯也。故夫知效一官，行比一鄉，德合一君，而徵一國者，其自視也亦若此矣。而宋榮子猶然笑之。且舉世而譽之而不加勸，舉世而非之而不加沮，定乎內外之分，辯乎榮辱之竟，斯已矣。彼其於世，未數數然也。雖然，猶有未樹也。夫列子御風而行，泠然善也，旬有五日而反。彼於致福者，未數數然也。此雖免乎行，猶有所待者也。若夫乘天地之正，而御六氣之辯，以遊無窮者，彼且惡乎待哉！故曰：至人無己，神人無功，聖人無名。

not the alternation of day and night. The chrysalis knows not the alternation of spring and autumn. Theirs are short years.

But in the State of Ch'u there is a tortoise whose spring and autumn are each of five hundred years' duration. And in former days there was a large tree which had a spring and autumn each of eight thousand years' duration. Yet, P'eng Tsu is still, alas! an object of envy to all.

It was on this very subject that the Emperor T'ang spoke to Chi, as follows:—"At the barren north there is a great sea, the Celestial Lake. In it there is a fish, several thousand li in breadth, and I know not how many in length. It is called the Leviathan. There is also a bird, called the Rukh, with a back like Mount T'ai, and wings like clouds across the sky. Upon a typhoon it soars up to a height of ninety thousand li, beyond the clouds and atmosphere, with only the clear sky above it. And then it directs its flight towards the south pole.

"A quail laughed, and said: Pray, what may that creature be going to do? I rise but a few yards in the air, and settle again after flying around among the reeds. That is the most I can manage. Now, where ever can this creature be going to?"

Such, indeed, is the difference between small and great. Take, for instance, a man who creditably fills some small office, or who is a pattern of virtue in his neighbourhood, or who influences his prince to right government of the State,—his opinion of himself will be much the same as that quail's. The philosopher Yung laughs at such a one. He, if the whole world flattered him, would not be affected thereby, nor if the whole world blamed him would he lose his faith in himself. For Yung can distinguish between the intrinsic and the extrinsic, between honour and shame,—and such men are rare in their generation. But even he has not established himself.

There was Lieh Tzu again. He could ride upon the wind, and travel whithersoever he wished, staying away as long as fifteen days. Among mortals who attain happiness, such a man is rare. Yet although Lieh Tzu was able to dispense with walking, he was still dependent upon something.

But had he been charioted upon the eternal fitness of Heaven and Earth, driving before him the elements as his team while roaming through the realms of For-Ever,—upon what, then, would he have had to depend?

堯讓天下於許由，曰：「日月出矣而爝火不息，其於光也，不亦難乎！時雨降矣而猶浸灌，其於澤也，不亦勞乎！夫子立而天下治，而我猶尸之，吾自視缺然。請致天下。」許由曰：「子治天下，天下既已治也。而我猶代子，吾將為名乎？名者，實之賓也，吾將為賓乎？鷦鷯巢於深林，不過一枝；偃鼠飲河，不過滿腹。歸休乎君，予無所用天下為！庖人雖不治庖，尸祝不越樽俎而代之矣。」

肩吾問於連叔曰：「吾聞言於接輿，大而無當，往而不返。吾驚怖其言，猶河漢而無極也，大有徑庭，不近人情焉。」連叔曰：「其言謂何哉？」曰：「藐姑射之山，有神人居焉，肌膚若冰雪，淖約若處子。不食五穀，吸風飲露。乘雲氣，御飛龍，而遊乎四海之外。其神凝，使

Thus it has been said, "The perfect man ignores self; the divine man ignores action; the true Sage ignores reputation."

The Emperor Yao wished to abdicate in favour of Hsu Yu, saying, "If, when the sun and moon are shining, you persist in lighting a torch, is not that a misapplication of fire? If, when the rainy season is at its height, you still continue to water the ground, is not this a waste of labour? Now, sir, do you assume the reins of government, and the empire will be at peace. I am but a dead body, conscious of my own deficiency. I beg you will ascend the throne."

"Ever since you, sire, have directed the administration," replied Hsu Yu, "the empire has enjoyed tranquillity. Supposing, therefore, that I were to take your place now, should I gain any reputation thereby? Besides, reputation is but the shadow of reality; and should I trouble myself about the shadow? The tit, building its nest in the mighty forest, occupies but a single twig. The tapir slakes its thirst from the river, but drinks enough only to fill its belly. To you, sire, belongs the reputation: the empire has no need for me. If a cook is unable to dress his funeral sacrifices, the boy who impersonates the corpse may not step over the wines and meats and do it for him."

Chien Wu said to Lien Shu, "I heard Chieh Yu utter something unjustifiably extravagant and without either rhyme or reason.

I was greatly startled at what he said, for it seemed to me boundless as the Milky Way, though very improbable and removed from the experiences of mortals."

"What was it?" asked Lien Shu.

"He declared," replied Chien Wu, "that on the Miao-ku-she mountain there lives a divine man whose flesh is like ice or snow, whose demeanour is that of a virgin, who eats no fruit of the earth, but lives on air and dew, and who, riding on clouds with flying dragons for his team, roams beyond the limits of mortality. This being is absolutely inert. Yet he wards off corruption from all things, and causes the crops to thrive. Now I call that nonsense, and do not believe it."

"Well," answered Lien Shu, "you don't ask a blind man's opinion of a picture, nor do you invite a deaf man to a concert. And blindness and deafness are not physical only. There is blindness and deafness of the mind, diseases from which I fear you yourself are suffering. The good influence

物不疵癘而年穀熟。吾以是狂而不信也。」連叔曰：「然，瞽者無以與乎文章之觀，聾者無以與乎鐘鼓之聲。豈唯形骸有聾盲哉？夫知亦有之。是其言也，猶時女也。之人也，之德也，將旁礡萬物以為一世蘄乎亂，孰弊弊焉以天下為事！之人也，物莫之傷，大浸稽天而不溺，大旱金石流土山焦而不熱。是其塵垢秕糠，將猶陶鑄堯舜者也，孰肯以物為事！」

宋人資章甫而適越，越人斷髮文身，無所用之。堯治天下之民，平海內之政。往見四子藐姑射之山，汾水之陽，窅然喪其天下焉。

惠子謂莊子曰：「魏王貽我大瓠之種，我樹之成而實五石。以盛水漿，其堅不能自舉也。剖之以為瓢，則瓠落無所容。非不呺然大也，吾為其無用而掊之。」莊子曰：「夫子固拙於用大矣。宋人有善為不龜手之藥者，世世以洴澼

of that man fills all creation. Yet because a paltry generation cries for reform, you would have him condescend to the details of an empire!

"Objective existences cannot harm him. In a flood which reached to the sky, he would not be drowned. In a drought, though metals ran liquid and mountains were scorched up, he would not be hot. Out of his very dust and siftings you might fashion two such men as Yao and Shun. And you would have him occupy himself with objectives!"

A man of the Sung State carried some sacrificial caps into the Yueh State, for sale. But the men of Yueh used to cut off their hair and paint their bodies, so that they had no use for such things. And so, when the Emperor Yao, the ruler of all under heaven and pacificator of all within the shores of ocean, paid a visit to the four sages of the Miao-ku-she mountain, on returning to his capital at Fen-yang, the empire existed for him no more.

Hui Tzu said to Chuang Tzu, "The Prince of Wei gave me a seed of a large-sized kind of gourd. I planted it, and it bore a fruit as big as a five-bushel measure. Now had I used this for holding liquids, it would have been too heavy to lift; and had I cut it in half for ladles, the ladles would have been ill adapted for such purpose. It was uselessly large, so I broke it up."

"Sir," replied Chuang Tzu, "it was rather you who did not know how to use large things. There was a man of Sung who had a recipe for salve for chapped hands, his family having been silk-washers for generations. Well, a stranger who had heard of it, came and offered him 100 oz. of silver for this recipe; whereupon he called together his clansmen and said, 'We have never made much money by silk-washing. Now, we can make 100 oz. in a single day. Let the stranger have the recipe.'

"So the stranger got it, and went and informed the Prince of Wu who was just then at war with the Yueh State. Accordingly, the Prince used it in a naval battle fought at the beginning of winter with the Yueh State, the result being that the latter was totally defeated. The stranger was rewarded with territory and a title. Thus, while the efficacy of the salve to cure chapped hands was in both cases the same, its application was different. Here, it secured a title; there, a capacity for washing silk.

"Now as to your five-bushel gourd, why did you not make a boat of it, and float about over river and lake? You could not then have complained of

絖為事。客聞之，請買其方百金。聚族而謀曰：『我世世為洴澼絖，不過數金；今一朝而鬻技百金，請與之。』客得之，以說吳王。越有難，吳王使之將。冬，與越人水戰，大敗越人，裂地而封之。能不龜手，一也；或以封，或不免於洴澼絖，則所用之異也。今子有五石之瓠，何不慮以為大樽而浮乎江湖，而憂其瓠落無所容？則夫子猶有蓬之心也夫！」

惠子謂莊子曰：「吾有大樹，人謂之樗。其大本擁腫而不中繩墨，其小枝卷曲而不中規矩。立之塗，匠者不顧。今子之言，大而無用，眾所同去也。」莊子曰：「子獨不見狸狌乎？卑身而伏，以候敖者；東西跳梁，不避高下；中於機辟，死於罔罟。今夫斄牛，其大若垂天之雲。此能為大矣，而不能執鼠。今子有大樹，患其無用，何不樹之於無何有之鄉，廣莫之野，彷徨乎無為其側，逍遙乎寢臥其下。不夭斤斧，物無害者，無所可用，安所困苦哉！」

its not holding anything! But I fear you are rather woolly inside."

Hui Tzu said to Chuang Tzu, "Sir, I have a large tree, of a worthless kind. Its trunk is so irregular and knotty that it cannot be measured out for planks; while its branches are so twisted as to admit of no geometrical subdivision whatever. It stands by the roadside, but no carpenter will look at it. And your words, sir, are like that tree;—big and useless, not wanted by anybody."

"Sir," rejoined Chuang Tzu, "have you never seen a wild cat, crouching down in wait for its prey? Right and left it springs from bough to bough, high and low alike,—until perchance it gets caught in a trap or dies in a snare. On the other hand, there is the yak with its great huge body. It is big enough in all conscience, but it cannot catch mice.

"Now if you have a big tree and are at a loss what to do with it, why not plant it in the domain of non-existence, whither you might betake yourself to inaction by its side, to blissful repose beneath its shade?

There it would be safe from the axe and from all other injury; for being of no use to others, itself would be free from harm."

# 齊物論第二

南郭子綦隱机而坐，仰天而噓，荅焉似喪其耦。顏成子游立侍乎前，曰：「何居乎？形固可使如槁木，而心固可使如死灰乎？今之隱机者，非昔之隱机者也？」子綦曰：「偃，不亦善乎，而問之也！今者吾喪我，汝知之乎？女聞人籟而未聞地籟，女聞地籟而未聞天籟夫！」子游曰：「敢問其方。」子綦曰：「夫大塊噫氣，其名為風。是唯無作，作則萬竅怒呺。而獨不聞之翏翏乎？山林之畏佳，大木百圍之竅穴，似鼻，似口，似耳，似枅，似圈，似臼，似洼者，似污者；激者、謞者、叱者、吸者、叫者、譹者、宎者、咬者，前者唱于而隨者唱喁。泠風則小和，飄風則大和，厲風濟則眾竅為虛。而獨不見之調調，之刀刀乎？」子游曰：「地籟則眾竅是已，人籟則比竹是已，敢問天籟。」子綦曰：「夫吹萬不同，而使其自已也。咸其自取，怒者其誰邪？」

大知閑閑，小知間間；大言炎炎，小言詹詹。其寐也魂交，其覺也形開。與接為構，日以心鬥。縵者、窖者、密者。小恐惴惴，大恐縵縵。其

# CHAPTER II

## The Identity of Contraries

Tzu Ch'i of Nan-kuo sat leaning on a table. Looking up to heaven, he sighed and became absent, as though soul and body had parted.

Yen Ch'eng Tzu Yu, who was standing by him, exclaimed, "What are you thinking about that your body should become thus like dry wood, your mind like dead ashes? Surely the man now leaning on the table is not he who was here just now."

"My friend," replied Tzu Ch'i, "your question is apposite. To-day I have buried myself.... Do you understand?... Ah! perhaps you only know the music of Man, and not that of Earth. Or even if you have heard the music of Earth, you have not heard the music of Heaven."

"Pray explain," said Tzu Yu.

"The breath of the universe," continued Tzu Ch'i, "is called wind. At times, it is inactive. But when active, every aperture resounds to the blast. Have you never listened to its growing roar?

"Caves and dells of hill and forest, hollows in huge trees of many a span in girth;—these are like nostrils, like mouths, like ears, like beam-sockets, like goblets, like mortars, like ditches, like bogs. And the wind goes rushing through them, sniffing, snoring, singing, soughing, puffing, purling, whistling, whirring, now shrilly treble, now deeply bass, now soft, now loud; until, with a lull, silence reigns supreme. Have you never witnessed among the trees such a disturbance as this?"

"Well, then," enquired Tzu Yu, "since the music of earth consists of nothing more than holes, and the music of man of pipes and flutes,—of what consists the music of Heaven?"

"The effect of the wind upon these various apertures," replied Tzu Ch'i, "is not uniform. But what is it that gives to each the individuality, to all the potentiality, of sound?

"Great knowledge embraces the whole: small knowledge, a part only. Great speech is universal: small speech is particular.

"For whether when the mind is locked in sleep or whether when in waking hours the body is released, we are subject to daily mental perturbations,—indecision, want of penetration, concealment, fretting fear, and

發若機栝，其司是非之謂也；其留如詛盟，其守勝之謂也；其殺若秋冬，以言其日消也；其溺之所為之，不可使復之也；其厭也如緘，以言其都溜也；近死之心，莫使復陽也。喜怒哀樂，慮歎變熱，姚佚啟態；樂出虛，蒸成菌。日夜相代乎前，而莫知其所萌。已乎，已乎！旦暮得此，其所由以生乎！非彼無我，非我無所取。是亦近矣，而不知其所為使。若有真宰，而特不得其眹。可行己信，而不見其形，有情而無形。百骸、九竅、六藏，賅而存焉，吾誰與為親？汝皆說之乎？其有私焉？如是皆有為臣妾乎？其臣妾不足以相治乎？其遞相為君臣乎？其有真君存焉？如求得其情與不得，無益損乎其真。一受其成形，不亡以待盡。與物相刃相靡，其行盡如馳，

trembling terror. Now like a javelin the mind flies forth, the arbiter of right and wrong.

Now like a solemn covenanter it remains firm, the guardian of rights secured.

Then, as under autumn and winter's blight, comes gradual decay, a passing away, like the flow of water, never to return. Finally, the block when all is choked up like an old drain,—the failing mind which shall not see light again.

"Joy and anger, sorrow and happiness, caution and remorse, come upon us by turns, with ever-changing mood. They come like music from hollowness, like mushrooms from damp. Daily and nightly they alternate within us, but we cannot tell whence they spring. Can we then hope in a moment to lay our finger upon their very Cause?

"But for these emotions I should not be. But for me, they would have no scope. So far we can go; but we do not know what it is that brings them into play. 'Twould seem to be a soul; but the clue to its existence is wanting. That such a Power operates, is credible enough, though we cannot see its form. It has functions without form.

"Take the human body with all its manifold divisions. Which part of it does a man love best? Does he not cherish all equally, or has he a preference? Do not all equally serve him? And do these servitors then govern themselves, or are they subdivided into rulers and subjects? Surely there is some soul which sways them all.

"But whether or not we ascertain what are the functions of this soul, it matters but little to the soul itself. For coming into existence with this mortal coil of mine, with the exhaustion of this mortal coil its mandate will also be exhausted. To be harassed by the wear and tear of life, and to pass rapidly through it without possibility of arresting one's course,— is not this pitiful indeed? To labour without ceasing, and then, without living to enjoy the fruit, worn out, to depart, suddenly, one knows not whither,—is not that a just cause for grief?

"What advantage is there in what men call not dying? The body decomposes, and the mind goes with it. This is our real cause for sorrow. Can the world be so dull as not to see this? Or is it I alone who am dull, and others not so?

"If we are to be guided by the criteria of our own minds, who shall be

而莫之能止，不亦悲乎！終身役役而不見其成功，苶然疲役而不知其所歸，可不哀邪！人謂之不死，奚益！其形化，其心與之然，可不謂大哀乎？人之生也，固若是芒乎？其我獨芒，而人亦有不芒者乎？夫隨其成心而師之，誰獨且無師乎？奚必知代而心自取者有之？愚者與有焉！未成乎心而有是非，是今日適越而昔至也。是以無有為有。無有為有，雖有神禹，且不能知，吾獨且奈何哉！

夫言非吹也，言者有言。其所言者特未定也。果有言邪？其未嘗有言邪？其以為異於鷇音，亦有辯乎？其無辯乎？道惡乎隱而有真偽？言惡乎隱而有是非？道惡乎往而不存？言惡乎存而不可？道隱於小成，言隱於榮華。故有儒墨之是非，以是其所非而非其所是。欲是其所非而非其所是，則莫若以明。物無非彼，物無非是。自彼則不見，自知則知之。故曰：彼出於是，是亦

without a guide?

What need to know of the alternations of passion, when the mind thus affords scope to itself?—verily even the minds of fools! Whereas, for a mind without criteria to admit the idea of contraries, is like saying, I went to Yueh to-day, and got there yesterday.

Or, like placing nowhere somewhere,—topography which even the Great Yu would fail to understand; how much more I?

"Speech is not mere breath. It is differentiated by meaning. Take away that, and you cannot say whether it is speech or not. Can you even distinguish it from the chirping of young birds?

"But how can Tao be so obscured that we speak of it as true and false? And how can speech be so obscured that it admits the idea of contraries? How can Tao go away and yet not remain?

How can speech exist and yet be impossible?

"Tao is obscured by our want of grasp. Speech is obscured by the gloss of this world.

Hence the affirmatives and negatives of the Confucian and Mihist schools, each denying what the other affirmed and affirming what the other denied. But he who would reconcile affirmative with negative and negative with affirmative, must do so by the light of nature.

"There is nothing which is not objective: there is nothing which is not subjective. But it is impossible to start from the objective. Only from subjective knowledge is it possible to proceed to objective knowledge. Hence it has been said,

'The objective emanates from the subjective; the subjective is consequent upon the objective. This is the Alternation Theory.' Nevertheless, when one is born, the other dies. When one is possible, the other is impossible. When one is affirmative the other is negative. Which being the case, the true sage rejects all distinctions of this and that. He takes his refuge in God, and places himself in subjective relation with all things.

"And inasmuch as the subjective is also objective, and the objective also subjective, and as the contraries under each are indistinguishably blended, does it not become impossible for us to say whether subjective and objective really exist at all?

"When subjective and objective are both without their correlates, that is the very axis of Tao. And when that axis passes through the centre at

因彼。彼是方生之說也。雖然，方生方死，方死方生；方可方不可，方不可方可；因是因非，因非因是。是以聖人不由，而照之於天，亦因是也。是亦彼也，彼亦是也。彼亦一是非，此亦一是非，果且有彼是乎哉？果且無彼是乎哉？彼是莫得其偶，謂之道樞。樞始得其環中，以應無窮。是亦一無窮，非亦一無窮也。故曰：莫若以明。

以指喻指之非指，不若以非指喻指之非指也；以馬喻馬之非馬，不若以非馬喻馬之非馬也。天地一指也，萬物一馬也。可乎可，不可乎不可。道行之而成，物謂之而然。惡乎然？然於然。惡乎不然？不然於不然。物固有所然，物固有所可。無物不然，無物不可。故為是舉莛與楹，厲與西施，恢詭譎怪，道通為一。其分也，成也；其成也，毀也。凡物無成與毀，復通為一。

which all Infinities converge, positive and negative alike blend into an infinite One. Hence it has been said that there is nothing like the light of nature.

"To take a finger in illustration of a finger not being a finger is not so good as to take something which is not a finger. To take a horse in illustration of a horse not being a horse is not so good as to take something which is not a horse.

"So with the universe and all that in it is. These things are but fingers and horses in this sense. The possible is possible: the impossible is impossible. Tao operates, and given results follow. Things receive names and are what they are. They achieve this by their natural affinity for what they are and their natural antagonism to what they are not. For all things have their own particular constitutions and potentialities. Nothing can exist without these.

"Therefore it is that, viewed from the standpoint of Tao, a beam and a pillar are identical.

So are ugliness and beauty, greatness, wickedness, perverseness, and strangeness. Separation is the same as construction: construction is the same as destruction. Nothing is subject either to construction or to destruction, for these conditions are brought together into One.

"Only the truly intelligent understand this principle of the identity of all things. They do not view things as apprehended by themselves, subjectively; but transfer themselves into the position of the things viewed.

And viewing them thus they are able to comprehend them, nay, to master them;—and he who can master them is near. So it is that to place oneself in subjective relation with externals, without consciousness of their objectivity,—this is Tao. But to wear out one's intellect in an obstinate adherence to the individuality of things, not recognising the fact that all things are One,—this is called Three in the Morning."

"What is Three in the Morning?" asked Tzu Yu.

"A keeper of monkeys," replied Tzu Ch'i, "said with regard to their rations of chestnuts that each monkey was to have three in the morning and four at night. But at this the monkeys were very angry, so the keeper said they might have four in the morning and three at night, with which arrangement they were all well pleased. The actual number of the chestnuts remained the same, but there was an adaptation to the likes and dislikes

唯達者知通為一，為是不用而寓諸庸。庸也者，用也；用也者，通也；通也者，得也。適得而幾矣。因是已，已而不知其然，謂之道。勞神明為一而不知其同也，謂之「朝三」。何謂「朝三？」曰：「狙公賦芧，曰：『朝三而暮四。』眾狙皆怒。曰：『然則朝四而暮三。』眾狙皆悅。」名實未虧而喜怒為用，亦因是也。是以聖人和之以是非而休乎天鈞，是之謂兩行。

古之人，其知有所至矣。惡乎至？有以為未始有物者，至矣，盡矣，不可以加矣！其次以為有物矣，而未始有封也。其次以為有封焉，而未始有是非也。是非之彰也，道之所以虧也。道之所以虧，愛之所以成。果且有成與虧乎哉？果且無成與虧乎哉？有成與虧，故昭氏之鼓琴也；

of those concerned. Such is the principle of putting oneself into subjective relation with externals.

"Wherefore the true Sage, while regarding contraries as identical, adapts himself to the laws of Heaven. This is called following two courses at once.

"The knowledge of the men of old had a limit. It extended back to a period when matter did not exist. That was the extreme point to which their knowledge reached.

"The second period was that of matter, but of matter unconditioned.

"The third epoch saw matter conditioned, but contraries were still unknown. When these appeared, Tao began to decline. And with the decline of Tao, individual bias arose.

"Have then these states of falling and rising real existences? Surely they are but as the falling and rising of Chao Wen's music,—the consequences of his playing.

Chao Wen played the guitar. Shih K'uang wielded the baton. Hui Tzu argued. Herein these three men excelled, and in the practice of such arts they passed their lives.

"Hui Tzu's particular views being very different from those of the world in general, he was correspondingly anxious to enlighten people. But he did not enlighten them as he should have done, and consequently ended in the obscurity of the 'hard and white.'

Subsequently, his son searched his works for some clue, but never succeeded in establishing the principle. And indeed if such were possible to be established, then even I am established; but if not, then neither I nor anything in the universe is established!

"Therefore what the true Sage aims at is the light which comes out of darkness. He does not view things as apprehended by himself, subjectively, but transfers himself into the position of the things viewed. This is called using the light.

"There remains, however, Speech. Is that to be enrolled under either category of contraries, or not? Whether it is so enrolled or not, it will in any case belong to one or the other, and thus be as though it had an objective existence. At any rate, I should like to hear some speech which belongs to neither category.

"If there was a beginning, then there was a time before that beginning.

無成與虧，故昭氏之不鼓琴也。昭文之鼓琴也，師曠之枝策也，惠子之據梧也，三子之知幾乎，皆其盛者也，故載之末年。唯其好之也，以異於彼，其好之也，欲以明之。彼非所明而明之，故以堅白之昧終。而其子又以文之綸終，終身無成。若是而可謂成乎？雖我亦成也。若是而不可謂成乎？物與我無成也。是故滑疑之耀，聖人之所鄙也。為是不用而寓諸庸，此之謂「以明」。

今且有言於此，不知其與是類乎？其與是不類乎？類與不類，相與為類，則與彼無以異矣。雖然，請嘗言之。有始也者，有未始有始也者，有未始有夫未始有始也者。有有也者，有無也者，有未始有無也者，有未始有夫未始有無也者。俄而有無矣，而未知有無之果孰有孰無也。今

And a time before the time which was before the time of that beginning.

"If there is existence, there must have been non-existence. And if there was a time when nothing existed, then there must have been a time before that—when even nothing did not exist. Suddenly, when nothing came into existence, could one really say whether it belonged to the category of existence or of non-existence? Even the very words I have just now uttered,—I cannot say whether they have really been uttered or not.

"There is nothing under the canopy of heaven greater than the tip of an autumn spikelet. A vast mountain is a small thing. Neither is there any age greater than that of a child cut off in infancy. P'eng Tsu himself died young. The universe and I came into being together; and I, and everything therein, are One.

"If then all things are One, what room is there for Speech? On the other hand, since I can utter these words, how can Speech not exist?

"If it does exist, we have One and Speech = two; and two and one = three. From which point onwards even the best mathematicians will fail to reach: how much more then will ordinary people fail?

"Hence, if from nothing you can proceed to something, and subsequently reach three, it follows that it would be still more easy if you were to start from something. To avoid such progression, you must put yourself into subjective relation with the external.

"Before conditions existed, Tao was. Before definitions existed, Speech was. Subjectively, we are conscious of certain delimitations which are,—
Right and Left
Relationship and Obligation
Division and Discrimination
Emulation and Contention
These are called the Eight Predicables.
For the true Sage, beyond the limits of an external world, they exist, but are not recognised. By the true Sage, within the limits of an external world, they are recognised, but are not assigned. And so, with regard to the wisdom of the ancients, as embodied in the canon of Spring and Autumn, the true Sage assigns, but does not justify by argument. And thus, classifying he does not classify; arguing, he does not argue."

"How can that be?" asked Tzu Yu.

"The true Sage," answered Tzu Ch'i, "keeps his knowledge with-

我則已有謂矣，而未知吾所謂之其果有謂乎？其果無謂乎？夫天下莫大於秋豪之末，而大山為小；莫壽於殤子，而彭祖為夭。天地與我並生，而萬物與我為一。既已為一矣，且得有言乎？既已謂之一矣，且得無言乎？一與言為二，二與一為三。自此以往，巧歷不能得，而況其凡乎！故自無適有以至於三，而況自有適有乎！無適焉，因是已！

夫道未始有封，言未始有常，為是而有畛也。請言其畛：有左，有右，有倫，有義，有分，有辯，有競，有爭，此之謂八德。六合之外，聖人存而不論；六合之內，聖人論而不議。春秋經世先王之志，聖人議而不辯。故分也者，有不分也；辯也者，有不辯也。曰：「何也？」「聖人懷之，眾人辯之以相示也。故曰：辯也者，有不見也。」夫大道不稱，大辯不言，大仁不仁，大廉不嗛，大勇不忮。道昭而不道，言辯而不及，

in him, while men in general set forth theirs in argument, in order to convince each other. And therefore it is said that in argument he does not manifest himself.

"Perfect Tao does not declare itself. Nor does perfect argument express itself in words. Nor does perfect charity show itself in act. Nor is perfect honesty absolutely incorruptible. Nor is perfect courage absolutely unyielding.

"For the Tao which shines forth is not Tao. Speech which argues falls short of its aim. Charity which has fixed points loses its scope. Honesty which is absolute is wanting in credit. Courage which is absolute misses its object. These five are, as it were, round, with a strong bias towards squareness. Therefore that knowledge which stops at what it does not know, is the highest knowledge.

"Who knows the argument which can be argued without words?— the Tao which does not declare itself as Tao? He who knows this may be said to be of God. To be able to pour in without making full, and pour out without making empty, in ignorance of the power by which such results are accomplished,—this is accounted Light."

Of old, the Emperor Yao said to Shun, "I would smite the Tsungs, and the Kueis, and the Hsu-aos. Ever since I have been on the throne I have had this desire. What do you think?"

"These three States," replied Shun, "are paltry out-of-the-way places. Why can you not shake off this desire? Once upon a time, ten suns came out together, and all things were illuminated thereby. How much more then should virtue excel suns?"

Yeh Ch'ueh asked Wang I, saying, "Do you know for certain that all things are subjectively the same?"

"How can I know?" answered Wang I. "Do you know what you do not know?"

"How can I know?" replied Yeh Ch'ueh. "But can then nothing be known?"

"How can I know?" said Wang I. "Nevertheless, I will try to tell you. How can it be known that what I call knowing is not really not knowing, and that what I call not knowing is not really knowing? Now I would ask you this. If a man sleeps in a damp place, he gets lumbago and dies. But how about an eel? And living up in a tree is precarious and trying to the

仁常而不成，廉清而不信，勇忮而不成。五者圓而幾向方矣！故知止其所不知，至矣。孰知不言之辯，不道之道？若有能知，此之謂天府。注焉而不滿，酌焉而不竭，而不知其所由來，此之謂葆光。故昔者堯問於舜曰：「我欲伐宗、膾、胥敖，南面而不釋然。其故何也？」舜曰：「夫三子者，猶存乎蓬艾之間。若不釋然何哉！昔者十日並出，萬物皆照，而況德之進乎日者乎！」

齧缺問乎王倪曰：「子知物之所同是乎？」曰：「吾惡乎知之！」「子知子之所不知邪？」曰：「吾惡乎知之！」「然則物無知邪？」曰：「吾惡乎知之！」雖然，嘗試言之。庸詎知吾所謂知之非不知邪？庸詎知吾所謂不知之非知邪？且吾嘗試問乎女：民濕寢則腰疾偏死，鰍然乎哉？木處則惴慄恂懼，猿猴然乎哉？三者孰知正處？民食芻豢，麋鹿食薦，蝍且甘帶，鴟鴉耆鼠，四者孰知正味？猿猵狙以為雌，麋與鹿交，鰍與魚游。毛嬙麗姬，

nerves;—but how about monkeys? Of the man, the eel, and the monkey, whose habitat is the right one, absolutely? Human beings feed on flesh, deer on grass, centipedes on snakes, owls and crows on mice. Of these four, whose is the right taste, absolutely? Monkey mates with monkey, the buck with the doe; eels consort with fishes, while men admire Mao Ch'iang and Li Chi, at the sight of whom fishes plunge deep down in the water, birds soar high in the air, and deer hurry away.

Yet who shall say which is the correct standard of beauty? In my opinion, the standard of human virtue, and of positive and negative, is so obscured that it is impossible to actually know it as such."

"If you then," asked Yeh Ch'ueh, "do not know what is bad for you, is the Perfect Man equally without this knowledge?"

"The Perfect Man," answered Wang I, "is a spiritual being. Were the ocean itself scorched up, he would not feel hot. Were the Milky Way frozen hard, he would not feel cold. Were the mountains to be riven with thunder, and the great deep to be thrown up by storm, he would not tremble. In such case, he would mount upon the clouds of heaven, and driving the sun and the moon before him, would pass beyond the limits of this external world, where death and life have no more victory over man;—how much less what is bad for him?"

人之所美也；魚見之深入，鳥見之高飛，麋鹿見之決驟，四者孰知天下之正色哉？自我觀之，仁義之端，是非之塗，樊然殽亂，吾惡能知其辯！」

齧缺曰：「子不知利害，則至人固不知利害乎？」

王倪曰：「至人神矣！大澤焚而不能熱，河漢冱而不能寒，疾雷破山、飄風振海而不能驚。若然者，乘雲氣，騎日月，而游乎四海之外，死生無變於己，而況利害之端乎！」

瞿鵲子問乎長梧子曰：「吾聞諸夫子，聖人不從事於務，不就利，不違害，不喜求，不緣道；無謂有謂，有謂無謂，而遊乎塵垢之外。夫子以為孟浪之言，而我以為妙道之行也。吾子以為奚若？」長梧子曰：「是黃帝之所聽熒也，而丘也何足以知之！且女亦大早計，見卵而求時夜，見彈而求鴞炙。予嘗為女妄言之，女以妄聽之。奚旁日月，挾宇宙？為其吻合，置其滑涽，以隸相尊。眾人役役，聖人愚芚，參萬歲而一成純。萬物盡然，而以是相蘊。予惡乎知說生之非惑邪！予惡乎知惡死之非弱喪而不知歸者邪！麗之姬，艾封人之子也。晉國之始得之也，

Chu Ch'iao addressed Chang Wu Tzu as follows:—"I heard Confucius say, 'The true sage pays no heed to mundane affairs. He neither seeks gain nor avoids injury. He asks nothing at the hands of man. He adheres, without questioning, to Tao. Without speaking, he can speak; and he can speak and yet say nothing. And so he roams beyond the limits of this dusty world. These,' added Confucius, 'are wild words.'

Now to me they are the skilful embodiment of Tao. What, Sir, is your opinion?"

"Points upon which the Yellow Emperor doubted," replied Chang Wu Tzu, "how should Confucius know?

You are going too fast. You see your egg, and expect to hear it crow. You look at your cross-bow, and expect to have broiled duck before you. I will say a few words to you at random, and do you listen at random.

"How does the Sage seat himself by the sun and moon, and hold the universe in his grasp? He blends everything into one harmonious whole, rejecting the confusion of this and that. Rank and precedence, which the vulgar prize, the Sage stolidly ignores. The revolutions of ten thousand years leave his Unity unscathed. The universe itself may pass away, but he will flourish still.

"How do I know that love of life is not a delusion after all? How do I know but that he who dreads to die is not as a child who has lost the way and cannot find his home?

"The lady Li Chi was the daughter of Ai Feng. When the Duke of Chin first got her, she wept until the bosom of her dress was drenched with tears. But when she came to the royal residence, and lived with the Duke, and ate rich food, she repented of having wept. How then do I know but that the dead repent of having previously clung to life?

"Those who dream of the banquet, wake to lamentation and sorrow. Those who dream of lamentation and sorrow wake to join the hunt. While they dream, they do not know that they dream. Some will even interpret the very dream they are dreaming; and only when they awake do they know it was a dream. By and by comes the Great Awakening, and then we find out that this life is really a great dream. Fools think they are awake now, and flatter themselves they know if they are really princes or peasants. Confucius and you are both dreams; and I who say you are dreams,— I am but a dream myself. This is a paradox. Tomorrow a sage may arise to

涕泣沾襟；及其至於王所，與王同筐床，食芻豢，而後悔其泣也。予惡乎知夫死者不悔其始之蘄生乎？夢飲酒者，旦而哭泣；夢哭泣者，旦而田獵。方其夢也，不知其夢也。夢之中又占其夢焉，覺而後知其夢也。且有大覺而後知此其大夢也，而愚者自以為覺，竊竊然知之。君乎，牧乎，固哉！丘也與女，皆夢也；予謂女夢，亦夢也。是其言也，其名為吊詭。萬世之後而一遇大聖，知其解者，是旦暮遇之也。既使我與若辯矣，若勝我，我不若勝，若果是也？我果非也邪？我勝若，若不吾勝，我果是也？而果非也邪？其或是也？其或非也邪？其俱是也？其俱非也邪？我與若不能相知也。則人固受其黮闇，吾誰使正之？使同乎若者正之？既與若同矣，惡能正之！使同乎我者正之？既同乎我矣，惡能正之！使異乎我與若者正

explain it; but that tomorrow will not be until ten thousand generations have gone by.

"Granting that you and I argue. If you beat me, and not I you, are you necessarily right and I wrong? Or if I beat you and not you me, am I necessarily right and you wrong? Or are we both partly right and partly wrong? Or are we both wholly right and wholly wrong? You and I cannot know this, and consequently the world will be in ignorance of the truth.

"Who shall I employ as arbiter between us? If I employ some one who takes your view, he will side with you. How can such a one arbitrate between us? If I employ some one who takes my view, he will side with me. How can such a one arbitrate between us? And if I employ some one who either differs from, or agrees with, both of us, he will be equally unable to decide between us. Since then you, and I, and man, cannot decide, must we not depend upon Another?

Such dependence is as though it were not dependence. We are embraced in the obliterating unity of God. There is perfect adaptation to whatever may eventuate; and so we complete our allotted span.

"But what is it to be embraced in the obliterating unity of God? It is this. With reference to positive and negative, to that which is so and that which is not so,—if the positive is really positive, it must necessarily be different from its negative: there is no room for argument. And if that which is so really is so, it must necessarily be different from that which is not so: there is no room for argument.

"Take no heed of time, nor of right and wrong. But passing into the realm of the Infinite, take your final rest therein."

之?既異乎我與若矣，惡能正之！使同乎我與若者正之？既同乎我與若矣，惡能正之！然則我與若與人俱不能相知也，而待彼也邪？」「何謂和之以天倪？」曰:「是不是，然不然。是若果是也，則是之異乎不是也亦無辯；然若果然也，則然之異乎不然也亦無辯。化聲之相待、若其不相待。和之以天倪，因之以曼衍，所以窮年也。忘年忘義，振於無竟，故寓諸無竟。

罔兩問景曰:「曩子行，今子止；曩子坐，今子起。何其無特操與？」景曰:「吾有待而然者邪？吾所待又有待而然者邪？吾待蛇蚹蜩翼邪？惡識所以然？惡識所以不然？」

昔者莊周夢為胡蝶，栩栩然胡蝶也。自喻適志與！不知周也。俄然覺，則蘧蘧然周也。不知周之夢為胡蝶與？胡蝶之夢為周與？周與胡蝶，則必有分矣。此之謂物化。

The Penumbra said to the Umbra, "At one moment you move: at another you are at rest. At one moment you sit down: at another you get up. Why this instability of purpose?" "I depend," replied the Umbra, "upon something which causes me to do as I do; and that something depends in turn upon something else which causes it to do as it does. My dependence is like that of a snake's scales or of a cicada's wings.

How can I tell why I do one thing, or why I do not do another?"

Once upon a time, I, Chuang Tzu, dreamt I was a butterfly, fluttering hither and thither, to all intents and purposes a butterfly. I was conscious only of following my fancies as a butterfly, and was unconscious of my individuality as a man. Suddenly, I awaked, and there I lay, myself again. Now I do not know whether I was then a man dreaming I was a butterfly, or whether I am now a butterfly dreaming I am a man. Between a man and a butterfly there is necessarily a barrier. The transition is called Metempsychosis.

# 養生主第三

　　吾生也有涯，而知也無涯。以有涯隨無涯，殆已！已而為知者，殆而已矣！為善無近名，為惡無近刑，緣督以為經，可以保身，可以全生，可以養親，可以盡年。

　　庖丁為文惠君解牛，手之所觸，肩之所倚，足之所履，膝之所踦，砉然響然，奏刀騞然，莫不中音，合於桑林之舞，乃中經首之會。文惠君曰：「嘻，善哉！技蓋至此乎？」庖丁釋刀對曰：「臣之所好者道也，進乎技矣。始臣之解牛之時，所見無非全牛者；三年之后，未嘗見全牛也；方今之時，臣以神遇而不以目視，官知止而神欲行。依乎天理，批大郤，導大窾，因其固然。技經肯綮之未嘗微礙，而況大軱乎！良庖歲更刀，割也；族庖月更刀，折也；今臣之刀十九年矣，

# CHAPTER III

## NOURISHMENT OF THE SOUL

My life has a limit, but my knowledge is without limit. To drive the limited in search of the limitless, is fatal; and the knowledge of those who do this is fatally lost.

In striving for others, avoid fame. In striving for self, avoid disgrace. Pursue a middle course. Thus you will keep a sound body, and a sound mind, fulfil your duties, and work out your allotted span.

Prince Hui's cook was cutting up a bullock. Every blow of his hand, every heave of his shoulders, every tread of his foot, every thrust of his knee, every whshh of rent flesh, every chhk of the chopper, was in perfect harmony,—rhythmical like the dance of the Mulberry Grove, simultaneous like the chords of the Ching Shou.

"Well done!" cried the Prince. "Yours is skill indeed."

"Sire," replied the cook; "I have always devoted myself to Tao. It is better than skill. When I first began to cut up bullocks, I saw before me simply whole bullocks. After three years' practice, I saw no more whole animals.

And now I work with my mind and not with my eye. When my senses bid me stop, but my mind urges me on, I fall back upon eternal principles. I follow such openings or cavities as there may be, according to the natural constitution of the animal. I do not attempt to cut through joints: still less through large bones.

"A good cook changes his chopper once a year,—because he cuts. An ordinary cook, once a month,—because he hacks. But I have had this chopper nineteen years, and although I have cut up many thousand bullocks, its edge is as if fresh from the whetstone. For at the joints there are always interstices, and the edge of a chopper being without thickness, it remains only to insert that which is without thickness into such an interstice.

By these means the interstice will be enlarged, and the blade will find plenty of room. It is thus that I have kept my chopper for nineteen years as though fresh from the whetstone.

"Nevertheless, when I come upon a hard part where the blade meets

所解數千牛矣，而刀刃若新發於硎。彼節者有閒，而刀刃者無厚，以無厚入有閒，恢恢乎其於游刃必有餘地矣。是以十九年而刀刃若新發於硎。雖然，每至於族，吾見其難為，怵然為戒，視為止，行為遲，動刀甚微，謋然已解，牛不知其死也，如土委地。提刀而立，為之而四顧，為之躊躇滿志，善刀而藏之。」文惠君曰：「善哉！吾聞庖丁之言，得養生焉。」

公文軒見右師而驚曰：「是何人也？惡乎介也？天與？其人與？」曰：「天也，非人也。天之生是使獨也，人之貌有與也。以是知其天也，非人也。」

澤雉十步一啄，百步一飲，不蘄畜乎樊中。神雖王，不善也。

with a difficulty, I am all caution. I fix my eye on it. I stay my hand, and gently apply my blade, until with a hwah the part yields like earth crumbling to the ground. Then I take out my chopper, and stand up, and look around, and pause, until with an air of triumph I wipe my chopper and put it carefully away."

"Bravo!" cried the Prince. "From the words of this cook I have learnt how to take care of my life."

When Hsien, of the Kung-wen family, beheld a certain official, he was horrified, and said, "Who is that man? How came he to lose a foot? Is this the work of God, or of man?

"Why, of course," continued Hsien, "it is the work of God, and not of man. When God brought this man into the world, he wanted him to be unlike other men. Men always have two feet. From this it is clear that God and not man made him as he is.

"Now, wild fowl get a peck once in ten steps, a drink once in a hundred. Yet they do not want to be fed in a cage. For although they would thus be able to command food, they would not be free."

老聃死，秦失弔之，三號而出。弟子曰：「非夫子之友邪？」曰：「然。」「然則弔焉若此，可乎？」曰：「然。始也吾以為其人也，而今非也。向吾入而弔焉，有老者哭之，如哭其子；少者哭之，如哭其母。彼其所以會之，必有不蘄言而言，不蘄哭而哭者。是遁天倍情，忘其所受，古者謂之遁天之刑。適來，夫子時也；適去，夫子順也。安時而處順，哀樂不能入也，古者謂是帝之縣解。」指窮於為薪，火傳也，不知其盡也。

When Lao Tzu died, Ch'in Shih went to mourn. He uttered three yells and departed.

A disciple asked him saying, "Were you not our Master's friend?"

"I was," replied Ch'in Shih.

"And if so, do you consider that a sufficient expression of grief at his loss?" added the disciple.

"I do," said Ch'in Shih. "I had believed him to be the man of all men, but now I know that he was not. When I went in to mourn, I found old persons weeping as if for their children, young ones wailing as if for their mothers. And for him to have gained the attachment of those people in this way, he too must have uttered words which should not have been spoken, and dropped tears which should not have been shed, thus violating eternal principles, increasing the sum of human emotion, and forgetting the source from which his own life was received. The ancients called such emotions the trammels of mortality. The Master came, because it was his time to be born; he went, because it was his time to die. For those who accept the phenomenon of birth and death in this sense, lamentation and sorrow have no place. The ancients spoke of death as of God cutting down a man suspended in the air. The fuel is consumed, but the fire may be transmitted, and we know not that it comes to an end."

# 人間世第四

顏回見仲尼，請行。曰：「奚之？」曰：「將之衛。」曰：「奚為焉？」曰：「回聞衛君，其年壯，其行獨。輕用其國，而不見其過。輕用民死，死者以國量乎澤，若蕉，民其無如矣！回嘗聞之夫子曰：'治國去之，亂國就之。醫門多疾。'願以所聞，思其所行，庶幾其國有瘳乎！」仲尼曰：「譆，若殆往而刑耳！夫道不欲雜，雜則多，多則擾，擾則憂，憂而不救。古之至人，先存諸己而后存諸人。所存於己者未定，何暇至於暴人之所行！且若亦知夫德之所蕩而知之所為出乎哉？德蕩乎名，知出乎爭。名也者，相軋也；知也者，爭之器也。二者凶器，非所以盡行也。且德厚信矼，未達人氣；名聞不爭，未達人心。而強以仁義繩墨之言衒暴人之前者，是以人惡有其美也，命之曰菑人。菑人者，人必反菑之。若殆為人菑夫。且苟為人悅賢而惡不肖，惡用而求有以異？若唯無詔，王公必將乘人而鬥其捷。而目將熒之，而色將平之，口將營之，容將形之，心且成之。是以火救火，以水救水，名之曰益多。

# CHAPTER IV

## MAN AMONG MEN

Yen Hui went to take leave of Confucius.

"Whither are you bound?" asked the Master.

"I am going to the State of Wei," was the reply.

"And what do you propose to do there?" continued Confucius.

"I hear," answered Yen Hui, "that the Prince of Wei is of mature age, but of an unmanageable disposition. He behaves as if the State were of no account, and will not see his own faults. Consequently, the people perish; and their corpses lie about like so much undergrowth in a marsh. They are at extremities. And I have heard you, Sir, say that if a State is well governed it may be neglected; but that if it is badly governed, then we should visit it.

The science of medicine embraces many various diseases. I would test my knowledge in this sense, that perchance I may do some good to that State."

"Alas!" cried Confucius, "you will only succeed in bringing evil upon yourself. For Tao must not be distributed. If it is, it will lose its unity. If it loses its unity, it will be uncertain; and so cause mental disturbance,—from which there is no escape.

"The sages of old first got Tao for themselves, and then got it for others. Before you possess this yourself, what leisure have you to attend to the doings of wicked men? Besides, do you know what Virtue results in and where Wisdom ends? Virtue results in a desire for fame; Wisdom ends in contentions. In the struggle for fame men crush each other, while their wisdom but provokes rivalry. Both are baleful instruments, and may not be incautiously used.

"Besides, those who, before influencing by their own solid virtue and unimpeachable sincerity, and before reaching the heart by the example of their own disregard for name and fame, go and preach charity and duty to one's neighbour to wicked men,—only make these men hate them for their very goodness' sake. Such persons are called evil speakers. And those who speak evil of others are apt to be evil spoken of themselves. That, alas! will be your end.

順始無窮，若殆以不信厚言，必死於暴人之前矣！且昔者桀殺關龍逢，紂殺王子比干，是皆修其身以下傴拊人之民，以下拂其上者也，故其君因其修以擠之。是好名者也。昔者堯攻叢、枝、胥、敖，禹攻有扈。國為虛厲，身為刑戮。其用兵不止，其求實無已，是皆求名實者也，而獨不聞之乎？名實者，聖人之所不能勝也，而況若乎！雖然，若必有以也，嘗以語我來。」顏回曰「端而虛，勉而一，則可乎？」曰：「惡！惡可！夫以陽為充孔揚，采色不定，常人之所不違，因案人之所感，以求容與其心。名之曰日漸之德不成，而況大德乎！將執而不化，外合而內不訾，其庸詎可乎！」「然則我內直而外曲，成而上比。內直者，與天為徒。與天為徒者，知天子之與己，皆天之所子，而獨以己言蘄乎而人善之，蘄乎而人不善之邪？若然者，人謂之童子，是之謂與天為徒。外曲者，與人之為徒也。擎跽曲拳，人臣之禮也。人皆為之，吾敢不為邪？為人之所為者，人亦無疵焉，是之謂與人為徒。成而上比者，與古為徒。其言雖教，適之實也，古之

"On the other hand, if the Prince loves the good and hates the bad, what object will you have in inviting him to change his ways? Before you have opened your mouth to preach, the Prince himself will have seized the opportunity to wrest the victory from you. Your eye will fall, your expression fade, your words will stick, your face will change, and your heart will die within you. It will be as though you took fire to quell fire, water to quell water, which is popularly known as 'pouring oil on the flames.' And if you begin with concessions, there will be no end to them. Neglect this sound advice, and you will be the victim of that violent man.

"Of old, Chieh murdered Kuan Lung Feng, and Chou slew Prince Pi Kan. Their victims were both men who cultivated virtue themselves in order to secure the welfare of the people. But in doing this they offended their superiors; and therefore, because of that very moral culture, their superiors got rid of them, in order to guard their own reputations.

"Of old, Yao attacked the Ts'ung-chih and Hsu-ao countries, and Yu attacked the Yu-hu country. Homes were desolated and families destroyed by the slaughter of the inhabitants. Yet they fought without ceasing, and strove for victory to the last. These are instances known to all. Now if the Sages of old failed in their efforts against this love of fame, this desire for victory,— are you likely to succeed? But of course you have a scheme. Tell it to me."

"Gravity of demeanour," replied Yen Hui, "and dispassionateness; energy and singleness of purpose,—will this do?"

"Alas!" said Confucius, "that will not do. If you make a show of being perfect and obtrude yourself, the Prince's mood will be doubtful. Ordinarily, he is not opposed, and so he has come to take actual pleasure in trampling upon the feelings of others. And if he has thus failed in the practice of routine virtues, do you expect that he will take readily to higher ones? You may insist, but without result. Outwardly you will be right, but inwardly wrong. How then will you make him mend his ways?"

"Just so," replied Yen Hui. "I am inwardly straight, and outwardly crooked, completed after the models of antiquity.

"He who is inwardly straight is a servant of God. And he who is a servant of God knows that the Son of Heaven and himself are equally the children of God. Shall then such a one trouble whether man visits him with evil or with good? Man indeed regards him as a child; and this is to

有也，非吾有也。若然者，雖直而不病，是之謂與古為徒。若是則可乎？」仲尼曰：「惡！惡可！大多政法而不諜。雖固亦無罪。雖然，止是耳矣，夫胡可以及化！猶師心者也。」顏回曰：「吾無以進矣，敢問其方。」仲尼曰：「齋，吾將語若。有心而為之，其易邪？易之者，皥天不宜。」顏回曰：「回之家貧，唯不飲酒不茹葷者數月矣。如此則可以為齋乎？」曰：「是祭祀之齋，非心齋也。」回曰：「敢問心齋。」仲尼曰：「若一志，無聽之以耳而聽之以心；無聽之以心而聽之以氣。耳止於聽，心止於符。氣也者，虛而待物者也。唯道集虛。虛者，心齋也」顏回曰：「回之未始得使，實有回也；得使之也，未始有回也，可謂虛乎？」夫子曰：「盡矣！吾語若：若能入游其樊而無感其名，入則鳴，不入則止。無門無毒，

be a servant of God.

"He who is outwardly crooked is a servant of man. He bows, he kneels, he folds his hands;—such is the ceremonial of a minister. What all men do, shall I dare not to do? What all men do, none will blame me for doing. This is to be a servant of man.

"He who is completed after the models of antiquity is a servant of the Sages of old. Although I utter the words of warning and take him to task, it is the Sages of old who speak, and not I. Thus my uprightness will not bring me into trouble, the servant of the Sages of old.—Will this do?"

"Alas!" replied Confucius, "No. Your plans are too many, and are lacking in prudence. However, your firmness will secure you from harm; but that is all. You will not influence him to such an extent that he shall seem to follow the dictates of his own heart."

"Then," said Yen Hui, "I am without resource, and venture to ask for a method."

Confucius said, "FAST.... Let me explain. You have a method, but it is difficult to practise. Those which are easy are not from God."

"Well," replied Yen Hui, "my family is poor, and for many months we have tasted neither wine nor flesh. Is not that fasting?"

"The fasting of religious observance it is," answered Confucius, "but not the fasting of the heart."

"And may I ask," said Yen Hui, "in what consists the fasting of the heart?"

"Cultivate unity," replied Confucius.

"You hear not with the ears, but with the mind; not with the mind, but with your soul.

But let hearing stop with the ears. Let the working of the mind stop with itself. Then the soul will be a negative existence, passively responsive to externals. In such a negative existence, only Tao can abide. And that negative state is the fasting of the heart."

"Then," said Yen Hui, "the reason I could not get the use of this method is my own individuality. If I could get the use of it, my individuality would have gone. Is this what you mean by the negative state?"

"Exactly so," replied the Master. "Let me tell you. If you can enter this man's domain without offending his amour propre, cheerful if he hears you, passive if he does not; without science, with out drugs, simply living

一宅而寓於不得已，則幾矣。「絕跡易，無行地難。為人使易以偽，為天使難以偽。聞以有翼飛者矣，未聞以無翼飛者也；聞以有知知者矣，未聞以無知知者也。瞻彼闋者，虛室生白，吉祥止止。夫且不止，是之謂坐馳。夫徇耳目內通而外於心知，鬼神將來舍，而況人乎！是萬物之化也，禹舜之紐也，伏戲、几蘧之所行終，而況散焉者乎！」

葉公子高將使於齊，問於仲尼曰：「王使諸梁也甚重。齊之待使者，蓋將甚敬而不急。匹夫猶未可動，而況諸侯乎！吾甚慄之。子常語諸梁也曰：‘凡事若小若大，寡不道以懽成。事若不成，則必有人道之患；事若成，則必有陰陽之患。若成若不成而后無患者，唯有德者能之。’吾食也執粗而不臧，爨無欲清之人。今吾朝受命而夕飲冰，我其內熱與！吾未至乎事之情，而既有陰陽之患矣！事若不成，必有人道之患，是兩也。為人臣者不足以任之，子其有以語我來！」仲尼曰：「天下有大戒二：其一，命也，其一，義也。子之愛親，命也，不可解於心；

there in a state of complete indifference,—you will be near success. It is easy to stop walking: the trouble is to walk without touching the ground. As an agent of man, it is easy to deceive; but not as an agent of God. You have heard of winged creatures flying. You have never heard of flying without wings. You have heard of men being wise with wisdom. You have never heard of men wise without wisdom.

"Look at that window. Through it an empty room becomes bright with scenery; but the landscape stops outside. Were this not so, we should have an exemplification of sitting still and running away at one and the same time.

"In this sense, you may use your ears and eyes to communicate within, but shut out all wisdom from the mind.

And there where the supernatural can find shelter, shall not man find shelter too? This is the method for regenerating all creation.

It was the instrument which Yu and Shun employed. It was the secret of the success of Fu Hsi and Chi Chu. Shall it not then be adopted by mankind in general?"

Tzu Kao, Duke of She, being about to go on a mission to the Ch'i State, asked Confucius, saying, "The mission my sovereign is sending me on is a most important one. Of course, I shall be received with all due respect, but they will not take the same interest in the matter that I shall. And as an ordinary person cannot be pushed, still less a Prince, I am in a state of great alarm.

"Now you, Sir, have told me that in all undertakings great and small, Tao alone leads to a happy issue. Otherwise that, failing success, there is to be feared punishment from without, and with success, punishment from within; while exemption in case either of success or non-success falls only to the share of those who possess the virtue required.

"Well, I am not dainty with my food; neither am I always wanting to cool myself when hot. However, this morning I received my orders, and this evening I have been drinking iced water. I am so hot inside. Before I have put my hand to the business I am suffering punishment from within; and if I do not succeed I am sure to suffer punishment from without. Thus I get both punishments, which is really more than I can bear. Kindly tell me what there is to be done."

"There exist two sources of safety," Confucius replied. "One is Desti-

臣之事君，義也，無適而非君也，無所逃於天地之間。是之謂大戒。是以夫事其親者，不擇地而安之，孝之至也；夫事其君者，不擇事而安之，忠之盛也；自事其心者，哀樂不易施乎前，知其不可奈何而安之若命，德之至也。為人臣幾者，固有所不得已。行事之情而忘其身，何暇至於悅生而惡死！夫子其行可矣！丘請復以所聞：凡交近則必相靡以信，交遠則必忠之以言。言必或傳之。夫傳兩喜兩怒之言，天下之難者也。夫兩喜必多溢美之言，兩怒必多溢惡之言。凡溢之類妄，妄則其信之也莫，莫則傳言者殃。故法言曰：『傳其常情，無傳其溢言，則幾乎全。』且以巧斗力者，始乎陽，常卒乎陰，泰至則多奇巧；以禮飲酒者，始乎治，常卒乎亂，泰至則多奇樂。凡事亦然，始乎諒，常卒乎鄙；其作始也簡，其將畢也必巨。「言者，風波也；行

ny: the other is Duty. A child's love for its parents is destiny. It is inseparable from the child's life. A subject's allegiance to his sovereign is duty.
Beneath the canopy of heaven there is no place to which he can escape
from it. These two sources of safety may be explained as follows. To serve
one's parents without reference to place but only to the service, is the acme
of filial piety. To serve one's prince without reference to the act but only to
the service, is the perfection of a subject's loyalty. To serve one's own heart
so as to permit neither joy nor sorrow within, but to cultivate resignation
to the inevitable,—this is the climax of Virtue.

"Now a minister often finds himself in circumstances over which he
has no control. But if he simply confines himself to his work, and is utterly
oblivious of self, what leisure has he for loving life or hating death? And so
you may safely go.

"But I have yet more to tell you. All intercourse, if personal, should be
characterised by sincerity. If from a distance, it should be carried on in loyal terms. These terms will have to be transmitted by some one. Now the
transmission of messages of good- or ill-will is the hardest thing possible.
Messages of good-will are sure to be overdone with fine phrases; messages
of ill-will with harsh ones. In each case the result is exaggeration, and a
consequent failure to carry conviction, for which the envoy suffers. Therefore it was said in the Fa-yen,

'Confine yourself to simple statements of fact, shorn of all superfluous
expression of feeling, and your risk will be small.'

"In trials of skill, at first all is friendliness; but at last it is all antagonism. Skill is pushed too far. So on festive occasions, the drinking which
is in the beginning orderly enough, degenerates into riot and disorder.
Festivity is pushed too far. It is in fact the same with all things: they begin with good faith and end with contempt. From small beginnings come
great endings.

"Speech is like wind to wave. Action is liable to divergence from its
true goal. By wind, waves are easily excited. Divergence from the true goal
is fraught with danger. Thus angry feelings rise up without a cause. Specious words and dishonest arguments follow, as the wild random cries of
an animal at the point of death. Both sides give way to passion. For where
one party drives the other too much into a corner, resistance will always be
provoked without apparent cause. And if the cause is not apparent, how

者，實喪也。夫風波易以動，實喪易以危。故
忿設無由，巧言偏辭。獸死不擇音，氣息茀然，
於是並生厲心。剋核太至，則必有不肖之心應之，
而不知其然也。苟為不知其然也，孰知其所終！
故法言曰：『無遷令，無勸成。過度益也。』遷
令勸成殆事。美成在久，惡成不及改，可不慎與！
且夫乘物以游心，託不得已以養中，至矣。何
作為報也！莫若為致命，此其難者。」

顏闔將傅衛靈公太子，而問於蘧伯玉曰；「有
人於此，其德天殺。與之為無方，則危吾國，
與之為有方，則危吾身。其知適足以知人之過，
而不知其所以過。若然者，吾奈之何？」蘧伯玉
曰：「善哉問乎！戒之，慎之，正汝身也哉！形莫
若就，心莫若和。雖然，之二者有患。就不欲入，
和不欲出。形就而入，且為顛為滅，為崩為蹶
；心和而出，且為聲為名，為妖為孽。彼且為
嬰兒，亦與之為嬰兒；彼且為無町畦，亦與之
為無町畦；彼且為無崖，亦與之為無崖；達之
入於無疵。汝不知夫螳螂乎？怒其臂以當車轍，

much less will the ultimate effect be so?

"Therefore it is said in the Fa-yen, 'Neither deviate from nor travel beyond your instructions.

To pass the limit is to go to excess.'

"To deviate from, or to travel beyond instructions, may imperil the negotiation. A settlement to be successful must be lasting. It is too late to change an evil settlement once made.

"Therefore let yourself be carried along without fear, taking refuge in no alternative to preserve you from harm on either side. This is the utmost you can do. What need for considering your obligations? Better leave all to Destiny, difficult as this may be."

Yen Ho was about to become tutor to the eldest son of Prince Ling of the Wei State. Accordingly he observed to Chu Poh Yu,

"Here is a man whose disposition is naturally of a low order. To let him take his own unprincipled way is to endanger the State. To try to restrain him is to endanger one's personal safety. He has just wit enough to see faults in others, but not to see his own. I am consequently at a loss what to do."

"A good question indeed," replied Chu Poh Yu, "You must be careful, and begin by self-reformation. Outwardly you may adapt yourself, but inwardly you must keep up to your own standard. In this there are two points to be guarded against. You must not let the outward adaptation penetrate within, nor the inward standard manifest itself without. In the former case, you will fall, you will be obliterated, you will collapse, you will lie prostrate. In the latter case, you will be a sound, a name, a bogie, an uncanny thing. If he would play the child, do you play the child too. If he cast aside all sense of decorum, do you do so too. As far as he goes, do you go also. Thus you will reach him without offending him.

"Don't you know the story of the praying mantis? In its rage it stretched out its arms to prevent a chariot from passing, unaware that this was beyond its strength, so admirable was its energy!

Be cautious. If you are always offending others by your superiority, you will probably come to grief.

"Do you not know that those who keep tigers do not venture to give them live animals as food, for fear of exciting their fury when killing the prey? Also, that whole animals are not given, for fear of exciting the tigers'

不知其不勝任也，是其才之美者也。戒之，慎之，積伐而美者以犯之，幾矣！汝不知夫養虎者乎？不敢以生物與之，為其殺之之怒也；不敢以全物與之，為其決之之怒也。時其飢飽，達其怒心。虎之與人異類，而媚養己者，順也；故其殺者，逆也。夫愛馬者，以筐盛矢，以蜃盛溺。適有蚊虻僕緣，而拊之不時，則缺銜毀首碎胸。意有所至而愛有所亡。可不慎邪！」

匠石之齊，至於曲轅，見櫟社樹。其大蔽數千牛，絜之百圍，其高臨山，十仞而后有枝，其可以為舟者旁十數。觀者如市，匠伯不顧，遂行不輟。弟子厭觀之，走及匠石，曰：「自吾執斧斤以隨夫子，未嘗見材如此其美也。先生不肯視，行不輟，何邪？」曰：「已矣，勿言之矣！散木也。以為舟，則沉；以為棺槨，則速腐；以為器，則速毀；以為門戶，則液樠；以為柱，則蠹。是不材之木也。無所可用，故能若是之壽。」匠石歸，櫟社見夢曰：「女將惡乎比予哉？若將比予於文木邪？夫柤梨橘柚，果蓏之屬，實熟則剝，剝則辱。大枝折，小枝泄。此以其能

fury when rending them? The periods of hunger and repletion are careful-ly watched in order to prevent such outbursts. The tiger is of a different species from man; but the latter too is manageable if properly managed, unmanageable if excited to fury.

"Those who are fond of horses surround them with various conveni-ences. Sometimes mosquitoes or flies trouble them; and then, unexpect-edly to the animal, a groom will brush them off, the result being that the horse breaks his bridle, and hurts his head and chest. The intention is good, but there is a want of real care for the horse. Against this you must be on your guard."

A certain artisan was travelling to the Ch'i State. On reaching Ch'u-yuan, he saw a sacred li tree, large enough to hide an ox behind it, a hundred spans in girth, towering up ten cubits over the hill top, and carrying behind it branches, many tens of the smallest of which were of a size for boats. Crowds stood gazing at it, but our artisan took no notice, and went on his way with out even casting a look behind. His apprentice however gazed his fill, and when he caught up his master, said, "Ever since I have handled an adze in your service, I have never seen such a splendid piece of timber as that. How was it that you, sir, did not care to stop and look at it?"

"It's not worth talking about," replied his master. "It's good for nothing. Make a boat of it,—'twould sink. A coffin,—'twould rot. Fur-niture,—'twould soon break down. A door,—'twould sweat. A pil-lar,—'twould be worm-eaten. It is wood of no quality, and of no use. That is why it has attained its present age."

When the artisan reached home, he dreamt that the tree appeared to him in a dream and spoke as follows:—"What is it that you compare me with? Is it with the more elegant trees?—The cherry-apple, the pear, the orange, the pumelo, and other fruit-bearers, as soon as their fruit ripens are stripped and treated with indignity. The great boughs are snapped off, the small ones scattered abroad. Thus do these trees by their own value injure their own lives. They cannot fulfil their allotted span of years, but perish prematurely in mid-career from their entanglement with the world around them. Thus it is with all things. For a long period my aim was to be useless. Many times I was in danger, but at length I succeeded, and so became useful as I am to-day. But had I then been of use, I

苦其生者也。故不終其天年而中道夭，自掊擊於世俗者也。物莫不若是。且予求無所可用久矣！幾死，乃今得之，為予大用。使予也而有用，且得有此大也邪？且也若與予也皆物也，奈何哉其相物也？而幾死之散人，又惡知散木！」匠石覺而診其夢。弟子曰：「趣取無用，則為社，何邪？」曰：「密！若無言！彼亦直寄焉！以為不知己者詬厲也。不為社者，且幾有翦乎！且也，彼其所保與眾異，而以義喻之，不亦遠乎！」

南伯子綦游乎商之丘，見大木焉，有異：結駟千乘，將隱芘其所藾。子綦曰：「此何木也哉！此必有異材夫！」仰而視其細枝，則拳曲而不可以為棟梁；俯而視其大根，則軸解而不可以為棺槨；咶其葉，則口爛而為傷；嗅之，則使人狂酲，三日而不已。子綦曰：「此果不材之木也，

should not now be of the great use I am. Moreover, you and I belong both to the same category of things. Have done then with this criticism of others. Is a good-for-nothing fellow whose dangers are not yet passed a fit person to talk of a good-for-nothing tree?"

When our artisan awaked and told his dream, his apprentice said, "If the tree aimed at uselessness, how was it that it became a sacred tree?"

"What you don't understand," replied his master, "don't talk about. That was merely to escape from the attacks of its enemies. Had it not become sacred, how many would have wanted to cut it down! The means of safety adopted were different from ordinary means, and to test these by ordinary canons leaves one far wide of the mark."

Tzu Ch'i of Nan-poh was travelling on the Shang mountain when he saw a large tree which astonished him very much. A thousand chariot teams could have found shelter under its shade.

"What tree is this?" cried Tzu Ch'i. "Surely it must have unusually fine timber." Then looking up, he saw that its branches were too crooked for rafters; while as to the trunk he saw that its irregular grain made it valueless for coffins. He tasted a leaf, but it took the skin off his lips; and its odour was so strong that it would make a man as it were drunk for three days together.

"Ah!" said Tzu Ch'i. "This tree is good for nothing, and that is how it has attained this size. A wise man might well follow its example."

以至於此其大也。嗟乎神人，以此不材。」宋有荊氏者，宜楸柏桑。其拱把而上者，求狙猴之杙者斬之；三圍四圍，求高名之麗者斬之；七圍八圍，貴人富商之家求樿傍者斬之。故未終其天年，而中道之夭於斧斤，此材之患也。故解之以牛之白顙者，與豚之亢鼻者，與人有痔病者，不可以適河。此皆巫祝以知之矣，所以為不祥也。此乃神人之所以為大祥也。

支離疏者，頤隱於臍，肩高於頂，會撮指天，五管在上，兩髀為脅。挫鍼治繲，足以餬口；鼓筴播精，足以食十人。上徵武士，則支離攘臂而游於其間；上有大役，則支離以有常疾不受功；上與病者粟，則受之三鍾與十束薪。夫支離者其形者，猶足以養其身，終其天年，又況支離其德者乎！

In the State of Sung there is a place called Ching-shih, where thrive the beech, the cedar, and the mulberry. Such as are of a one-handed span or so in girth are cut down for monkey-cages. Those of two or three two-handed spans are cut down for the beams of fine houses. Those of seven or eight such spans are cut down for the solid sides of rich men's coffins.

Thus they do not fulfil their allotted span of years, but perish in mid-career beneath the axe. Such is the misfortune which overtakes worth.

For the sacrifices to the River God, neither bulls with white cheeks, nor pigs with large snouts, nor men suffering from piles, were allowed to be used. This had been revealed to the soothsayers, and these characteristics were consequently regarded as inauspicious. The wise, however, would regard them as extremely auspicious.

There was a hunchback named Su. His jaws touched his navel. His shoulders were higher than his head. His hair knot looked up to the sky. His viscera were upside down. His buttocks were where his ribs should have been. By tailoring, or washing, he was easily able to earn his living. By sifting rice he could make enough to support a family of ten.

When orders came down for a conscription, the hunchback stood unconcerned among the crowd. And similarly, in matters of public works, his deformity shielded him from being employed.

On the other hand, when it came to donations of grain, the hunchback received as much as three chung, and of firewood, ten faggots. And if physical deformity was thus enough to preserve his body until its allotted end, how much more would not moral and mental deformity avail!

　　孔子適楚，楚狂接輿游其門曰：「鳳兮鳳兮，何如德之衰也！來世不可待，往世不可追也。天下有道，聖人成焉；天下無道，聖人生焉。方今之時，僅免刑焉。福輕乎羽，莫之知載；禍重乎地，莫之知避。已乎已乎！臨人以德。殆乎殆乎！畫地而趨。迷陽迷陽，無傷吾行；吾行郤曲，無傷吾足。」山木，自寇也；膏火，自煎也。桂可食，故伐之；漆可用，故割之。人皆知有用之用，而莫知無用之用也。

When Confucius was in the Ch'u State, the eccentric Chieh Yu passed his door, saying, "O phoenix, O phoenix, how has thy virtue fallen!— unable to wait for the coming years or to go back into the past.

If Tao prevails on earth, prophets will fulfil their mission. If Tao does not prevail, they will but preserve themselves. At the present day they will but just escape.

"The honours of this world are light as feathers, yet none estimate them at their true value. The misfortunes of this life are weighty as the earth itself, yet none can keep out of their reach. No more, no more, seek to influence by virtue. Beware, beware, move cautiously on! O ferns, O ferns, wound not my steps! Through my tortuous journey wound not my feet! Hills suffer from the trees they produce. Fat burns by its own combustibility. Cinnamon trees furnish food: therefore they are cut down. The lacquer tree is felled for use. All men know the use of useful things; but they do not know the use of useless things."

# 德充符第五

魯有兀者王駘，從之游者，與仲尼相若。常季問於仲尼曰：「王駘，兀者也，從之游者，與夫子中分魯。立不教，坐不議。虛而往，實而歸。固有不言之教，無形而心成者邪？是何人也？」仲尼曰：「夫子，聖人也，丘也直後而未往耳！丘將以為師，而況不若丘者乎！奚假魯國，丘將引天下而與從之。」常季曰：「彼兀者也，而王先生，其與庸亦遠矣。若然者，其用心也獨若之何？」仲尼曰：「死生亦大矣，而不得與之變；雖天地覆墜，亦將不與之遺；審乎無假而不與物遷，命物之化而守其宗也。」常季曰：「何謂也？」仲尼曰：「自其異者視之，肝膽楚越也；自其同者視之，萬物皆一也。夫若然者，且不知耳目之所宜，而游心乎德之和。物視其所一而不見其所喪，視喪其足猶遺土也。」常季曰：「彼為己，以其知得其心，以其心得其常心。物何為最之哉？」仲尼曰：「人莫鑑於流水，而

# CHAPTER V

## THE EVIDENCE OF VIRTUE COMPLETE

In the State of Lu there was a man, named Wang T'ai, who had had his toes cut off. His disciples were as numerous as those of Confucius.

Ch'ang Chi asked Confucius, saying, "This Wang T'ai has been mutilated, yet he divides with you, Sir, the teaching of the Lu State. He neither preaches nor discusses; yet those who go to him empty, depart full. He must teach the doctrine which does not find expression in words; and although his shape is imperfect, his mind is perhaps complete. What manner of man is this?"

"He is a prophet," replied Confucius, "whose instruction I have been late in seeking. I will go and learn from him. And if I,—why not those who are not equal to me? And I will take with me, not the State of Lu only, but the whole world."

"The fellow has been mutilated," said Ch'ang Chi, "and yet people call him Master. He must be very different from the ordinary run. But how does he use his mind in this sense?"

"Life and Death are all powerful," answered Confucius, "but they cannot affect it.

Heaven and earth may collapse, but that will remain. If this is found to be without flaw, it will not share the fate of all things. It can cause other things to change, while preserving its own constitution intact."

"How so?" asked Ch'ang Chi.

"From the point of view of difference," replied Confucius, "we distinguish between the liver and the gall, between the Ch'u State and the Yueh State. From the point of view of sameness, all things are ONE. Such is the position of Wang T'ai. He does not trouble about what reaches him through the senses of hearing and sight, but directs his whole mind towards the very climax of virtue. He beholds all things as though ONE, without observing their discrepancies. And thus the discrepancy of his toes is to him as would be the loss of so much mud."

"He devotes himself in fact to himself," said Ch'ang Chi, "and uses his wisdom to perfect his mind, until it becomes perfect. But how then is it that people make so much of him?"

鑑於止水。唯止能止眾止。受命於地，唯松柏獨也正，在冬夏青青；受命於天，唯堯舜獨也正，在萬物之首。幸能正生，以正眾生。夫保始之徵，不懼之實，勇士一人，雄入於九軍。將求名而能自要者，而猶若是，而況官天地、府萬物、直寓六骸、象耳目、一知之所知，而心未嘗死者乎！彼且擇日而登假，人則從是也。彼且何肯以物為事乎！」

申徒嘉，兀者也，而與鄭子產同師於伯昏無人。子產謂申徒嘉曰：「我先出則子止，子先出則我止。」其明日，又與合堂同席而坐。子產謂申徒嘉曰：「我先出則子止，子先出則我止。今我將出，子可以止乎？其未邪？且子見執政而不違，子齊執政乎？」申徒嘉曰：「先生之門固有執政焉如此哉？子而悅子之執政而后人者也。聞之：『鑑明則塵垢不止，止則不明也。久與賢人處則無過。』今子之所取大者，先生也，而猶出言若是，不亦過乎！」子產曰：「子既若是矣，猶與堯爭善。計子之德，不足以自反邪？」申徒嘉曰：「自狀其過，以不當亡者眾；不狀其過，

"A man," replied Confucius, "does not seek to see himself in running water, but in still water. For only what is itself still can instil stillness into others.

"The grace of earth has reached only to pines and cedars;—winter and summer alike they are green. The grace of God has reached to Yao and to Shun alone;—the first and foremost of all creation. Happily they were able to regulate their own lives and thus regulate the lives of all mankind.

"By nourishment of physical courage, the sense of fear may be so eliminated that a man will, single-handed, brave a whole army. And if such a result can be achieved in search of fame, how much more by one who extends his sway over heaven and earth and influences all things; and who, lodging within the confines of a body with its channels of sight and sound, brings his knowledge to know that all things are ONE, and that his soul endures for ever! Besides, he awaits his appointed hour, and men flock to him of their own accord. He makes no effort to attract them."

Shen T'u Chia had had his toes cut off. Subsequently, he studied under Poh Hun Wu Jen at the same time as Tzu Ch'an of the Cheng State. The latter said to him, "When I leave first, do you remain awhile. When you leave first, I will remain behind."

Next day, when they were again together in the lecture-room, Tzu Ch'an said, "When I leave first, do you remain awhile. When you leave first, I will remain. I am now about to go. Will you remain or not? I notice you show no respect to a Minister of State. Perhaps you think yourself my equal?"

"Dear me!" replied Shen T'u Chia, "I didn't know we had a Minister of State in the class. Perhaps you think that because you are one you should take precedence over the rest. Now I have heard that if a mirror is perfectly bright, dust and dirt will not collect on it. That if they do, it is because the mirror was not bright. He who associates for long with the wise will be without fault. Now you have been improving yourself at the feet of our Master, yet you can utter words like these. Is not the fault in you?"

"You are a fine fellow, certainly," retorted Tzu Ch'an, "you will be emulating the virtue of Yao next. To look at you, I should say you had enough to do to attend to your own shortcomings!"

"Those who disguise their faults," said Shen T'u Chia, "so as not

以不當存者寡。知不可奈何，而安之若命，唯有德者能之。游於羿之彀中。中央者，中地也；然而不中者，命也。人以其全足笑吾不全足者多矣，我怫然而怒，而適先生之所，則廢然而反。不知先生之洗我以善邪？吾之自寐邪？吾與夫子游十九年矣，而未嘗知吾兀者也。今子與我游於形骸之內，而子索我於形骸之外，不亦過乎！」子產蹴然改容更貌曰：「子無乃稱！」

魯有兀者叔山無趾，踵見仲尼。仲尼曰：「子不謹，前既犯患若是矣。雖今來，何及矣！」無趾曰：「吾唯不知務而輕用吾身，吾是以亡足。今吾來也，猶有尊足者存，吾是以務全之也。夫天無不覆，地無不載，吾以夫子為天地，安知夫子之猶若是也！」孔子曰：「丘則陋矣！夫子

to lose their toes, are many in number. Those who do not disguise their faults, and so fail to keep them, are few. To recognise the inevitable and to quietly acquiesce in Destiny, is the achievement of the virtuous man alone. He who should put himself in front of the bull's-eye when Hou I

was shooting, would be hit. If he was not hit, it would be destiny. Those with toes who laugh at me for having no toes are many. This used to make me angry. But since I have studied under our Master, I have ceased to trouble about it. It may be that our Master has so far succeeded in purifying me. At any rate I have been with him nineteen years without being aware of the loss of my toes. Now you and I are engaged in studying the internal. Do you not then commit a fault by thus dragging me back to the external?"

At this Tzu Ch'an began to fidget, and changing countenance, begged Shen T'u Chia to say no more.

There was a man of the Lu State who had been mutilated,—Shu Shan No-toes. He came walking on his heels to see Confucius; but Confucius said, "You did not take care, and so brought this misfortune upon yourself. What is the use of coming to me now?"

"In my ignorance," replied No-toes, "I made free with my body and lost my toes. But I come with something more precious than toes which I now seek to keep. There is no man, but Heaven covers him: there is no man, but Earth supports him;—and I thought that you, sir, would be as Heaven and Earth. I little expected to hear these words from you."

"I must apologise," said Confucius. "Pray walk in and let us discuss." But No-toes walked out.

"There!" said Confucius to his disciples. "There is a criminal without toes who seeks to learn in order to make atonement for his previous misdeeds. And if he, how much more those who have no misdeeds for which to atone?"

No-toes went off to Lao Tzu and said, "Is Confucius a sage, or is he not? How is it he has so many disciples? He aims at being a subtle dialectician, not knowing that such a reputation is regarded by real sages as the fetters of a criminal."

"Why do you not meet him with the continuity of life and death, the identity of can and can not," answered Lao Tzu, "and so release him from these fetters?"

胡不入乎？請講以所聞。」無趾出。 孔子曰：「弟子勉之！夫無趾，兀者也，猶務學以復補前行之惡，而況全德之人乎！」無趾語老聃曰：「孔丘之於至人，其未邪？彼何賓賓以學子為？彼且以蘄以諔詭幻怪之名聞，不知至人之以是為己桎梏邪？」老聃曰：「胡不直使彼以死生為一條，以可不可為一貫者，解其桎梏，其可乎？」無趾曰：「天刑之，安可解！」

魯哀公問於仲尼曰：「衛有惡人焉，曰哀駘它。丈夫與之處者，思而不能去也；婦人見之，請於父母曰：‘與為人妻，寧為夫子妾’者，十數而未止也。未嘗有聞其唱者也，常和人而已矣。無君人之位以濟乎人之死，無聚祿以望人之腹，又以惡駭天下，和而不唱，知不出乎四域，且而雌雄合乎前，是必有異乎人者也。寡人召而觀之，果以惡駭天下。與寡人處，不至以月數，而寡人有意乎其為人也；不至乎期年，而寡人信之。國無宰，寡人傳國焉。悶然而後應，氾然而若辭。寡人醜乎，卒授之國。無幾何也，去寡人而行。寡人恤焉若有亡也，若無與樂是

"He has been thus punished by God," replied
No-toes. "It would be impossible to release him."

Duke Ai of the Lu State said to Confucius, "In the Wei State there is a leper, named Ai T'ai T'o. The men who live with him like him and make no effort to get rid of him. Of the women who have seen him, many have said to their parents, Rather than be another man's wife, I would be his concubine.

"He never preaches at people, but puts himself into sympathy with them. He wields no power by which he may protect men's bodies. He has at his disposal no appointments by which to gratify their hearts. He is loathsome to a degree. He sympathises, but does not instruct. His knowledge is limited to his own State. Yet males and females alike all congregate around him.

"So thinking that he must be different from ordinary men, I sent for him, and saw that he was indeed loathsome to a degree. Yet we had not been many months together ere my attention was fixed upon his conduct. A year had not elapsed ere I trusted him thoroughly; and as my State wanted a Prime Minister, I offered the post to him. He accepted it sullenly, as if he would much rather have declined. Perhaps he didn't think me good enough for him! At any rate, he took it; but in a very short time he left me and went away. I grieved for him as for a lost friend, and as though there were none left with whom I could rejoice. What manner of man is this?

"When I was on a mission to the Ch'u State," replied Confucius, "I saw a litter of young pigs sucking their dead mother. After a while they looked at her, and then they all left the body and went off. For their mother did not look at them any more, nor did she any more seem to be of their kind. What they loved was their mother; not the body which contained her, but that which made the body what it was.

"When a man is killed in battle, his arms are not buried with him.

A man whose toes have been cut off does not value a present of boots. In each case the function of such things is gone.

"The concubines of the Son of Heaven do not cut their nails or pierce their ears.

He who has a marriageable daughter keeps her away from menial work. To preserve her beauty is quite enough occupation for her. How

國也。是何人者也！」仲尼曰：「丘也嘗使於楚矣，適見純子食於其死母者。少焉眴若，皆棄之而走。不見己焉爾，不得類焉爾。所愛其母者，非愛其形也，愛使其形者也。戰而死者，其人之葬也不以翣資；刖者之屨，無為愛之。皆無其本矣。為天子之諸御：不翦爪，不穿耳；取妻者止於外，不得復使。形全猶足以為爾，而況全德之人乎！今哀駘它未言而信，無功而親，使人授己國，唯恐其不受也，是必才全而德不形者也。」哀公曰：「何謂才全？」仲尼曰：「死生存亡、窮達貧富、賢與不肖、毀譽、飢渴寒暑，是事之變、命之行也。日夜相代乎前，而知不能規乎其始者也。故不足以滑和，不可入於靈府。使之和豫通，而不失於兌。使日夜無郤，而與物

much more so for a man of perfect virtue?

"Now Ai T'ai T'o says nothing, and is trusted. He does nothing, and is sought after. He causes a man to offer him the government of his own State, and the only fear is lest he should decline.

Truly his talents are perfect and his virtue without outward form!"

"What do you mean by his talents being perfect?" asked the Duke.

"Life and Death," replied Confucius, "existence and non-existence, success and non-success, poverty and wealth, virtue and vice, good and evil report, hunger and thirst, warmth and cold,—these all revolve upon the changing wheel of Destiny. Day and night they follow one upon the other, and no man can say where each one begins. Therefore they cannot be allowed to disturb the harmony of the organism, nor enter into the soul's domain. Swim however with the tide, so as not to offend others. Do this day by day without break, and live in peace with mankind. Thus you will be ready for all contingencies, and may be said to have your talents perfect."

"And virtue without outward form; what is that?"

"In a water-level," said Confucius, "the water is in a most perfect state of repose. Let that be your model. The water remains quietly within, and does not overflow. It is from the cultivation of such harmony that virtue results. And if virtue takes no outward form, man will not be able to keep aloof from it."

Some days afterwards Duke Ai told Min Tzu, saying, "When first I took the reins of government in hand, I thought that in caring for my people's lives I had done all my duty as a ruler. But now that I have heard what a perfect man is, I fear that I have not been succeeding, but foolishly using my body and working destruction to my State. Confucius and I are not prince and minister, but merely friends with a care for each other's moral welfare."

A certain hunchback, named Wu Ch'un, whose heels did not touch the ground, had the ear of Duke Ling of Wei. The Duke took a great fancy to him; and as for well-formed men, he thought their necks were too short.

Another man, with a goitre as big as a large jar, had the ear of Duke Huan of Ch'i. The Duke took a great fancy to him; and as for well-formed men, he thought their necks were too thin.

為春，是接而生時於心者也。是之謂才全。」「何謂德不形？」曰：「平者，水停之盛也。其可以為法也，內保之而外不蕩也。德者，成和之修也。德不形者，物不能離也。」哀公異日以告閔子曰：「始也吾以南面而君天下，執民之紀而憂其死，吾自以為至通矣。今吾聞至人之言，恐吾無其實，輕用吾身而亡其國。吾與孔丘非君臣也，德友而已矣！」

闉跂支離無脤說衛靈公，靈公說之，而視全人，其脰肩肩。甕瓷大癭說齊桓公，桓公說之，而視全人，其脰肩肩。故德有所長，而形有所忘。人不忘其所忘，而忘其所不忘，此所謂誠忘。故聖人有所游，而知為孽，約為膠，德為接，工為商。聖人不謀，惡用知？不斫，惡用膠？無喪，惡用德？不貨，惡用商？四者，天鬻也。天鬻者，天食也。既受食於天，又惡用人！有人之形，無人之情。有人之形，故群於人；無人之情，故是非不得於身。眇乎小哉，所以屬於人也；警乎大哉，獨成其天。

Thus it is that virtue should prevail and outward form be forgotten. But mankind forgets not that which is to be forgotten, forgetting that which is not to be forgotten. This is forgetfulness indeed! And thus with the truly wise, wisdom is a curse, sincerity like glue, virtue only a means to acquire, and skill nothing more than a commercial capacity. For the truly wise make no plans, and therefore require no wisdom. They do not separate, and therefore require no glue. They want nothing, and therefore need no virtue. They sell nothing, and therefore are not in want of a commercial capacity. These four qualifications are bestowed upon them by God and serve as heavenly food to them. And those who thus feed upon the divine have little need for the human. They wear the forms of men, without human passions. Because they wear the forms of men, they associate with men. Because they have not human passions, positives and negatives find in them no place. Infinitesimal indeed is that which makes them man: infinitely great is that which makes them divine!

　　惠子謂莊子曰：「人故無情乎？」莊子曰：「然。」惠子曰：「人而無情，何以謂之人？」莊子曰：「道與之貌，天與之形，惡得不謂之人？」惠子曰：「既謂之人，惡得無情？」莊子曰：「是非吾所謂情也。吾所謂無情者，言人之不以好惡內傷其身，常因自然而不益生也。」惠子曰：「不益生，何以有其身？」莊子曰：「道與之貌，天與之形，無以好惡內傷其身。今子外乎子之神，勞乎子之精，倚樹而吟，據槁梧而瞑。天選之形，子以堅白鳴。」

Hui Tzu said to Chuang Tzu, "Are there then men who have no passions?"

Chuang Tzu replied, "Certainly."

"But if a man has no passions," argued Hui Tzu, "what is it that makes him a man?"

"Tao," replied Chuang Tzu, "gives him his expression, and God gives him his form. How should he not be a man?"

"If then he is a man," said Hui Tzu, "how can he be without passions?"

"What you mean by passions," answered Chuang Tzu, "is not what I mean. By a man without passions I mean one who does not permit good and evil to disturb his internal economy, but rather falls in with whatever happens, as a matter of course, and does not add to the sum of his mortality."

"But whence is man to get his body," asked Hui Tzu, "if there is to be no adding to the sum of mortality?"

"Tao gives him his expression," said Chuang Tzu, "and God gives him his form. He does not permit good and evil to disturb his internal economy. But now you are devoting your intelligence to externals, and wearing out your mental powers. You prop yourself against a tree and mutter, or lean over a table with half-closed eyes.

God has made you a shapely sight,
Yet your only thought is the hard and white."

# 大宗師第六

知天之所為，知人之所為者，至矣！知天之所為者，天而生也；知人之所為者，以其知之所知，以養其知之所不知，終其天年而不中道夭者，是知之盛也。雖然，有患，夫知有所待而後當，其所待者特未定也。庸詎知吾所謂天之非人乎？所謂人之非天乎？且有真人而後有真知。何謂真人？古之真人，不逆寡，不雄成，不謨士。若然者，過而弗悔，當而不自得也。若然者，登高不慄，入水不濡，入火不熱，是知之能登假於道者也若此。古之真人，其寢不夢，其覺無憂，其食不甘，其息深深。真人之息以踵，眾人之息以喉。屈服者，其嗌言若哇。其耆欲深者，其天機淺。古之真人，不知說生，不知惡死。其出不訢，其入不距。翛然而往，翛然而來而已矣。不忘其所始，不求其所終。受而喜之，忘而復之。是之謂不以心損道，不以人助天，是之謂真人。若然者，其心忘，其容寂，其顙頯。淒然似秋，煖然似春，喜怒通四時，與物有宜而莫知其極。故聖人之用兵也，亡國而不失人心。

# CHAPTER VI

## THE GREAT SUPREME

He who knows what God is, and who knows what Man is, has attained. Knowing what God is, he knows that he himself proceeded therefrom. Knowing what Man is, he rests in the knowledge of the known, waiting for the knowledge of the unknown. Working out one's allotted span, and not perishing in mid career,—this is the fulness of knowledge.

God is a principle which exists by virtue of its own intrinsicality, and operates spontaneously, without self-manifestation.

Herein, however, there is a flaw. Knowledge is dependent upon fulfilment. And as this fulfilment is uncertain, how can it be known that my divine is not really human, my human really divine?

We must have pure men, and then only can we have pure knowledge.

But what is a pure man?—The pure men of old acted without calculation, not seeking to secure results. They laid no plans. Therefore, failing, they had no cause for regret; succeeding, no cause for congratulation. And thus they could scale heights without fear; enter water without becoming wet; fire, without feeling hot. So far had their wisdom advanced towards Tao.

The pure men of old slept without dreams, and waked without anxiety. They ate without discrimination, breathing deep breaths. For pure men draw breath from their uttermost depths; the vulgar only from their throats.

Out of the crooked, words are retched up like vomit. If men's passions are deep, their divinity is shallow.

The pure men of old did not know what it was to love life or to hate death. They did not rejoice in birth, nor strive to put off dissolution. Quickly come, and quickly go;—no more. They did not forget whence it was they had sprung, neither did they seek to hasten their return thither. Cheerfully they played their allotted parts, waiting patiently for the end. This is what is called not to lead the heart astray from Tao, nor to let the human seek to supplement the divine.

And this is what is meant by a pure man.

Such men are in mind absolutely free; in demeanour, grave; in expres-

利澤施乎萬世，不為愛人。故樂通物，非聖人也；有親，非仁也；天時，非賢也；利害不通，非君子也；行名失己，非士也；亡身不真，非役人也。若狐不偕、務光、伯夷、叔齊、箕子、胥余、紀他、申徒狄，是役人之役，適人之適，而不自適其適者也。古之真人，其狀義而不朋，若不足而不承；與乎其觚而不堅也，張乎其虛而不華也；邴乎其似喜也，崔乎其不得已也，滀乎進我色也，與乎止我德也，廣乎其似世也，警乎其未可制也，連乎其似好閉也，悗乎忘其言也。以刑為體，以禮為翼，以知為時，以德為循。以刑為體者，綽乎其殺也；以禮為翼者，所以行於世也；以知為時者，不得已於事也；以德為循者，言其與有足者至於丘也，而人真以為勤行者也。故其好之也一，其弗好之也一。其一也一，其不一也一。其一與天為徒，其不一與人為徒，天與人不相勝也，是之謂真人。

死生，命也；其有夜旦之常，天也。人之有所不得與，皆物之情也。彼特以天為父，而身猶愛之，而況其卓乎！人特以有君為愈乎己，而

sion, cheerful. If it is freezing cold, it seems to them like autumn; if blazing hot, like spring. Their passions occur like the four seasons.

They are in harmony with all creation, and none know the limit thereof.

And so it is that a perfect man can destroy a kingdom and yet not lose the hearts of the people, while the benefits he hands down to ten thousand generations do not proceed from love of his fellow-man.

He who delights in man, is himself not a perfect man. His affection is not true charity.

Depending upon opportunity, he has not true worth.

He who is not conversant with both good and evil is not a superior man.

He who disregards his reputation is not what a man should be.

He who is not absolutely oblivious of his own existence can never be a ruler of men.

Thus Hu Pu Hsieh, Wu Kuang, Poh I, Shu Ch'i, Chi Tzu Hsu Yu, Chi T'o, and Shen T'u Ti, were the servants of rulers, and did the behests of others, not their own.

The pure men of old did their duty to their neighbours, but did not associate with them.

They behaved as though wanting in themselves, but without flattering others. Naturally rectangular, they were not uncompromisingly hard. They manifested their independence without going to extremes. They appeared to smile as if pleased, when the expression was only a natural response.

Their outward semblance derived its fascination from the store of goodness within. They seemed to be of the world around them, while proudly treading beyond its limits. They seemed to desire silence, while in truth they had dispensed with language.

They saw in penal laws a trunk; in social ceremonies, wings; in wisdom, a useful accessory; in morality, a guide. For them penal laws meant a merciful administration; social ceremonies, a passport through the world; wisdom, an excuse for doing what they could not help; and morality, walking like others upon the path.

And thus all men praised them for the worthy lives they led.

For what they cared for could be reduced to ONE, and what they did not care for to ONE also. That which was ONE was ONE, and that which

身猶死之，而況其真乎！泉涸，魚相與處於陸，相呴以濕，相濡以沫，不如相忘於江湖。與其譽堯而非桀也，不如兩忘而化其道。夫藏舟於壑，藏山於澤，謂之固矣！然而夜半有力者負之而走，昧者不知也。藏小大有宜，猶有所遯。若夫藏天下於天下而不得所遯，是恆物之大情也。特犯人之形而猶喜之。若人之形者，萬化而未始有極也，其為樂可勝計邪？故聖人將游於物之所不得遯而皆存。善夭善老，善始善終，人猶效之，而況萬物之所系，而一化之所待乎！夫道，有情有信，無為無形；可傳而不可受，可得而不可見；自本自根，未有天地，自古以固存；神鬼神帝，生天生地；在太極之先而不為高，在六極之下而不為深，先天地生而不為久，長於上古而不為老。狶韋氏得之，以挈天地；伏戲氏

was not

ONE was likewise ONE. In that which was ONE, they were of God; in that which was not ONE, they were of Man. And so between the human and the divine no conflict ensued. This was to be a pure man.

Life and Death belong to Destiny. Their sequence, like day and night, is of God, beyond the interference of man, an inevitable law.

A man looks upon God as upon his father, and loves him in like measure. Shall he then not love that which is greater than God?

A man looks upon a ruler of men as upon some one better than himself, for whom he would sacrifice his life. Shall he not then do so for the Supreme Ruler of Creation?

When the pond dries up, and the fishes are left upon dry ground, to moisten them with the breath or to damp them with spittle is not to be compared with leaving them in the first instance in their native rivers and lakes. And better than praising Yao and blaming Chieh would be leaving them both and attending to the development of Tao.

Tao gives me this form, this toil in manhood, this repose in old age, this rest in death. And surely that which is such a kind arbiter of my life is the best arbiter of my death.

A boat may be hidden in a creek, or in a bog, safe enough.

But at midnight a strong man may come and carry away the boat on his back. The dull of vision do not perceive that however you conceal things, small ones in larger ones, there will always be a chance of losing them.

But if you conceal the whole universe in the whole universe, there will be no place left wherein it may be lost. The laws of matter make this to be so.

To have attained to the human form must be always a source of joy. And then, to undergo countless transitions, with only the infinite to look forward to,—what incomparable bliss is that!

Therefore it is that the truly wise rejoice in that which can never be lost, but endures alway.

For if we can accept early death, old age, a beginning, and an end, why not that which informs all creation and is of all phenomena the Ultimate Cause?

Tao has its laws, and its evidences. It is devoid both of action and of

得之，以襲氣母；維斗得之，終古不忒；日月得之，終古不息；堪坏得之，以襲昆侖；馮夷得之，以游大川；肩吾得之，以處大山；黃帝得之，以登雲天；顓頊得之，以處玄宮；禺強得之，立乎北極；西王母得之，坐乎少廣，莫知其始，莫知其終；彭祖得之，上及有虞，下及五伯；傅說得之，以相武丁，奄有天下，乘東維、騎箕尾而比於列星。

南伯子葵問乎女偊曰：「子之年長矣，而色若孺子，何也？」曰：「吾聞道矣。」南伯子葵曰：「道可得學邪？」曰：「惡！惡可！子非其人也。夫卜梁倚有聖人之才而無聖人之道，我有聖人之道而無聖人之才。吾欲以教之，庶幾其果為聖人乎？不然，以聖人之道告聖人之才，亦易矣。吾猶守而告之，三日而後能外天下；已外天下矣，吾又守之，七日而後能外物；已外物矣，吾又守之，九日而後能外生；已外生矣，而後能朝徹；朝徹而後能見獨；見獨而後能無

form. It may be transmitted, but cannot be received.

It may be obtained, but cannot be seen. Before heaven and earth were, Tao was. It has existed without change from all time. Spiritual beings drew their spirituality therefrom, while the universe became what we can see it now. To Tao, the zenith is not high, nor the nadir low; no point in time is long ago, nor by lapse of ages has it grown old.

Hsi Wei obtained Tao, and so set the universe in order.

Fu Hsi obtained it, and was able to establish eternal principles.

The Great Bear obtained it, and has never erred from its course. The sun and moon obtained it, and have never ceased to revolve. K'an P'i obtained it, and established the K'un-lun mountains.

P'ing I obtained it, and rules over the streams. Chien Wu obtained it, and dwells on Mount T'ai.

The Yellow Emperor obtained it, and soared upon the clouds to heaven.

Chuan Hsu obtained it, and dwells in the Dark Palace.

Yu Ch'iang obtained it, and fixed himself at the North Pole.

Hsi Wang Mu obtained it, and settled at Shao Kuang; since when, no one knows; until when, no one knows either.

P'eng Tsu obtained it, and lived from the time of Shun until the time of the Five Princes.

Fu Yueh obtained it, and as the Minister of Wu Ting got the empire under his control. And now, charioted upon one constellation and drawn by another, he has been enrolled among the stars of heaven.

Nan Po Tzu K'uei said to Nu Yu,

"You are old, Sir, and yet your countenance is like that of a child. How is this?"

Nu Yu replied, "I have learnt Tao."

"Could I get Tao by studying it?" asked the other.

"I fear not," said Nu Yu. "You are not the sort of man. There was Pu Liang I. He had all the qualifications of a sage, but not Tao. Now I had Tao, though none of the qualifications. But do you imagine that much as I wished it I was able to teach Tao to him so that he should be a perfect sage? Had it been so, then to teach Tao to one who has the qualifications of a sage would be an easy matter. No, Sir. I imparted as though withholding; and in three days, for him, this sublunary state had ceased to exist.

古今；無古今，而後能入於不死不生。殺生者
不死，生生者不生。其為物無不將也，無不迎也，
無不毀也，無不成也。其名為攖寧。攖寧也者，
攖而後成者也。」南伯子葵曰：「子獨惡乎聞之？」
曰：「聞諸副墨之子，副墨之子聞諸洛誦之孫，
洛誦之孫聞之瞻明，瞻明聞之聶許，聶許聞之
需役，需役聞之於謳，於謳聞之玄冥，玄冥聞
之參寥，參寥聞之疑始。」

　　子祀、子輿、子犁、子來四人相與語，曰：「孰
能以無為首，以生為脊，以死為尻；孰知死生
存亡之一體者，吾與之友矣！」四人相視而笑，
莫逆於心，遂相與為友。俄而子輿有病，子祀
往問之。曰：「偉哉，夫造物者將以予為此拘拘
也。」曲僂發背，上有五管，頤隱於齊，肩高於
頂，句贅指天，陰陽之氣有沴，其心閒而無事，
跰𨇤而鑑於井，曰：「嗟乎！夫造物者又將以予
為此拘拘也。」子祀曰：「女惡之乎？」曰：「亡，
予何惡！浸假而化予之左臂以為雞，予因以求時
夜；浸假而化予之右臂以為彈，予因以求鴞炙
；浸假而化予之尻以為輪，以神為馬，予因以

When he had attained to this, I withheld again; and in seven days more, for him, the external world had ceased to be. And so again for another nine days, when he became unconscious of his own existence. He became first etherealised, next possessed of perfect wisdom, then without past or present, and finally able to enter there where life and death are no more,—where killing does not take away life, nor does prolongation of life add to the duration of existence.

In that state, he is ever in accord with the exigencies of his environment; and this is to be Battered but not Bruised. And he who can be thus battered but not bruised is on the way to perfection."

"And how did you manage to get hold of all this?" asked Nan Po Tzu K'uei.

"I got it from books," replied Nu Yu; "and the books got it from learning, and learning from investigation, and investigation from co-ordination, and co-ordination from application, and application from desire to know, and desire to know from the unknown, and the unknown from the great void, and the great void from infinity!"

Four men were conversing together, when the following resolution was suggested:—"Whosoever can make Inaction the head, Life the backbone, and Death the tail, of his existence,—that man shall be admitted to friendship with us." The four looked at each other and smiled; and tacitly accepting the conditions, became friends forthwith.

By-and-by, one of them, named Tzu Yu, fell ill, and another, Tzu Ssu, went to see him. "Verily God is great!" said the sick man. "See how he has doubled me up. My back is so hunched that my viscera are at the top of my body. My cheeks are level with my navel. My shoulders are higher than my neck. My hair grows up towards the sky.

The whole economy of my organism is deranged. Nevertheless, my mental equilibrium is not disturbed." So saying, he dragged himself painfully to a well, where he could see himself, and continued, "Alas, that God should have doubled me up like this!"

"Are you afraid?" asked Tzu Ssu.

"I am not," replied Tzu Yu. "What have I to fear? Ere long I shall be decomposed. My left shoulder will become a cock, and I shall herald the approach of morn. My right shoulder will become a cross-bow, and I shall be able to get broiled duck. My buttocks will become wheels; and with

乘之，豈更駕哉！且夫得者，時也；失者，順也。安時而處順，哀樂不能入也，此古之所謂縣解也，而不能自解者，物有結之。且夫物不勝天久矣，吾又何惡焉！」俄而子來有病，喘喘然將死。其妻子環而泣之。子犁往問之，曰：「叱！避！無怛化！」倚其戶與之語曰：「偉哉造化！又將奚以汝為？將奚以汝適？以汝為鼠肝乎？以汝為虫臂乎？」子來曰：「父母於子，東西南北，唯命之從。陰陽於人，不翅於父母。彼近吾死而我不聽，我則悍矣，彼何罪焉？夫大塊以載我以形，勞我以生，佚我以老，息我以死。故善吾生者，乃所以善吾死也。今大冶鑄金，金踊躍曰：'我且必為鏌琊！'大冶必以為不祥之金。今一犯人之形，而曰：'人耳人耳'夫造化者必以為不祥之人。今一以天地為大鑪，以造化為大冶，惡乎往而不可哉！」成然寐，蘧然覺。

　　子桑戶、孟子反、子琴張三人相與語曰：「孰能相與於無相與，相為無相為，孰能登天遊霧，撓挑無極，相忘以生，無所終窮？」三人相視而笑，莫逆於心，遂相與為友。莫然有間，而子桑戶

my soul for a horse, I shall be able to ride in my own chariot. I obtained life because it was my time: I am now parting with it in accordance with the same law. Content with the natural sequence of these states, joy and sorrow touch me not. I am simply, as the ancients expressed it, hanging in the air, unable to cut myself down, bound with the trammels of material existence. But man has ever given way before God: why, then, should I be afraid?"

By-and-by, another of the four, named Tzu Lai, fell ill, and lay gasping for breath, while his family stood weeping around. The fourth friend, Tzu Li, went to see him. "Chut!" cried he to the wife and children; "begone! you balk his decomposition." Then, leaning against the door, he said,

"Verily, God is great! I wonder what he will make of you now. I wonder whither you will be sent. Do you think he will make you into a rat's liver or into the shoulders of a snake?"

"A son," answered Tzu Lai, "must go whithersoever his parents bid him. Nature is no other than a man's parents.

If she bid me die quickly, and I demur, then I am an unfilial son. She can do me no wrong. Tao gives me this form, this toil in manhood, this repose in old age, this rest in death. And surely that which is such a kind arbiter of my life is the best arbiter of my death.

"Suppose that the boiling metal in a smelting-pot were to bubble up and say, 'Make of me an Excalibur;' I think the caster would reject that metal as uncanny. And if a sinner like myself were to say to God, 'Make of me a man, make of me a man;' I think he too would reject me as uncanny. The universe is the smelting-pot, and God is the caster. I shall go whithersoever I am sent, to wake unconscious of the past, as a man wakes from a dreamless sleep."

Tzu Sang Hu, Meng Tzu Fan, and Tzu Ch'in Chang, were conversing together, when it was asked, "Who can be, and yet not be?

Who can do, and yet not do?

Who can mount to heaven, and roaming through the clouds, pass beyond the limits of space, oblivious of existence, for ever and ever without end?"

The three looked at each other and smiled; and as neither had any misgivings, they became friends accordingly.

死，未葬。孔子聞之，使子貢往侍事焉。或編曲，或鼓琴，相和而歌曰：「嗟來桑戶乎！嗟來桑戶乎！而已反其真，而我猶為人猗！」子貢趨而進曰：「敢問臨尸而歌，禮乎？」二人相視而笑曰：「是惡知禮意！」子貢反，以告孔子曰：「彼何人者邪？修行無有，而外其形骸，臨尸而歌，顏色不變，無以命之。彼何人者邪？」孔子曰：「彼游方之外者也，而丘，游方之內者也。外內不相及，而丘使女往弔之，丘則陋矣！彼方且與造物者為人，而游乎天地之一氣。彼以生為附贅縣疣，以死為決病潰癰。夫若然者，又惡知死生先後之所在！假於異物，托於同體；忘其肝膽，遺其耳目；反復終始，不知端倪；芒然仿徨乎塵垢之外，逍遙乎無為之業。彼又惡能憒憒然

Shortly afterwards Tzu Sang Hu died; whereupon Confucius sent Tzu Kung to take part in the mourning. But Tzu Kung found that one had composed a song which the other was accompanying on the lute, as follows:—

> Ah! Wilt thou come back to us, Sang Hu?
> Ah! Wilt thou come back to us, Sang Hu?
> Thou hast already returned to thy God,
> While we still remain here as men,—alas!

Tzu Kung hurried in and said, "How can you sing alongside of a corpse? Is this decorum?"

The two men looked at each other and laughed, saying, "What should this man know of decorum indeed?"

Tzu Kung went back and told Confucius, asking him, "What manner of men are these? Their object is nothingness and a separation from their corporeal frames.

They can sit near a corpse and yet sing, unmoved. There is no class for such. What are they?"

"These men," replied Confucius, "travel beyond the rule of life. I travel within it. Consequently, our paths do not meet; and I was wrong in sending you to mourn. They consider themselves as one with God, recognising no distinctions between human and divine. They look on life as a huge tumour from which death sets them free. All the same they know not where they were before birth, nor where they will be after death. Though admitting different elements, they take their stand upon the unity of all things. They ignore their passions. They take no count of their ears and eyes. Backwards and forwards through all eternity, they do not admit a beginning or end. They stroll beyond the dust and dirt of mortality, to wander in the realms of inaction. How should such men trouble themselves with the conventionalities of this world, or care what people may think of them?"

"But if such is the case," said Tzu Kung, "why should we stick to the rule?"

"Heaven has condemned me to this," replied Confucius. "Nevertheless, you and I may perhaps escape from it."

"By what method?" asked Tzu Kung.

"Fishes," replied Confucius, "are born in water. Man is born in Tao. If

為世俗之禮，以觀眾人之耳目哉！」子貢曰：「然
則夫子何方之依？」孔子曰：「丘，天之戮民也。
雖然，吾與汝共之。」子貢曰：「敢問其方？」孔
子曰：「魚相造乎水，人相造乎道。相造乎水者，
穿池而養給；相造乎道者，無事而生定。故曰：
魚相忘乎江湖，人相忘乎道術。」子貢曰：「敢
問畸人？」曰：「畸人者，畸於人而侔於天。故曰：
天之小人，人之君子；人之君子，天之小人也。」

顏回問仲尼曰：「孟孫才，其母死，哭泣無涕，
中心不戚，居喪不哀。無是三者，以善處喪蓋
魯國，固有無其實而得其名者乎？回壹怪之。」
仲尼曰：「夫孟孫氏盡之矣，進於知矣，唯簡之
而不得，夫已有所簡矣。孟孫氏不知所以生，
不知所以死。不知就先，不知就後。若化為物，

fishes get ponds to live in, they thrive. If man gets Tao to live in, he may live his life in peace.

Hence the saying, 'All that a fish wants is water; all that a man wants is Tao.'"

"May I ask," said Tzu Kung, "about divine men?"

"Divine men," replied Confucius, "are divine to man, but ordinary to God. Hence the saying that the meanest being in heaven would be the best on earth; and the best on earth, the meanest in heaven."

Yen Hui said to Confucius, "When Meng Sun Ts'ai's mother died, he wept, but without snivelling; he grieved but his grief was not heartfelt; he wore mourning but without howling. Yet although wanting in these three points, he is considered the best mourner in the State of Lu. Surely this is the name and not the reality. I am astonished at it."

"Meng Sun," said Confucius, "did all that was required. He has made an advance towards wisdom.

He could not do less; while all the time actually doing less.

"Meng Sun knows not whence we come nor whither we go. He knows not whether the end will come early or late. Passing into life as a man, he quietly awaits his passage into the unknown. What should the dead know of the living, or the living know of the dead? Even you and I may be in a dream from which we have not yet awaked.

"Then again, he adapts himself physically, while avoiding injury to his higher self.

He regards a dying man simply as one who is going home. He sees others weep, and he naturally weeps too.

"Besides, a man's personality is something of which he is subjectively conscious. It is impossible for him to say if he is really that which he is conscious of being. You dream you are a bird, and soar to heaven. You dream you are a fish, and dive into the ocean's depths. And you cannot tell whether the man now speaking is awake or in a dream.

"A pleasurable sensation precedes the smile it evokes. The smile itself is not dependent upon a reminding nudge.

Resign yourself, unconscious of all changes, and you shall enter into the pure, the divine, the One."

I Erh Tzu went to see Hsu Yu. The latter asked him, saying, "How has Yao benefited you?"

以待其所不知之化已乎。且方將化，惡知不化哉？方將不化，惡知已化哉？吾特與汝，其夢未始覺者邪！且彼有駭形而無損心，有旦宅而無耗精。孟孫氏特覺，人哭亦哭，是自其所以乃。且也相與吾之耳矣，庸詎知吾所謂吾之非吾乎？且汝夢為鳥而厲乎天，夢為魚而沒於淵。不識今之言者，其覺者乎？其夢者乎？造適不及笑，獻笑不及排，安排而去化，乃入於寥天一。」

意而子見許由，許由曰：「堯何以資汝？」意而子曰：「堯謂我：汝必躬服仁義而明言是非。」許由曰：「而奚來為軹？夫堯既已黥汝以仁義，而劓汝以是非矣。汝將何以游夫遙蕩恣睢轉徙之塗乎？」意而子曰：「雖然，吾愿游於其藩。」許由曰：「不然。夫盲者無以與乎眉目顏色之好，

"He bade me," replied the former, "practise charity and do my duty, and distinguish clearly between right and wrong."

"Then what do you want here?" said Hsu Yu.

"If Yao has already branded you with charity and duty, and cut off your nose with right and wrong, what do you do in this free-and-easy, care-for-nobody, topsy-turvy neighbourhood?"

"Nevertheless," replied I Erh Tzu, "I should like to be on its confines."

"If a man has lost his eyes," retorted Hsu Yu, "it is impossible for him to join in the appreciation of beauty. A man with a film over his eyes cannot tell a blue sacrificial robe from a yellow one."

"Wu Chuang's disregard of her beauty," answered I Erh Tzu, "Chu Liang's disregard of his strength, the Yellow Emperor's abandonment of wisdom,—all these were brought about by a process of filing and hammering. And how do you know but that God would rid me of my brands, and give me a new nose, and make me fit to become a disciple of yourself?"

"Ah!" replied Hsu Yu, "that cannot be known. But I will just give you an outline. The Master I serve succours all things, and does not account it duty. He continues his blessings through countless generations, and does not account it charity. Dating back to the remotest antiquity, he does not account himself old. Covering heaven, supporting earth, and fashioning the various forms of things, he does not account himself skilled. He it is whom you should seek."

瞽者無以與乎青黃黼黻之觀。」意而子曰：「夫無莊之失其美，據梁之失其力，黃帝之亡其知，皆在鑪捶之間耳。庸詎知夫造物者之不息我黥而補我劓，使我乘成以隨先生邪？」許由曰：「噫！未可知也。我為汝言其大略：吾師乎！吾師乎齏萬物而不為義，澤及萬世而不為仁，長於上古而不為老，覆載天地刻雕眾形而不為巧。此所游已！」

顏回曰：「回益矣。」仲尼曰：「何謂也？」曰：「回忘禮樂矣！」曰：「可矣，猶未也。」他日復見，曰：「回益矣。」曰：「何謂也？」曰：「回忘仁義矣。」曰：「可矣，猶未也。」他日復見，曰：「回益矣！」曰：「何謂也？」曰：「回坐忘矣。」仲尼蹴然曰：「何謂坐忘？」顏回曰：「墮肢體，黜聰明，離形去知，同於大通，此謂坐忘。」仲尼曰：「同則無好也，化則無常也。而果其賢乎！丘也請從而後也。」

"I am getting on," observed Yen Hui to Confucius.

"How so?" asked the latter.

"I have got rid of charity and duty," replied the former.

"Very good," replied Confucius, "but not perfect."

Another day Yen Hui met Confucius and said, "I am getting on."

"How so?" asked Confucius.

"I have got rid of ceremonial and music," answered Yen Hui.

"Very good," said Confucius, "but not perfect."

On a third occasion Yen Hui met Confucius and said, "I am getting on."

"How so?" asked the Sage.

"I have got rid of everything," replied Yen Hui.

"Got rid of everything!" said Confucius eagerly. "What do you mean by that?"

"I have freed myself from my body," answered Yen Hui. "I have discarded my reasoning powers. And by thus getting rid of body and mind, I have become One with the Infinite. This is what I mean by getting rid of everything."

"If you have become One," cried Confucius, "there can be no room for bias. If you have passed into space, you are indeed without begin ning or end. And if you have really attained to this, I trust to be allowed to follow in your steps."

　　子輿與子桑友。而霖雨十日，子輿曰：「子桑殆病矣！」裹飯而往食之。至子桑之門，則若歌若哭，鼓琴曰：「父邪！母邪！天乎！人乎！」有不任其聲而趨舉其詩焉。子輿入，曰：「子之歌詩，何故若是？」曰：「吾思夫使我至此極者而弗得也。父母豈欲吾貧哉？天無私覆，地無私載，天地豈私貧我哉？求其為之者而不得也！然而至此極者，命也夫！」

Tzu Yu and Tzu Sang were friends. Once when it had rained for ten days, Tzu Yu said, "Tzu Sang is dangerously ill." So he packed up some food and went to see him.

Arriving at the door, he heard something between singing and lamentation, accompanied with the sound of music, as follows:—

"O father! O mother! O Heaven! O Man!"

These words seemed to be uttered with a great effort; whereupon Tzu Yu went in and asked what it all meant.

"I was trying to think who could have brought me to this extreme," replied Tzu Sang, "but I could not guess. My father and mother would hardly wish me to be poor. Heaven covers all equally. Earth supports all equally. How can they make me in particular poor? I was seeking to know who it was, but without success. Surely then I am brought to this extreme by Destiny."

# 應帝王第七

　　齧缺問於王倪，四問而四不知。齧缺因躍而大喜，行以告蒲衣子。蒲衣子曰：「而乃今知之乎？有虞氏不及泰氏。有虞氏，其猶藏仁以要人，亦得人矣，而未始出於非人。泰氏，其臥徐徐，其覺于于。一以己為馬，一以己為牛。其知情信，其德甚真，而未始入於非人。」

　　肩吾見狂接輿。狂接輿曰：「日中始何以語女？」肩吾曰：「告我君人者以己出經式義度，人孰敢不聽而化諸！」狂接輿曰：「是欺德也。其於治天下也，猶涉海鑿河，而使蚊負山也。夫聖人之治也，治外夫？正而後行，確乎能其事者而已矣。且鳥高飛以避矰弋之害，鼷鼠深穴乎神丘之下，以避熏鑿之患，而曾二虫之無知？」

# CHAPTER VII

## HOW TO GOVERN

Yeh Ch'ueh asked Wang I

four questions, none of which he could answer. Thereat the former was greatly delighted, and went off and told P'u I Tzu.

"Have you only just found that out?" said P'u I Tzu. "The Emperor Shun was not equal to T'ai Huang.

Shun was all for charity in his zeal for mankind; but although he succeeded in government, he himself never rose above the level of artificiality. Now

T'ai Huang was peaceful when asleep and inactive when awake. At one time he would think himself a horse; at another, an ox.

His wisdom was substantial and above suspicion. His virtue was genuine indeed. And yet he never sank to the level of artificiality."

Chien Wu meeting the eccentric Chieh Yu, the latter enquired, saying, "What did Jih Chung Shih teach you?"

"He taught me," replied Chien Wu, "about the laws and regulations which princes evolve, and which he said none would venture not to hear and obey."

"That is a false teaching indeed," replied Chieh Yu. "To attempt to govern mankind thus,—as well try to wade through the sea, to hew a passage through a river, or make a mosquito fly away with a mountain!

"The government of the truly wise man has no concern with externals. He first perfects himself, and then by virtue thereof he is enabled to accomplish what he wants.

"The bird flies high to avoid snare and dart.

The mouse burrows down below the hill to avoid being smoked or cut out of its nest. Is your wit below that of these two creatures?"

T'ien Ken was travelling on the south of the Yin mountain. He had reached the river Liao when he met a certain Sage to whom he said, "I beg to ask about the government of the empire."

"Begone!" cried the Sage. "You are a low fellow, and your question is ill timed. God has just turned me out a man. That is enough for me. Borne on light pinions I can soar beyond the cardinal points, to the land of

天根游於殷陽，至蓼水之上，適遭無名人而問焉，曰：「請問為天下。」無名人曰：「去！汝鄙人也，何問之不豫也！予方將與造物者為人，厭，則又乘夫莽眇之鳥，以出六極之外，而游無何有之鄉，以處壙垠之野。汝又何帛以治天下感予之心為？」又復問，無名人曰：「汝游心於淡，合氣於漠，順物自然而無容私焉，而天下治矣。」

陽子居見老聃，曰：「有人於此，嚮疾強梁，物徹疏明，學道不卷，如是者，可比明王乎？」老聃曰：「是於聖人也，胥易技係，勞形怵心者也。且也虎豹之文來田，猿狙之便來藉。如是者，可比明王乎？」陽子居蹴然曰：「敢問明王之治。」老聃曰：「明王之治：功蓋天下而似不自己，化貸萬物而民弗恃。有莫舉名，使物自喜。立乎不測，而游於無有者也。」

鄭有神巫曰季咸，知人之死生存亡、禍福壽夭，期以歲月旬日若神。鄭人見之，皆棄而走。列子見之而心醉，歸，以告壺子，曰：「始吾以夫子之道為至矣，則又有至焉者矣。」壺子曰：

nowhere, in the domain of nothingness. And you come to worry me with government of the empire!"

But T'ien Ken enquired a second time, and the Sage replied, "Resolve your mental energy into abstraction, your physical energy into inaction. Allow yourself to fall in with the natural order of phenomena, without admitting the element of self,—and the empire will be governed."

Yang Tzu Chu went to see Lao Tzu, and said, "Suppose a man were ardent and courageous, acquainted with the order and principles of things, and untiring in the pursuit of Tao—would he be accounted a wise ruler?"

"From the point of view of a truly wise man," replied Lao Tzu, "such a one would be a mere handicraftsman, wearing out body and mind alike. The tiger and the pard suffer from the beauty of their skins. The cleverness of the monkey, the tractability of the ox, bring them both to the tether. It is not on such grounds that a ruler may be accounted wise."

"But in what, then," cried Yang Tzu Chu, "does the government of a wise man consist?"

"The goodness of a wise ruler," answered Lao Tzu, "covers the whole empire, yet he himself seems to know it not. It influences all creation, yet none is conscious thereof. It appears under countless forms, bringing joy to all things. It is based upon the baseless, and travels through the realms of Nowhere."

In the State of Cheng there was a wonderful magician, named Chi Han. He knew all about birth and death, gain and loss, misfortune and happiness, long life and short life,—predicting events to a day with supernatural accuracy. The people of Cheng used to flee at his approach; but Lieh Tzu went to see him, and became so infatuated that on his return he said to Hu Tzu,

"I used to look upon your Tao as perfect. Now I know something more perfect still."

"So far," replied Hu Tzu, "I have only taught you the ornamentals, not the essentials, of Tao; and yet you think you know all about it. Without cocks in your poultry-yard, what sort of eggs do the hens lay? If you go about trying to force Tao down people's throats, you will be simply exposing yourself. Bring your friend with you, and let me show myself to him."

So next day Lieh Tzu went with Chi Han to see Hu Tzu, and when they came out Chi Han said, "Alas! your teacher is doomed. He cannot

「吾與汝既其文，未既其實。而固得道與？眾雌而無雄，而又奚卵焉！而以道與世亢，必信，夫故使人得而相汝。嘗試與來，以予示之。」明日，列子與之見壺子。出而謂列子曰：「嘻！子之先生死矣！弗活矣！不以旬數矣！吾見怪焉，見濕灰焉。」列子入，泣涕沾襟以告壺子。壺子曰：「鄉吾示之以地文，萌乎不震不止，是殆見吾杜德機也。嘗又與來。」明日，又與之見壺子。出而謂列子曰：「幸矣！子之先生遇我也，有瘳矣！全然有生矣！吾見其杜權矣！」列子入，以告壺子。壺子曰：「鄉吾示之以天壤，名實不入，而機發於踵。是殆見吾善者機也。嘗又與來。」明日，又與之見壺子。出而謂列子曰：「子之先生不齊，吾無得而相焉。試齊，且復相之。」列子入，以告壺子。壺子曰：「吾鄉示之以太沖莫勝，是殆見吾衡氣機也。鯢桓之審為淵，止水之審為淵，流水之審為淵。淵有九名，此處三焉。嘗又與來。」

live. I hardly give him ten days. I am astonished at him. He is but wet ashes."

Lieh Tzu went in and wept bitterly, and told Hu Tzu; but the latter said, "I showed myself to him just now as the earth shows us its outward form, motionless and still, while production is all the time going on. I merely prevented him from seeing my pent-up energy within. Bring him again."

Next day the interview took place as before; but as they were leaving Chi Han said to Lieh Tzu, "It is lucky for your teacher that he met me. He is better. He will recover. I saw he had recuperative power."

Lieh Tzu went in and told Hu Tzu; whereupon the latter replied, "I showed myself to him just now as heaven shows itself in all its dispassionate grandeur, letting a little energy run out of my heels. He was thus able to detect that I had some. Bring him here again."

Next day a third interview took place, and as they were leaving, Chi Han said to Lieh Tzu, "Your teacher is never one day like another. I can tell nothing from his physiognomy. Get him to be regular, and I will then examine him again."

This being repeated to Hu Tzu as before, the latter said, "I showed myself to him just now in a state of harmonious equilibrium. Where the whale disports itself,—is the abyss. Where water is at rest,—is the abyss. Where water is in motion,—is the abyss. The abyss has nine names. These are three of them."

Next day the two went once more to see Hu Tzu; but Chi Han was unable to stand still, and in his confusion turned and fled.

"Pursue him!" cried Hu Tzu; whereupon Lieh Tzu ran after him, but could not overtake him, so he returned and told Hu Tzu that the fugitive had disappeared.

"I showed myself to him just now," said Hu Tzu,

"as Tao appeared before time was. I was to him as a great blank, existing of itself. He knew not who I was. His face fell. He became confused. And so he fled."

Upon this Lieh Tzu stood convinced that he had not yet acquired any real knowledge, and at once set to work in earnest, passing three years without leaving the house. He helped his wife to cook the family dinner, and fed his pigs just like human beings. He discarded the artificial and

明日，又與之見壺子。立未定，自失而走。壺子曰：「追之！」列子追之不及。反，以報壺子曰：「已滅矣，已失矣，吾弗及已。」壺子曰：「鄉吾示之以未始出吾宗。吾與之虛而委蛇，不知其誰何，因以為弟靡，因以為波流，故逃也。」然後列子自以為未始學而歸。三年不出，為其妻爨，食豕如食人，於事無與親。雕琢復朴，塊然獨以其形立。紛而封哉，一以是終。

無為名尸，無為謀府，無為事任，無為知主。體盡無窮，而游無朕。盡其所受乎天，而無見得，亦虛而已！至人之用心若鏡，不將不迎，應而不藏，故能勝物而不傷。

南海之帝為儵，北海之帝為忽，中央之帝為渾沌。儵與忽時相下遇於渾沌之地，渾沌待之甚善。儵與忽謀報渾沌之德，曰：「人皆有七竅以視聽食息此獨無有，嘗試鑿之。」日鑿一竅，七日而渾沌死。

reverted to the natural. He became merely a shape. Amidst confusion, he was unconfounded. And so he continued to the end.

By Inaction, fame comes as the spirits of the dead come to the boy who impersonates the corpse.

By Inaction, one can become the centre of thought, the focus of responsibility, the arbiter of wisdom. Full allowance must be made for others, while remaining unmoved oneself. There must be a thorough compliance with divine principles, without any manifestation thereof.

All of which may be summed up in the one word passivity. For the perfect man employs his mind as a mirror. It grasps nothing: it refuses nothing.

It receives, but does not keep. And thus he can triumph over matter, without injury to himself.

The ruler of the southern sea was called Shu. The ruler of the northern sea was called Hu. The ruler of the central zone was called Hun Tun.

Shu and Hu often met on Hun Tun's territory, and being always well treated by him, determined to repay his kindness.

They said, "All men have seven holes,—for seeing, hearing, eating, and breathing. Hun Tun alone has none. We will bore some for him."

So every day they bored one hole; but on the seventh day Hun Tun died.

# 駢拇第八

駢拇枝指，出乎性哉！而侈於德。附贅縣疣，出乎形哉！而侈於性。多方乎仁義而用之者，列於五藏哉！而非道德之正也。是故駢於足者，連無用之肉也；枝於手者，樹無用之指也；多方駢枝於五藏之情者，淫僻於仁義之行，而多方於聰明之用也。是故駢於明者，亂五色，淫文章，青黃黼黻之煌煌非乎？而離朱是已！多於聰者，亂五聲，淫六律，金石絲竹黃鐘大呂之聲非乎？而師曠是已！枝於仁者，擢德塞性以收名聲，使天下簧鼓以奉不及之法非乎？而曾、史是已。駢於辯者，累瓦結繩竄句，游心於堅白同異之間，而敝跬譽無用之言非乎？而楊墨是已。故此皆多駢旁枝之道，非天下之至正也。彼正正者，不失其性命之情。故合者不為駢，而枝者不為跂；長者不為有餘，短者不為不足。是故鳧脛雖短，續之則憂；鶴脛雖長，斷之則悲。故性長非所斷，性短非所續，無所去憂也。意仁義其非人情乎！彼仁人何其多憂也？且夫駢於拇者，決之則泣；枝於手者，齕之則啼。二者，或有餘於數，

# CHAPTER VIII

## JOINED TOES

Joined toes and extra fingers are an addition to nature, though, functionally speaking, superfluous. Wens and tumours are an addition to the bodily form, though, as far as nature is concerned, superfluous. And similarly, to include charity and duty to one's neighbour among the functions of man's organism, is not true Tao.

For just as joined toes are but useless lumps of flesh, and extra fingers but useless excrescences, so are any artificial additions to our internal economy but harmful adjuncts to real charity and duty to one's neighbour, and are moreover prejudicial to the right use of intelligence.

People with extra keenness of vision muddle themselves over the five colours, exaggerate the value of shades, and of distinctions of greens and yellows for sacrificial robes. Of such was Li Chu.

People with extra keenness of hearing muddle themselves over the five notes, exaggerate the tonic differences of the six pitch-pipes, and the various timbres of metal, stone, silk, and bamboo, of the Huang-chung, and of the Ta-lu. Of such was Shih K'uang.

People who graft on charity, force themselves to display this virtue in order to gain reputation and to enjoy the applause of the world for that which is of no account. Of such were Tseng and Shih.

People who refine in argument do but pile up tiles or knot ropes in their maunderings over the hard and white, the like and the unlike, wearing themselves out over mere useless terms. Of such were Yang and Mih.

Therefore every addition to or deviation from nature belongs not to the ultimate perfection of all.

He who would attain to such perfection never loses sight of the natural conditions of his existence. With him the joined is not united, nor the separated apart, nor the long in excess, nor the short wanting. For just as a duck's legs, though short, cannot be lengthened without pain to the duck, and a crane's legs, though long, cannot be shortened without misery to the crane, so that which is long in man's moral nature cannot be cut off, nor that which is short be lengthened. All sorrow is thus avoided.

Intentional charity and intentional duty to one's neighbour are surely

或不足於數，其於憂一也。今世之仁人，蒿目而憂世之患；不仁之人，決性命之情而饕貴富。故意仁義其非人情乎！自三代以下者，天下何其囂囂也？且夫待鉤繩規矩而正者，是削其性也；待繩約膠漆而固者，是侵其德者也；屈折禮樂，呴俞仁義，以慰天下之心者，此失其常然也。天下有常然，常然者，曲者不以鉤，直者不以繩，圓者不以規，方者不以矩，附離不以膠漆，約束不以纆索。故天下誘然皆生，而不知其所以生；同焉皆得，而不知其所以得。故古今不二，不可虧也。則仁義又奚連連如膠漆纆索而游乎道德之間為哉！使天下惑也！夫小惑易方，大惑易性，何以知其然邪？自虞氏招仁義以撓天下也，天下莫不奔命於仁義。是非以仁義易其性與？

故嘗試論之，自三代以下者，天下莫不以物易其性矣！小人則以身殉利；士則以身殉名；大夫則以身殉家；聖人則以身殉天下。故此數子者，事業不同，名聲異號，其於傷性以身為殉，一也。臧與穀，二人相與牧羊，而俱亡其羊。問臧奚事，則挾策讀書；問穀奚事，則博塞以游。二人者，

not included in our moral nature. Yet what sorrow these have involved. Divide your joined toes and you will howl: bite off your extra finger and you will scream. In one case there is too much, in the other too little; but the sorrow is the same. And the charitable of the age go about sorrowing over the ills of the age, while the non-charitable cut through the natural conditions of things in their greed after place and wealth. Surely then intentional charity and duty to one's neighbour are not included in our moral nature. Yet from the time of the Three Dynasties downwards what a fuss has been made about them!

Those who cannot make perfect without arc, line, compasses, and square, injure the natural constitu tion of things. Those who require cords to bind and glue to stick, interfere with the natural functions of things. And those who seek to satisfy the mind of man by hampering with ceremonies and music and preaching charity and duty to one's neighbour, thereby destroy the intrinsicality of things.

For such intrinsicality does exist, in this sense:—Things which are curved require no arcs; things which are straight require no lines; things which are round require no compasses; things which are rectangular require no squares; things which stick require no glue; things which hold together require no cords. And just as all things are produced, and none can tell how they are produced, so do all things possess their own intrinsic qualities and none can tell how they possess them. From time immemorial this has always been so, without variation. Why then should charity and duty to one's neighbour be as it were glued or corded on, and introduced into the domain of Tao, to give rise to doubt among mankind?

Lesser doubts change the rule of life; greater doubts change man's nature.

How do we know this? By the fact that ever since the time when Shun bid for charity and duty to one's neighbour in order to secure the empire, men have devoted their lives to the pursuit thereof. Is it not then charity and duty to one's neighbour which change the nature of man?

Therefore I have tried to show that from the time of the Three Dynasties it has always been the external which has changed the nature of man. If a mean man, he will die for gain. If a superior man, he will die for fame. If a man of rank, he will die for his ancestral honours. If a Sage, he will die for the world. The pursuits and ambitions of these men differ, but the in-

事業不同，其於亡羊均也。伯夷死名於首陽之下，盜跖死利於東陵之上。二人者，所死不同，其於殘生傷性均也。奚必伯夷之是而盜跖之非乎？天下盡殉也。彼其所殉仁義也，則俗謂之君子；其所殉貨財也，則俗謂之小人。其殉一也，則有君子焉，有小人焉；若其殘生損性，則盜跖亦伯夷已，又惡取君子小人於其間哉！且夫屬其性乎仁義者，雖通如曾、史，非吾所謂臧也；屬其性於五味，雖通如俞兒，非吾所謂臧也；屬其性乎五聲，雖通如師曠，非吾所謂聰也；屬其性乎五色，雖通如離朱，非吾所謂明也。吾所謂臧者，非所謂仁義之謂也，臧於其德而已矣；吾所謂臧者，非所謂仁義之謂也，任其性命之情而已矣；吾所謂聰者，非謂其聞彼也，自聞而已矣；吾所謂明者，非謂其見彼也，自見而已矣。夫不自見而見彼，不自得而得彼者，是得人之得而不自得其得者也，適人之適而不自適其適者也。夫適人之適而不自適其適，雖盜跖與伯夷，是同為淫僻也。余愧乎道德，是以上不敢為仁義之操，而下不敢為淫僻之行也。

jury to their natures involved in the sacrifice of their lives is the same.

Tsang and Ku were shepherds, both of whom lost their flocks. On inquiry, it appeared that Tsang had been engaged in reading, while Ku had gone to take part in some trials of strength. Their occupations had been different, but the result was in each case loss of the sheep.

Poh I died for fame at the foot of Mount Shou-yang.

Robber Che died for gain on Mount T'ai.

Their deaths were not the same, but the injury to their lives and natures was in each case the same. How then can we applaud the former and blame the latter?

And so, if a man dies for charity and duty to his neighbour the world calls him a noble fellow; but if he dies for gain, the world calls him a low fellow. The dying being the same, one is nevertheless called noble and the other low. But in point of injury to life and nature, the robber Che and Poh I are one. Where then does the distinction of noble and low come in?

Were a man to apply himself to charity and duty towards his neighbour until he were the equal of Tseng or Shih, this would not be what I mean by perfection. Or to flavours, until he were the equal of Yu Erh.

Or to sounds, until he were the equal of Shih K'uang. Or to colours, until he were the equal of Li Chu. What I mean by perfection is not what is meant by charity and duty to one's neighbour. It is found in the cultivation of Tao. And those whom I regard as cultivators of Tao are not those who cultivate charity and duty to one's neighbour. They are those who yield to the natural conditions of things. What I call perfection of hearing is not hearing others but oneself. What I call perfection of vision is not seeing others but oneself.

For a man who sees not himself but others, takes not possession of himself but of others, thus taking what others should take and not what he himself should take.

Instead of being himself, he in fact becomes some one else. And if a man thus becomes some one else instead of himself, this is a fatal error of which both the robber Che and Poh I can be equally guilty.

And so, conscious of my own deficiency in regard to Tao, I do not venture at my best to practise the principles of charity and duty to my neighbour, nor at my worst to fall into the fatal error above-mentioned.

# 馬蹄第九

馬，蹄可以踐霜雪，毛可以御風寒。齕草飲水，翹足而陸，此馬之真性也。雖有義臺路寢，無所用之。及至伯樂，曰：「我善治馬。」燒之，剔之，刻之，雒之。連之以羈馽，編之以皂棧，馬之死者十二三矣；飢之，渴之，馳之，驟之，整之，齊之，前有橛飾之患，而後有鞭筴之威，而馬之死者已過半矣！陶者曰：「我善治埴。圓者中規，方者中矩。」匠人曰：「我善治木。」曲者中鉤，直者應繩。夫埴木之性，豈欲中規矩鉤繩哉？然且世世稱之曰：「伯樂善治馬，而陶匠善治埴木。」此亦治天下者之過也。吾意善治天下者不然。彼民有常性，織而衣，耕而食，是謂同德；一而不黨，命曰天放。故至德之世，其行填填，其視顛顛。當是時也，山無蹊隧，澤無舟梁；萬物群生，連屬其鄉；禽獸成群，草木遂長。是故禽獸可係羈而游，鳥鵲之巢可攀援而闚。夫至德之世，同與禽獸居，族與萬物並。惡乎知君子小人哉！同乎無知，其德不離；同乎無欲，是謂素樸。素樸而民性得矣。

# CHAPTER IX

## HORSES' HOOFS

Horses have hoofs to carry them over frost and snow; hair, to protect them from wind and cold. They eat grass and drink water, and fling up their heels over the champaign. Such is the real nature of horses. Palatial dwellings are of no use to them.

One day Poh Loh appeared, saying, "I understand the management of horses."

So he branded them, and clipped them, and pared their hoofs, and put halters on them, tying them up by the head and shackling them by the feet, and disposing them in stables, with the result that two or three in every ten died. Then he kept them hungry and thirsty, trotting them and galloping them, and grooming, and trimming, with the misery of the tasselled bridle before and the fear of the knotted whip behind, until more than half of them were dead.

The potter says, "I can do what I will with clay. If I want it round, I use compasses; if rectangular, a square."

The carpenter says, "I can do what I will with wood. If I want it curved, I use an arc; if straight, a line."

But on what grounds can we think that the natures of clay and wood desire this application of compasses and square, of arc and line? Nevertheless, every age extols Poh Loh for his skill in managing horses, and potters and carpenters for their skill with clay and wood. Those who govern the empire make the same mistake.

Now I regard government of the empire from quite a different point of view.

The people have certain natural instincts;—to weave and clothe themselves, to till and feed themselves. These are common to all humanity, and all are agreed thereon. Such instincts are called "Heaven-sent."

And so in the days when natural instincts prevailed, men moved quietly and gazed steadily. At that time, there were no roads over mountains, nor boats, nor bridges over water. All things were produced, each for its own proper sphere. Birds and beasts multiplied; trees and shrubs grew up. The former might be led by the hand; you could climb up and peep into

及至聖人，蹩躠為仁，踶跂為義，而天下始疑矣。澶漫為樂，摘辟為禮，而天下始分矣。故純樸不殘，孰為犧尊！白玉不毀，孰為珪璋！道德不廢，安取仁義！性情不離，安用禮樂！五色不亂，孰為文采！無聲不亂，孰應六律！夫殘樸以為器，工匠之罪也；毀道德以為仁義，聖人之過也。夫馬，陸居則食草飲水，喜則交頸相靡，怒則分背相踶。馬知已此矣！夫加之以衡扼，齊之以月題，而馬知介倪闉扼鷙曼詭銜竊轡。故馬之知而能至盜者，伯樂之罪也。夫赫胥氏之時，民居不知所為，行不知所之，含哺而熙，鼓腹而游。民能以此矣！及至聖人，屈折禮樂以匡天下之形，縣跂仁義以慰天下之心，而民乃始踶跂好知，爭歸於利，不可止也。此亦聖人之過也。

the raven's nest. For then man dwelt with birds and beasts, and all creation was one. There were no distinctions of good and bad men. Being all equally without knowledge, their virtue could not go astray. Being all equally without evil desires, they were in a state of natural integrity, the perfection of human existence.

But when Sages appeared, tripping people over charity and fettering with duty to one's neighbour, doubt found its way into the world. And then with their gushing over music and fussing over ceremony, the empire became divided against itself.

Were the natural integrity of things left unharmed, who could make sacrificial vessels? Were white jade left unbroken, who could make the regalia of courts? Were Tao not abandoned, who could introduce charity and duty to one's neighbour? Were man's natural instincts his guide, what need would there be for music and ceremonies? Were the five colours not confused, who would practise decoration? Were the five notes not confused, who would adopt the six pitch-pipes?

Destruction of the natural integrity of things, in order to produce articles of various kinds,—this is the fault of the artisan. Annihilation of Tao in order to practise charity and duty to one's neighbour,—this is the error of the Sage.

Horses live on dry land, eat grass and drink water. When pleased, they rub their necks together. When angry, they turn around and kick up their heels at each other. Thus far only do their natural dispositions carry them. But bridled and bitted, with a plate of metal on their foreheads, they learn to cast vicious looks, to turn the head to bite, to resist, to get the bit out of the mouth or the bridle into it. And thus their natures become depraved,—the fault of Poh Loh.

In the days of Ho Hsu the people did nothing in particular when at rest, and went nowhere in particular when they moved. Having food, they rejoiced; having full bellies, they strolled about. Such were the capacities of the people. But when the Sages came to worry them with ceremonies and music in order to rectify the form of government, and dangled charity and duty to one's neighbour before them in order to satisfy their hearts,—then the people began to develop a taste for knowledge and to struggle one with the other in their desire for gain. This was the error of the Sages.

# 胠篋第十

　　將為胠篋探囊發匱之盜而為守備，則必攝緘縢，固扃鐍，此世俗之所謂知也。然而巨盜至，則負匱揭篋擔囊而趨，唯恐緘縢扃鐍之不固也。然則鄉之所謂知者，不乃為大盜積者也？故嘗試論之，世俗之所謂知者，有不為大盜積者乎？所謂聖者，有不為大盜守者乎？何以知其然邪？昔者齊國鄰邑相望，雞狗之音相聞，罔罟之所布，耒耨之所刺，方二千餘里。闔四竟之內，所以立宗廟社稷，治邑屋州閭鄉曲者，曷嘗不法聖人哉？然而田成子一旦殺齊君而盜其國，所盜者豈獨其國邪？並與其聖知之法而盜之，故田成子有乎盜賊之名，而身處堯舜之安；小國不敢非，大國不敢誅，十二世有齊國。則是不乃竊齊國，並與其聖知之法以守其盜賊之身乎？嘗試論之，世俗之所謂至知者，有不為大盜積者乎？所謂至聖者，有不為大盜守者乎？何以知其然邪？昔者龍逢斬，比干剖，萇弘胣，子胥靡。故四子之賢而身不免乎戮。故跖之徒問跖曰：「盜亦有道乎？」跖曰：「何適而無有道邪？」夫妄意室中

# CHAPTER X

## OPENING TRUNKS

The precautions taken against thieves who open trunks, search bags, or ransack tills, consist of securing with cords and fastening with bolts and locks. This is what the world calls wit.

But a strong thief comes who carries off the till on his shoulders, with box and bag to boot. And his only fear is that the cords and locks should not be strong enough!

Therefore, what the world calls wit, simply amounts to assistance given to the strong thief.

And I venture to state that nothing of that which the world calls wit, is otherwise than serviceable to strong thieves; and that nothing of that which the world calls wisdom is other than a protection to strong thieves.

How can this be shown?—In the State of Ch'i a man used to be able to see from one town to the next, and hear the barking and crowing of its dogs and cocks.

The area covered by the nets of fishermen and fowlers, and pricked by the plough, was a square of two thousand and odd li.

And within its four boundaries not a temple or shrine was dedicated, nor a district or hamlet governed, but in accordance with the rules laid down by the Sages.

Yet one morning

T'ien Ch'eng Tzu slew the Prince of Ch'i, and stole his kingdom. And not his kingdom only, but the wisdom-tricks which he had got from the Sages as well; so that although T'ien Ch'eng Tzu acquired the reputation of a thief, he lived as comfortably as ever did either Yao or Shun. The small States did not venture to blame, nor the great States to punish him; and so for twelve generations his descendants ruled over Ch'i.

Was not this stealing the State of Ch'i and the wisdom-tricks of the Sages as well in order to secure himself from the consequences of such theft?

This amounts to what I have already said, namely that nothing of what the world esteems great wit is otherwise than serviceable to strong thieves, and that nothing of what the world calls great wisdom is other than a pro-

之藏，聖也；入先，勇也；出後，義也；知可否，知也；分均，仁也。五者不備而能成大盜者，天下未之有也。」由是觀之，善人不得聖人之道不立，跖不得聖人之道不行；天下之善人少而不善人多，則聖人之利天下也少而害天下也多。故曰：脣竭則齒寒，魯酒薄而邯鄲圍，聖人生而大盜起。掊擊聖人，縱舍盜賊，而天下始治矣。夫川竭而谷虛，丘夷而淵實。聖人已死，則大盜不起，天下平而無故矣！聖人不死，大盜不止。雖重聖人而治天下，則是重利盜跖也。為之斗斛以量之，則并與斗斛而竊之；為之權衡以稱之，則并與權衡而竊之；為之符璽以信之，則并與符璽而竊之；為之仁義以矯之，則并與仁義而竊之。何以知其然邪？彼竊鉤者誅，竊國者為諸侯，諸侯之門而仁義存焉。則是非竊仁義聖知邪？故逐於大盜，揭諸侯，竊仁義并斗斛權衡符璽之利者，雖有軒冕之賞弗能勸，斧鉞之威弗能禁。此重利盜跖而使不可禁者，是乃聖人之過也。故曰：「魚不可脫於淵，國之利器不可以示人。」彼聖人者，天下之利器也，非所以明天下

tection to strong thieves.

Let us take another example. Of old, Lung Feng was beheaded, Pi Kan was disembowelled, Chang Hung was sliced to death, Tzu Hsu was chopped to mince-meat.

All these four were Sages, but their wisdom could not preserve them from death.

An apprentice to Robber Che asked him saying, "Is there then Tao in thieving?"

"Pray tell me of something in which there is not Tao," Che replied. "There is the wisdom by which booty is located. The courage to go in first, and the heroism of coming out last. There is the shrewdness of calculating success, and justice in the equal division of the spoil. There has never yet been, a great robber who was not possessed of these five."

Thus the doctrine of the Sages is equally indispensable to good men and to Che. But good men are scarce and bad men plentiful, so that the good the Sages do to the world is little and the evil great.

Therefore it has been said, "If the lips are gone, the teeth will be cold." It was the thinness of the wine of Lu which caused the siege of Han Tan.

It was the appearance of Sages which caused the appearance of great robbers.

Drive out the Sages and leave the robbers alone,—then only will the empire be governed. As when the stream ceases the gully dries up, and when the hill is levelled the chasm is filled; so when Sages are extinct, there will be no more robbers, but the empire will rest in peace.

On the other hand, unless Sages disappear, neither will great robbers disappear; nor if you double the number of Sages wherewithal to govern the empire will you do more than double the profits of Robber Che.

If pecks and bushels are used for measurement, they will also be stolen.

If scales and steelyards are used for weighing, they will also be stolen. If tallies and signets are used for good faith, they will also be stolen. If charity and duty to one's neighbour are used for rectification, they will also be stolen.

How is this so?—One man steals a purse, and is punished. Another steals a State, and becomes a Prince. But charity and duty to one's neighbour are integral parts of princedom. Does he not then steal charity and

也。 故絕聖棄知， 大盜乃止；擿玉毀珠， 小盜不起；焚符破璽， 而民朴鄙；掊斗折衡， 而民不爭；殫殘天下之聖法， 而民始可與論議。 擢亂六律， 鑠絕竽瑟， 塞瞽曠之耳， 而天下始人含其聰矣；滅文章， 散五采， 膠離朱之目， 而天下始人含其明矣；毀絕鉤繩而棄規矩， 攦工倕之指， 而天下始人有其巧矣。 故曰：大巧若拙。削曾、 史之行， 鉗楊、 墨之口， 攘棄仁義， 而天下之德始玄同矣。彼人含其明，則天下不鑠矣；人含其聰， 則天下不累矣；人含其知， 則天下不惑矣；人含其德，則天下不僻矣。 彼曾、史、楊、墨、 師曠、 工倕、 離朱者， 皆外立其德， 而以爛亂天下者也， 法之所無用也。

duty to one's neighbour together with the wisdom of the Sages?

So it is that to attempt to drive out great robbers is simply to help them to steal principalities, charity, duty to one's neighbour, together with measures, scales, tallies, and signets. No reward of official regalia and uniform will dissuade, nor dread of sharp instruments of punishment will deter such men from their course. These do but double the profits of robbers like Che, and make it impossible to get rid of them,—for which the Sages are responsible.

Therefore it has been said, "Fishes cannot be taken away from water: the instruments of government cannot be delegated to others."

In the wisdom of Sages the instruments of government are found. This wisdom is not fit for enlightening the world.

Away then with wisdom and knowledge, and great robbers will disappear! Discard jade and destroy pearls, and petty thieves will cease to exist. Burn tallies and break signets, and the people will revert to their natural integrity. Split measures and smash scales, and the people will not fight over quantities. Utterly abolish all the restrictions of Sages, and the people will begin to be fit for the reception of Tao.

Confuse the six pitch-pipes, break up organs and flutes, stuff up the ears of Shih K'uang,—and each man will keep his own sense of hearing to himself.

Put an end to decoration, disperse the five categories of colour, glue up the eyes of Li Chu,—and each man will keep his own sense of sight to himself.

Destroy arcs and lines, fling away square and compasses, snap off the fingers of Kung Ch'ui,— and each man will use his own natural skill.

Wherefore the saying, "Great skill is as clumsiness."

Restrain the actions of Tseng and Shih, stop the mouths of Yang and Mih, get rid of charity and duty to one's neighbour,—and the virtue of the people will become one with God.

If each man keeps to himself his own sense of sight, the world will escape confusion. If each man keeps to himself his own sense of hearing, the world will escape entanglements. If each man keeps his knowledge to himself, the world will escape doubt. If each man keeps his own virtue to himself, the world will avoid deviation from the true path.

Tseng, Shih, Yang, Mih, Shih K'uang, Kung Ch'ui, and Li Chu, all set

子獨不知至德之世乎？昔者容成氏、大庭氏、伯皇氏、中央氏、栗陸氏、驪畜氏、軒轅氏、赫胥氏、尊盧氏、祝融氏、伏犧氏、神農氏，當是時也，民結繩而用之。甘其食，美其服，樂其俗，安其居，鄰國相望，雞狗之音相聞，民至老死而不相往來。若此之時，則至治已。今遂至使民延頸舉踵，曰「某所有賢者」，贏糧而趣之，則內棄其親，而外去其主之事，足跡接乎諸侯之境，車軌結乎千里之外。則是上好知之過也。上誠好知而無道，則天下大亂矣。何以知其然邪？夫弓弩畢弋機變之知多，則鳥亂於上矣；鉤餌罔罟罾笱之知多，則魚亂於水矣；削格羅落罝罘之知多，則獸亂於澤矣；知詐漸毒、頡滑堅白、解垢同異之變多，則俗惑於辯矣。

up their virtue outside themselves and involve the world in such angry discussions that nothing definite is accomplished.

Have you never heard of the Golden Age,— the days of Yung Ch'eng, Ta T'ing, Poh Huang, Chung Yang, Li Lu, Li Hsu, Hsien Yuan, He Hsu, Tsun Lu, Chu Yung, Fu Hsi, and Shen Nung?

Then the people used knotted cords.

They were contented with what food and raiment they could get. They lived simple and peaceful lives. Neighbouring districts were within sight, and the cocks and dogs of one could be heard in the other, yet the people grew old and died without ever interchanging visits.

In those days, government was indeed perfect. But nowadays any one can excite the people by saying, "In such and such a place there is a Sage."

Immediately they put together a few provisions and hurry off, neglecting their parents at home and their master's business abroad, filing in unbroken line through territories of Princes, with a string of carts and carriages a thousand li in length. Such is the evil effect of an exaggerated desire for knowledge among our rulers. And if rulers aim at knowledge and neglect Tao, the empire will be overwhelmed in confusion.

How can it be shown that this is so?—Bows and cross-bows and hand-nets and harpoon-arrows, involve much knowledge in their use; but they carry confusion among the birds of the air. Hooks and bait and nets and traps, involve much knowledge in their use; but they carry confusion among the fishes of the deep. Fences and nets and snares, involve much knowledge in their use; but they carry confusion among the beasts of the field. In the same way the sophistical fallacies of the hard and white and the like and the unlike of schoolmen involve much knowledge of argument; but they overwhelm the world in doubt.

故天下每每大亂，罪在於好知。故天下皆知求其所不知而不知求其所已知者，皆知非其所不善而不知非其所已善者，是以大亂。故上悖日月之明，下爍山川之精，中墮四時之施；惴耎之蟲，肖翹之物，莫不失其性。甚矣夫好知之亂天下也！自三代以下者是已，舍夫種種之機而悅夫役役之佞；釋夫恬淡無為而悅夫啍啍之意，啍啍已亂天下矣！

Therefore it is that whenever there is great confusion, love of knowledge is ever at the bottom of it. For all men strive to grasp what they do not know, while none strive to grasp what they already know; and all strive to discredit what they do not excel in, while none strive to discredit what they do excel in. The result is overwhelming confusion.

Thus, above, the splendour of the heavenly bodies is dimmed; below, the energy of land and water is disturbed; while midway the influence of the four seasons is destroyed. There is not one tiny creature which moves on earth or flies in air but becomes other than by nature it should be. So overwhelming is the confusion which desire for knowledge has brought upon the world ever since the time of the Three Dynasties downwards! The simple and the guileless have been set aside; the specious and the false have been exalted. Tranquil inaction has given place to a love of disputation; and by disputation has confusion come upon the world.

# 在宥第十一

聞在宥天下，不聞治天下也。在之也者，恐天下之淫其性也；宥之也者，恐天下之遷其德也。天下不淫其性，不遷其德，有治天下者哉？昔堯之治天下也，使天下欣欣焉人樂其性，是不恬也；桀之治天下也，使天下瘁瘁焉人苦其性，是不愉也。夫不恬不愉。非德也。非德也而可長久者，天下無之。人大喜邪？毗於陽；大怒邪，毗於陰。陰陽並毗，四時不至，寒暑之和不成，其反傷人之形乎！使人喜怒失位，居處無常，思慮不自得，中道不成章。於是乎天下始喬詰卓鷙，而後有盜跖、曾、史之行。故舉天下以賞其善者不足，舉天下以罰其惡者不給。故天下之大不足以賞罰。自三代以下者，匈匈焉終以賞罰為事，彼何暇安其性命之情哉！而且說明邪？是淫於色也；說聰邪？是淫於聲也；說仁邪？是亂於德也；說義邪？是悖於理也；說禮邪？是相於技也；說樂邪？是相於淫也；說聖邪？是相於藝也；說知邪？是相於疵也。天下將安其性命之情，之八者，存可也，亡可也；天下將不安其性命之情，之

# CHAPTER XI

# ON LETTING ALONE

There has been such a thing as letting mankind alone; there has never been such a thing as governing mankind.

Letting alone springs from fear lest men's natural dispositions be perverted and their virtue laid aside. But if their natural dispositions be not perverted nor their virtue laid aside, what room is there left for government?

Of old, when Yao governed the empire, he caused happiness to prevail to excess in man's nature; and consequently the people were not satisfied. When Chieh governed the empire he caused sorrow to prevail to excess in man's nature; and consequently the people were not contented. Dissatisfaction and discontent are subversive of virtue; and without virtue there is no such thing for an empire as stability.

When man rejoices greatly he gravitates towards the positive pole. When he sorrows deeply he gravitates towards the negative pole.

If the equilibrium of positive and negative is disturbed, the four seasons are interrupted, the balance of heat and cold is destroyed, and man himself suffers physically thereby.

Because men are made to rejoice and to sorrow and to displace their centre of gravity, they lose their steadiness, and are unsuccessful in thought and action. And thus it is that the idea of surpassing others first came into the world, followed by the appearance of such men as Robber Che, Tseng, and Shih, the result being that the whole world could not furnish enough rewards for the good nor distribute punishments enough for the evil among mankind. And as this great world is not equal to the demand for rewards and punishments; and as, ever since the time of the Three Dynasties downwards, men have done nothing but struggle over rewards and punishments,—what possible leisure can they have had for adapting themselves to the natural conditions of their existence?

Besides, over-refinement of vision leads to debauchery in colour; over-refinement of hearing leads to debauchery in sound; over-refinement of charity leads to confusion in virtue; over-refinement of duty towards one's neighbour leads to perversion of principle; over-refinement of cere-

八者，乃始臠卷愴囊而亂天下也。而天下乃始尊之惜之，甚矣天下之惑也！豈直過也而去之邪！乃齊戒以言之，跪坐以進之，鼓歌以儛之。吾若是何哉？故君子不得已而臨蒞天下，莫若無為。無為也而後安其性命之情。故貴以身於為天下，則可以托天下；愛以身於為天下，則可以寄天下。故君子苟能無解其五藏，無擢其聰明；尸居而龍見，淵默而雷聲，神動而天隨，從容無為而萬物炊累焉。吾又何暇治天下哉！

崔瞿問於老聃曰：「不治天下，安藏人心？」老聃曰：「汝慎無攖人心。人心排下而進上，上下囚殺，淖約柔乎剛強，廉劌雕琢，其熱焦火，其寒凝冰。其疾俯仰之間而再撫四海之外。其居也淵而靜，其動也縣而天。僨驕而不可係者，其唯人心乎！昔者黃帝始以仁義攖人之心，堯、舜於是乎股無胈，脛無毛，以養天下之形，愁其五藏以為仁義，矜其血氣以規法度。然猶有不勝也，堯於是放讙兜於崇山，投三苗於三峗，流共工於幽都，此不勝天下也。夫施及三王而天下大駭矣。下有桀、跖，上有曾、史，而儒

monial leads to divergence from the true object; over-refinement of music leads to lewdness of thought; over-refinement of wisdom leads to an extension of mechanical art; and over-refinement of shrewdness leads to an extension of vice.

If people adapt themselves to the natural conditions of existence, the above eight may be or may not be; it matters not. But if people do not adapt themselves to the natural conditions of existence, then these eight become hindrances and spoilers, and throw the world into confusion.

In spite of this, the world reverences and cherishes them, thereby greatly increasing the sum of human error. And not as a passing fashion, but with admonitions in words, with humility in prostrations, and with the stimulus of music and song. What then is left for me?

Therefore, for the perfect man who is unavoidably summoned to power over his fellows, there is naught like Inaction.

By means of inaction he will be able to adapt himself to the natural conditions of existence. And so it is that he who respects the State as his own body is fit to support it, and he who loves the State as his own body, is fit to govern it.

And if I can refrain from injuring my internal economy, and from taxing my powers of sight and hearing, sitting like a corpse while my dragon-power is manifested around, in profound silence while my thunder-voice resounds, the powers of heaven responding to every phase of my will, as under the yielding influence of inaction all things are brought to maturity and thrive,—what leisure then have I to set about governing the world?

Ts'ui Chu asked Lao Tzu, saying, "If the empire is not to be governed, how are men's hearts to be kept in order?"

"Be careful," replied Lao Tzu, "not to interfere with the natural goodness of the heart of man. Man's heart may be forced down or stirred up. In each case the issue is fatal.

"By gentleness, the hardest heart may be softened. But try to cut and polish it,—'twill glow like fire or freeze like ice. In the twinkling of an eye it will pass beyond the limits of the Four Seas. In repose, profoundly still; in motion, far away in the sky. No bolt can bar, no bond can bind,—such is the human heart."

"Of old, the Yellow Emperor first caused charity and duty to one's

墨畢起。於是乎喜怒相疑，愚知相欺，善否相非，誕信相譏，而天下衰矣；大德不同，而性命爛漫矣；天下好知，而百姓求竭矣。於是乎釿鋸制焉，繩墨殺焉，椎鑿決焉。天下脊脊大亂，罪在攖人心。故賢者伏處大山嵁巖之下，而萬乘之君憂慄乎廟堂之上。今世殊死者相枕也，桁楊者相推也，刑戮者相望也，而儒墨乃始離跂攘臂乎桎梏之間。意，甚矣哉！其無愧而不知恥也甚矣！吾未知聖知之不為桁楊椄槢也，仁義之不為桎梏鑿枘也，焉知曾、史之不為桀、跖嚆矢也！故曰：絕聖棄知，而天下大治。」

neighbour to interfere with the natural goodness of the heart of man. In consequence of which, Yao and Shun wore the hair off their legs in endeavouring to feed their people. They disturbed their internal economy in order to find room for charity and duty to one's neighbour. They exhausted their energies in framing laws and statutes. Still they did not succeed.

"Thereupon, Yao confined Huan Tou on Mount Tsung; drove the chief of San-miao and his people into San-wei, and kept them there; and banished the Minister of Works to Yu Island.

But they were not equal to their task, and through the times of the Three Princes the empire was in a state of great unrest. Among the bad men were Chieh and Che; among the good were Tseng and Shih. By and by, the Confucianists and the Mihists arose; and then came exultation and anger of rivals, fraud between the simple and the cunning, recrimination between the virtuous and the evil, slander between the honest and the dishonest,—until decadence set in, men fell away from their original virtue, their natures became corrupt, and there was a general rush for knowledge.

"The next thing was to coerce by all kinds of physical torture, thus bringing utter confusion into the empire, the blame for which rests upon those who would interfere with the natural goodness of the heart of man.

"In consequence, virtuous men sought refuge in mountain caves, while rulers of States sat trembling in their ancestral halls. Then, when dead men lay about pillowed on each others' corpses, when cangued prisoners and condemned criminals jostled each other in crowds,—then the Confucianists and the Mihists, in the midst of gyves and fetters, stood forth to preach!

Alas, they know not shame, nor what it is to blush!

"Until I can say that the wisdom of Sages is not a fastener of cangues, and that charity and duty to one's neighbour are not bolts for gyves, how should I know that Tseng and Shih are not the forerunners of Chieh and Che?

"Therefore I said, 'Abandon wisdom and discard knowledge, and the empire will be at peace.'"

The Yellow Emperor sat on the throne for nineteen years, and his laws obtained all over the empire.

Hearing that Kuang Ch'eng Tzu was living on Mount K'ung-t'ung, he went thither to see him, and said, "I am told, Sir, that you are in pos-

　　黃帝立為天子十九年，令行天下，聞廣成子在於空同之山，故往見之，曰：「我聞吾子達於至道，敢問至道之精。吾欲取天地之精，以佐五穀，以養民人。吾又欲官陰陽，以遂群生，為之奈何？」廣成子曰：「而所欲問者，物之質也；而所欲官者，物之殘也。自而治天下，雲氣不待族而雨，草木不待黃而落，日月之光益以荒矣。而佞人之心翦翦者，又奚足以語至道？」黃帝退，捐天下，築特室，席白茅，閒居三月，復往邀之。廣成子南首而臥，黃帝順下風膝行而進，再拜稽首而問曰：「聞吾子達於至道，敢問，治身奈何而可以長久？」廣成子蹶然而起，曰：「善哉問乎！來，吾語女至道。至道之精，窈窈冥冥；至道之極，昏昏默默。無視無聽，抱神以靜，形將自正。必靜必清，無勞女形，無搖女精，乃可以長生。目無所見，耳無所聞，心無所知，女神將守形，形乃長生。慎女內，閉女外，多知為敗。我為女遂於大明之上矣，至彼至陽之原也；為女入於窈冥之門矣，至彼至陰之原也。天地有官，陰陽有藏。慎守女身，物將自

session of perfect Tao. May I ask in what perfect Tao consists? I desire to avail myself of the good influence of heaven and earth in order to secure harvests and feed my people. I should also like to control the Two Powers of nature in order to the protection of all living things. How can I accomplish this?"

"What you desire to avail yourself of," replied Kuang Ch'eng Tzu, "is the primordial integrity of matter. What you wish to control are the disintegrators thereof. Ever since the empire has been governed by you, the clouds have rained without waiting to thicken, the foliage of trees has fallen without waiting to grow yellow, the brightness of the sun and moon has paled, and the voice of the flatterer is heard on every side. How then speak of perfect Tao?"

The Yellow Emperor withdrew. He resigned the Throne. He built himself a solitary hut. He lay upon straw. For three months he remained in seclusion, and then went again to see Kuang Ch'eng Tzu.

The latter was lying down with his face to the south. The Yellow Emperor approached after the manner of an inferior, upon his knees. Prostrating himself upon the ground he said, "I am told, Sir, that you are in possession of perfect Tao. May I ask how my self may be preserved so as to last?"

Kuang Ch'eng Tzu jumped up with a start. "A good question indeed!" cried he. "Come, and I will speak to you of perfect Tao.

"The essence of perfect Tao is profoundly mysterious; its extent is lost in obscurity.

"See nothing; hear nothing; let your soul be wrapped in quiet; and your body will begin to take proper form. Let there be absolute repose and absolute purity; do not weary your body nor disturb your vitality,—and you will live for ever. For if the eye sees nothing, and the ear hears nothing, and the mind thinks nothing, the soul will preserve the body, and the body will live for ever.

"Cherish that which is within you, and shut off that which is without; for much knowledge is a curse. Then I will place you upon that abode of Great Light which is the source of the positive Power, and escort you through the gate of Profound Mystery which is the source of the negative Power. These Powers are the controllers of heaven and earth, and each contains the other.

壯。我守其一，以處其和。故我修身千二百歲矣，吾形未常衰。」黃帝再拜稽首曰：「廣成子之謂天矣！」廣成子曰：「來！余語女：彼其物無窮，而人皆以為有終；彼其物無測，而人皆以為有極。得吾道者，上為皇而下為王；失吾道者，上見光而下為土。今夫百昌皆生於土而反於土。故余將去女，入無窮之門，以遊無極之野。吾與日月參光，吾與天地為常。當我，緡乎！遠我，昏乎！人其盡死，而我獨存乎！」

雲將東游，過扶搖之枝而適遭鴻蒙。鴻蒙方將拊脾雀躍而遊。雲將見之，倘然止，贄然立，曰：「叟何人邪？叟何為此？」鴻蒙拊脾雀躍不輟，對雲將曰：「遊！」雲將曰：「朕願有問也。」鴻蒙仰而視雲將曰：「吁！」雲將曰：「天氣不和，地氣鬱結，六氣不調，四時不節。今我願合六氣之精，以育群生，為之奈何？」鴻蒙拊脾雀躍掉頭曰：「吾弗知！吾弗知！」雲將不得問。又三年，東游，過有宋之野，而適遭鴻蒙。雲將大喜，行趨而進曰：「天忘朕邪？天忘朕邪？」再拜稽首，願聞於鴻蒙。鴻蒙曰：「浮游，不知所求；猖狂，

"Cherish and preserve your own self, and all the rest will prosper of itself.

I preserve the original One, while resting in harmony with externals. It is because I have thus cared for my self now for twelve hundred years that my body has not decayed."

The Yellow Emperor prostrated himself and said, "Kuang Ch'eng Tzu is surely God...."

Whereupon the latter continued, "Come, I will tell you. That self is eternal; yet all men think it mortal. That self is infinite; yet all men think it finite. Those who possess Tao are princes in this life and rulers in the hereafter. Those who do not possess Tao, behold the light of day in this life and become clods of earth in the hereafter.

"Nowadays, all living things spring from the dust and to the dust return. But I will lead you through the portals of Eternity into the domain of Infinity. My light is the light of sun and moon. My life is the life of heaven and earth. I know not who comes nor who goes. Men may all die, but I endure for ever."

The Spirit of the Clouds when passing eastwards through the expanse of Air happened to fall in with the Vital Principle. The latter was slapping his ribs and hopping about; whereupon the Spirit of the Clouds said, "Who are you, old man, and what are you doing here?"

"Strolling!" replied the Vital Principle, without stopping.

"I want to know something," continued the Spirit of the Clouds.

"Ah!" uttered the Vital Principle, in a tone of disapprobation.

"The relationship of heaven and earth is out of harmony," said the Spirit of the Clouds; "the six influences do not combine, and the four seasons are no longer regular. I desire to blend the six influences so as to nourish all living beings. What am I to do?"

"I do not know!" cried the Vital Principle, shaking his head, while still slapping his ribs and hopping about; "I do not know!"

So the Spirit of the Clouds did not press his question; but three years later, when passing eastwards through the Yu-sung territory, he again fell in with the Vital Principle. The former was overjoyed, and hurrying up, said, "Has your Holiness forgotten me?"

He then prostrated himself, and desired to be allowed to interrogate the Vital Principle; but the latter said, "I wander on without knowing

不知所往；遊者鞅掌，以觀無妄。朕又何知！」
雲將曰：「朕也自以為猖狂，而民隨予所往；朕
也不得已於民，今則民之放也！願聞一言。」鴻
蒙曰：「亂天之經，逆物之情，玄天弗成；解獸
之群，而鳥皆夜鳴；災及草木，禍及止蟲。意！
治人之過也。」雲將曰：「然則吾奈何？」鴻蒙
曰：「意！毒哉！僊僊乎歸矣。」雲將曰：「吾遇天
難，願聞一言。」鴻蒙曰：「意！心養。汝徒處無
為，而物自化。墮爾形體，吐爾聰明，倫與物忘；
大同乎涬溟。解心釋神，莫然無魂。萬物云云，
各復其根，各復其根而不知；渾渾沌沌，終身
不離；若彼知之，乃是離之。無問其名，無闚
其情，物故自生。」雲將曰：「天降朕以德，示
朕以默。躬身求之，乃今也得。」再拜稽首，起
辭而行。

　　世俗之人，皆喜人之同乎己而惡人之異於己
也。同於己而欲之，異於己而不欲者，以出乎
眾為心也。夫以出乎眾為心者，曷常出乎眾哉！
因眾以寧，所聞不如眾技眾矣。而欲為人之國

what I want. I roam about without knowing where I am going. I stroll in this ecstatic manner, simply awaiting events. What should I know?"

"I too roam about," answered the Spirit of the Clouds; "but the people depend upon my movements. I am thus unavoidably summoned to power; and under these circumstances I would gladly receive some advice."

"That the scheme of empire is in confusion," said the Vital Principle, "that the conditions of life are violated, that the will of God does not triumph, that the beasts of the field are disorganised, that the birds of the air cry at night, that blight reaches the trees and herbs, that destruction spreads among creeping things,—this, alas! is the fault of government."

"True," replied the Spirit of the Clouds, "but what am I to do?"

"It is here," cried the Vital Principle, "that the poison lurks! Go back!"

"It is not often," urged the Spirit of the Clouds, "that I meet with your Holiness. I would gladly receive some advice."

"Feed then your people," said the Vital Principle, "with your heart.

Rest in inaction, and the world will be good of itself. Cast your slough. Spit forth intelligence. Ignore all differences. Become one with the infinite. Release your mind. Free your soul. Be vacuous. Be Nothing!

"Let all things revert to their original constitution. If they do this, without knowledge, the result will be a simple purity which they will never lose; but knowledge will bring with it a divergence therefrom. Seek not the names nor the relations of things, and all things will flourish of themselves."

"Your Holiness," said the Spirit of the Clouds, as he prostrated himself and took leave, "has informed me with power and filled me with mysteries. What I had long sought, I have now found."

The men of this world all rejoice in others being like themselves, and object to others not being like themselves.

Those who make friends with their likes and do not make friends with their unlikes, are influenced by a desire to differentiate themselves from others. But those who are thus influenced by a desire to differentiate themselves from others,—how will they find it possible to do so?

To subordinate oneself to the majority in order to gratify personal ambition, is not so good as to let that majority look each one after his own affairs. Those who desire to govern kingdoms, clutch at the advantages of the Three Princes without seeing the troubles involved. In fact, they trust

者，此攬乎三王之利而不見其患者也。此以人之國僥倖也。幾何僥倖而不喪人之國乎！其存人之國也，無萬分之一；而喪人之國也，一不成而萬有餘喪矣。悲夫，有土者之不知也！夫有土者，有大物也。有大物者，不可以物；物而不物，故能物物。明乎物物者之非物也，豈獨治天下百姓而已哉！出入六合，遊乎九州，獨往獨來，是謂獨有。獨有之人，是之謂至貴。

大人之教，若形之於影，聲之於響。有問而應之，盡其所懷，為天下配。處乎無響。行乎無方。挈汝適復之撓撓，以遊無端；出入無旁，與日無始；頌論形軀，合乎大同，大同而無己。無己，惡乎得有有！睹有者，昔之君子；睹無者，天地之友。

賤而不可不任者，物也；卑而不可不因者，民也；匿而不可不為者，事也；麤而不可不陳者，法也；遠而不可不居者，義也；親而不可不廣者，仁也；節而不可不積者，禮也；中而不可不高者，德也；一而不可不易者，道也；神而不可不為者，天也。故聖人觀於天而不助，成於德而不累，

to luck. But in thus trusting to luck not to destroy the kingdom, their chances of preserving it do not amount to one in ten thousand, while their chances of destroying it are ten thousand to nothing and even more. Such, alas! is the ignorance of rulers.

For, given territory, there is the great thing—Man. Given man, he must not be managed as if he were a mere thing; though by not managing him at all he may actually be managed as if he were a mere thing. And for those who understand that the management of man as if he were a mere thing is not the way to manage him, the issue is not confined to mere government of the empire. Such men may wander at will between the six limits of space or travel over the continent of earth, unrestrained in coming and in going. This is to be distinguished from one's fellows, and this distinction is the highest attainable by man.

The doctrine of the perfect man is to him as shadow to form, as echo to sound. Ask and it responds, fulfilling its mission as the help-mate of humanity. Noiseless in repose, objectless in motion, it guides you to the goal, free to come and free to go for ever without end. Alone in its exits and its entrances, it rivals the eternity of the sun.

As for his body, that is in accordance with the usual standard. Being in accordance with the usual standard it is not distinguished in any way. But if not distinguished in any way, what becomes of the distinction by which he is distinguished?

Those who see what is to be seen,—of such were the perfect men of old. Those who see what is not to be seen,—they are the chosen of the universe.

Low in the scale, but still to be allowed for,—matter. Humble, but still to be followed,— mankind. Of others, but still to be attended to,—affairs. Harsh, but still necessary to be set forth,—the law. Far off, but still claiming our presence,—duty to one's neighbour. Near, but still claiming extension,—charity. Of sparing use, but still to be of bounteous store,—ceremony. Of middle course, but still to be of lofty scope,—virtue. One, but not to be without modification,—Tao. Spiritual, yet not to be devoid of action,—God.

Therefore the true Sage looks up to God, but does not offer to aid. He perfects his virtue, but does not involve himself. He guides himself by Tao, but makes no plans. He identifies himself with charity, but does not rely

出於道而不謀，會於仁而不恃，薄於義而不積，應於禮而不諱，接於事而不辭，齊於法而不亂，恃於民而不輕，因於物而不去。物者莫足為也，而不可不為。不明於天者，不純於德；不通於道者，無自而可；不明於道者，悲夫！何謂道？有天道，有人道。無為而尊者，天道也；有為而累者，人道也。主者，天道也；臣者，人道也。天道之與人道也，相去遠矣，不可不察也。

on it. He extends to duty towards his neighbour, but does not store it up. He responds to ceremony, without tabooing it.

He undertakes affairs without declining them. He metes out law without confusion. He relies on his fellow-men and does not make light of them. He accommodates himself to matter and does not ignore it.

While there should be no action, there should be also no inaction.

He who is not divinely enlightened will not be sublimely pure. He who has not clear apprehension of Tao will find this beyond his reach. And he who is not enlightened by Tao,—alas indeed for him!

What then is Tao?—There is the Tao of God, and the Tao of man. Inaction and compliance make the Tao of God: action and entanglement the Tao of man. The Tao of God is fundamental: the Tao of man is accidental. The distance which separates them is great. Let us all take heed thereto!

# 天地第十二

天地雖大，其化均也；萬物雖多，其治一也；人卒雖眾，其主君也。君原天德而成於天。故曰：玄古之君天下，無為也，天德而已矣。以道觀言而天下之君正，以道觀分而君臣之義明，以道觀能而天下之官治，以道汎觀而萬物之應備。故通於天地者，德也；行於萬物者，道也；上治人者，事也；能有所藝者，技也。技兼於事，事兼於義，義兼於德，德兼於道，道兼於天。故曰：古之畜天下者，無欲而天下足，無為而萬物化，淵靜而百姓定。《記》曰：「通於一而萬事畢，無心得而鬼神服。」

夫子曰：「夫道，覆載萬物者也，洋洋乎大哉！君子不可以不刳心焉。無為為之之謂天，無為言之之謂德，愛人利物之謂仁，不同同之之謂大，

# CHAPTER XII

## THE UNIVERSE

Vast as is the universe, its phenomena are regular. Countless though its contents, the laws which govern these are uniform. Many though its inhabitants, that which dominates them is sovereignty. Sovereignty begins in virtue and ends in God. Therefore it is called divine.

Of old, the empire was under the sovereignty of inaction. There was the virtue of God,—nothing more.

Words being in accordance with Tao, the sovereignty of the empire was correct. Delimitations being in accordance with Tao, the duties of prince and subject were clear. Abilities being in accordance with Tao, the officials of the empire governed. The point of view being always in accordance with Tao, all things responded thereto.

Thus, virtue was the connecting link between God and man, while Tao spread throughout all creation. Men were controlled by outward circumstances, applying their in-born skill to the development of civilised life. This skill was bound up with the circumstances of life, and these with duty, and duty with virtue, and virtue with Tao, and Tao with God.

Therefore it has been said, "As for those who nourished the empire of old, having no desires for themselves, the empire was not in want. They did nothing, and all things proceeded on their course. They preserved a dignified repose, and the people rested in peace."

The Record says, "By converging to One, all things may be accomplished. By the virtue which is without intention, even the supernatural may be subdued."

The Master said, "Tao covers and supports all things,"—so vast is its extent. Each man should prepare his heart accordingly.

"To act by means of inaction is God. To speak by means of inaction is Virtue. To love men and care for things is Charity. To recognise the unlike as the like is breadth of view. To make no distinctions is liberal. To possess variety is wealth. And so, to hold fast to virtue is strength. To complete virtue is establishment. To follow Tao is to be prepared. And not to run counter to the natural bias of things is to be perfect.

"He who fully realises these ten points, by storing them within enlarg-

行不崖異之謂寬，有萬不同之謂富。故執德之謂紀，德成之謂立，循於道之謂備，不以物挫志之謂完。君子明於此十者，則韜乎其事心之大也，沛乎其為萬物逝也。若然者，藏金於山，藏珠於淵，不利貨財，不近貴富；不樂壽，不哀夭；不榮通，不醜窮；不拘一世之利以為己私分，不以王天下為己處顯。顯則明。萬物一府，死生同狀。」

夫子曰：「夫道，淵乎其居也，漻乎其清也。金石不得，無以鳴。故金石有聲，不考不鳴。萬物孰能定之！夫王德之人，素逝而恥通於事，立之本原而知通於神，故其德廣。其心之出，有物採之。故形非道不生，生非德不明。存形窮生，立德明道，非王德者邪！蕩蕩乎！忽然出，勃然動，而萬物從之乎！此謂王德之人。視乎冥冥，聽乎無聲。冥冥之中，獨見曉焉；無聲之中，獨聞和焉。故深之又深而能物焉；神之又神而能精焉。故其與萬物接也，至無而供其求，時騁而要其宿，大小、長短、修遠。」

es his heart, and with this enlargement brings all creation to himself. Such a man will bury gold on the hillside and cast pearls into the sea. He will not struggle for wealth, nor strive for fame. He will not rejoice at old age, nor grieve over early death. He will find no pleasure in success, no chagrin in failure. He will not account a throne as his own private gain, nor the empire of the world as glory personal to himself. His glory is to know that all things are One, and that life and death are but phases of the same existence!"

The Master said, "How profound in its repose, how infinite in its purity, is Tao!

"If metal and stone were without Tao, they would not be capable of emitting sound. And just as they possess the property of sound but will not emit sound unless struck, so surely is the same principle applicable to all creation.

"The man of complete virtue remains blankly passive as regards what goes on around him. He is as originally by nature, and his knowledge extends to the supernatural. Thus, his virtue expands his heart, which goes forth to all who come to take refuge therein.

"Without Tao, form cannot be endued with life. Without virtue, life cannot be endued with intelligence. To preserve one's form, live out one's life, establish one's virtue, and realise Tao,—is not this complete virtue?

"Issuing forth spontaneously, moving without premeditation, all things following in his wake,—such is the man of complete virtue!

"He can see where all is dark. He can hear where all is still. In the darkness he alone can see light. In the stillness he alone can detect harmony. He can sink to the lowest depths of materialism. To the highest heights of spirituality he can soar. This because he stands in due relation to all things. Though a mere abstraction, he can minister to their wants, and ever and anon receive them into rest,—the great, the small, the long, the short, for ever without end."

The Yellow Emperor travelled to the north of the Red Lake and ascended the K'un-lun Mountains. Returning south he lost his magic pearl.

He employed Intelligence to find it, but without success. He employed Sight to find it, but without success. He employed Speech to find it, but without success. Finally, he employed Nothing, and Nothing got it.

"Strange indeed," quoth the Emperor, "that Nothing should have been

黃帝遊乎赤水之北，登乎崑崙之丘而南望，還歸，遺其玄珠。使知索之而不得，使離朱索之而不得，使喫詬索之而不得也。乃使象罔，象罔得之。黃帝曰：「異哉，象罔乃可以得之乎？」

堯之師曰許由，許由之師曰齧缺，齧缺之師曰王倪，王倪之師曰被衣。堯問於許由曰：「齧缺可以配天乎？吾藉王倪以要之。」許由曰：「殆哉圾乎天下！齧缺之為人也，聰明睿知，給數以敏，其性過人，而又乃以人受天。彼審乎禁過，而不知過之所由生。與之配天乎？彼且乘人而無天。方且本身而異形，方且尊知而火馳，方且為緒使，方且為物絯，方且四顧而物應，方且應眾宜，方且與物化而未始有恆。夫何足以配天乎！雖然，有族，有祖，可以為眾父，而不可以為眾父父。治，亂之率也，北面之禍也，南面之賊也。」

堯觀乎華。華封人曰：「嘻，聖人！請祝聖人，使聖人壽。」堯曰：「辭。」「使聖人富。」堯曰：「辭。」「使聖人多男子。」堯曰：「辭。」封人曰：「壽，富，多男子，人之所欲也。女獨不欲，何邪？」堯曰：

able to get it!"

Yao's tutor was Hsu Yu. The latter's tutor was Yeh Ch'ueh, and Yeh Ch'ueh's tutor was Wang I, whose tutor was Pei I.

Yao enquired of Hsu Yu, saying, "Would Yeh Ch'ueh do to be emperor? I am going to get Wang I to ask him."

"Alas!" cried Hsu Yu, "that would be bad indeed for the empire. Yeh Ch'ueh is a clever and capable man. He is by nature better than most men, but he seeks by means of the human to reach the divine. He strives to do no wrong; but he is ignorant of the source from which wrong springs. Emperor forsooth! He avails himself of the artificial and neglects the natural. He lacks unity in himself. He worships intelligence and is always in a state of ferment. He is a slave to circumstances and to things. Wherever he looks, his surroundings respond. He himself responds to his surroundings.

He is always undergoing modifications and is wanting in fixity. How should such a one be fit for emperor? Still every clan has its elder. He may be leader of a clan, but not a leader of leaders. A captain who has been successful in suppressing rebellion, as minister is a bane, as sovereign, a thief."

Yao went to visit Hua. The border-warden of Hua said "Ha! a Sage. My best respects to you, Sir. I wish you a long life."

"Don't!" replied Yao.

"I wish you plenty of money," continued the border-warden.

"Don't!" replied Yao.

"And many sons," added he.

"Don't!" replied Yao.

"Long life, plenty of money, and many sons," cried the warden, "these are what all men desire. How is it you alone do not want them?"

"Many sons," answered Yao, "are many anxieties. Plenty of money means plenty of trouble. Long life involves much that is not pleasant to put up with. These three gifts do not advance virtue; therefore I declined them."

"At first I took you for a Sage," said the warden, "but now I find you are a mere man. God, in sending man into the world, gives to each his proper function. If you have many sons and give to each his proper function, what cause have you for anxiety?

"And similarly, if you have wealth and allow others to share it, what troubles will you have?"

「多男子則多懼，富則多事，壽則多辱。是三者，非所以養德也，故辭。」封人曰：「始也我以女為聖人邪，今然君子也。天生萬民，必授之職。多男子而授之職，則何懼之有！富而使人分之，則何事之有！夫聖人鶉居而鷇食，鳥行而無彰；天下有道，則與物皆昌；天下無道，則修德就閒。千歲厭世，去而上僊，乘彼白雲，至於帝鄉；三患莫至，身常無殃，則何辱之有？」封人去之，堯隨之，曰：「請問。」封人曰：「退已！」

堯治天下，伯成子高立為諸侯。堯授舜，舜授禹，伯成子高辭為諸侯而耕。禹往見之，則耕在野。禹趨就下風，立而問焉，曰：「昔堯治天下，吾子立為諸侯。堯授舜，舜授予，而吾子辭為諸侯而耕。敢問，其故何也？」子高曰：「昔者堯治天下，不賞而民勸，不罰而民畏。今子賞罰而民且不仁，德自此衰，刑自此立，後世之亂，自此始矣！夫子闔行邪？無落吾事！」俋俋乎耕而不顧。

"The true Sage dwells like the quail and feeds like a fledgeling.

He travels like the bird, leaving no trace behind.

If there be Tao in the empire, he and all things are in harmony. If there be not Tao, he cultivates virtue in retirement. After a thousand years of this weary world, he mounts aloft, and riding upon the white clouds passes into the kingdom of God, whither the three evils do not reach, and where he rests secure in eternity. What is there to put up with in that?"

Thereupon the border-warden went off, and Yao followed him; saying, "May I ask——," to which the warden only replied "Begone!"

When Yao was Emperor, Poh Ch'eng Tzu Kao was one of his vassals. But when Yao handed over the empire to Shun, and Shun to the Great Yu, Poh Ch'eng Tzu Kao resigned his fief and betook himself to agriculture.

The Great Yu going to visit him, found him working in the fields; whereupon he approached humbly, saying, "When Yao was emperor, you, Sir, were a vassal; but when Yao handed over the empire to Shun, and Shun to me, you resigned your fief and betook yourself to agriculture. May I enquire the reason of this?"

"When Yao ruled the empire," said Tzu Kao,

"the people exerted themselves without reward and behaved themselves without punishment. But now you reward and punish them, and yet they are not good. From this point virtue will decline, the reign of force will begin, and the troubles of after ages will date their rise. Away with you! Do not interrupt my work." And he quietly went on ploughing as before.

At the beginning of the beginning, even Nothing did not exist. Then came the period of the Nameless.

When One came into existence, there was One, but it was formless. When things got that by which they came into existence, it was called their virtue.

That which was formless, but divided, though without interstice, was called destiny.

Then came the movement which gave life, and things produced in accordance with the principles of life had what is called form. When form encloses the spiritual part, each with its own characteristics, that is its nature. By cultivating this nature, we are carried back to virtue; and if this is perfected, we become as all things were in the beginning. We become

泰初有無，無有無名。一之所起，有一而未形。物得以生，謂之德；未形者有分，且然無間，謂之命；留動而生物，物成生理，謂之形；形體保神，各有儀則，謂之性。性修反德，德至同於初。同乃虛，虛乃大。合喙鳴；喙鳴合，與天地為合。其合緡緡，若愚若昏，是謂玄德，同乎大順。

夫子問於老聃曰：「有人治道若相放，可不可，然不然。辯者有言曰：『離堅白若縣宇。』若是則可謂聖人乎？」老聃曰：「是胥易技係勞形怵心者也。執留之狗成思，蝯狙之便自山林來。丘，予告若，而所不能聞與而所不能言。凡有首有趾、無心無耳者眾；有形者與無形無狀而皆存者盡無。其動，止也；其死，生也；其廢，起也，此又非其所以也。有治在人，忘乎物，忘乎天，其名為忘己。忘己之人，是之謂入於天。」

將閭葂見季徹曰：「魯君謂葂也曰：『請受教。』辭不獲命，既已告矣，未知中否。請嘗薦之。吾謂魯君曰：『必服恭儉，拔出公忠之屬而無阿私，民孰敢不輯！』」季徹局局然笑曰：「若

unconditioned, and the unconditioned is great. As birds join their beaks in chirping, and beaks to chirp must be joined,—to be thus joined with the universe without being more conscious of it than an idiot, this is divine virtue, this is accordance with the eternal fitness of things.

Confucius asked Lao Tzu, saying, "There are persons who cultivate Tao according to fixed rules of possible and impossible, fit and unfit, just as the schoolmen speak of separating hardness from whiteness as though these could be hung up on different pegs.

Could such persons be termed sages?"

"That," replied Lao Tzu, "is but the skill of the handicraftsman, wearing out body and soul alike. The powers of the hunting-dog involve it in trouble; the cleverness of the monkey brings it down from the mountain.

Ch'iu, what I mean you cannot understand, neither can you put it into words.

Those who have a head and feet, but no mind nor ears, are many. Those who have a body without a body or appearance of one, and yet there they are,—are none. Movement and rest, life and death, rise and fall, are not at the beck and call of man. Cultivation of self is in his own hands. To be unconscious of objective existences and of God, this is to be unconscious of one's own personality. And he who is unconscious of his own personality, combines in himself the human and the divine."

Chiang Lu Mien went to see Chi Ch'e, and said, "The Prince of Lu begged me to instruct him, but I declined. However, he would take no refusal, so I was obliged to do so. I don't know if I was correct in my doctrine or not. Please note what I said. I told him to be decorous and thrifty;

to advance the public-spirited and loyal, and to have no partialities. Then, I said, no one would venture to oppose him."

Chi Ch'e sniggered and said, "Your remarks on the virtues of Princes may be compared with the mantis stretching out its feelers and trying to stop a carriage,—not likely to effect the object proposed.

Besides, he would be placing himself in the position of a man who builds a lofty tower and makes a display of his valuables where all his neighbours will come and gaze at them."

"Alas! I fear I am but a fool," replied Chiang Lu Mien. "Nevertheless, I should be glad to be instructed by you in the proper course to pursue."

"The government of the perfect Sage," explained Chi Ch'e, "consists in

夫子之言，於帝王之德，猶螳螂之怒臂以當車軼，則必不勝任矣！且若是，則其自為處危，其觀臺多物將往投跡者眾。」將閭葂覤覤然驚曰：「葂也汒若於夫子之所言矣！雖然，願先生之言其風也。」季徹曰：「大聖之治天下也，搖蕩民心，使之成教易俗，舉滅其賊心而皆進其獨志。若性之自為，而民不知其所由然。若然者，豈兄堯、舜之教民，溟涬然弟之哉？欲同乎德而心居矣！」

　　子貢南游於楚，反於晉，過漢陰，見一丈人方將為圃畦，鑿隧而入井，抱甕而出灌，搰搰然用力甚多而見功寡。子貢曰：「有械於此，一日浸百畦，用力甚寡而見功多，夫子不欲乎？」為圃者卬而視之曰：「奈何？」曰：「鑿木為機，後重前輕，挈水若抽，數如泆湯，其名為槔。」為圃者忿然作色而笑曰：「吾聞之吾師，有機械者必有機事，有機事者必有機心。機心存於胸中，則純白不備；純白不備，則神生不定，神生不定者，道之所不載也。吾非不知，羞而不為也。」子貢瞞然慚，俯而不對。有間，為圃者曰：「子奚為者邪？」曰：「孔丘之徒也。」為圃者曰：「子

influencing the hearts of the people so as to cause them to complete their education, to reform their manners, to subdue the rebel mind, and to exert themselves one and all for the common good. This influence operates in accordance with the natural disposition of the people, who are thus unconscious of its operation. He who can so act has no need to humble himself before the teachings of Yao and Shun. He makes the desires of the people coincident with virtue, and their hearts rest therein."

When Tzu Kung went south to the Ch'u State on his way back to the Chin State, he passed through Han-yin. There he saw an old man engaged in making a ditch to connect his vegetable garden with a well. He had a pitcher in his hand, with which he was bringing up water and pouring it into the ditch,—great labour with very little result.

"If you had a machine here," cried Tzu Kung, "in a day you could irrigate a hundred times your present area. The labour required is trifling as compared with the work done. Would you not like to have one?"

"What is it?" asked the gardener.

"It is a contrivance made of wood," replied Tzu Kung, "heavy behind and light in front. It draws up water as you do with your hands, but in a constantly overflowing stream. It is called a well-sweep."

Thereupon the gardener flushed up and said, "I have heard from my teacher that those who have cunning implements are cunning in their dealings, and that those who are cunning in their dealings have cunning in their hearts, and that those who have cunning in their hearts cannot be pure and incorrupt, and that those who are not pure and incorrupt are restless in spirit, and that those who are restless in spirit are not fit vehicles for Tao.

It is not that I do not know of these things. I should be ashamed to use them."

At this Tzu Kung was much abashed, and said nothing. Then the gardener asked him who he was, to which Tzu Kung replied that he was a disciple of Confucius.

"Are you not one who extends his learning with a view to being a Sage; who talks big in order to put himself above the rest of mankind; who plays in a key to which no one can sing so as to spread his reputation abroad? Rather become unconscious of self and shake off the trammels of the flesh,—and you will be near. But if you cannot govern your own self, what

非夫博學以擬聖，於于以蓋眾，獨弦哀歌以賣名聲於天下者乎？汝方將忘汝神氣，墮汝形骸，而庶幾乎！而身之不能治，而何暇治天下乎！子往矣，無乏吾事。」子貢卑陬失色，頊頊然不自得，行三十里而後愈。　其弟子曰：「向之人何為者邪？夫子何故見之變容失色，終日不自反邪？」曰：「始吾以為天下一人耳，不知復有夫人也。　吾聞之夫子，事求可，功求成。　用力少，見功多者，聖人之道。　今徒不然。　執道者德全，德全者形全，形全者神全。　神全者，聖人之道也。　托生與民並行而不知其所之，汒乎淳備哉！功利機巧，必忘夫人之心。　若夫人者，非其志不之，非其心不為。　雖以天下譽之，得其所謂，謷然不顧；以天下非之，失其所謂，儻然不受。　天下之非譽，無益損焉，是謂全德之人哉！我之謂風波之民。」反於魯，以告孔子。　孔子曰：「彼假修渾沌氏之術者也。識其一，不知其二；治其內，而不治其外。夫明白入素，無為復朴，體性抱神，以遊世俗之間者，汝將固驚邪？且渾沌氏之術，予與汝何足以識之哉！」

leisure have you for governing the empire? Begone! Do not interrupt my work."

Tzu Kung changed colour and slunk away, being not at all pleased with this rebuff; and it was not before he had travelled some thirty li that he recovered his usual appearance.

"What did the man we met do," asked a disciple, "that you should change colour and not recover for such a long time?"

"I used to think there was only one man in all the world," replied Tzu Kung.

"I did not know that there was also this man. I have heard the Master say that the test of a scheme is its practicability, and that success must be certain. The minimum of effort with the maximum of success,—such is the way of the Sage.

"Not so this manner of man. Aiming at Tao, he perfects his virtue. By perfecting his virtue he perfects his body, and by perfecting his body he perfects his spiritual part. And the perfection of the spiritual part is the Tao of the Sage. Coming into life he is as one of the people, knowing not whither he is bound. How complete is his purity? Success, profit, skill,— these have no place in his heart. Such a man, if he does not will it, he does not stir; if he does not wish it, he does not act. If all the world praises him, he does not heed. If all the world blames him, he does not repine.

The praise and the blame of the world neither advantage him nor otherwise. He may be called a man of perfect virtue. As for me, I am but a mere creature of impulse."

So he went back to Lu to tell Confucius. But Confucius said, "That fellow pretends to a knowledge of the science of the ante-mundane. He knows something, but not much. His government is of the internal, not of the external. What is there wonderful in a man by clearness of intelligence becoming pure, by inaction reverting to his original integrity, and with his nature and his spiritual part wrapped up in a body, passing through this common world of ours? Besides, to you and to me the science of the ante-mundane is not worth knowing."

As Chun Mang was starting eastwards to the ocean, he fell in with Yuan Feng on the shore of the eastern sea.

"Whither bound?" cried the latter.

"I am going to the ocean," replied Chun Mang.

諄芒將東之大壑，適遇苑風於東海之濱。苑風曰：「子將奚之？」曰：「將之大壑。」曰：「奚為焉？」曰：「夫大壑之為物也，注焉而不滿，酌焉而不竭。吾將遊焉！」苑風曰：「夫子無意於橫目之民乎？願聞聖治。」諄芒曰：「聖治乎？官施而不失其宜，拔舉而不失其能，畢見其情事而行其所為行，言自為而天下化。手撓顧指，四方之民莫不俱至，此之謂聖治。」「願聞德人。」曰：「德人者，居無思，行無慮，不藏是非美惡。四海之內共利之之謂悅，共給之之謂安；怊乎若嬰兒之失其母也，儻乎若行而失其道也。財用有餘，而不知其所自來，飲食取足，而不知其所從，此謂德人之容。」「願聞神人。」曰：「上神乘光，與形滅亡，是謂照曠。致命盡情，天地樂而萬事銷亡，萬物復情，此之謂混冥。」

門無鬼與赤張滿稽觀於武王之師，赤張滿稽曰：「不及有虞氏乎！故離此患也。」門無鬼曰：「天

"What are you going to do there?" asked Yuan Feng.

"The ocean," said Chun Mang, "is a thing you cannot fill by pouring in, nor empty by taking out. I am simply on a trip."

"But surely you have intentions with regard to the straight-browed people?... Come, tell me how the Sage governs."

"Oh, the government of the Sage," answered

Chun Mang. "The officials confine themselves to their functions. Ability is secure of employment. The voice of the people is heard, and action is taken accordingly. Men's words and deeds are their own affairs, and so the empire is at peace. A beck or a call, and the people flock together from all sides. This is how the Sage governs."

"Tell me about the man of perfect virtue," said Yuan Feng.

"The man of perfect virtue," replied Chun Mang, "in repose has no thoughts, in action no anxiety. He recognises no right, nor wrong, nor good, nor bad. Within the Four Seas, when all profit—that is his pleasure; when all share—that is his repose. Men cling to him as children who have lost their mothers; they rally round him as wayfarers who have missed their road. He has wealth and to spare, but he knows not whence it comes. He has food and drink more than sufficient, but knows not who provides it. Such is a man of virtue."

"And now," said Yuan Feng, "tell me about the divine man."

"The divine man," replied Chun Mang, "rides upon the glory of the sky where his form can no longer be discerned. This is called absorption into light. He fulfils his destiny. He acts in accordance with his nature. He is at one with God and man. For him all affairs cease to exist, and all things revert to their original state. This is called envelopment in darkness."

Men Wu Kuei and Ch'ih Chang Man Chi were looking at Wu Wang's troops.

"He is not equal to the Great Yu," said the latter; and consequently "we are involved in all these troubles."

"May I ask," replied Men Wu Kuei, "if the empire was under proper government when the Great Yu began to govern it, or had he first to quell disorder and then to proceed to government?"

"If the empire had all been under proper government," said the other, "what would there have been for the Great Yu to do? He was as ointment

下均治而有虞氏治之邪？其亂而後治之與？」赤張滿稽曰：「天下均治之為願，而何計以有虞氏為！有虞氏之藥瘍也，禿而施髢，病而求醫。孝子操藥以修慈父，其色燋然，聖人羞之。至德之世，不尚賢，不使能；上如標枝，民如野鹿。端正而不知以為義，相愛而不知以為仁，實而不知以為忠，當而不知以為信，蠢動而相使，不以為賜。是故行而無跡，事而無傳。」

孝子不諛其親，忠臣不諂其君，臣、子之盛也。親之所言而然，所行而善，則世俗謂之不肖子；君之所言而然，所行而善，則世俗謂之不肖臣。而未知此其必然邪？俗之所謂然而然之，所謂善而善之，則不謂之道諛之人也！然則俗故嚴於親而尊於君邪？謂己道人，則勃然作色；謂己諛人，則怫然作色。而終身道人也，終身諛人也，合譬飾辭聚眾也，是終始本末不相坐。垂衣裳，設采色，動容貌，以媚一世，而不自謂道諛；與夫人之為徒，通是非，而不自謂眾人也，愚之至也。知其愚者，非大愚也；知其惑者，非不惑也。大惑者，終身不解；大愚者，終身不靈。

to a sore. Only bald men use wigs; only sick people want doctors. And the Sage blushes when a filial son, with anxious look, administers medicine to cure his loving father.

"In the Golden Age, good men were not appreciated; ability was not conspicuous. Rulers were mere beacons, while the people were free as the wild deer. They were upright without being conscious of duty to their neighbours. They loved one another without being conscious of charity. They were true without being conscious of loyalty. They were honest without being conscious of good faith. They acted freely in all things without recognising obligations to any one. Thus, their deeds left no trace; their affairs were not handed down to posterity.

"A filial son does not humour his parents. A loyal minister does not flatter his prince. This is the acme of filial piety and loyalty. To assent to whatever a parent or a prince says, and to praise whatever a parent or a prince does, this is what the world calls unfilial and disloyal conduct, though apparently unaware that the principle is of universal application. For though a man assents to whatever the world says, and praises whatever the world does, he is not dubbed a toady; from which one might infer that the world is severer than a father and more to be respected than a prince!

"If you tell a man he is a wheedler, he will not like it. If you tell him he is a flatterer, he will be angry. Yet he is everlastingly both. But all such sham and pretence is what the world likes, and consequently people do not punish each other for doing what they do themselves. For a man to arrange his dress, or make a display, or suit his expression so as to get into the good graces of the world, and yet not to call himself a flatterer; to identify himself in every way with the yeas and nays of his fellows, and yet not call himself one of them;—this is the height of folly.

"A man who knows that he is a fool is not a great fool. A man who knows his error is not greatly in error. Great error can never be shaken off; a great fool never becomes clear-headed. If three men are travelling and one man makes a mistake, they may still arrive at their destination, error being in the minority. But if two of them make a mistake, then they will not succeed, error being in the majority. And now, as all the world is in error, I, though I know the true path, am alas! unable to guide.

"Grand music does not appeal to vulgar ears. Give them the Che-yang or the Huang-hua, and they will roar with laughter. And likewise great

三人行而一人惑，所適者猶可致也，惑者少也；二人惑則勞而不至，惑者勝也。而今也以天下惑，予雖有祈嚮，不可得也。不亦悲乎！大聲不入於里耳，折楊、皇荂，則嗑然而笑。是故高言不止於眾人之心；至言不出，俗言勝也。以二垂鐘惑，而所適不得矣。而今也以天下惑，予雖有祈嚮，其庸可得邪！知其不可得也而強之，又一惑也！故莫若釋之而不推。不推，誰其比憂！厲之人夜半生其子，遽取火而視之，汲汲然唯恐其似己也。

truths do not take hold of the hearts of the masses. And great truths not finding utterance, common-places carry the day. Two earthen instruments will drown the sound of one metal one; and the result will not be melodious.

"And now, as all the world is in error, I, though I know the true path,—how shall I guide? If I know that I cannot succeed and yet try to force success, this would be but another source of error. Better, then, to desist and strive no more. But if I strive not, who will?

"An ugly man who has a son born to him in the middle of the night will hurry up with a light, in dread lest the child should be like himself.

百年之木，破為犧尊，青黃而文之，其斷在溝中。比犧尊於溝中之斷，則美惡有間矣，其於失性一也。跖與曾、史，行義有間矣，然其失性均也。且夫失性有五：一曰五色亂目，使目不明；二曰五聲亂耳，使耳不聰；三曰五臭熏鼻，困惾中顙；四曰五味濁口，使口厲爽；五曰趣舍滑心，使性飛揚。此五者，皆生之害也。而楊、墨乃始離跂自以為得，非吾所謂得也。夫得者困，可以為得乎？則鳩鴞之在於籠也，亦可以為得矣。且夫趣舍聲色以柴其內，皮弁鷸冠，搢笏紳修以約其外。內支盈於柴柵，外重纆繳，睆睆然在纆繳之中而自以為得，則是罪人交臂歷指而虎豹在於囊檻，亦可以為得矣！

"An old tree is cut down to make sacrificial vessels, which are then ornamented with colour. The stump remains in a ditch. The sacrificial vessels and the stump in the ditch are very differently treated as regards honour and dishonour; equally, as far as destruction of the woods original nature is concerned. Similarly, the acts of Robber Che and of Tseng and Shih are very different; but the loss of original nature is in each case the same.

"The causes of this loss are five in number; viz.—The five colours confuse the eye, and the eyes fail to see clearly. The five sounds confuse the ear, and the ear fails to hear accurately. The five scents confuse the nose, and obstruct the sense of smell. The five tastes cloy the palate, and vitiate the sense of taste. Finally, likes and dislikes cloud the understanding, and cause dispersion of the original nature.

"These five are the banes of life; yet Yang and Mih regarded them as the summum bonum.

They are not my summum bonum. For if men who are thus fettered can be said to have attained the summum bonum, then pigeons and owls in a cage may also be said to have attained the summum bonum!

"Besides, to stuff one's inside with likes and dislikes and sounds and colours; to encompass one's outside with fur caps, feather hats, the carrying of tablets, or girding of sashes—full of rubbish inside while swathed in magnificence without—and still to talk of having attained the summum bonum;—then the prisoner with arms tied behind him and fingers in the squeezer, the tiger or the leopard which has just been put in a cage, may justly consider that they too have attained the summum bonum!"

# 天道第十三

天道運而無所積，故萬物成；帝道運而無所積，故天下歸；聖道運而無所積，故海內服。明於天，通於聖，六通四辟於帝王之德者，其自為也，昧然無不靜者矣！聖人之靜也，非曰靜也善，故靜也；萬物無足以鐃心者，故靜也。水靜則明燭鬚眉，平中準，大匠取法焉。水靜猶明，而況精神！聖人之心靜乎！天地之鑒也，萬物之鏡也。夫虛靜恬淡寂漠無為者，天地之平而道德之至也。故帝王聖人休焉。休則虛，虛則實，實則倫矣。虛則靜，靜則動，動則得矣。靜則無為，無為也，則任事者責矣。無為則俞俞。俞俞者，憂患不能處，年壽長矣。夫虛靜恬淡寂漠無為者，萬物之本也。明此以南鄉，堯之為君也；明此以北面，舜之為臣也。以此處上，帝王天子之德也；以此處下，玄聖素王之道也。以此退居而閒遊江海，山林之士服；以此進為而撫世，則功大名顯而天下一也。靜而聖，動而王，無為也而尊，樸素而天下莫能與之爭美。夫明白於天地之德者，此之謂大本大宗，與天

# CHAPTER XIII

## THE TAO OF GOD

The Tao of God operates ceaselessly; and all things are produced. The Tao of the sovereign operates ceaselessly; and the empire rallies around him. The Tao of the Sage operates ceaselessly; and all within the limit of surrounding ocean acknowledge his sway. He who apprehends God, who is in relation with the Sage, and who recognises the radiating virtue of the sovereign,—his actions will be to him unconscious, the actions of repose.

The repose of the Sage is not what the world calls repose. His repose is the result of his mental attitude. All creation could not disturb his equilibrium: hence his repose.

When water is still, it is like a mirror, reflecting the beard and the eyebrows. It gives the accuracy of the water-level, and the philosopher makes it his model. And if water thus derives lucidity from stillness, how much more the faculties of the mind? The mind of the Sage being in repose becomes the mirror of the universe, the speculum of all creation.

Repose, tranquillity, stillness, inaction,—these were the levels of the universe, the ultimate perfection of Tao.

Therefore wise rulers and Sages rest therein. Resting therein they reach the unconditioned, from which springs the conditioned; and with the conditioned comes order.

Again, from the unconditioned comes repose, and from repose comes movement, and from movement comes attainment. Further, from repose comes inaction, and from inaction comes potentiality of action.

And inaction is happiness; and where there is happiness no cares can abide, and life is long.

Repose, tranquillity, stillness, inaction,—these were the source of all things. Due perception of this was the secret of Yao's success as a ruler, and of Shun's success as his minister. Due perception of this constitutes the virtue of sovereigns on the throne, the Tao of the inspired Sage and of the uncrowned King below. Keep to this in retirement, and the lettered denizens of sea and dale will recognise your power. Keep to this when coming forward to pacify a troubled world, and your merit shall be great and your name illustrious, and the empire united into one. In your repose

和者也；所以均調天下，與人和者也。 與人和者，
謂之人樂；與天和者，謂之天樂。 莊子曰：「吾
師乎，吾師乎！韲萬物而不為戾，澤及萬世而不
為仁，長於上古而不為壽，覆載天地、刻雕眾
形而不為巧。」此之謂天樂。 故曰：『知天樂者，
其生也天行，其死也物化。 靜而與陰同德，動
而與陽同波。』故知天樂者，無天怨，無人非，
無物累，無鬼責。 故曰：『其動也天，其靜也地，
一心定而王天下；其鬼不祟，其魂不疲，一心
定而萬物服。』言以虛靜推於天地，通於萬物，
此之謂天樂。 天樂者，聖人之心，以畜天下也。」

夫帝王之德，以天地為宗，以道德為主，以
無為為常。 無為也，則用天下而有餘；有為也，
則為天下用而不足。 故古之人貴夫無為也。 上
無為也，下亦無為也，是下與上同德。 下與上
同德則不臣。 下有為也，上亦有為也，是上與

you will be wise; in your movements, powerful. By inaction you will gain honour; and by confining yourself to the pure and simple, you will hinder the whole world from struggling with you for show.

To fully apprehend the scheme of the universe, this is called the great secret of being in accord with God, whereby the empire is so administered that the result is accord with man. To be in accord with man is human happiness; to be in accord with God is the happiness of God.

Chuang Tzu said, "O my exemplar! Thou who destroyest all things, and dost not account it cruelty; thou who benefitest all time, and dost not account it charity; thou who art older than antiquity and dost not account it age; thou who supportest the universe, shaping the many forms therein, and dost not account it skill;—this is the happiness of God!"

Therefore it has been said, "Those who enjoy the happiness of God, when born into the world, are but fulfilling their divine functions; when they die, they do but undergo a physical change. In repose, they exert the influence of the Negative; in motion, they wield the power of the Positive."

Thus, those who enjoy the happiness of God have no grievance against God, no grudge against man. Nothing material injures them; nothing spiritual punishes them. Accordingly it has been said, "Their motion is that of heaven; their repose is that of earth. Mental equilibrium gives them the empire of the world. Evil spirits do not harass them without; demons do not trouble them within. Mental equilibrium gives them sovereignty over all creation." Which signifies that in repose to extend to the whole universe and to be in relation with all creation,—this is the happiness of God. This enables the mind of the Sage to cherish the whole empire.

For the virtue of the wise ruler is modelled upon the universe, is guided by Tao, and is ever occupied in inaction. By inaction, he administers the empire, and has energy to spare; but by action he finds his energy inadequate to the administration of the empire. Therefore the men of old set great store by inaction.

But if rulers practise inaction and the ruled also practise inaction, the ruled will equal the rulers, and will not be as their subjects. On the other hand, if the ruled practise action and rulers also practise action, rulers will assimilate themselves to the ruled, and will not be as their masters. Rulers must practise inaction in order to administer the empire. The ruled must practise action in order to subserve the interests of the empire. This is an

下同道。上與下同道則不主。上必無為而用天下，下必有為為天下用。 此不易之道也。 故古之王天下者，知雖落天地，不自慮也；辯雖雕萬物，不自說也；能雖窮海內，不自為也。 天不產而萬物化，地不長而萬物育，帝王無為而天下功。故曰：莫神於天，莫富於地，莫大於帝王。 故曰：帝王之德配天地。 此乘天地，馳萬物，而用人群之道也。

本在於上，末在於下；要在於主，詳在於臣。三軍五兵之運，德在末也；賞罰利害，五刑之辟，教之末也；禮法度數，形名比詳，治之末也；鐘鼓之音，羽旄之容，樂之末也；哭泣衰絰，隆殺之服，哀之末也。 此五末者，須精神之運，心術之動，然後從之者也。 末學者，古人有之，而非所以先也。 君先而臣從，父先而子從，兄先而弟從，長先而少從，男先而女從，夫先而婦從。 夫尊卑先後，天地之行也，故聖人取象焉。 天尊，地卑，神明之位也；春夏先，秋冬後，四時之序也；萬物化作，萌區有狀；盛衰之殺，變化之流也。 夫天地至神，而有尊卑先後之序，

unchangeable law.

Thus, the men of old, although their knowledge did not extend throughout the universe, were not troubled in mind. Although their intellectual powers beautified all creation, they did not rejoice. Although their abilities exhausted all things within the limits of ocean, they did not act.

Heaven has no parturitions, yet all things are evolved. Earth knows no increment, yet all things are nourished. The wise ruler practises inaction, and the empire applauds him. Therefore it has been said, "There is nothing more mysterious than heaven, nothing richer than earth, nothing greater than the wise ruler." Wherefore also it has been said, "The virtue of the wise ruler makes him the peer of heaven and earth." Charioted upon the universe, with all creation for his team, he passes along the highway of mortality.

The essential is in the ruler; the accidental in the ruled.

The ultima ratio lies with the prince; representation is the duty of the minister.

Appeal to arms is the lowest form of virtue. Rewards and punishments are the lowest form of education. Ceremonies and laws are the lowest form of government. Music and fine clothes are the lowest form of happiness. Weeping and mourning are the lowest form of grief. These five should follow the movements of the mind.

The ancients indeed cultivated the study of accidentals, but they did not allow it to precede that of essentials. The prince precedes, the minister follows. The father precedes, the son follows. The elder brother precedes, the younger follows. Seniors precede, juniors follow. Men precede, women follow. Husbands precede, wives follow. Distinctions of rank and precedence are part of the scheme of the universe, and the Sage adopts them accordingly. In point of spirituality, heaven is honourable, earth is lowly. Spring and summer precede autumn and winter: such is the order of the seasons. In the constant production of all things, there are phases of existence. There are the extremes of maturity and decay, the perpetual tide of change. And if heaven and earth, divinest of all, admit of rank and precedence, how much more man?

In the ancestral temple, parents rank before all; at court, the most honourable; in the village, the elders; in matters to be accomplished, the most trustworthy. Such is the order which appertains to Tao. He who in

而況人道乎！宗廟尚親，朝廷尚尊，鄉黨尚齒，行事尚賢，大道之序也。語道而非其序者，非其道也；語道而非其道者，安取道哉！是故古之明大道者，先明天而道德次之，道德已明而仁義次之，仁義已明而分守次之，分守已明而形名次之，形名已明而因任次之，因任已明而原省次之，原省已明而是非次之，是非已明而賞罰次之，賞罰已明而愚知處宜，貴賤履位，仁賢不肖襲情，必分其能，必由其名。以此事上，以此畜下，以此治物，以此修身，知謀不用，必歸其天，此之謂太平，治之至也。故書曰：「有形有名。」形名者，古人有之，而非所以先也。古之語大道者，五變而形名可舉，九變而賞罰可言也。驟而語形名，不知其本也；驟而語賞罰，不知其始也。倒道而言，迕道而說者，人之所治也，安能治人！驟而語形名賞罰，此有知治之具，非知治之道。可用於天下，不足以用天下。此之謂辯士，一曲之人也。禮法數度，形名比詳，古人有之。此下之所以事上，非上之所以畜下也。昔者舜問於堯曰：「天王之用心何如？」堯曰：「吾

considering Tao disregards this order, thereby disregards Tao; and he who in considering Tao disregards Tao,—whence will he secure Tao?

Therefore, those of old who apprehended Tao, first apprehended God. Tao came next, and then charity and duty to one's neighbour, and then the functions of public life, and then forms and names, and then employment according to capacity, and then distinctions of good and bad, and then discrimination between right and wrong, and then rewards and punishments. Thus wise men and fools met with their dues; the exalted and the humble occupied their proper places. And the virtuous and the worthless being each guided by their own natural instincts, it was necessary to distinguish capabilities, and to adopt a corresponding nomenclature, in order to serve the ruler, nourish the ruled, administer things generally, and elevate self. Where knowledge and plans are of no avail, one must fall back upon the natural. This is perfect peace, the acme of good government. Therefore it has been written, "Wherever there is form, there is also its name." Forms and names indeed the ancients had, but did not give precedence to them.

Thus, those of old who considered Tao, passed through five phases before forms and names were reached, and nine before rewards and punishments could be discussed.

To rise per saltum to forms and names is to be ignorant of their source; to rise per saltum to rewards and punishments is to be ignorant of their beginning. Those who invert the process of discussing Tao, arguing in a directly contrary sense, are rather to be governed by others than able to govern others themselves.

To rise per saltum to forms and names and rewards and punishments, this is to understand the instrumental part of government, but not to understand the great principle of government.

This is to be of use in the administration of the empire, but not to be able to administer the empire. This is to be a sciolist, a man of narrow views.

Ceremonies and laws were indeed cultivated by the ancients; but they were employed in the service of the rulers by the ruled. Rulers did not employ them as a means of nourishing the ruled.

Of old, Shun asked Yao, saying, "How does your Majesty employ your faculties?"

"I am not arrogant towards the defenceless," replied Yao. "I do not ne-

不敖無告，不廢窮民，苦死者，嘉孺子而哀婦人，此吾所以用心已。」舜曰：「美則美矣，而未大也。」堯曰：「然則何如？」舜曰：「天德而出寧，日月照而四時行，若晝夜之有經，雲行而雨施矣！」堯曰：「膠膠擾擾乎！子，天之合也；我，人之合也。」夫天地者，古之所大也，而黃帝、堯、舜之所共美也。故古之王天下者，奚為哉？天地而已矣！

孔子西藏書於周室。子路謀曰：「由聞周之徵藏史有老聃者，免而歸居，夫子欲藏書，則試往因焉。」孔子曰：「善。」往見老聃，而老聃不許，於是繙十二經以說。老聃中其說，曰：「大謾，願聞其要。」孔子曰：「要在仁義。」老聃曰：「請問仁義，人之性邪？」孔子曰：「然。君子不仁則不成，不義而不生。仁義，真人之性也，

glect the poor. I grieve for those who die. I pity the orphan. I sympathise with the widow. Beyond this, nothing."

"Good indeed!" cried Shun, "but yet not great."

"How so?" inquired Yao.

"Be passive," said Shun, "like the virtue of God. The sun and moon shine; the four seasons revolve; day and night alternate; clouds come and rain falls."

"Alas!" cried Yao, "what a muddle I have been making. You are in accord with God; I am in accord with man."

Of old, heaven and earth were considered great; and the Yellow Emperor and Yao and Shun all thought them perfection. Consequently, what did those do who ruled the empire of old? They did what heaven and earth do; no more.

When Confucius was going west to place his works in the Imperial library of the House of Chou, Tzu Lu counselled him, saying, "I have heard that a certain librarian of the Cheng department, by name Lao Tan, has resigned and retired into private life. Now as you, Sir, wish to deposit your works, it would be advisable to go and interview him."

"Certainly," said Confucius; and he thereupon went to see Lao Tzu. The latter would not hear of the proposal; so Confucius began to expound the doctrines of his twelve canons, in order to convince Lao Tzu.

"This is all nonsense," cried Lao Tzu, interrupting him. "Tell me what are your criteria."

"Charity," replied Confucius, "and duty towards one's neighbour."

"Tell me, please," asked Lao Tzu, "are these part of man's original nature?"

"They are," answered Confucius. "Without charity, the superior man could not become what he is. Without duty to one's neighbour, he would be of no effect. These two belong to the original nature of a pure man. What further would you have?"

"Tell me," said Lao Tzu, "in what consist charity and duty to one's neighbour?"

"They consist," answered Confucius, "in a capacity for rejoicing in all things; in universal love, without the element of self. These are the characteristics of charity and duty to one's neighbour."

"What stuff!" cried Lao Tzu. "Does not universal love contradict it-

又將奚為矣?」老聃曰:「請問,何謂仁義?」孔子曰:「中心物愷,兼愛無私,此仁義之情也。」老聃曰:「意,幾乎後言!夫兼愛,不亦迂夫!無私焉,乃私也。夫子若欲使天下無失其牧乎?則天地固有常矣,日月固有明矣,星辰固有列矣,禽獸固有群矣,樹木固有立矣。夫子亦放德而行,遁遁而趨,已至矣;又何偈偈乎揭仁義,若擊鼓而求亡子焉?意,夫子亂人之性也!」

　　士成綺見老子而問曰:「吾聞夫子聖人也。吾固不辭遠道而來願見,百舍重趼而不敢息。今吾觀子,非聖人也,鼠壤有餘蔬而棄妹,不仁也!生熟不盡於前,而積斂無崖。」老子漠然不應。士成綺明日復見,曰:「昔者吾有刺於子,今吾心正郤矣,何故也?」老子曰:「夫巧知神

self?

Is not your elimination of self a positive manifestation of self?

Sir, if you would cause the empire not to lose its source of nourishment,—there is the universe, its regularity is unceasing; there are the sun and moon, their brightness is unceasing; there are the stars, their groupings never change; there are birds and beasts, they flock together without varying; there are trees and shrubs, they grow upwards without exception, Be like these; follow Tao; and you will be perfect. Why then these vain struggles after charity and duty to one's neighbour, as though beating a drum in search of a fugitive. Alas! Sir, you have brought much confusion into the mind of man."

Shih Ch'eng Ch'i visited Lao Tzu, and addressed him, saying, "Having heard, Sir, that you were a Sage, I put aside all thought of distance to come and visit you. Travelling many stages, the soles of my feet thickened, but I did not venture to rest. And now I see you are not a Sage. While rats feasted off your leavings, you turned your sister out of doors. This is not charity. Though you have no lack of food, raw and cooked, you are stingy beyond all bounds."

At this Lao Tzu was silent and made no reply; and the next day Shih Ch'eng Ch'i came again and said, "Before, I was rude to you; now, I am sorry. How is this?"

"I have no pretension," replied Lao Tzu, "to be possessed of cunning knowledge nor of divine wisdom. Had you yesterday called me an ox, I should have considered myself an ox. Had you called me a horse, I should have considered myself a horse.

"For if men class you in accordance with truth, and you reject the classification, you only double the reproach. My humility is natural humility. It is not humility for humility's sake."

Shih Ch'eng Ch'i moved respectfully away.

Then he advanced again, also respectfully, and said, "May I ask you about personal cultivation?"

Lao Tzu said, "Your countenance is a strange one. Your eyes protrude. Your jaws are heavy. Your lips are parted. Your demeanour is self-satisfied. You look like a man on a tethered horse.

You are too confident. You are too hasty. You think too much of your own powers. Such men are not trusted. Those who are found on the

聖之人，吾自以為脫焉。昔者子呼我牛也而謂之牛，呼我馬也而謂之馬。苟有其實，人與之名而弗受，再受其殃。吾服也恆服，吾非以服有服。」士成綺雁行避影，履行遂進而問：「修身若何？」老子曰：「而容崖然，而目衝然，而顙頯然，而口闞然，而狀義然。似繫馬而止也。動而持，發也機，察而審，知巧而睹於泰，凡以為不信。邊竟有人焉，其名為竊。」

老子曰：「夫道，於大不終，於小不遺，故萬物備。廣廣乎其無不容也，淵淵乎其不可測也。形德仁義，神之末也，非至人孰能定之！夫至人有世，不亦大乎，而不足以為之累。天下奮柄而不與之偕；審乎無假而不與利遷，極物之真，能守其本。故外天地，遺萬物，而神未嘗有所困也。通乎道，合乎德，通仁義，賓禮樂，至人之心有所定矣！」

世之所貴道者，書也。書不過語，語有貴也。語之所貴者，意也，意有所隨。意之所隨者，不可以言傳也，而世因貴言傳書。世雖貴之哉，猶不足貴也，為其貴非其貴也。故視而可見者，

wrong side of a boundary line are called thieves."

Lao Tzu said, "Tao is not too small for the greatest, nor too great for the smallest. Thus all things are embosomed therein; wide indeed its boundless capacity, unfathomable its depth.

"Form, and virtue, and charity, and duty to one's neighbour, these are the accidentals of the spiritual. Except he be a perfect man, who shall determine their place? The world of the perfect man, is not that vast? And yet it is not able to involve him in trouble. All struggle for power, but he does not join. Though discovering nothing false, he is not tempted astray. In spite of the utmost genuineness, he still confines himself to essentials.

"He thus places himself outside the universe, beyond all creation, where his soul is free from care. Apprehending Tao, he is in accord with virtue. He leaves charity and duty to one's neighbour alone. He treats ceremonies and music as adventitious. And so the mind of the perfect man is at peace.

"Books are what the world values as representing Tao. But books are only words, and the valuable part of words is the thought therein contained. That thought has a certain bias which cannot be conveyed in words, yet the world values words as being the essence of books. But though the world values them, they are not of value; as that sense in which the world values them is not the sense in which they are valuable.

"That which can be seen with the eye is form and colour; that which can be heard with the ear is sound and noise. But alas! the people of this generation think that form, and colour, and sound, and noise, are means by which they can come to understand the essence of Tao. This is not so. And as those who know, do not speak, while those who speak do not know, whence should the world derive its knowledge?"

Duke Huan. was one day reading in his hall, when a wheelwright who was working below, flung down his hammer and chisel, and mounting the steps said, "What words may your Highness be studying?"

"I am studying the words of the Sages," replied the Duke.

"Are the Sages alive?" asked the wheelwright.

"No," answered the Duke; "they are dead."

"Then the words your Highness is studying," rejoined the wheelwright, "are only the dregs of the ancients."

"What do you mean, sirrah!" cried the Duke, "by interfering with

形與色也；聽而可聞者，名與聲也。悲夫！世人以形色名聲為足以得彼之情。夫形色名聲，果不足以得彼之情，則知者不言，言者不知，而世豈識之哉！桓公讀書於堂上，輪扁斲輪於堂下，釋椎鑿而上，問桓公曰：「敢問：「公之所讀者，何言邪？」公曰：「聖人之言也。」曰：「聖人在乎？」公曰：「已死矣。」曰：「然則君之所讀者，古人之糟魄已夫！」桓公曰：「寡人讀書，輪人安得議乎！有說則可，無說則死！」輪扁曰：「臣也以臣之事觀之。斲輪，徐則甘而不固，疾則苦而不入，不徐不疾，得之於手而應於心，口不能言，有數存焉於其間。臣不能以喻臣之子，臣之子亦不能受之於臣，是以行年七十而老斲輪。古之人與其不可傳也死矣，然則君之所讀者，古人之糟魄已夫！」

what I read? Explain yourself, or you shall die."

"Let me take an illustration," said the wheelwright, "from my own trade. In making a wheel, if you work too slowly, you can't make it firm; if you work too fast, the spokes won't fit in. You must go neither too slowly nor too fast. There must be co-ordination of mind and hand. Words cannot explain what it is, but there is some mysterious art herein. I cannot teach it to my son; nor can he learn it from me. Consequently, though seventy years of age, I am still making wheels in my old age. If the ancients, together with what they could not impart, are dead and gone, then what your Highness is studying must be the dregs."

# 天運第十四

「天其運乎？地其運乎？日月其爭於所乎？孰主張是？孰維綱是？孰居無事推而行是？意者其有機緘而不得已邪？意者其運轉而不能自止邪？雲者為雨乎？雨者為雲乎？孰隆施是？孰居無事淫樂而勸是？風起北方，一西一東，有上彷徨。孰噓吸是？孰居無事而披拂是？敢問何故？」巫咸袑曰：「來！吾語女。天有六極五常，帝王順之則治，逆之則凶。九洛之事，治成德備，監照下土，天下戴之，此謂上皇。」

商大宰蕩問仁於莊子。莊子曰：「虎狼，仁也。」曰：「何謂也？」莊子曰：「父子相親，何為不仁！」曰：「請問至仁。」莊子曰：「至仁無親。」大宰曰：「蕩聞之，無親則不愛，不愛則不孝。謂至仁不孝，可乎？」莊子曰：「不然，夫至仁尚矣，孝固不足以言之。此非過孝之言也，不及孝之言也。夫南行者至於郢，北面而不見冥山，

# CHAPTER XIV

## THE CIRCLING SKY

"The sky turns round; the earth stands still; sun and moon pursue one another. Who causes this? Who directs this? Who has leisure enough to see that such movements continue?

"Some think there is a mechanical arrangement which makes these bodies move as they do. Others think that they revolve without being able to stop.

"The clouds cause rain; rain causes clouds. Whose kindly bounty is this? Who has leisure enough to see that such, result is achieved?

"Wind comes from the north. It blows now east, now west; and now it whirls aloft. Who puffs it forth? Who has leisure enough to be flapping it this way or that? I should like to know the cause of all this."

Wu Han Chao said, "Come here, and I will tell you. Above there are the Six Influences and the Five Virtues.

If a ruler keeps in harmony with these, his rule is good; if not, it is bad. By following the nine chapters of the Lo book, his rule will be a success and his virtue complete; he will watch over the interests of his people, and all the empire will owe him gratitude. This is to be an eminent ruler."

Tang, a high official of Sung, asked Chuang Tzu about charity. Chuang Tzu said, "Tigers and wolves have it."

"How so?" asked Tang.

"The natural love between parents and offspring," replied Chuang Tzu,—"is not that charity?"

Tang then inquired about perfect charity.

"Perfect charity," said Chuang Tzu, "does not admit of love for the individual."

"Without such love," replied Tang, "it appears to me there would be no such thing as affection, and without affection no filial piety. Does perfect charity not admit of filial piety?"

"Not so," said Chuang Tzu. "Perfect charity is the more extensive term. Consequently, it was unnecessary to mention filial piety. It was not that filial piety was omitted. It was merely not particularised.

"A man who travels southwards to Ying, cannot see Mount Ming in

是何也？則去之遠也。故曰：以敬孝易，以愛孝難；以愛孝易，以忘親難；忘親易，使親忘我難；使親忘我易，兼忘天下難；兼忘天下易，使天下兼忘我難。夫德遺堯、舜而不為也，利澤施於萬世，天下莫知也，豈直大息而言仁孝乎哉！夫孝悌仁義，忠信貞廉，此皆自勉以役其德者也，不足多也。故曰：至貴，國爵并焉；至富，國財并焉；至願，名譽并焉。是以道不渝。」

北門成問於黃帝曰：「帝張咸池之樂於洞庭之野，吾始聞之懼，復聞之怠，卒聞之而惑；蕩蕩默默，乃不自得。」帝曰：「汝殆其然哉！吾奏之以人，徵之以天，行之以禮義，建之以大清。四時迭起，萬物循生；一盛一衰，文武倫經；一清一濁，陰陽調和，流光其聲；蟄蟲始作，吾驚之以雷霆；其卒無尾，其始無首；一死一生，一債一起；所常無窮，而一不可待。女故懼也。吾又奏之以陰陽之和，燭之以日月之明；其聲能短能長，能柔能剛，變化齊一，不主故常；在谷滿谷，在坑滿坑；塗郤守神，以物為量。其聲揮綽，其名高明。是故鬼神守其幽，日月

the north. Why? Because he is too far off.

"Therefore it has been said that it is easy to be respectfully filial, but difficult to be affectionately filial.

But even that is easier than to become unconscious of one's natural obligations, which is in turn easier than to cause others to be unconscious of the operations thereof.

Similarly, this is easier than to become altogether unconscious of the world, which again is easier than to cause the world to be unconscious of one's influence upon it.

"True virtue does nothing, yet it leaves Yao and Shun far behind. Its good influence extends to ten thousand generations, yet no man knoweth it to exist. What boots it then to sigh after charity and duty to one's neighbour?

"Filial piety, fraternal love, charity, duty to one's neighbour, loyalty, truth, chastity, and honesty,—these are all studied efforts, designed to aid the development of virtue. They are only parts of a whole.

"Therefore it has been said, 'Perfect honour includes all the honour a country can give. Perfect wealth includes all the wealth a country can give. Perfect ambition includes all the reputation one can desire.' And by parity of reasoning, Tao does not admit of sub-division."

Pei Men Ch'eng said to the Yellow Emperor, "When your Majesty played the Han-ch'ih in the wilds of Tung-t'ing, the first time I heard it I was afraid, the second time I was amazed, and the last time I was confused, speechless, overwhelmed."

"You are not far from the truth," replied the Yellow Emperor. "I played as a man, drawing inspiration from God. The execution was punctilious, the expression sublime.

"Perfect music first shapes itself according to a human standard; then it follows the lines of the divine; then it proceeds in harmony with the five virtues; then it passes into spontaneity. The four seasons are then blended, and all creation is brought into accord. As the seasons come forth in turn, so are all things produced. Now fulness, now decay, now soft and loud in turn, now clear, now muffled, the harmony of Yin and Yang. Like a flash was the sound which roused you as the insect world is roused, followed by a thundering peal, without end and without beginning, now dying, now living, now sinking, now rising, on and on without a moment's break. And

星辰行其紀。吾止之於有窮，流之於無止。子欲慮之而不能知也，望之而不能見也，逐之而不能及也；儻然立於四虛之道，倚於槁梧而吟。目知窮乎所欲見，力屈乎所欲逐，吾既不及已夫！形充空虛，乃至委蛇。女委蛇，故怠。吾又奏之以無怠之聲，調之以自然之命。故若混逐叢生，林樂而無形，布揮而不曳，幽昏而無聲。動於無方，居於窈冥；或謂之死，或謂之生；或謂之實，或謂之榮；行流散徙，不主常聲。世疑之，稽於聖人。聖也者，達於情而遂於命也。天機不張而五官皆備。此之謂天樂，無言而心說。故有焱氏為之頌曰：『聽之不聞其聲，視之不見其形，充滿天地，苞裹六極。』女欲聽之而無接焉，而故惑也。樂也者，始於懼，懼故祟；吾又次之以怠，怠故遁；卒之於惑，惑故愚；愚故道，道可載而與之俱也。」

孔子西遊於衛，顏淵問師金曰：「以夫子之行為奚如？」師金曰：「惜乎！而夫子其窮哉！」顏淵曰：「何也？」師金曰：「夫芻狗之未陳也，盛以篋衍，巾以文繡，尸祝齋戒以將之。及其

so you were afraid.

"When I played again, it was the harmony of the Yin and Yang, lighted by the glory of sun and moon; now broken, now prolonged, now gentle, now severe, in one unbroken, unfathomable volume of sound. Filling valley and gorge, stopping the ears and dominating the senses, adapting itself to the capacities of things,—the sound whirled around on all sides, with shrill note and clear. The spirits of darkness kept to their domain. Sun, moon, and stars, pursued their appointed course. When the melody was exhausted I stopped; if the melody did not stop, I went on.

You would have sympathised, but you could not understand. You would have looked, but you could not see. You would have pursued, but you could not overtake. You stood dazed in the middle of the wilderness, leaning against a tree and crooning, your eye conscious of exhausted vision, your strength failing for the pursuit, and so unable to overtake me. Your frame was but an empty shell. You were completely at a loss, and so you were amazed.

"Then I played in sounds which produce no amazement, the melodious law of spontaneity, springing forth like nature's countless buds, in manifold but formless joy, as though poured forth to the dregs, in deep but soundless bass. Beginning nowhere, the melody rested in void; some would say dead, others alive, others real, others ornamental, as it scattered itself on all sides in never to be anticipated chords.

"The wondering world enquires of the Sage. He is in relation with its variations and follows the same eternal law.

"When no machinery is set in motion, and yet the instrumentation is complete, this is the music of God. The mind awakes to its enjoyment with out waiting to be called. Accordingly, Yu Piao praised it, saying, 'Listening you cannot hear its sound; gazing you cannot see its form.

It fills heaven and earth. It embraces the six cardinal points.' Now you desired to listen to it, but you were not able to grasp its existence. And so you were confused.

"My music first induced fear; and as a consequence, respect. I then added amazement, by which you were isolated.

And lastly, confusion; for confusion means absence of sense, and absence of sense means Tao, and Tao means absorption therein."

When Confucius travelled west to the Wei State, Yen Yuan asked Shih

已陳也，行者踐其首脊，蘇者取而爨之而已；將復取而盛以篋衍，巾以文繡，遊居寢臥其下，彼不得夢，必且數眯焉。今而夫子亦取先王已陳芻狗，聚弟子遊居寢臥其下。故伐樹於宋，削跡於衛，窮於商周，是非其夢邪？圍於陳蔡之間，七日不火食，死生相與鄰，是非其眯邪？夫水行莫如用舟，而陸行莫如用車。以舟之可行於水也，而求推之於陸，則沒世不行尋常。古今非水陸與？周魯非舟車與？今蘄行周於魯，是猶推舟於陸也！勞而無功，身必有殃。彼未知夫無方之傳，應物而不窮者也。且子獨不見夫桔槔者乎？引之則俯，舍之則仰。彼，人之所引，非引人者也。故俯仰而不得罪於人。故夫三皇五帝之禮義法度，不矜於同而矜於治。故譬三

Chin, saying, "What think you of my Master?"

"Alas!" replied Shih Chin, "he is not a success."

"How so?" enquired Yen Yuan.

"Before the straw dog has been offered in sacrifice," replied Shih Chin, "it is kept in a box, wrapped up in an embroidered cloth, and the augur fasts before using it. But when it has once been offered up, passers-by trample over its body, and fuel-gatherers pick it up for burning. Then, if any one should take it, and again putting it in a box and wrapping it up in an embroidered cloth, watch and sleep alongside, he would not only dream, but have nightmare into the bargain.

"Now your Master has been thus treating the ancients, who are like the dog which has already been offered in sacrifice. He causes his disciples to watch and sleep alongside of them. Consequently, his tree has been cut down in Sung; they will have none of him in Wei; in fact, his chances among the Shangs and the Chous are exhausted. Is not this the dream? And then to be surrounded by the Ch'ens and the Ts'ais, seven days without food, death staring him in the face,—is not this the nightmare?

"For travelling by water there is nothing like a boat. For travelling by land there is nothing like a cart. This because a boat moves readily in water; but were you to try to push it on land you would never succeed in making it go.

Now ancient and modern times may be likened unto water and land; Chou and Lu to the boat and the cart. To try to make the customs of Chou succeed in Lu, is like pushing a boat on land: great trouble and no result, except certain injury to oneself. Your Master has not yet learnt the doctrine of non-angularity, of self-adaptation to externals.

"Have you never seen a well-sweep? You pull it, and down it comes. You release it, and up it goes. It is the man who pulls the well-sweep, and not the well-sweep which pulls the man; so that both in coming down and going up, it does not run counter to the wishes of the man. And so it was that the ceremonial and obligations and laws of the Three Emperors and Five Rulers did not aim at uniformity of application but at good government of the empire. Their ceremonial, obligations, laws, etc., were like the cherry-apple, the pear, the orange, and the pumelo,—all differing in flavour but each palatable. They changed with the changing season.

"Dress up a monkey in the robes of Chou Kung, and it will not be

皇五帝之禮義法度，其猶柤梨橘柚邪！其味相反而皆可於口。故禮義法度者，應時而變者也。今取猨狙而衣以周公之服，彼必齕齧挽裂，盡去而後慊。觀古今之異，猶猨狙之異乎周公也。故西施病心而矉其里，其里之醜人見之而美之，歸亦捧心而矉其里。其里之富人見之，堅閉門而不出；貧人見之，挈妻子而去走。彼知矉美而不知矉之所以美。惜乎，而夫子其窮哉！」

孔子行年五十有一而不聞道，乃南之沛見老聃。老聃曰：「子來乎？吾聞子，北方之賢者也，子亦得道乎？」孔子曰：「未得也。」老子曰：「子惡乎求之哉？」曰：「吾求之於度數，五年而未得也。」老子曰：「子又惡乎求之哉？」曰：「吾求之於陰陽，十有二年而未得也。」老子曰：「然，使道而可獻，則人莫不獻之於其君；使道而可進，則人莫不進之於其親；使道而可以告人，則人莫不告其兄弟；使道而可以與人，則人莫不與其子孫。然而不可者，無它也，中無主而不止，外無正而不行。由中出者，不受於外，聖人不出；由外入者，無主於中，聖人不隱。名，公器也，

happy until they are torn to shreds. And the difference between past and present is much the same as the difference between Chou Kung and a monkey.

"When Hsi Shih was distressed in mind, she knitted her brows. An ugly woman of the village, seeing how beautiful she looked, went home, and having worked herself into a fit frame of mind, knitted her brows. The result was that the rich people of the place barred up their doors and would not come out, while the poor people took their wives and children and departed elsewhere. That woman saw the beauty of knitted brows, but she did not see wherein the beauty of knitted brows lay.

Alas! your Master is emphatically not a success."

Confucius had lived to the age of fifty-one without hearing Tao, when he went south to P'ei, to see Lao Tzu.

Lao Tzu said, "So you have come, Sir, have you? I hear you are considered a wise man up north. Have you got Tao?"

"Not yet," answered Confucius.

"In what direction," asked Lao Tzu, "have you sought for it?"

"I sought it for five years," replied Confucius, "in the science of numbers, but did not succeed."

"And then?..." continued Lao Tzu.

"Then," said Confucius, "I spent twelve years seeking for it in the doctrine of the Yin and Yang, also without success."

"Just so," rejoined Lao Tzu. "Were Tao something which could be presented, there is no man but would present it to his sovereign, or to his parents. Could it be imparted or given, there is no man but would impart it to his brother or give it to his child. But this is impossible, for the following reason. Unless there is a suitable endowment within, Tao will not abide. Unless there is outward correctness, Tao will not operate. The external being unfitted for the impression of the internal, the true Sage does not seek to imprint. The internal being unfitted for the reception of the external, the true Sage does not seek to receive.

"Reputation is public property; you may not appropriate it in excess. Charity and duty to one's neighbour are as caravanserais established by wise rulers of old; you may stop there one night, but not for long, or you will incur reproach.

"The perfect men of old took their road through charity, stopping a

不可多取。仁義，先王之蘧廬也，止可以一宿而不可久處。覯而多責。古之至人，假道於仁，託宿於義，以游逍遙之墟，食於苟簡之田，立於不貸之圃。逍遙，無為也；苟簡，易養也；不貸，無出也。古者謂是采真之遊。以富為是者，不能讓祿；以顯為是者，不能讓名；親權者，不能與人柄，操之則慄，舍之則悲，而一無所鑒，以闚其所不休者，是天之戮民也。怨、恩、取、與、諫、教、生殺八者，正之器也，唯循大變無所湮者為能用之。故曰：正者，正也。其心以為不然者，天門弗開矣。」

孔子見老聃而語仁義。老聃曰：「夫播糠眯目，則天地四方易位矣；蚊虻噆膚，則通昔不寐矣。夫仁義憯然，乃憤吾心，亂莫大焉。吾子使天下無失其朴，吾子亦放風而動，總德而立矣！又奚傑然若負建鼓而求亡子者邪！夫鵠不日浴而白，烏不日黔而黑。黑白之朴，不足以為辯；名譽之觀，不足以為廣。泉涸，魚相與處於陸，相呴以濕，相濡以沫，不若相忘於江湖。」

night with duty to their neighbour, on their way to ramble in transcendental space. Feeding on the produce of non-cultivation, and establishing themselves in the domain of no obligations, they enjoyed their transcendental inaction. Their food was ready to hand; and being under no obligations to others, they did not put any one under obligation to themselves. The ancients called this the outward visible sign of an inward and spiritual grace.

"Those who make wealth their all in all, cannot bear loss of money. Those who make distinction their all in all, cannot bear loss of fame. Those who affect power will not place authority in the hands of others. Anxious while holding, distressed if losing, yet never taking warning from the past and seeing the folly of their pursuit,—such men are the accursed of God.

"Resentment, gratitude, taking, giving, censure of self, instruction of others, power of life and death,—these eight are the instruments of right; but only he who can adapt himself to the vicissitudes of fortune, without being carried away, is fit to use them. Such a one is an upright man among the upright. And he whose heart is not so constituted,—the door of divine intelligence is not yet opened for him."

Confucius visited Lao Tzu, and spoke of charity and duty to one's neighbour.

Lao Tzu said, "The chaff from winnowing will blind a man's eyes so that he cannot tell the points of the compass. Mosquitoes will keep a man awake all night with their biting. And just in the same way this talk of charity and duty to one's neighbour drives me nearly crazy. Sir! strive to keep the world to its own original simplicity. And as the wind bloweth where it listeth, so let Virtue establish itself. Wherefore such undue energy, as though searching for a fugitive with a big drum?

"The snow-goose is white without a daily bath. The raven is black without daily colouring itself. The original simplicity of black and of white is beyond the reach of argument. The vista of fame and reputation is not worthy of enlargement. When the pond dries up and the fishes are left upon dry ground, to moisten them with the breath or to damp them with a little spittle is not to be compared with leaving them in the first instance in their native rivers and lakes."

On returning from this visit to Lao Tzu, Confucius did not speak for

孔子見老聃歸，三日不談。弟子問日：「夫子見老聃，亦得將何規哉？」孔子日：「吾乃今於是乎見龍！龍，合而成體，散而成章，乘乎雲氣而養乎陰陽。予口張而不能嚼，予又何規老聃哉？」子貢日：「然則人固有尸居而龍見，雷聲而淵默，發動如天地者乎？賜亦可得而觀乎？」遂以孔子聲見老聃。老聃方將倨堂而應，微日：「予年運而往矣，子將何以戒我乎？」子貢日：「夫三皇五帝之治天下不同，其係聲名一也。而先生獨以為非聖人，如何哉？」老聃日：「小子少進！子何以謂不同？」對日：「堯授舜，舜授禹。禹用力而湯用兵，文王順紂而不敢逆，武王逆紂而不肯順，故日不同。」老聃日：「小子少進，余語女三皇五帝之治天下。黃帝之治天下，使民心一，民有其親死不哭而民不非也。堯之治天下，使民心親。民有為其親殺其服而民不非也。舜之治天下，使民心競。民孕婦十月生子，子生五月而能言，不至乎孩而始誰，則人始有

three days. A disciple asked him, saying, "Master, when you saw Lao Tzu, in what direction did you admonish him?"

"I saw a Dragon," replied Confucius, "—a Dragon which by convergence showed a body, by radiation became colour, and riding upon the clouds of heaven, nourished the two Principles of Creation. My mouth was agape: I could not shut it. How then do you think I was going to admonish Lao Tzu?"

Upon this Tzu Kung remarked, "Ha! then a man can sit corpse-like manifesting his dragon-power around, his thunder-voice heard though profound silence reigns, his movements like those of the universe? I too would go and see him."

So on the strength of his connection with Confucius, Tzu Kung obtained an interview. Lao Tzu received him distantly and with dignity, saying in a low voice, "I am old, Sir. What injunctions may you have to give me?"

"The administration of the Three Kings and of the Five Rulers," replied Tzu Kung, "was not uniform; but their reputation has been identical. How then, Sir, is it that you do not regard them as Sages?"

"Come nearer, my son," said Lao Tzu. "What mean you by not uniform?"

"Yao handed over the empire to Shun," replied Tzu Kung; "and Shun to Yu. Yu employed labour, and T'ang employed troops. Wen Wang followed Chou Hsin and did not venture to oppose him. Wu Wang opposed him and would not follow. Therefore I said not uniform."

"Come nearer, my son," said Lao Tzu, "and I will tell you about the Three Kings and the Five Rulers.

"The Yellow Emperor's administration caused the affections of the people to be catholic. Nobody wept for the death of his parents, and nobody found fault.

"The administration of Yao diverted the affections of the people into particular channels. If a man slew the slayer of his parents, nobody blamed him.

"The administration of Shun brought a spirit of rivalry among the people. Children were born after ten months' gestation; when five months old, they could speak; and ere they were three years of age, could already tell one person from another. And so early death came into the world.

夭矣。禹之治天下，使民心變，人有心而兵有順，殺盜非殺，人自為種而天下耳。是以天下大駭，儒墨皆起。其作始有倫，而今乎婦女，何言哉！余語汝，三皇五帝之治天下，名曰治之，而亂莫甚焉。三皇之知，上悖日月之明，下睽山川之精，中墮四時之施。其知憯於蠣蠆之尾，鮮規之獸，莫得安其性命之情者，而猶自以為聖人，不可恥乎？其無恥也！」子貢蹴蹴然立不安。

孔子謂老聃曰：「丘治《詩》、《書》、《禮》、《樂》、《易》、《春秋》六經，自以為久矣，孰知其故矣；以奸者七十二君，論先王之道而明周、召之跡，一君無所鉤用。甚矣夫！人之難說也，道之難明邪？」老子曰：「幸矣，子之不遇治世之君也！夫六經，先王之陳跡也，豈其所以跡哉！今子之所言，猶跡也。夫跡，履之所出，而跡豈履哉！夫

"The administration of Yu wrought a change in the hearts of the people. Individuality prevailed, and force was called into play. Killing robbers was not accounted murder; and throughout the empire people became sub-divided into classes. There was great alarm on all sides, and the Confucianists and the Mihists arose. At first the relationships were duly observed; but what about the women of to-day?

"Let me tell you. The government of the Three Kings and Five Rulers was so only in name. In reality, it was utter confusion. The wisdom of the Three Kings was opposed to the brilliancy of the sun and moon above, destructive of the energy of land and water below, and subversive of the influence of the four seasons between.

That wisdom is more harmful than a hornet's tail, preventing the very animals from putting themselves into due relation with the conditions of their existence—and yet they call themselves Sages! Is not their shamelessness shameful indeed?"

At this Tzu Kung became ill at ease.

Confucius said to Lao Tzu, "I arranged the Six Canons of Poetry, History, Rites, Music, Changes, and Spring and Autumn. I spent much time over them, and I am well acquainted with their purport. I used them in admonishing seventy-two rulers, by discourses on the wisdom of ancient sovereigns and illustrations from the lives of Chou and Shao. Yet not one ruler has in any way adopted my suggestions. Alas that man should be so difficult to persuade, and wisdom so difficult to illustrate."

"It is well for you, Sir," replied Lao Tzu, "that you did not come across any real ruler of mankind. Your Six Canons are but the worn-out foot-prints of ancient Sages. And what are foot-prints? Why, the words you now utter are as it were foot-prints. Foot-prints are made by the shoe: they are not the shoe itself.

白鶂之相視，眸子不運而風化；蟲，雄鳴於上風，雌應於下風而化。類自為雌雄，故風化。性不可易，命不可變，時不可止，道不可壅。苟得於道，無自而不可；失焉者，無自而可。」孔子不出三月，復見，曰：「丘得之矣。烏鵲孺，魚傅沫，細要者化，有弟而兄啼。久矣，夫丘不與化為人！不與化為人，安能化人。」老子曰：「可，丘得之矣！」

"Fish-hawks gaze at each other with motionless eyes,—and their young are produced. The male of a certain insect chirps with the wind while the female chirps against it,—and their offspring is produced. There is another animal which, being an hermaphrodite, produces its own offspring. Nature cannot be changed. Destiny cannot be altered. Time cannot stop. Tao cannot be obstructed. Once attain to Tao, and there is nothing which you cannot accomplish. Without it, there is nothing which you can accomplish."

For three months after this Confucius did not leave his house. Then he again visited Lao Tzu and said, "I have attained. Birds lay eggs, fish spawn, insects undergo metamorphosis, and mammals suckle their young.

For a long time I have not been enlightened. And he who is not enlightened himself,—how should he enlighten others?"

Lao Tzu said, "Ch'iu, you have attained!"

# 刻意第十五

刻意尚行，離世異俗，高論怨誹，為亢而已矣。此山谷之士，非世之人，枯槁赴淵者之所好也。語仁義忠信，恭儉推讓，為修而已矣。此平世之士，教誨之人，遊居學者之所好也。語大功，立大名，禮君臣，正上下，為治而已矣。此朝廷之士，尊主彊國之人，致功并兼者之所好也。就藪澤，處閒曠，釣魚閒處，無為而已矣。此江海之士，避世之人，閒暇者之所好也。吹呴呼吸，吐故納新，熊經鳥申，為壽而已矣。此道引之士，養形之人，彭祖壽考者之所好也。若夫不刻意而高，無仁義而修，無功名而治，無江海而閒，不道引而壽，無不忘也，無不有也。澹然無極而眾美從之。此天地之道，聖人之德也。

# CHAPTER XV

## SELF-CONCEIT

Self-conceit and assurance, which lead men to quit society, and be different from their fellows, to indulge in tall talk and abuse of others,—these are nothing more than personal over-estimation, the affectation of recluses and those who have done with the world and have closed their hearts to mundane influences.

Preaching of charity and duty to one's neighbour, of loyalty and truth, of respect, of economy, and of humility,—this is but moral culture, affected by would-be pacificators and teachers of mankind, and by scholars at home or abroad.

Preaching of meritorious services, of fame, of ceremonial between sovereign and minister, of due relationship between upper and lower classes,—this is mere government, affected by courtiers or patriots who strive to extend the boundaries of their own State and to swallow up the territory of others.

Living in marshes or in wildernesses, and passing one's days in fishing—this is mere inaction, affected by wanderers who have turned their backs upon the world and have nothing better to do.

Exhaling and inhaling, getting rid of the old and assimilating the new, stretching like a bear and craning like a bird,—

—this is but valetudinarianism, affected by professors of hygiene and those who try to preserve the body to the age of P'eng Tsu.

But in self-esteem without self-conceit, in moral culture without charity and duty to one's neighbour, in government without rank and fame, in retirement without solitude, in health without hygiene,—there we have oblivion absolute coupled with possession of all things; an infinite calm which becomes an object to be attained by all.

Such is the Tao of the universe, such is the virtue of the Sage. Wherefore it has been said, "In tranquillity, in stillness, in the unconditioned, in inaction, we find the levels of the universe, the very constitution of Tao."

Wherefore it has been said, "The Sage is a negative quantity, and is consequently in a state of passivity. Being passive he is in a state of repose. And where passivity and repose are, there sorrow and anxiety do not enter,

故日：夫恬惔寂漠，虛無無為，此天地之平而道德之質也。故日：聖人休休焉則平易矣。平易則恬淡矣。平易恬惔，則憂患不能入，邪氣不能襲，故其德全而神不虧。故日，聖人之生也天行，其死也物化。靜而與陰同德，動而與陽同波。不為福先，不為禍始。感而後應，迫而後動，不得已而後起。去知與故，遁天之理。故無天災，無物累，無人非，無鬼責。其生若浮，其死若休。不思慮，不豫謀。光矣而不耀，信矣而不期。其寢不夢，其覺無憂。其神純粹，其魂不罷。虛無恬惔，乃合天德。故日，悲樂者，德之邪；喜怒者，道之過；好惡者，德之失。故心不憂樂，德之至也；一而不變，靜之至也；無所於忤，虛之至也；不與物交，淡之至也；無所於逆，粹之至也。故日，形勞而不休則弊，精用而不已則勞，勞則竭。水之性，不雜則清，莫動則平；鬱閉而不流，亦不能清；天德之象也。故日：純粹而不雜，靜一而不變，淡而無為，

and foul influences do not collect. And thus his virtue is complete and his spirituality unimpaired."

Wherefore it has been said, "The birth of the Sage is the will of God; his death is but a modification of existence. In repose, he shares the passivity of the Yin; in action, the energy of the Yang. He will have nothing to do with happiness, and so has nothing to do with misfortune.

He must be influenced ere he will respond. He must be urged ere he will move. He must be compelled ere he will arise. Ignoring the future and the past, he resigns himself to the laws of God.

"And therefore no calamity comes upon him, nothing injures him, no man is against him, no spirit punishes him. He floats through life to rest in death. He has no anxieties; he makes no plans. His honour does not make him illustrious. His good faith reflects no credit upon himself.

His sleep is dreamless, his awaking without pain. His spirituality is pure, and his soul vigorous. Thus unconditioned and in repose, he is a partaker of the virtue of God."

Wherefore it has been said, "Sorrow and happiness are the heresies of virtue; joy and anger lead astray from Tao; love and hate cause the loss of virtue. The heart unconscious of sorrow and happiness,—that is perfect virtue. One, without change,—that is perfect repose. Without any obstruction,—that is the perfection of the unconditioned. Holding no relations with the external world,—that is perfection of the negative state. Without blemish of any kind,—that is the perfection of purity."

Wherefore it has been said, "If the body toils without rest, it dies. If the mind is employed without ceasing, it becomes wearied; and being wearied, its power is gone."

Pure water is by nature clear. If untouched, it is smooth. If dammed, it will not flow, neither will it be clear. It is an emblem of the virtue of God. Wherefore it has been said, "Pure, without admixture; uniform, without change; negative, without action; moved, only at the will of God;—such would be the spirituality nourished according to Tao."

Those who possess blades from Kan or Yueh, keep them carefully in their scabbards, and do not venture to use them. For they are precious in the extreme. The spirit spreads forth on all sides: there is no point to which it does not reach, attaining heaven above, embracing earth beneath. Influencing all creation, its form cannot be portrayed. Its name is then Of-

動而以天行，此養神之道也。夫有干越之劍者，柙而藏之，不敢用也，寶之至也。精神四達並流，無所不極，上際於天，下蟠於地，化育萬物，不可為象，其名為同帝。純素之道，唯神是守。守而勿失，與神為一。一之精通，合於天倫。野語有之曰：「眾人重利，廉士重名，賢士尚志，聖人貴精。」故素也者，謂其無所與雜也；純也者，謂其不虧其神也。能體純素，謂之真人。

God.

The Tao of the pure and simple consists in preserving spirituality. He who preserves his spirituality and loses it not, becomes one with that spirituality. And through that unity the spirit operates freely, and comes into due relationship with God.

A vulgar saying has it, "The masses value money; honest men, fame; virtuous men, resolution; and Sages, the soul."

Thus, the pure is that in which there is nothing mixed; the simple is that which implies no injury to the spirituality. And he who can keep the pure and simple within himself,—he is a divine man.

# 繕性第十六

　　繕性於俗，學以求復其初；滑欲於俗，思以求致其明；謂之蔽蒙之民。古之治道者，以恬養知。生而無以知為也，謂之以知養恬。知與恬交相養，而和理出其性。夫德，和也；道，理也。德無不容，仁也；道無不理，義也；義明而物親，忠也；中純實而反乎情，樂也；信行容體而順乎文，禮也。禮樂遍行，則天下亂矣。彼正而蒙己德，德則不冒。冒則物必失其性也。古之人，在混芒之中，與一世而得澹漠焉。當是時也，陰陽和靜，鬼神不擾，四時得節，萬物不傷，群生不夭，人雖有知，無所用之，此之謂至一。當是時也，莫之為而常自然。逮德下衰，及燧人、伏羲始為天下，是故順而不一。德又下衰，及神農、黃帝始為天下，是故安而不順。德又下衰，及唐、虞始為天下，興治化之流，澆淳散朴，離道以善，險德以行，然後去性而從於心。心與心識知而不足以定天下，然後附之以文，益之以博。文滅質，博溺心，然後民始惑亂，無以反其性情而復其初。

# CHAPTER XVI

## EXERCISE OF FACULTIES

Those who exercise their faculties in mere worldly studies, hoping thereby to revert to their original condition; and those who sink their aspirations in mundane thoughts, hoping thereby to reach enlightenment;—these are the dullards of the earth.

The ancients, in cultivating Tao, begat knowledge out of repose. When born, this knowledge was not applied to any purpose; and so it may be said that out of knowledge they begat repose. Knowledge and repose thus mutually producing each other, harmony and order were developed. Virtue is harmony; Tao is order.

Virtue all-embracing,—hence charity. Tao all-influencing,—hence duty to one's neighbour. From the establishment of these two springs loyalty. Then comes music, an expression of inward purity and truth; followed by ceremonial, or sincerity expressed in ornamental guise. If music and ceremonial are ill regulated, the empire is plunged into confusion. And to attempt to correct others while one's own virtue is clouded, is to set one's own virtue a task for which it is inadequate, the result being that the natural constitution of the object will suffer.

Primeval man enjoyed perfect tranquillity throughout life. In his day, the Positive and Negative principles were peacefully united; spiritual beings gave no trouble; the four seasons followed in due order; nothing suffered any injury; death was unknown; men had knowledge, but no occasion to use it. This may be called perfection of unity.

At that period, nothing was ever made so; but everything was so.

By and by, virtue declined. Sui Jen and Fu Hsi ruled the empire. There was still natural adaptation, but the unity was gone.

A further decline in virtue. Shen Nung and Huang Ti ruled the empire. There was peace, but the natural adaptation was gone.

Again virtue declined. Yao and Shun ruled the empire. Systems of government and moral reform were introduced. Man's original integrity was scattered. Goodness led him astray from Tao; his actions imperilled his virtue.

Then he discarded natural instinct and took up with the intellectual. Mind was pitted against mind, but it was impossible thus to settle the

由是觀之，世喪道矣，道喪世矣，世與道交相喪也。道之人何由興乎世，世亦何由興乎道哉！道無以興乎世，世無以興乎道，雖聖人不在山林之中，其德隱矣。隱，故不自隱。古之所謂隱士者，非伏其身而弗見也，非閉其言而不出也，非藏其知而不發也，時命大謬也。當時命而大行乎天下，則反一無跡；不當時命而大窮乎天下，則深根寧極而待：此存身之道也。古之存身者，不以辯飾知，不以知窮天下，不以知窮德，危然處其所而反其性已，又何為哉！道固不小行，德固不小識。小識傷德，小行傷道。故曰：正己而已矣。樂全之謂得志。古之所謂得志者，非軒冕之謂也，謂其無以益其樂而已矣。今之所謂得志者，軒冕之謂也。軒冕在身，非性命也，物之儻來，寄者也。寄之，其來不可圉，其去不可止。故不為軒冕肆志，不為窮約趨俗，其樂彼與此同，故無憂而已矣！今寄去則不樂。由是觀之，雖樂，未嘗不荒也。故曰：喪己於物，失性於俗者，謂之倒置之民。

empire. So art and learning were added. But art obliterated the original constitution, and learning overwhelmed mind; upon which confusion set in, and man was unable to revert to his natural instincts, to the condition in which he at first existed.

Thus it may be said that the world destroys Tao, and that Tao destroys the world. And the world and Tao thus mutually destroying each other, how can the men of Tao elevate the world, and how can the world elevate Tao? Tao cannot elevate the world; neither can the world elevate Tao. Though the Sages were not to dwell on mountain and in forest, their virtue would still be hidden;—hidden, but not by themselves.

Those of old who were called retired scholars, were not men who hid their bodies, or kept back their words, or concealed their wisdom. It was that the age was not suitable for their mission. If the age was suitable and their mission a success over the empire, they simply effaced themselves in the unity which prevailed. If the age was unsuitable and their mission at failure, they fell back upon their own resources and waited. Such is the way to preserve oneself.

Those of old who preserved themselves, did not ornament their knowledge with rhetoric. They did not exhaust the empire with their knowledge. They did not exhaust virtue. They kept quietly to their own spheres, and reverted to their natural instincts. What then was left for them to do?

Tao does not deal with detail. Virtue does not take cognizance of trifles. Trifles injure virtue; detail injures Tao. Wherefore it has been said, "Self-reformation is enough." He whose happiness is complete has attained his desire.

Of old, attainment of desire did not mean office. It meant that nothing could be added to the sum of happiness. But now it does mean office, though office is external and is not a part of oneself. That which is adventitious, comes. Coming, you cannot prevent it; going, you cannot arrest it. Therefore, not to look on office as the attainment of desire, and not because of poverty to become a toady, but to be equally happy under all conditions,—this is to be without sorrow.

But now-a-days, both having and not having are causes of unhappiness. From which we may infer that even happiness is not exempt from sorrow.

Wherefore it has been said, "Those who over-estimate the external and lose their natural instincts in worldliness,—these are the people of topsy-turvydom."

# 秋水第十七

　　秋水時至，百川灌河。涇流之大，兩涘渚崖之間，不辯牛馬。於是焉河伯欣然自喜，以天下之美為盡在己。順流而東行，至於北海，東面而視，不見水端。於是焉河伯始旋其面目，望洋向若而嘆曰：「野語有之曰：『聞道百，以為莫己若者。』我之謂也。且夫我嘗聞少仲尼之聞，而輕伯夷之義者，始吾弗信。今我睹子之難窮也，吾非至於子之門則殆矣，吾長見笑於大方之家。」北海若曰：「井蛙不可以語於海者，拘於虛也；夏蟲不可以語於冰者，篤於時也；曲士不可以語於道者，束於教也。今爾出於崖涘，觀於大海，乃知爾醜，爾將可與語大理矣。天下之水，莫大於海，萬川歸之，不知何時止而不盈；尾閭泄之，不知何時已而不虛；春秋不變，水旱不知。此其過江河之流，不可為量數。而吾未嘗以此自多者，自以比形於天地，而受氣於陰陽，吾在於天地之間，猶小石小木之在大山也。方存乎見小，又奚以自多！計四海之在

# CHAPTER XVII

## AUTUMN FLOODS

It was the time of autumn floods. Every stream poured into the river, which swelled in its turbid course. The banks receded so far from one another that it was impossible to tell a cow from a horse.

Then the Spirit of the River laughed for joy that all the beauty of the earth was gathered to himself. Down with the stream he journeyed east, until he reached the ocean. There, looking eastwards and seeing no limit to its waves, his countenance changed. And as he gazed over the expanse, he sighed and said to the Spirit of the Ocean, "A vulgar proverb says that he who has heard but part of the truth thinks no one equal to himself. And such a one am I.

"When formerly I heard people detracting from the learning of Confucius or underrating the heroism of Poh I,

I did not believe. But now that I have looked upon your inexhaustibility—alas for me had I not reached your abode, I should have been for ever a laughing-stock to those of comprehensive enlightenment!"

To which the Spirit of the Ocean replied, "You cannot speak of ocean to a well-frog,—the creature of a narrower sphere. You cannot speak of ice to a summer insect,—the creature of a season. You cannot speak of Tao to a pedagogue: his scope is too restricted. But now that you have emerged from your narrow sphere and have seen the great ocean, you know your own insignificance, and I can speak to you of great principles.

"There is no body of water beneath the canopy of heaven which is greater than ocean. All streams pour into it without cease, yet it does not overflow. It is constantly being drained off, yet it is never empty. Spring and autumn bring no change; floods and droughts are equally unknown. And thus it is immeasurably superior to mere rivers and brooks,—though I would not venture to boast on this account, for I get my shape from the universe, my vital power from the Yin and Yang. In the universe I am but as a small stone or a small tree on a vast mountain. And conscious thus of my own insignificance, what is there of which I can boast?

"The Four Seas,—are they not to the universe but like puddles in a marsh? The Middle Kingdom,—is it not to the surrounding ocean like a

天地之間也，不似礨空之在大澤乎？計中國之在海內不似稊米之在太倉乎？號物之數謂之萬，人處一焉；人卒九州，穀食之所生，舟車之所通，人處一焉；此其比萬物也，不似豪末之在於馬體乎？五帝之所連，三王之所爭，仁人之所憂，任士之所勞，盡此矣！伯夷辭之以為名，仲尼語之以為博。此其自多也，不似爾向之自多於水乎？」

河伯曰：「然則吾大天地而小豪末，可乎？」北海若曰：「否。夫物，量無窮，時無止，分無常，終始無故。是故大知觀於遠近，故小而不寡，大而不多：知量無窮。證曏今故，故遙而不悶，掇而不跂，知時無止；察乎盈虛，故得而不喜，失而不憂，知分之無常也；明乎坦塗，故生而不說，死而不禍，知終始之不可故也。計人之所知，不若其所不知；其生之時，不若未生之時；以其至小，求窮其至大之域，是故迷亂而不能自得也。由此觀之，又何以知毫末之足以定至細之倪，又何以知天地之足以窮至大之域！」

tare-seed in a granary? Of all the myriad created things, man is but one. And of all those who inhabit the land, live on the fruit of the earth, and move about in cart and boat, an individual man is but one. Is not he, as compared with all creation, but as the tip of a hair upon a horse's skin?

"The succession of the Five Rulers, the contentions of the Three Kings, the griefs of the philanthropist, the labours of the administrator, are but this and nothing more.

Poh I refused the throne for fame's sake. Confucius discoursed to get a reputation for learning. This over-estimation of self on their part, was it not very much your own in reference to water?"

"Very well," replied the Spirit of the River, "am I then to regard the universe as great and the tip of a hair as small?"

"Not at all," said the Spirit of the Ocean. "Dimensions are limitless; time is endless. Conditions are not invariable; terms are not final. Thus, the wise man looks into space, and does not regard the small as too little, nor the great as too much; for he knows that there is no limit to dimension. He looks back into the past, and does not grieve over what is far off, nor rejoice over what is near; for he knows that time is without end.

He investigates fulness and decay, and does not rejoice if he succeeds, nor lament if he fails; for he knows that conditions are not invariable.

He who clearly apprehends the scheme of existence, does not rejoice over life, nor repine at death; for he knows that terms are not final.

"What man knows is not to be compared with what he does not know. The span of his existence is not to be compared with the span of his non-existence. With the small to strive to exhaust the great, necessarily lands him in confusion, and he does not attain his object. How then should one be able to say that the tip of a hair is the ne plus ultra of smallness, or that the universe is the ne plus ultra of greatness?"

"Dialecticians of the day," replied the Spirit of the River, "all say that the infinitesimally small has no form, and that the infinitesimally great is beyond all measurement. Is that so?"

"If we regard greatness as compared with that which is small," said the Spirit of the Ocean, "there is no limit to it; and if we regard smallness as compared with that which is great, it eludes our sight.

The infinitesimal is a subdivision of the small; the colossal is an extension of the great. In this sense the two fall into different categories.

　河伯曰：「世之議者皆曰：『至精無形，至大不可圍。』是信情乎？」北海若曰：「夫自細視大者不盡，自大視細者不明。夫精，小之微也；郛，大之殷也：故異便。此勢之有也。夫精粗者，期於有形者也；無形者，數之所不能分也；不可圍者，數之所不能窮也。可以言論者，物之粗也；可以意致者，物之精也；言之所不能論，意之所不能察致者，不期精粗焉。是故大人之行，不出乎害人，不多仁恩；動不為利，不賤門隸；貨財弗爭，不多辭讓；事焉不借人，不多食乎力，不賤貪污；行殊乎俗，不多辟異；為在從眾，不賤佞諂；世之爵祿不足以為勸，戮恥不足以為辱；知是非之不可為分，細大之不可為倪。聞曰：『道人不聞，至德不得，大人無己。』約分之至也。」

　河伯曰：「若物之外，若物之內，惡至而倪貴賤？惡至而倪小大？」北海若曰：「以道觀之，物無貴賤；以物觀之，自貴而相賤；以俗觀之，貴賤不在己。以差觀之，因其所大而大之，則萬物莫不大；因其所小而小之，則萬物莫不小。

"Both small and great things must equally possess form. The mind cannot picture to itself a thing without form, nor conceive a form of unlimited dimensions. The greatness of anything may be a topic of discussion, or the smallness of anything may be mentally realized. But that which can be neither a topic of discussion nor be realized mentally, can be neither great nor small.

"Therefore, the truly great man, although he does not injure others, does not credit himself with charity and mercy.

He seeks not gain, but does not despise his followers who do. He struggles not for wealth, but does not take credit for letting it alone. He asks help from no man, but takes no credit for his self-reliance, neither does he despise those who seek preferment through friends. He acts differently from the vulgar crowd, but takes no credit for his exceptionality; nor because others act with the majority does he despise them as hypocrites. The ranks and emoluments of the world are to him no cause for joy; its punishments and shame no cause for disgrace. He knows that positive and negative cannot be distinguished, that great and small cannot be defined.

"I have heard say, the man of Tao has no reputation; perfect virtue acquires nothing; the truly great man ignores self;—this is the height of self-discipline."

"But how then," asked the Spirit of the River, "are the internal and external extremes of value and worthlessness, of greatness and smallness, to be determined?"

"From the point of view of Tao," replied the Spirit of the Ocean, "there are no such extremes of value or worthlessness. Men individually value themselves and hold others cheap. The world collectively withholds from the individual the right of appraising himself.

"If we say that a thing is great or small because it is relatively great or small, then there is nothing in all creation which is not great, nothing which is not small. To know that the universe is but as a tare-seed, and that the tip of a hair is a mountain,—this is the expression of relativity.

"If we say that something exists or does not exist, in deference to the function it fulfils or does not fulfil, then there is nothing which does not exist, nothing which does exist. To know that east and west are convertible and yet necessary terms,—this is the due adjustment of functions.

"If we say that anything is good or evil because it is either good or evil

知天地之為稊米也，知毫末之為丘山也，則差數睹矣。以功觀之，因其所有而有之，則萬物莫不有；因其所無而無之，則萬物莫不無。知東西之相反而不可以相無，則功分定矣。以趣觀之，因其所然而然之，則萬物莫不然；因其所非而非之，則萬物莫不非。知堯、桀之自然而相非，則趣操睹矣。昔者堯、舜讓而帝，之、噲讓而絕；湯、武爭而王，白公爭而滅。由此觀之，爭讓之禮，堯、桀之行，貴賤有時，未可以為常也。梁麗可以衝城，而不可以窒穴，言殊器也；騏驥驊騮，一日而馳千里，捕鼠不如狸狌，言殊技也；鴟鵂夜撮蚤，察毫末，晝出瞋目而不見丘山，言殊性也。故曰，蓋師是而無非，師治而無亂乎？是未明天地之理，萬物之情也。是猶師天而無地，師陰而無陽，其不可行明矣！然且語而不舍，非愚則誣也！帝王殊禪，三代殊繼。差其時，逆其俗者，謂之篡夫；當其時，順其俗者，謂之義之徒。默默乎河伯！女惡知貴賤之門，小大之家！」

in our eyes, then there is nothing which is not good, nothing which is not evil. To know that Yao and Chieh were both good and both evil from their opposite points of view,—this is the expression of a standard.

"Of old Yao abdicated in favour of Shun, and the latter ruled. Kuei abdicated in favour of Chih, and the latter failed.

T'ang and Wu got the empire by fighting. By fighting, Poh Kung lost it.

From which it may be seen that the rationale of abdicating or fighting, of acting like Yao or like Chieh, must be determined according to the opportunity, and may not be regarded as a constant quantity.

"A battering-ram can knock down a wall, but it cannot repair the breach.

Different things are differently applied.

"Ch'ih-Chi and Hua Liu could travel 1,000 li in one day, but for catching rats they were not equal to a wild cat.

Different animals possess different aptitudes.

"An owl can catch fleas at night, and see the tip of a hair, but if it comes out in the daytime its eyes are so dazzled it cannot see a mountain. Different creatures are differently constituted.

"Thus, as has been said, those who would have right without its correlative, wrong; or good government without its correlative, misrule,—they do not apprehend the great principles of the universe nor the conditions to which all creation is subject. One might as well talk of the existence of heaven without that of earth, or of the negative principle without the positive, which is clearly absurd. Such people, if they do not yield to argument, must be either fools or knaves.

"Rulers have abdicated under different conditions, dynasties have been continued under different conditions. Those who did not hit off a favourable time and were in opposition to their age,—they were called usurpers. Those who did hit off the right time and were in harmony with their age,—they were called patriots. Fair and softly, my River friend; what should you know of value and worthlessness, of great and small?"

"In this case," replied the Spirit of the River, "what am I to do and what am I not to do? How am I to arrange my declinings and receivings, my takings-hold and my lettings-go?"

"From the point of view of Tao," said the Spirit of the Ocean, "value

　河伯曰：「然則我何為乎？何不為乎？吾辭受趣舍，吾終奈何？」北海若曰：「以道觀之，何貴何賤，是謂反衍；無拘而志，與道大蹇。何少何多，是謂謝施；無一而行，與道參差。嚴乎若國之有君，其無私德；繇繇乎若祭之有社，其無私福；汎汎乎其若四方之無窮，其無所畛域。兼懷萬物，其孰承翼？是謂無方。萬物一齊，孰短孰長？道無終始，物有死生，不恃其功。一虛一滿，不位乎其形。年不可舉，時不可止。消息盈虛，終則有始。是所以語大義之方，論萬物之理也。物之生也，若驟若馳。無動而不變，無時而不移。何為乎，何不為乎？夫固將自化。」河伯曰：「然則何貴於道邪？」

　北海若曰：「知道者必達於理，達於理者必明於權，明於權者不以物害己。至德者，火弗

and worthlessness are like slopes and plains.

To consider either as absolutely such would involve great injury to Tao. Few and many are like giving and receiving presents. These must not be regarded from one side, or there will be great confusion to Tao.

Be discriminating, as the ruler of a State whose administration is impartial. Be dispassionate, as the worshipped deity whose dispensation is impartial. Be expansive, like the points of the compass, to whose boundlessness no limit is set. Embrace all creation, and none shall be more sheltered than another. This is the unconditioned. And where all things are equal, how can we have the long and the short?

"Tao is without beginning, without end. Other things are born and die. They are impermanent; and now for better, now for worse, they are ceaselessly changing form. Past years cannot be recalled: time cannot be arrested. The succession of states is endless; and every end is followed by a new beginning. Thus it may be said that man's duty to his neighbour is embodied in the eternal principles of the universe.

"The life of man passes by like a galloping horse, changing at every turn, at every hour. What should he do, or what should he not do, other than let his decomposition go on?"

"If this is the case," retorted the Spirit of the River, "pray what is the value of Tao?"

"Those who understand Tao," answered the Spirit of the Ocean, "must necessarily apprehend the eternal principles above mentioned and be clear as to their application. Consequently, they do not suffer any injury from without.

"The man of perfect virtue cannot be burnt by fire, nor drowned in water, nor hurt by frost or sun, nor torn by wild bird or beast. Not that he makes light of these; but that he discriminates between safety and danger. Happy under prosperous and adverse circumstances alike, cautious as to what he discards and what he accepts;—nothing can harm him.

"Therefore it has been said that the natural abides within, the artificial without. Virtue abides in the natural. Knowledge of the action of the natural and of the artificial has its root in the natural, its development in virtue. And thus, whether in motion or at rest, whether in expansion or in contraction, there is always a reversion to the essential and to the ultimate."

"What do you mean," enquired the Spirit of the River, "by the natural

能熱，水弗能溺，寒暑弗能害，禽獸弗能賊。非謂其薄之也，言察乎安危，寧於禍福，謹於去就，莫之能害也。故曰，天在內，人在外，德在乎天。知天人之行，本乎天，位乎得；蹢躅而屈伸，反要而語極。」曰：「何謂天？何謂人？」北海若曰：「牛馬四足，是謂天；落馬首，穿牛鼻，是謂人。故曰，無以人滅天，無以故滅命，無以得殉名。謹守而勿失，是謂反其真。」

　　夔憐蚿，蚿憐蛇，蛇憐風，風憐目，目憐心。夔謂蚿曰：「吾以一足趻踔而行，予無如矣。今子之使萬足，獨奈何？」蚿曰：「不然。子不見夫唾者乎？噴則大者如珠，小者如霧，雜而下者不可勝數也。今予動吾天機，而不知其所以然。」

and the artificial?"

"Horses and oxen," answered the Spirit of the Ocean, "have four feet. That is the natural. Put a halter on a horse's head, a string through a bullock's nose,—that is the artificial.

"Therefore it has been said, do not let the artificial obliterate the natural; do not let will obliterate destiny; do not let virtue be sacrificed to fame. Diligently observe these precepts without fail, and thus you will revert to the divine."

The walrus envies the centipede; the centipede envies the snake; the snake envies the wind; the Wind envies the eye; the eye envies the mind;

The walrus said to the centipede, "I hop about on one leg, but not very successfully. How do you manage all these legs you have?"

"I don't manage them," replied the centipede. "Have you never seen saliva? When it is ejected, the big drops are the size of pearls, the small ones like mist. They fall promiscuously on the ground and cannot be counted. And so it is that my mechanism works naturally, without my being conscious of the fact."

The centipede said to the snake, "With all my legs I do not move as fast as you with none. How is that?"

"One's natural mechanism," replied the snake, "is not a thing to be changed. What need have I for legs?"

The snake said to the wind, "I can manage to wriggle along, but I have a form. Now you come blustering down from the north sea to bluster away to the south sea, and you seem to be without form. How is that?"

"'Tis true," replied the wind, "that I bluster as you say; but any one who can point at me or kick at me, excels me.

On the other hand, I can break huge trees and destroy large buildings. That is my strong point. Out of all the small things in which I do not excel I make one great one in which I do excel.

And to excel in great things is given only to the Sages."

When Confucius visited K'uang, the men of Sung surrounded him closely.

Yet he went on playing and singing to his guitar without ceasing.

"How is it, Sir," enquired Tzu Lu, "that you are so cheerful?"

"Come here," replied Confucius, "and I will tell you. For a long time I have been struggling against failure, but in vain. Fate is against me. For a

蚿謂蛇曰：「吾以眾足行，而不及子之無足，何也？」蛇曰：「夫天機之所動，何可易邪？吾安用足哉！」蛇謂風曰：「予動吾脊脅而行，則有似也。今子蓬蓬然起於北海，蓬蓬然入於南海，而似無有，何也？」風曰：「然，予蓬蓬然起於北海而入於南海也，然而指我則勝我，鰌我亦勝我。雖然，夫折大木，蜚大屋者，唯我能也。故以眾小不勝為大勝也。為大勝者，唯聖人能之。」

孔子游於匡，宋人圍之數匝，而弦歌不輟。子路入見，曰：「何夫子之娛也？」孔子曰：「來，吾語女。我諱窮久矣，而不免，命也；求通久矣，而不得，時也。當堯、舜而天下無窮人，非知得也；當桀、紂而天下無通人，非知失也：時勢適然。夫水行不避蛟龍者，漁父之勇也；陸行不避兕虎者，獵夫之勇也；白刃交於前，視死若生者，烈士之勇也；知窮之有命，知通之有時，臨大難而不懼者，聖人之勇也。由處矣！吾命有所制矣！」無幾何，將甲者進，辭曰：「以為陽虎也，故圍之；今非也，請辭而退。」

long time I have been seeking success, but in vain. The hour has not come.

"In the days of Yao and Shun, no man throughout the empire was a failure, though no one was conscious of the gain. In the days of Chieh and Chou, no man throughout the empire was a success, though no one was conscious of the loss. The times and circumstances were adapted accordingly.

"To travel by water and not avoid sea-serpents and dragons,—this is the courage of the fisherman. To travel by land and not avoid the rhinoceros and the tiger,—this is the courage of hunters. When bright blades cross, to look on death as on life,—this is the courage of the hero. To know that failure is fate and that success is opportunity, and to remain fearless in great danger,—this is the courage of the Sage. Yu! rest in this. My destiny is cut out for me."

Shortly afterwards, the captain of the troops came in and apologised, saying, "We thought you were Yang Hu; consequently we surrounded you. We find we have made a mistake." Whereupon he again apologised and retired.

Kung Sun Lung said to Mou of Wei, "When young I studied the Tao of the ancient Sages. When I grew up I knew all about the practice of charity and duty to one's neighbour, the identification of like and unlike, the separation of hardness and whiteness, and about making the not-so so, and the impossible possible. I vanquished the wisdom of all the philosophies. I

exhausted all the arguments that were brought against me. I thought that I had indeed reached the goal. But now that I have heard Chuang Tzu, I am lost in astonishment at his grandeur. I know not whether it is in arguing or in knowledge that I am not equal to him. I can no longer open my mouth. May I ask you to impart to me the secret?"

Kung Tzu Mou leant over the table and sighed. Then he looked up to heaven, and smiling replied, saying, "Have you never heard of the frog in the old well?—The frog said to the turtle of the eastern sea, 'Happy indeed am I! I hop on to the rail around the well. I rest in the hollow of some broken brick. Swimming, I gather the water under my arms and shut my mouth. I plunge into the mud, burying my feet and toes; and not one of the cockles, crabs, or tadpoles I see around me are my match. Why do you not come, Sir, and pay me a visit?'

公孫龍問於魏牟曰:「龍少學先王之道,長而明仁義之行;合同異,離堅白;然不然,可不可;困百家之知,窮眾口之辯:吾自以為至達已。今吾聞莊子之言,茫然異之。不知論之不及與?知之弗若與?今吾無所開吾喙,敢問其方。」公子牟隱機大息,仰天而笑曰:「子獨不聞夫坎井之蛙乎?謂東海之鱉曰:『吾樂與!吾跳梁乎井幹之上,入休乎缺甃之崖。赴水則接掖持頤,蹶泥則沒足滅跗。還虷蟹與科斗,莫吾能若也。且夫擅一壑之水,而跨跱坎井之樂,此亦至矣。夫子奚不時來入觀乎?』東海之鱉左足未入,而右膝已縶矣。於是逡巡而卻,告之海曰:『夫千里之遠,不足以舉其大;千仞之高,不足以極其深。禹之時,十年九潦,而水弗為加益;湯之時,八年七旱,而崖不為加損。夫不為頃久推移,不以多少進退者,此亦東海之大樂也。』於是坎井之蛙聞之,適適然驚,規規然自失也。且夫知不知是非之竟,而猶欲觀於莊子之言,是猶使蚊負山,商蚷馳河也,必不勝任矣。且夫知不知論極妙之言,而自適一時

"Now the turtle of the eastern sea had not got its left leg down ere its right had already stuck fast, so it shrank back and begged to be excused. It then described the sea, saying, 'A thousand li would not measure its breadth, nor a thousand fathoms its depth. In the days of the Great Yu, there were nine years of flood out of ten; but this did not add to its bulk. In the days of T'ang, there were seven years out of eight of drought; but this did not narrow its span. Not to be affected by duration of time, not to be affected by volume of water,—such is the great happiness of the eastern sea.'

"At this the well-frog was considerably astonished, and knew not what to say next. And for one whose knowledge does not reach to the positive-negative domain, to attempt to understand Chuang Tzu, is like a mosquito trying to carry a mountain, or an ant to swim a river,—they cannot succeed. And for one whose knowledge does not reach to the abstrusest of the abstruse, but is based only upon such victories as you have enumerated,—is not he like the frog in the well?

"Chuang Tzu moves in the realms below while soaring to heaven above. For him north and south do not exist; the four points are gone; he is engulphed in the unfathomable. For him east and west do not exist. Beginning with chaos, he has gone back to Tao; and yet you think you are going to examine his doctrines and meet them with argument! This is like looking at the sky through a tube, or pointing at the earth with an awl,—a small result.

之利者，是非埳井之蛙與？且彼方跐黃泉而登大皇，無南無北，奭然四解，淪於不測；無東無西，始於玄冥，反於大通。子乃規規然而求之以察，索之以辯，是直用管闚天，用錐指地也，不亦小乎？子往矣！且子獨不聞夫壽陵餘子之學於邯鄲與？未得國能，又失其故行矣，直匍匐而歸耳。今子不去，將忘子之故，失子之業。」公孫龍口呿而不合，舌舉而不下，乃逸而走。

莊子釣於濮水。楚王使大夫二人往先焉，曰：「願以竟內累矣！」莊子持竿不顧，曰：「吾聞楚有神龜，死已三千歲矣。王巾笥而藏之廟堂之上。此龜者，寧其死為留骨而貴乎？寧其生而曳尾於塗中乎？」二大夫曰：「寧生而曳尾塗中。」莊子曰：「往矣！吾將曳尾於塗中。」

"Have you never heard how the youth of Shou-ling went to study at Han-tan? They did not learn what they wanted at Han-tan, and forgot all they knew before into the bargain, so that they returned home in disgrace. And you, if you do not go away, you will forget all you know, and waste your time into the bargain."

Kung Sun Lung's jaw dropped; his tongue clave to his palate; and he slunk away.

Chuang Tzu was fishing in the P'u when the prince of Ch'u sent two high officials to ask him to take charge of the administration of the Ch'u State.

Chuang Tzu went on fishing, and without turning his head said, "I have heard that in Ch'u there is a sacred tortoise which has been dead now some three thousand years. And that the prince keeps this tortoise carefully enclosed in a chest on the altar of his ancestral temple. Now would this tortoise rather be dead and have its remains venerated, or be alive and wagging its tail in the mud?"

"It would rather be alive," replied the two officials, "and wagging its tail in the mud."

"Begone!" cried Chuang Tzu. "I too will wag my tail in the mud."

　　惠子相梁，莊子往見之。或謂惠子曰：「莊子來，欲代子相。」於是惠子恐，搜於國中三日三夜。莊子往見之，曰：「南方有鳥，其名鵷鶵，子知之乎？夫鵷鶵，發於南海而飛於北海，非梧桐不止，非練實不食，非醴泉不飲。於是鴟得腐鼠，鵷鶵過之，仰而視之曰：『嚇！』今子欲以子之梁國而嚇我邪？」

　　莊子與惠子游於濠梁之上。莊子曰：「儵魚出游從容，是魚之樂也。」惠子曰：「子非魚，安知魚之樂？」莊子曰：「子非我，安知我不知魚之樂？」惠子曰「我非子，固不知子矣；子固非魚也，子之不知魚之樂，全矣！」莊子曰：「請循其本。子曰『汝安知魚樂』云者，既已知吾知之而問我。我知之濠上也。」

Hui Tzu was prime minister in the Liang State. Chuang Tzu went thither to visit him.

Some one remarked, "Chuang Tzu has come. He wants to be minister in your place."

Thereupon Hui Tzu was afraid, and searched all over the State for three days and three nights to find him.

Then Chuang Tzu went to see Hui Tzu, and said, "In the south there is a bird. It is a kind of phoenix. Do you know it? It started from the south sea to fly to the north sea. Except on the wu-t'ung tree, it would not alight. It would eat nothing but the fruit of the bamboo, drink nothing but the purest spring water. An owl which had got the rotten carcass of a rat, looked up as the phoenix flew by, and screeched.

Are you not screeching at me over your kingdom of Liang?"

Chuang Tzu and Hui Tzu had strolled on to the bridge over the Hao, when the former observed, "See how the minnows are darting about! That is the pleasure of fishes."

"You not being a fish yourself," said Hui Tzu, "how can you possibly know in what consists the pleasure of fishes?"

"And you not being I," retorted Chuang Tzu, "how can you know that I do not know?"

"If I, not being you, cannot know what you know," urged Hui Tzu, "it follows that you, not being a fish, cannot know in what consists the pleasure of fishes."

"Let us go back," said Chuang Tzu, "to your original question. You asked me how I knew in what consists the pleasure of fishes. Your very question shows that you knew I knew.

I knew it from my own feelings on this bridge."

# 至樂第十八

天下有至樂無有哉？有可以活身者無有哉？今奚為奚據？奚避奚處？奚就奚去？奚樂奚惡？夫天下之所尊者，富貴壽善也；所樂者，身安厚味美服好色音聲也；所下者，貧賤夭惡也；所苦者，身不得安逸，口不得厚味，形不得美服，目不得好色，耳不得音聲。若不得者，則大憂以懼，其為形也亦愚哉！夫富者，苦身疾作，多積財而不得盡用，其為形也亦外矣！夫貴者，夜以繼日，思慮善否，其為形也亦疏矣！人之生也，與憂俱生。壽者惛惛，久憂不死，何之苦也！其為形也亦遠矣！烈士為天下見善矣，未足以活身。吾未知善之誠善邪？誠不善邪？若以為善矣，不足活身；以為不善矣，足以活人。故曰：「忠諫不聽，蹲循勿爭。」故夫子胥爭之以殘其形；不爭，名亦不成。誠有善無有哉？今俗之所為與其所樂，吾又未知樂之果樂邪？果不樂邪？吾觀夫俗之所樂舉群趣者，誙誙然如將不得已，而皆曰樂者，吾未之樂也，亦未之不樂也。果有樂無有哉？吾

# CHAPTER XVIII

## PERFECT HAPPINESS

Is perfect happiness to be found on earth, or not? Are there those who can enjoy life, or not? If so, what do they do, what do they affect, what do they avoid, what do they rest in, accept, reject, like, and dislike?

What the world esteems comprises wealth, rank, old age, and goodness of heart. What it enjoys comprises comfort, rich food, fine clothes, beauty, and music. What it does not esteem comprises poverty, want of position, early death, and evil behaviour. What it does not enjoy comprises lack of comfort for the body, lack of rich food for the palate, lack of fine clothes for the back, lack of beauty for the eye, and lack of music for the ear. If men do not get these, they are greatly miserable. Yet from the point of view of our physical frame, this is folly.

Wealthy people who toil and moil, putting together more money than they can possibly use,—from the point of view of our physical frame, is not this going beyond the mark?

Officials of rank who turn night into day in their endeavours to compass the best ends;—from the point of view of our physical frame, is not this a divergence?

Man is born to sorrow, and what misery is theirs whose old age with dulled faculties only means prolonged sorrow! From the point of view of our physical frame, this is going far astray.

Patriots are in the world's opinion admittedly good. Yet their goodness does not enable them to enjoy life; and so I know not whether theirs is veritable goodness or not. If the former, it does not enable them to enjoy life; if the latter, it at any rate enables them to cause others to enjoy theirs.

It has been said, "If your loyal counsels are not attended to, depart quietly without resistance." Thus, when Tzu Hsu resisted, his physical frame perished; yet had he not resisted, he would not have made his name. Is there then really such a thing as this goodness, or not?

As to what the world does and the way in which people are happy now, I know not whether such happiness be real happiness or not. The happiness of ordinary persons seems to me to consist in slavishly following the majority, as if they could not help it. Yet they all say they are happy.

以無為誠樂矣，又俗之所大苦也。故曰：「至樂無樂，至譽無譽。」天下是非果未可定也。雖然，無為可以定是非。至樂活身，唯無為幾存。請嘗試言之：天無為以之清，地無為以之寧。故兩無為相合，萬物皆化生。芒乎芴乎，而無從出乎！芴乎芒乎，而無有象乎！萬物職職，皆從無為殖。故曰：「天地無為也而無不為也。」人也孰能得無為哉！

莊子妻死，惠子吊之，莊子則方箕踞鼓盆而歌。惠子曰：「與人居，長子老身，死不哭亦足矣，又鼓盆而歌，不亦甚乎！」莊子曰：「不然。是其始死也，我獨何能無概然！察其始而本無生；非徒無生也，而本無形；非徒無形也，而本無氣。雜乎芒芴之間，變而有氣，氣變而有形，形變而有生。今又變而之死。是相與為春秋冬夏四時行也。人且偃然寢於巨室，而我噭噭然隨而哭之，自以為不通乎命，故止也。」

But I cannot say that this is happiness or that it is not happiness. Is there then, after all, such a thing as happiness?

I make true pleasure to consist in inaction, which the world regards as great pain. Thus it has been said, "Perfect happiness is the absence of happiness; perfect renown is the absence of renown."

Now in this sublunary world of ours it is impossible to assign positive and negative absolutely. Nevertheless, in inaction they can be so assigned. Perfect happiness and preservation of life are to be sought for only in inaction.

Let us consider. Heaven does nothing; yet it is clear. Earth does nothing; yet it enjoys repose.

From the inaction of these two proceed all the modifications of things. How vast, how infinite is inaction, yet without source! How infinite, how vast, yet without form!

The endless varieties of things around us all spring from inaction. Therefore it has been said, "Heaven and earth do nothing, yet there is nothing which they do not accomplish." But among men, who can attain to inaction?

When Chuang Tzu's wife died, Hui Tzu went to condole. He found the widower sitting on the ground, singing, with his legs spread out at a right angle, and beating time on a bowl.

"To live with your wife," exclaimed Hui Tzu, "and see your eldest son grow up to be a man, and then not to shed a tear over her corpse,—this would be bad enough. But to drum on a bowl, and sing; surely this is going too far."

"Not at all," replied Chuang Tzu. "When she died, I could not help being affected by her death. Soon, however, I remembered that she had already existed in a previous state before birth, without form, or even substance; that while in that unconditioned condition, substance was added to spirit; that this substance then assumed form; and that the next stage was birth. And now, by virtue of a further change, she is dead, passing from one phase to another like the sequence of spring, summer, autumn, and winter. And while she is thus lying asleep in Eternity, for me to go about weeping and wailing would be to proclaim myself ignorant of these natural laws. Therefore I refrain."

A hunchback and a one-legged man were looking at the tombs of de-

　　支離叔與滑介叔觀於冥伯之丘，崑崙之虛，黃帝之所休。俄而柳生其左肘，其意蹶蹶然惡之。支離叔曰：「子惡之乎？」滑介叔曰：「亡，予何惡！生者，假借也。假之而生生者，塵垢也。死生為晝夜。且吾與子觀化而化及我，我又何惡焉！」

　　莊子之楚，見空髑髏，髐然有形。撽以馬捶，因而問之，曰：「夫子貪生失理，而為此乎？將子有亡國之事、斧鉞之誅，而為此乎？將子有不善之行，愧遺父母妻子之醜而為此乎？將子有凍餒之患，而為此乎？將子之春秋故及此乎？」於是語卒，援髑髏，枕而臥。夜半，髑髏見夢曰：「子之談者似辯士，視子所言，皆生人之累也，死則無此矣。子欲聞死之說乎？」莊子曰：「然。」髑髏曰：「死，無君於上，無臣於下；亦無四時之事，從然以天地為春秋，雖南面王樂，不能過也。」莊子不信，曰：「吾使司命復生子形，為子骨肉肌膚，反子父母、妻子、閭里、知識，子欲之乎？」髑髏深矉蹙頞曰：「吾安能棄南面王樂而復為人間之勞乎！」

parted heroes, on the K'un-lun Mountains, where the Yellow Emperor rests. Suddenly, ulcers broke out upon their left elbows, of a very loathsome description.

"Do you loathe this?" asked the hunchback.

"Not I," replied the other, "why should I? Life is a loan with which the borrower does but add more dust and dirt to the sum total of existence. Life and death are as day and night; and while you and I stand gazing at the evidences of mortality around us, if the same mortality overtakes me, why should I loathe it?"

Chuang Tzu one day saw an empty skull, bleached, but still preserving its shape. Striking it with his riding whip, he said, "Wert thou once some ambitious citizen whose inordinate yearnings brought him to this pass?—some statesman who plunged his country in ruin and perished in the fray?—some wretch who left behind him a legacy of shame?—some beggar who died in the pangs of hunger and cold? Or didst thou reach this state by the natural course of old age?"

When he had finished speaking, he took the skull, and placing it under his head as a pillow, went to sleep. In the night, he dreamt that the skull appeared to him and said, "You speak well, Sir; but all you say has reference to the life of mortals, and to mortal troubles. In death there are none of these. Would you like to hear about death?"

Chuang Tzu having replied in the affirmative, the skull began:—"In death, there is no sovereign above, and no subject below. The workings of the four seasons are unknown. Our existences are bounded only by eternity. The happiness of a king among men cannot exceed that which we enjoy."

Chuang Tzu, however, was not convinced, and said, "Were I to prevail upon God to allow your body to be born again, and your bones and flesh to be renewed, so that you could return to your parents, to your wife, and to the friends of your youth,—would you be willing?"

At this, the skull opened its eyes wide and knitted its brows and said, "How should I cast aside happiness greater than that of a king, and mingle once again in the toils and troubles of mortality?"

When Yen Yuan went eastwards to the Ch'i State, Confucius was sad. Tzu Kung arose and said, "Is it, Sir, because Hui has gone east to Ch'i that you are sad?"

顏淵東之齊，孔子有憂色。子貢下席而問曰：「小子敢問，回東之齊，夫子有憂色，何邪？」孔子曰：「善哉女問！昔者管子有言，丘甚善之，曰：『褚小者不可以懷大，綆短者不可以汲深。』夫若是者，以為命有所成而形有所適也，夫不可損益。吾恐回與齊侯言堯、舜、黃帝之道，而重以燧人、神農之言。彼將內求於己而不得，不得則惑，人惑則死。且女獨不聞邪？昔者海鳥止於魯郊，魯侯御而觴之於廟，奏九韶以為樂，具太牢以為膳。鳥乃眩視憂悲，不敢食一臠，不敢飲一杯，三日而死。此以己養養鳥也，非以鳥養養鳥也。夫以鳥養養鳥者，宜栖之深林，遊之壇陸，浮之江湖，食之鰍鰷，隨行列而止，委蛇而處。彼唯人言之惡聞，奚以夫譊譊為乎！咸池九韶之樂，張之洞庭之野，鳥聞之而飛，獸聞之而走，魚聞之而下入，人卒聞之，相與還而觀之。魚處水而生，人處水而死。彼必相與異，其好惡故異也。故先聖不一其能，不同其事。名止於實，義設於適，是之謂條達而福持。」

"A good question," replied Confucius. "There is a saying by Kuan Chung of old which I highly esteem: 'Small bags won't hold big things; short ropes won't reach down deep wells.' Thus, destiny is a pre-arrangement, just as form has its limitations. From neither, to neither, can you either take away or add. And I fear lest Hui, on his visit to the prince of Ch'i, should preach the Tao of Yao and Shun, and dwell on the words of Sui Jen and Shen Nung. The prince will then search within himself, but will not find. And not finding, he will doubt. And when a man doubts, he will kill.

"Besides, have you not heard that of old when a sea-bird alighted outside the capital of Lu, the prince went out to receive it, and gave it wine in the temple, and had the Chiu Shao played to amuse it, and a bullock slaughtered to feed it? But the bird was dazed and too timid to eat or drink anything; and in three days it was dead. This was treating the bird like oneself, and not as a bird would treat a bird. Had he treated it as a bird would have treated a bird, he would have put it to roost in a deep forest, to wander over a plain, to swim in a river or lake, to feed upon fish, to fly in order, and to settle leisurely. When the bird was already terrified at human voices, fancy adding music! Play the Hsien Ch'ih or the Chiu Shao in the wilds of Tung-t'ing, and birds will fly away, beasts will take themselves off, and fishes will dive down below. But men will collect to hear.

"Water, which is life to fishes, is death to man. Being differently constituted, their likes and dislikes are different. Therefore the Sages of the past favoured not uniformity of skill or of occupation. Reputation was commensurate with reality; means were adapted to the end. This was called a due relationship with others coupled with advantage to oneself."

Lieh Tzu, being on a journey, was eating by the roadside, when he saw an old skull. Plucking a blade of grass, he pointed at it and said, "Only you and I know that there is no such thing as life and no such thing as death.

Are you really at peace? Or am I really happy?

"Certain germs, falling upon water, become duckweed. When they reach the junction of the land and the water, they become lichen. Spreading up the bank, they become the dog-tooth violet. Reaching rich soil, they become wu-tsu, the root of which becomes grubs, while the leaves comes from butterflies, or hsu. These are changed into insects, born in the chimney corner, which look like skeletons. Their name is ch'u-to. After a

　　列子行，食於道從，見百歲髑髏，攓蓬而指之曰：「唯予與女知而未嘗死，未嘗生也。若果養乎？予果歡乎？」種有機？得水則為㡭，得水土之際則為蛙蠙之衣，生於陵屯則為陵舄，陵舄得鬱棲則為烏足，烏足之根為蠐螬，其葉為胡蝶。胡蝶胥也化而為蟲，生於灶下，其狀若脫，其名為鴝掇。鴝掇千日為鳥，其名為乾餘骨。乾餘骨之沫為斯彌，斯彌為食醯。頤輅生乎食醯，黃軦生乎九猷，瞀芮生乎腐蠸。羊奚比乎不箰，久竹生青寧，青寧生程，程生馬，馬生人，人又反入於機。萬物皆出於機，皆入於機。」

thousand days, the ch'u-to becomes a bird, called Kan-yu-ku, the spittle of which becomes the ssu-mi. The ssu-mi becomes a wine fly, and that comes from an i-lu. The huang-k'uang produces the chiu-yu and the mou-jui produces the glow-worm. The yang-ch'i grafted to an old bamboo which has for a long time put forth no shoots, produces the ch'ing-ning, which produces the leopard, which produces the horse, which produces man.

"Then man goes back into the great Scheme, from which all things come and to which all things return."

# 達生第十九

　　達生之情者，不務生之所無以為；達命之情者，不務知之所無奈何。養形必先之以物，物有餘而形不養者有之矣；有生必先無離形，形不離而生亡者有之矣。生之來不能卻，其去不能止。悲夫！世之人以為養形足以存生；而養形果不足以存生，則世奚足為哉！雖不足為而不可不為者，其為不免矣！夫欲免為形者，莫如棄世。棄世則無累，無累則正平，正平則與彼更生，更生則幾矣！事奚足棄而生奚足遺？棄事則形不勞，遺生則精不虧。夫形全精復，與天為一。天地者，萬物之父母也。合則成體，散則成始。形精不虧，是謂能移。精而又精，反以相天。

　　子列子問關尹曰：「至人潛行不窒，蹈火不熱，行乎萬物之上而不慄。請問何以至於此？」關尹曰：「是純氣之守也，非知巧果敢之列。居，予語女！凡有貌象聲色者，皆物也，物與物何以相遠？夫奚足以至乎先？是色而已。則物之造乎不形，而止乎無所化。夫得是而窮之者，物焉得而止焉！彼將處乎不淫之度，而藏乎無端之紀，游乎

# CHAPTER XIX

## THE SECRET OF LIFE

Those who understand the conditions of life devote no attention to things which life cannot accomplish. Those who understand the conditions of destiny devote no attention to things over which knowledge has no control.

For the due nourishment of our physical frames, certain things are needful. Yet where such things abound, the physical frame is not always nourished. For the preservation of life it is necessary that there should be no abandonment of the physical frame. Yet where the physical frame is not abandoned, life does not always remain.

Life comes, and cannot be declined. It goes, and cannot be stopped. But alas! the world thinks that to nourish the frame is enough to keep life. And if indeed it is not enough, what then is the world to do?

Although not enough, it must still be done. It cannot be neglected. For if one is to neglect the physical frame, better far to retire at once from the world. By renouncing the world, one gets rid of the cares of the world. The result is a natural level, which is equivalent to a re-birth. And he who is re-born is near.

But what inducement is there to renounce the affairs of men, to become indifferent to life?—In the first case, the physical body suffers no wear and tear; in the second, the vitality is left unharmed. And he whose physical frame is perfect and whose vitality is in its original purity,—he is one with God.

Heaven and earth are the father and mother of all things. When they unite, the result is shape. When they disperse, the original condition is renewed.

But if body and vitality are both perfect, this state is called fit for translation.

Such perfection of vitality goes back to the minister of God.

Lieh Tzu asked Kuan Yin, saying, "The perfect man can walk through solid bodies without obstruction. He can pass through fire without being burnt. He can scale the highest heights without fear. How does he bring himself to this?"

萬物之所終始。壹其性，養其氣，合其德，以通乎物之所造。夫若是者，其天守全，其神無郤，物奚自入焉！夫醉者之墜車，雖疾不死。骨節與人同而犯害與人異，其神全也。乘亦不知也，墜亦不知也，死生驚懼不入乎其胸中，是故遻物而不慴。彼得全於酒而猶若是，而況全於天乎？聖人藏於天，故莫之能傷也。復讎者，不折鏌干；雖有忮心者，不怨飄瓦，是以天下平均。故無攻戰之亂，無殺戮之刑者，由此道也。不開人之天，而開天之天。開天者德生，開人者賊生。不厭其天，不忽於人，民幾乎以其真。」

仲尼適楚，出於林中，見佝僂者承蜩，猶掇之也。仲尼曰：「子巧乎，有道邪？」曰：「我有道也。五六月累丸二而不墜，則失者錙銖；累三而不墜，則失者十一；累五而不墜，猶掇之也。吾處身也，若厥株拘；吾執臂也，若槁木之枝。雖天地之大，萬物之多，而唯蜩翼之知。吾不反不側，不以萬物易蜩之翼，何為而不得！」孔子顧謂弟子曰：「用志不分，乃凝於神。其佝僂丈人之謂乎！」

"It is because he is in a condition of absolute purity," replied Kuan Yin. "It is not cunning which enables him to dare such feats. Be seated, and I will tell you.

"All that has form, sound, and colour, may be classed under the head thing. Man differs so much from the rest, and stands at the head of all things, simply because the latter are but what they appear and nothing more. But man can attain to formlessness and vanquish death. And with that which is in possession of the eternal, how can mere things compare?

"Man may rest in the eternal fitness; he may abide in the everlasting; and roam from the beginning to the end of all creation. He may bring his nature to a condition of ONE; he may nourish his strength; he may harmonize his virtue, and so put himself into partnership with God. Then, when his divinity is thus assured, and his spirit closed in on all sides, how can anything find a passage within?

"A drunken man who falls out of a cart, though he may suffer, does not die. His bones are the same as other people's; but he meets his accident in a different way. His spirit is in a condition of security. He is not conscious of riding in the cart; neither is he conscious of falling out of it. Ideas of life, death, fear, etc., cannot penetrate his breast; and so he does not suffer from contact with objective existences. And if such security is to be got from wine, how much more is it to be got from God. It is in God that the Sage seeks his refuge, and so he is free from harm.

"An avenger does not snap in twain the murderous weapon; neither does the most spiteful man carry his resentment to a tile which may have hit him on the head. And by the extension of this principle, the empire would be at peace; no more confusion of war, no more punishment of death.

"Do not develop your artificial intelligence, but develop that intelligence which is from God. From the latter, results virtue; from the former, cunning. And those who do not shrink from the natural, nor wallow in the artificial,—they are near to perfection."

When Confucius was on his way to the Ch'u State, he came to a forest where he saw a hunchback catching cicadas as though with his hand.

"How clever you are!" cried Confucius. "Have you any way of doing this?"

"I have a way," replied the hunchback. "In the fifth and sixth moons I

　　顏淵問仲尼曰：「吾嘗濟乎觴深之淵，津人操舟若神。吾問焉，曰:『操舟可學邪?』曰:『可。善游者數能。若乃夫沒人，則未嘗見舟而便操之也。』吾問焉而不吾告，敢問何謂也?」仲尼曰：「善游者數能，忘水也。若乃夫沒人之未嘗見舟而便操之也，彼視淵若陵，視舟之覆，猶其車卻也。覆卻萬方陳乎前而不得入其舍，惡往而不暇!以瓦注者巧，以鉤注者憚，以黃金注者殙。其巧一也，而有所矜，則重外也。凡外重者內拙。」

　　田開之見周威公，威公曰：「吾聞祝腎學生，吾子與祝腎游，亦何聞焉?」田開之曰：「開之操拔篲以侍門庭，亦何聞於夫子!」威公曰：「田子無讓，寡人願聞之。」開之曰:「聞之夫子曰:『善養生者，若牧羊然，視其後者而鞭之。』」威公曰:「何謂也?」田開之曰：「魯有單豹者，巖居而水飲，不與民共利，行年七十而猶有嬰兒之色，不幸遇餓虎，餓虎殺而食之。有張毅者，高門

practise balancing two balls one on top of the other.

If they do not fall, I do not miss many cicadas. When I can balance three balls, I only miss one in ten; and when five, then it is as though I caught the cicadas with my hand. My body is as motionless as the stump of a tree; my arms like dead branches. Heaven and earth and all creation may be around me, but I am conscious only of my cicada's wings. How should I not succeed?"

Confucius looked round at his disciples and said, "Singleness of purpose induces concentration of the faculties. Of such is the success of this hunchback."

Yen Yuan said to Confucius, "When I crossed over the Shang-shen rapid, the boatman managed his craft with marvellous skill. I asked him if handling a boat could be learnt. 'It can,' replied he. 'The way of those who know how to keep you afloat is more like sinking you. They row as if the boat wasn't there.'

"I enquired what this meant, but he would not tell me. May I ask its signification."

"It means," answered Confucius, "that such a man is oblivious of the water around him. He regards the rapid as though dry land. He looks upon an upset as an ordinary cart accident. And if a man can but be impervious to capsizings and accidents in general, whither should he not be able comfortably to go?

"A man who plays for counters will play well. If he stakes his girdle, he will be nervous; if yellow gold, he will lose his wits. His skill is the same in each case, but he is distracted by the value of his stake. And every one who attaches importance to the external, becomes internally without resource."

T'ien K'ai Chih had an audience of Duke Wei of Chou. The Duke asked him, saying, "I have heard that Chu Hsien is studying the art of life. As you are a companion of his, pray tell me anything you know about it."

"I do but ply the broom at his outer gate," replied T'ien K'ai Chih; "what should I know about my Master's researches?"

"Don't be so modest," said the Duke. "I am very anxious to hear about it."

"Well," replied T'ien, "I have heard my master say that keeping life is like keeping a flock of sheep. You look out for the laggards, and whip them up."

縣薄，無不走也，行年四十而有內熱之病以死。豹養其內而虎食其外，毅養其外而病攻其內。此二子者，皆不鞭其後者也。」仲尼曰：「無入而藏，無出而陽，柴立其中央。三者若得，其名必極。夫畏塗者，十殺一人，則父子兄弟相戒也，必盛卒徒而後敢出焉，不亦知乎！人之取畏者，衽席之上，飲食之間，而不知為之戒者，過也！」

祝宗人玄端以臨牢筴，說彘曰：「汝奚惡死！吾將三月豢汝，十日戒，三日齊，藉白茅，加汝肩尻乎雕俎之上，則汝為之乎？」為彘謀，曰：「不如食以糠糟而錯之牢筴之中。」自為謀，則苟生有軒冕之尊，死得於腞楯之上，聚僂之中則為之。為彘謀則去之，自為謀則取之，所異彘者何也！

桓公田於澤，管仲御，見鬼焉。公撫管仲之手曰：「仲父何見？」對曰：「臣無所見。」公反，誒詒為病，數日不出。齊士有皇子告敖者，曰：「公則自傷，鬼惡能傷公！夫忿滀之氣，散而不反，則為不足；上而不下，則使人善怒；下而不上，

"What does that mean?" asked the Duke.

"In the State of Lu," said T'ien, "there was a man named Shan Pao. He lived on the mountains and drank water. All worldly interests he had put aside. And at the age of seventy, his complexion was like that of a child. Unluckily, he one day fell in with a hungry tiger who killed and ate him.

"There was also a man named Chang I, who frequented the houses of rich and poor alike. At the age of forty he was attacked by some internal disease and died.

"Shan Pao took care of his inner self, and a tiger ate his external man. Chang I took care of himself externally, but disease attacked him internally. These two individuals both omitted to whip up the laggards."

Confucius said, "Neither affecting obscurity, nor courting prominence, but unconsciously occupying the happy mean,—he who can attain to these three will enjoy a surpassing fame.

"In dangerous parts, where one wayfarer out of ten meets his death, fathers and sons and brothers will counsel each other not to travel without a sufficient escort. Is not this wisdom? And there where men are also greatly in danger, in the lists of passion, in the banquet hour, not to warn them is error indeed."

The Grand Augur, in his ceremonial robes, approached the shambles and thus addressed the pigs:—

"How can you object to die? I shall fatten you for three months. I shall discipline myself for ten days and fast for three. I shall strew fine grass, and place you bodily upon a carved sacrificial dish. Does not this satisfy you?"

Then speaking from the pigs' point of view, he continued, "It is better perhaps after all to live on bran and escape the shambles...."

"But then," added he, speaking from his own point of view, "to enjoy honour when alive one would readily die on a war-shield or in the headsman's basket."

So he rejected the pigs' point of view and adopted his own point of view. In what sense then was he different from the pigs?

When Duke Huan was out hunting, with Kuan Chung as his charioteer, he saw a bogy. Catching hold of Kuan Chung's hand, he asked him, saying, "What do you see?"

"I see nothing," replied Kuan Chung. But when the Duke got home he

則使人善忘；不上不下，中身當心，則為病。」
桓公曰：「然則有鬼乎？」曰：「有。沈有履。灶
有髻。戶內之煩壤，雷霆處之；東北方之下者，
倍阿鮭蠪躍之；西北方之下者，則泆陽處之。
水有罔象，丘有峷，山有夔，野有彷徨，澤有
委蛇。」公曰：「請問委蛇之狀何如？」皇子曰：「委
蛇，其大如轂，其長如轅，紫衣而朱冠。其為物也，
惡聞雷車之聲，則捧其首而立。見之者殆乎霸。」
桓公輾然而笑曰：「此寡人之所見者也。」於是
正衣冠與之坐，不終日而不知病之去也。

　　紀渻子為王養鬥雞。十日而問：「雞已乎？」
曰：「未也，方虛憍而恃氣。」十日又問，曰：「未
也，猶應嚮景。」十日又問，曰：「未也，猶疾
視而盛氣。」十日又問，曰：「幾矣，雞雖有鳴者，
已無變矣，望之似木雞矣，其德全矣。異雞無
敢應者，反走矣。」

　　孔子觀於呂梁，縣水三十仞，流沫四十里，
黿鼉魚鱉之所不能游也。見一丈夫游之，以為
有苦而欲死也。使弟子並流而拯之。數百步而出，

became delirious, and for many days was unable to go out.

There came a certain Huang Tzu Kao Ngao of the Ch'i State and said, "Your Highness is self-injured. How could a bogy injure you? When the vital strength is dissipated in anger, and is not renewed, there is a deficiency. When its tendency is in one direction upwards, the result is to incline men to wrath. When its tendency is in one direction downwards, the result is loss of memory. When it remains stagnant, in the middle of the body, the result is disease."

"Very well," said the Duke, "but are there such things as bogies?"

"There are," replied Huang. "There is the mud spirit Li; the fire spirit Kao; Lei T'ing, the spirit of the dust-bin; P'ei O and Wa Lung, sprites of the north-east; Yi Yang of the north-west; Wang Hsiang of the water; the Hsin of the hills; the K'uei of the mountain; the P'ang Huang of the moor; the Wei I of the marsh."

"And what may the Wei I be like?" asked the Duke.

"The Wei I," replied Huang, "is as broad as a cart-wheel and as long as the shaft. It wears purple clothes and a red cap. It is a sentient being, and whenever it hears the rumble of thunder, it stands up in a respectful attitude. Those who see this bogy are like to be chieftains among men."

The Duke laughed exultingly and said, "The very one I saw!" Thereupon he dressed himself and sat up; and ere the day had closed, without knowing it, his sickness had left him.

Chi Hsing Tzu was training fighting cocks for the prince.

At the end of ten days the latter asked if they were ready. "Not yet," replied Chi; "they are in the stage of seeking fiercely for a foe."

Again ten days elapsed, and the prince made a further enquiry. "Not yet," replied Chi; "they are still excited by the sounds and shadows of other cocks."

Ten days more, and the prince asked again. "Not yet," answered Chi; "the sight of an enemy is still enough to excite them to rage."

But after another ten days, when the prince again enquired, Chi said, "They will do. Other cocks may crow, but they will take no notice. To look at them one might say they were of wood. Their virtue is complete. Strange cocks will not dare meet them, but will run."

Confucius was looking at the cataract at Lu-liang. It fell from a height of thirty jen, and its foam reached forty li away. No scaly, finny creature

被髮行歌而游於塘下。孔子從而問焉，曰：「吾以子為鬼，察子則人也。請問：蹈水有道乎？」曰：「亡，吾無道。吾始乎故，長乎性，成乎命。與齊俱入，與汩偕出，從水之道而不為私焉。此吾所以蹈之也。」孔子曰：「何謂始乎故，長乎性，成乎命？」曰：「吾生於陵而安於陵，故也；長於水而安於水，性也；不知吾所以然而然，命也。」

梓慶削木為鐻，鐻成，見者驚猶鬼神。魯侯見而問焉，曰：「子何術以為焉？」對曰：「臣工人，何術之有！雖然，有一焉。臣將為鐻，未嘗敢以耗氣也，必齊以靜心。齊三日，而不敢懷慶賞爵祿；齊五日，不敢懷非譽巧拙；齊七日，輒然忘吾有四枝形體也。當是時也，無公朝。其巧專而外骨消，然後入山林，觀天性；形軀至矣，然後成見鐻，然後加手焉；不然則已。則以天合天，器之所以疑神者，其是與！」

could enter therein.

Yet Confucius saw an old man go in, and thinking that he was suffering from some trouble and desirous of ending his life, bade a disciple run along the side to try and save him. The old man emerged about a hundred paces off, and with flowing hair went carolling along the bank. Confucius followed him and said, "I had thought, Sir, you were a spirit, but now I see you are a man. Kindly tell me, is there any way to deal thus with water?"

"No," replied the old man; "I have no way. There was my original condition to begin with; then habit growing into nature; and lastly acquiescence in destiny. Plunging in with the whirl, I come out with the swirl. I accommodate myself to the water, not the water to me. And so I am able to deal with it after this fashion."

"What do you mean," enquired Confucius, "by your original condition to begin with, habit growing into nature, and acquiescence in destiny?"

"I was born," replied the old man, "upon dry land, and accommodated myself to dry land. That was my original condition. Growing up on the water, I accommodated myself to the water. That was what I meant by nature.

And doing as I did without being conscious of any effort so to do, that was what I meant by destiny."

Ch'ing, the chief carpenter, was carving wood into a stand for hanging musical instruments. When finished, the work appeared to those who saw it as though of supernatural execution. And the prince of Lu asked him, saying, "What mystery is there in your art?"

"No mystery, your Highness," replied Ch'ing; "and yet there is something.

"When I am about to make such a stand, I guard against any diminution of my vital power. I first reduce my mind to absolute quiescence. Three days in this condition, and I become oblivious of any reward to be gained. Five days, and I become oblivious of any fame to be acquired. Seven days, and I become unconscious of my four limbs and my physical frame. Then, with no thought of the Court present to my mind, my skill becomes concentrated, and all disturbing elements from without are gone. I enter some mountain forest. I search for a suitable tree. It contains the form required, which is afterwards elaborated. I see the stand in my mind's eye, and then set to work. Otherwise, there is nothing. I bring my own natural

　　東野稷以御見莊公，進退中繩，左右旋中規。莊公以為文弗過也。使之鉤百而反。顏闔遇之，入見曰：「稷之馬將敗。」公密而不應。少焉，果敗而反。公曰：「子何以知之？」曰：「其馬力竭矣，而猶求焉，故曰敗。」

　　工倕旋而蓋規矩，指與物化而不以心稽，故其靈臺一而不桎。忘足，履之適也；忘要，帶之適也；知忘是非，心之適也；不內變，不外從，事會之適也；始乎適而未嘗不適者，忘適之適也。

　　有孫休者，踵門而詫子扁慶子曰：「休居鄉不見謂不修，臨難不見謂不勇。然而田原不遇歲，事君不遇世，賓於鄉里，逐於州部，則胡罪乎天哉？休惡遇此命也？」扁子曰：「子獨不聞夫至人之自行邪？忘其肝膽，遺其耳目，芒然彷徨乎塵垢之外，逍遙乎無事之業，是謂為而不恃，長而不宰。今汝飾知以驚愚，修身以明汙，昭昭乎若揭日月而行也。汝得全而形軀，具而九竅，無中道夭於聾盲跛蹇而比於人數，亦幸矣，又何暇乎天之怨哉！子往矣！」孫子出。扁子入坐，有間，仰天而歎。弟子問曰：「先生何

capacity into relation with that of the wood. What was suspected to be of supernatural execution in my work was due solely to this."

Tung Yeh Chi exhibited his charioteering skill before Duke Chuang.

Backwards and forwards he drove in lines which might have been ruled, sweeping round at each end in curves which might have been described by compasses.

The Duke, however, said that this was nothing more than weaving; and bidding him drive round and round a hundred times, returned home.

Yen Ho came upon him, and then went in and said to the Duke, "Chi's horses are on the point of breaking down."

The Duke remained silent, making no reply; and in a short time it was announced that the horses had actually broken down, and that Chi had gone away.

"How could you tell this?" said the Duke to Yen Ho.

"Because," replied the latter, "Chi was trying to make his horses perform a task to which they were unequal. Therefore I said they would break down."

Ch'ui the artisan could draw circles with his hand better than with compasses. His fingers seemed to accommodate themselves so naturally to the thing he was working at, that it was unnecessary to fix his attention. His mental faculties thus remained ONE, and suffered no hindrance.

To be unconscious of one's feet implies that the shoes are easy. To be unconscious of a waist implies that the girdle is easy. The intelligence being unconscious of positive and negative implies that the heart is at ease. No modifications within, no yielding to influences without,

—this is ease under all conditions. And he who beginning with ease, is never not at ease, is unconscious of the ease of ease.

A certain Sun Hsiu went to the house of Pien Ch'ing Tzu and complained, saying, "In peace I am not considered wanting in propriety. In times of trouble

I am not considered wanting in courage. Yet my crops fail; and officially I am not a success. From my village an outcast, I am an outlaw from my State. How have I offended against God that he should visit me with such a fate?"

"Have you not heard," replied Pien Tzu, "how the perfect man conducts himself? He is oblivious of his physical organisation. He is beyond

為歡乎?」扁子曰：「向者休來，吾告之以至人之德，吾恐其驚而遂至於惑也。」弟子曰:「不然。孫子之所言是邪?先生之所言非邪?非固不能惑是。孫子所言非邪?先生所言是邪?彼固惑而來矣，又奚罪焉!」扁子曰:「不然。昔者有鳥止於魯郊，魯君說之，為具太牢以饗之，奏九韶以樂之。鳥乃始憂悲眩視，不敢飲食。此之謂以己養養鳥也。若夫以鳥養養鳥者,宜棲之深林，浮之江湖，食之以委蛇，則平陸而已矣。今休，款啟寡聞之民也，吾告以至人之德，譬之若載鼷以車馬，樂鴳以鐘鼓也，彼又惡能無驚乎哉!」

the reach of sight and hearing. He moves outside the limits of this dusty world, rambling transcendentally in the domain of no-affairs. This is called acting but not from self-confidence, influencing but not from authority.

"But you, you make a show of your knowledge in order to startle fools. You cultivate yourself in contrast to the degradation of others. And you blaze along as though the sun and moon were under your arms.

Whereas, that you have a whole body in a whole skin, and have not perished in mid career, dumb, blind, or halt, but actually hold a place among men,

—this ought to be enough for you. Why rail at God? Begone!"

Sun Hsiu went away, and Pien Tzu went in and sat down. Shortly afterwards, he looked up to heaven and sighed; whereupon a disciple asked him what was the matter.

"When Hsiu was here just now," answered Pien Tzu, "I spoke to him of the virtue of the perfect man. I fear lest he be startled and so driven on to doubt."

"No, Sir," answered the disciple. "If he was right and you were wrong, wrong will never drive right into doubt. If, on the other hand, he was wrong and you were right, he brought his doubt with him, and you are not responsible."

"Not so," said Pien Tzu. "Of old, when a bird alighted outside the capital of Lu, the prince was delighted, and killed an ox to feed it and had the Chiu Shao played to entertain it. The bird, however, was timid and dazed and dared not to eat or drink. This was treating the bird like oneself. But to treat a bird as a bird would treat a bird, you must put it to roost in a deep forest, let it swim in river or lake, and feed at its ease on the plain. Now Sun Hsiu is a man of small understanding; and for me to speak to him of the perfect man is like setting a mouse to ride in a coach or a band of music to play to a quail. How should he not be startled?"

# 山木第二十

　　莊子行於山中，見大木，枝葉盛茂。伐木者止其旁而不取也。問其故，曰：「無所可用。」莊子曰：「此木以不材得終其天年。」夫子出於山，舍於故人之家。故人喜，命豎子殺雁而烹之。豎子請曰：「其一能鳴，其一不能鳴，請奚殺？」主人曰：「殺不能鳴者。」明日，弟子問於莊子曰：「昨日山中之木，以不材得終其天年；今主人之雁，以不材死。先生將何處？」莊子笑曰：「周將處夫材與不材之間。材與不材之間，似之而非也，故未免乎累。若夫乘道德而浮游則不然。無譽無訾，一龍一蛇，與時俱化，而無肯專為；一上一下，以和為量，浮游乎萬物之祖；物物而不物於物，則胡可得而累邪！此神農、黃帝之法則也。若夫萬物之情，人倫之傳，則不然。合則離，成則毀；廉則挫，尊則議，有為則虧，賢則謀，不肖則欺。胡可得而必乎哉！悲夫，弟子志之，其唯道德之鄉乎！」

　　市南宜僚見魯侯，魯侯有憂色。市南子曰：「君有憂色，何也？」魯侯曰：「吾學先王之道，修

# CHAPTER XX

## MOUNTAIN TREES

Chuang Tzu was travelling over a mountain when he saw a huge tree well covered with foliage. A woodsman had stopped near by, not caring to take it; and on Chuang Tzu enquiring the reason, he was told that it was of no use.

"This tree," cried Chuang Tzu, "by virtue of being good for nothing succeeds in completing its allotted span."

When Chuang Tzu left the mountain, he put up at the house of an old friend. The latter was delighted, and ordered a servant to kill a goose and cook it.

"Which shall I kill?" enquired the servant; "the one that cackles or the one that doesn't?"

His master told him to kill the one which did not cackle. And accordingly, the next day, a disciple asked Chuang Tzu, saying, "Yesterday, that tree on the mountain, because good for nothing, was to succeed in completing its allotted span. But now, our host's goose, which is good for nothing, has to die. Upon which horn of the dilemma will you rest?"

"I rest," replied Chuang Tzu with a smile, "halfway between the two. In that position, appearing to be what I am not, it is impossible to avoid the troubles of mortality; though, if charioted upon Tao and floating far above mortality, this would not be so. No praise, no blame; both great and small; changing with the change of time, but ever without special effort; both above and below; making for harmony with surroundings; reaching creation's First Cause; swaying all things and swayed by none;—how then shall such troubles come? This was the method of Shen Nung and Huang Ti.

"But amidst the mundane passions and relationships of man, such would not be the case. For where there is union, there is also separation; where there is completion, there is also destruction; where there is purity, there is also oppression;

where there is honour, there is also disparagement; where there is doing, there is also undoing; where there is openness, there is also underhandedness; and where there is no semblance, there is also deceit. How

先君之業；吾敬鬼尊賢，親而行之，無須臾離居。
然不免於患，吾是以憂。」市南子曰：「君之除
患之術淺矣！夫豐狐文豹，棲於山林，伏於巖穴，
靜也；夜行晝居，戒也；雖飢渴隱約，猶且胥
疏於江湖之上而求食焉，定也；然且不免於罔
羅機辟之患，是何罪之有哉？其皮為之災也。今
魯國獨非君之皮邪？吾願君刳形去皮，洒心去
欲，而游於無人之野。南越有邑焉，名為建德
之國。其民愚而朴，少私而寡欲；知作而不知藏，
與而不求其報；不知義之所適，不知禮之所將。
猖狂妄行，乃蹈乎大方。其生可樂，其死可葬。
吾願君去國捐俗，與道相輔而行。」君曰：「彼
其道遠而險，又有江山，我無舟車，奈何？」市
南子曰：「君無形倨，無留居，以為君車。」君
曰：「彼其道幽遠而無人，吾誰與為鄰？吾無糧，
我無食，安得而至焉？」市南子曰：「少君之費，
寡君之欲，雖無糧而乃足。君其涉於江而浮於
海，望之而不見其崖，愈往而不知其所窮。送

then can there be any fixed point? Alas indeed! Take note, my disciples, that such is to be found only in the domain of Tao."

I Liao of Shih-nan paid a visit to the prince of Lu. The latter wore a melancholy look; whereupon the philosopher of Shih-nan enquired what was the cause.

"I study the doctrines of the ancient Sages," replied the prince. "I carry on the work of my predecessors. I respect religion. I honour the good. Never for a moment do I relax in these points; yet I cannot avoid misfortune, and consequently I am sad."

"Your Highness' method of avoiding misfortune," said the philosopher of Shih-nan, "is but a shallow one. A handsome fox or a striped leopard will live in a mountain forest, hiding beneath some precipitous cliff. This is their repose. They come out at night and keep in by day. This is their caution. Though under the stress of hunger and thirst, they lie hidden, hardly venturing to slink secretly to the river bank in search of food. This is their resoluteness. Nevertheless, they do not escape the misfortune of the net and the trap. But what crime have they committed? 'Tis their skin which is the cause of their trouble; and is not the State of Lu your Highness' skin? I would have your Highness put away body and skin alike, and cleansing your heart and purging it of passion, betake yourself to the land where mortality is not.

"In Nan-yueh there is a district, called Established-Virtue. Its people are simple and honest, unselfish, and without passions. They can make, but cannot keep. They give, but look for no return. They are not conscious of fulfilling obligations. They are not conscious of subservience to etiquette.

Their actions are altogether uncontrolled, yet they tread in the way of the wise. Life is for enjoyment; death, for burial. And thither I would have your Highness proceed, power discarded and the world left behind, only putting trust in Tao."

"The road is long and dangerous," said the prince. "Rivers and hills to be crossed, and I without boat or chariot;—what then?"

"Unhindered by body and unfettered in mind," replied the philosopher, "your Highness will be a chariot to yourself."

"But the road is long and dreary," argued the prince, "and uninhabited. I shall have no one to turn to for help; and how, without food, shall I

君者皆自崖而反。君自此遠矣!故有人者累，見有於人者憂。故堯非有人，非見有於人也。吾願去君之累，除君之憂，而獨與道遊於大莫之國。方舟而濟於河，有虛船來觸舟，雖有惼心之人不怒；有一人在其上，則呼張歙之；一呼而不聞，再呼而不聞，於是三呼邪，則必以惡聲隨之。向也不怒而今也怒，向也虛而今也實。人能虛己以游世，其孰能害之!」

北宮奢為衛靈公賦斂以為鐘，為壇乎郭門之外。三月而成上下之縣。王子慶忌見而問焉，曰：「子何術之設?」奢曰：「一之間，無敢設也。奢聞之：『既雕既琢，復歸於朴。』侗乎其無識，儻乎其怠疑；萃乎芒乎，其送往而迎來；來者勿禁，往者勿止；從其彊梁，隨其曲傅，因其自窮。故朝夕賦斂而毫毛不挫，而況有大塗者乎!」

ever be able to get there?"

"Decrease expenditure and lessen desires," answered the philosopher, "and even though without provisions, there will be enough. And then through river and over sea your Highness will travel into shoreless illimitable space. From the border-land, those who act as escort will return; but thence onwards your Highness will travel afar.

"It is the human in ourselves which is our hindrance; and the human in others which causes our sorrow. The great Yao had not this human element himself, nor did he perceive it in others. And I would have your Highness put off this hindrance and rid yourself of this sorrow, and roam with Tao alone through the realms of Infinite Nought.

"Suppose a boat is crossing a river, and another empty boat is about to collide with it. Even an irritable man would not lose his temper. But supposing there was some one in the second boat. Then the occupant of the first would shout to him to keep clear. And if the other did not hear the first time, nor even when called to three times, bad language would inevitably follow. In the first case there was no anger, in the second there was; because in the first case the boat was empty, and in the second it was occupied. And so it is with man.

If he could only roam empty through life, who would be able to injure him?"

Pei Kung She, minister to Duke Ling of Wei, levied contributions for making bells. An altar was built outside the city gate; and in three months the bells, upper and lower, were all hung.

When Wang Tzu Ch'ing Chi saw them, he asked, saying, "How, Sir, did you manage this?"

"In the domain of ONE," replied She, "there may not be managing. I have heard say that which is carved and polished reverts nevertheless to its natural condition. And so I made allowances for ignorance and for suspicion. I betrayed no feeling when welcomed or dismissed. I forbade not those who came, nor detained those who went away. I showed no resentment towards the unwilling, nor gratitude towards those who gave. Every one subscribed what he liked; and thus in my daily collection of subscriptions, no injury was done.—

How much more then those who have the great WAY?"

When Confucius was hemmed in between Ch'en and Ts'ai, he passed

孔子圍於陳蔡之間，七日不火食。大公任往弔之，曰：「子幾死乎？」曰：「然。」「子惡死乎？」曰：「然。」任曰：「予嘗言不死之道。東海有鳥焉，名曰意怠。其為鳥也，翂翂翐翐，而似無能；引援而飛，迫脅而棲；進不敢為前，退不敢為後；食不敢先嘗，必取其緒。是故其行列不斥，而外人卒不得害，是以免於患。直木先伐，甘井先竭。子其意者飾知以驚愚，修身以明汙，昭昭乎如揭日月而行，故不免也。昔吾聞之大成之人曰：『自伐者無功，功成者墮，名成者虧。』孰能去功與名而還與眾人！道流而不明，居得行而不名處；純純常常，乃比於狂；削跡捐勢，不為功名。是故無責於人，人亦無責焉。至人不聞，子何喜哉！」孔子曰：「善哉！」辭其交游，去其弟子，逃於大澤，衣裘褐，食杼栗，入獸不亂群，入鳥不亂行。鳥獸不惡，而況人乎！

孔子問子桑雽曰：「吾再逐於魯，伐樹於宋，削跡於衛，窮於商周，圍於陳蔡之間。吾犯此數患，親交益疏，徒友益散，何與？」子桑雽曰：「子獨不聞假人之亡與？林回棄千金之璧，負赤子而

seven days without food.

The minister Jen went to condole with him, and said, "You were near, Sir, to death."

"I was indeed," replied Confucius.

"Do you fear death, Sir?" enquired Jen.

"I do," said Confucius.

"Then I will try to teach you," said Jen, "the way not to die.

"In the eastern sea there are certain birds, called the i-erh. They behave themselves in a modest and unassuming manner, as though unpossessed of ability. They fly simultaneously: they roost in a body. In advancing, none strives to be first; in retreating, none ventures to be last. In eating, none will be the first to begin; it is considered proper to take the leavings of others. Therefore, in their own ranks they are at peace, and the outside world is unable to harm them. And thus they escape trouble.

"Straight trees are the first felled. Sweet wells are soonest exhausted. And you, you make a show of your knowledge in order to startle fools. You cultivate yourself in contrast to the degradation of others. And you blaze along as though the sun and moon were under your arms; consequently, you cannot avoid trouble.

"Formerly, I heard a very wise man say, Self-praise is no recommendation. In merit achieved there is deterioration. In fame achieved there is loss. Who can discard both merit and fame and become one with the rest? Tao pervades all things but is not seen. Te moves through all things but its place is not known. In its purity and constancy, it may be compared with the purposeless. Remaining concealed, rejecting power, it works not for merit nor for fame. Thus, not censuring others, it is not censured by others.

"And if the perfect man cares not for fame, why, Sir, should you take pleasure in it?"

"Good indeed!" replied Confucius; and forthwith he took leave of his friends and dismissed his disciples and retired to the wilds, where he dressed himself in skins and serge and fed on acorns and chestnuts. He passed among the beasts and birds and they took no heed of him. And if so, how much more among men?

Confucius asked Tzu Sang Hu, saying, "I have been twice expelled from Lu. My tree was cut down in Sung. I have been tabooed in Wei. I am

趨。或曰：『為其布與？赤子之布寡矣；為其累與？赤子之累多矣；棄千金之璧，負赤子而趨，何也？』林回曰：『彼以利合，此以天屬也。』夫以利合者，迫窮禍患害相棄也；以天屬者，迫窮禍患害相收也。夫相收之與相棄亦遠矣，且君子之交淡若水，小人之交甘若醴。君子淡以親，小人甘以絕，彼無故以合者，則無故以離。」孔子曰：「敬聞命矣！」徐行翔佯而歸，絕學捐書，弟子無挹於前，其愛益加進。異日，桑雽又曰：「舜之將死，真泠禹曰：『汝戒之哉！形莫若緣，情莫若率。緣則不離，率則不勞。不離不勞，則不求文以待形；不求文以待形；固不待物。』」

a failure in Shang and Chou. I was surrounded between Ch'en and Ts'ai. And in addition to all these troubles, my friends have separated from me and my disciples are gone. How is this?"

"Have you not heard," replied Sang Hu, "how when the men of Kuo fled, one of them, named Lin Hui, cast aside most valuable regalia and carried away his child upon his back? Some one suggested that he was influenced by the value of the child;—but the child's value was small. Or by the inconvenience of the regalia;—but the inconvenience of the child would be much greater. Why then did he leave behind the regalia and carry off the child?

"Lin Hui himself said, 'The regalia involved a mere question of money. The child was from God.'

"And so it is that in trouble and calamity mere money questions are neglected, while we ever cling nearer to that which is from God. And between neglecting and clinging to, the difference is great.

"The friendship of the superior man is negative like water. The friendship of the mean man is full-flavoured like wine. That of the superior man passes from the negative to the affectionate. That of the mean man passes from the full-flavoured to nothing. The friendship of the mean man begins without due cause, and in like manner comes to an end.

"I hear and obey," replied Confucius; and forthwith he went quietly home, put an end to his studies and cast aside his books. His disciples no longer saluted him as teacher; but his love for them deepened every day.

On another occasion, Sang Hu said to him again, "When Shun was about to die, he commanded the Great Yu as follows:—Be careful. Act in accordance with your physical body. Speak in accordance with your feelings. You will thus not get into difficulty with the former nor suffer annoyance in the latter. And as under these conditions you will not stand in need of outward embellishment of any kind, it follows that you therefore will not stand in need of anything."

Chuang Tzu put on cotton clothes with patches in them, and arranging his girdle and tieing on his shoes, went to see the prince of Wei.

"How miserable you look, Sir!" cried the prince.

"It is poverty, not misery," replied Chuang Tzu.

"A man who has Tao cannot be miserable. Ragged clothes and old boots make poverty, not misery. Mine is what is called being out of harmo-

莊子衣大布而補之，正緳係履而過魏王。魏王曰：「何先生之憊邪？」莊子曰：「貧也，非憊也。士有道德不能行，憊也；衣弊履穿，貧也，非憊也，此所謂非遭時也。王獨不見夫騰猿乎？其得楠梓豫章也，攬蔓其枝而王長其間，雖羿、蓬蒙不能眄睨也。及其得柘棘枳枸之間也，危行側視，振動悼慄，此筋骨非有加急而不柔也，處勢不便，未足以逞其能也。今處昏上亂相之間，而欲無憊，奚可得邪？此比干之見剖心徵也夫！」

孔子窮於陳蔡之間，七日不火食。左據槁木，右擊槁枝，而歌猋氏之風，有其具而無其數，有其聲而無宮角。木聲與人聲，犁然有當於人之心。顏回端拱還目而窺之。仲尼恐其廣己而造大也，愛己而造哀也，曰：「回，無受天損易，無受人益難。無始而非卒也，人與天一也。夫今之歌者其誰乎！」回曰：「敢問無受天損易。」仲尼曰：「飢渴寒暑，窮桎不行，天地之行也，運物之泄也，言與之偕逝之謂也。為人臣者，不敢去之。執臣之道猶若是，而況乎所以待天乎？」「何謂無受人益難？」仲尼曰：「始用四達，

ny with one's age.

"Has your Highness never seen a climbing ape? Give it some large tree, and it will twist and twirl among the branches as though monarch of all it surveys. Yi and Feng Meng can never catch a glimpse of it.

"But put it in a bramble bush, and it will move cautiously with side-long glances, trembling all over with fear. Not that its muscles relax in the face of difficulty, but because it is at a disadvantage as regards position, and is unable to make use of its skill. And how should any one, living un-der foolish sovereigns and wicked ministers, help being miserable, even though he might wish not to be so?

"It was under such circumstances that Pi Kan was disembowelled."

When Confucius was hemmed in between Ch'en and Ts'ai and had gone seven days without food, then, holding in his left hand a piece of dry wood and in his right hand a dry stick, he sang a ballad of Piao Shih.

He had an instrument, but the gamut was wanting. There was sound, but no tune. The sound of the wood accompanied by the voice of the man yielded a harsh result, but it was in keeping with the feelings of his audi-ence.

Yen Hui, who was standing by in a respectful attitude, thereupon be-gan to turn his eyes about him; and Confucius, fearing lest he should be driven by exaltation into bragging, or by a desire for safety into sorrow, spoke to him as follows:—

"Hui! it is easy to escape injury from God; it is difficult to avoid the benefits of man. There is no beginning and there is no end. Man and God are ONE. Who then was singing just now?"

"Pray, Sir, what do you mean," asked Yen Hui, "by saying that it is easy to escape injury from God?"

"Hunger, thirst, cold, and heat," replied Confucius, "are but as fetters in the path of life. They belong to the natural laws which govern the uni-verse; and in obedience thereto I pass on my allotted course. The subject dares not disregard the mandates of his prince. And if this is man's duty to man, how much more shall it be his duty to God?"

"What is the meaning of difficult to avoid the benefits of man?" asked Yen Hui.

"If one begins," replied Confucius, "by adapta tion to surroundings, rank and power follow without cease. Such advantages are external; they

爵祿並至而不窮。物之所利，乃非己也，吾命有在外者也。君子不為盜，賢人不為竊，吾若取之，何哉？故曰：鳥莫知於鷾鴯，目之所不宜處，不給視，雖落其實，棄之而走。其畏人也，而襲諸人間。社稷存焉爾！」「何謂無始而非卒？」仲尼曰：「化其萬物而不知其禪之者，焉知其所終？焉知其所始？正而待之而已耳。」「何謂人與天一邪？」仲尼曰：「有人，天也；有天，亦天也。人之不能有天，性也。聖人晏然體逝而終矣！」

莊周游於雕陵之樊，睹一異鵲自南方來者。翼廣七尺，目大運寸，感周之顙，而集於栗林。莊周曰：「此何鳥哉！翼殷不逝，目大不睹。」蹇裳躩步，執彈而留之。睹一蟬，方得美蔭而忘其身。螳蜋執翳而搏之，見得而忘形；異鵲從

are not derived from oneself. And my life is more or less dependent upon the external. The superior man does not steal these; nor does the good man pilfer them. What then do I but take them as they come?

"Therefore it has been said that no bird is so wise as the swallow. If it sees a place unfit to dwell in, it will not bestow a glance thereon; and even though it should drop food there, it will leave the food and fly away. Now swallows fear man. Yet they dwell among men. Because there they find their natural abode."

"And what is the meaning," enquired Yen Hui, "of no beginning and no end?"

"The work goes on," replied Confucius, "and no man knoweth the cause. How then shall he know the end, or the beginning? There is nothing left to us but to wait."

"And that man and God are One," said Yen Hui. "What does that mean?"

"That man is," replied Confucius, "is from God. That God is, is also from God. That man is not God, is his nature.

The Sage quietly waits for death as the end."

When Chuang Tzu was wandering in the park at Tiao-ling, he saw a strange bird which came from the south. Its wings were seven feet across. Its eyes were an inch in circumference. And it flew close past Chuang Tzu's head to alight in a chestnut grove.

"What manner of bird is this?" cried Chuang Tzu. "With strong wings it does not fly away. With large eyes it does not see."

So he picked up his skirts and strode towards it with his cross-bow, anxious to get a shot. Just then he saw a cicada enjoying itself in the shade, forgetful of all else. And he saw a mantis spring and seize it, forgetting in the act its own body, which the strange bird immediately pounced upon and made its prey. And this it was which had caused the bird to forget its own nature.

"Alas!" cried Chuang Tzu with a sigh, "how creatures injure one another. Loss follows the pursuit of gain."

So he laid aside his bow and went home, driven away by the park-keeper who wanted to know what business he had there.

For three months after this, Chuang Tzu did not leave the house; and at length Lin Chu asked him, saying, "Master, how is it that you have not

而利之，見利而忘其真。莊周怵然曰：「噫！物固相累，二類相召也。」捐彈而反走，虞人逐而誶之。莊周反入，三日不庭。藺且從而問之，「夫子何為頃間甚不庭乎？」莊周曰：「吾守形而忘身，觀於濁水而迷於清淵。且吾聞諸夫子曰：『入其俗，從其俗。』今吾游於雕陵而忘吾身，異鵲感吾顙，游於栗林而忘真。栗林虞人以吾為戮，吾所以不庭也。」

陽子之宋，宿於逆旅。逆旅人有妾二人，其一人美，其一人惡。惡者貴而美者賤。陽子問其故，逆旅小子對曰：「其美者自美，吾不知其美也；其惡者自惡，吾不知其惡也。」陽子曰：「弟子記之：行賢而去自賢之行，安往而不愛哉！」

been out for so long?"

"While keeping my physical frame," replied Chuang Tzu, "I lost sight of my real self. Gazing at muddy water, I lost sight of the clear abyss. Besides, I have learnt from the Master as follows:—"When you go into the world, follow its customs."

Now when I strolled into the park at Tiao-ling, I forgot my real self. That strange bird which flew close past me to the chestnut grove, forgot its nature. The keeper of the chestnut grove took me for a thief. Consequently I have not been out."

When Yang Tzu went to the Sung State, he passed a night at an inn.

The innkeeper had two concubines, one beautiful, the other ugly. The latter he loved; the former, he hated.

Yang Tzu asked how this was; whereupon one of the inn servants said, "The beautiful one is so conscious of her beauty that one does not think her beautiful. The ugly one is so conscious of her ugliness that one does not think her ugly."

"Note this, my disciples!" cried Yang Tzu. "Be virtuous, but without being consciously so; and wherever you go, you will be beloved."

# 田子方第二十一

　　田子方侍坐於魏文侯，數稱谿工。文侯曰：「谿工，子之師邪？」子方曰：「非也，無擇之里人也。稱道數當故無擇稱之。」文侯曰：「然則子無師邪？」子方曰：「有。」曰：「子之師誰邪？」子方曰：「東郭順子。」文侯曰：「然則夫子何故未嘗稱之？」子方曰：「其為人也真。人貌而天虛，緣而葆真，清而容物。物無道，正容以悟之，使人之意也消。無擇何足以稱之！」子方出，文侯儻然，終日不言。召前立臣而語之曰：「遠矣，全德之君子！始吾以聖知之言、仁義之行為至矣。吾聞子方之師，吾形解而不欲動，口鉗而不欲言。吾所學者，直土埂耳！夫魏真為我累耳！」

　　溫伯雪子適齊，舍於魯。魯人有請見之者，溫伯雪子曰：「不可。吾聞中國之君子，明乎禮義而陋於知人心。吾不欲見也。」至於齊，反舍於魯，是人也又請見。溫伯雪子曰：「往也蘄見我，今也又蘄見我，是必有以振我也。」出而見客，

# CHAPTER XXI

## T'ien Tzu Fang

T'ien Tzu Fang was in attendance upon Prince Wen of Wei.

He kept on praising Ch'i Kung, until at length Prince Wen said, "Is Ch'i Kung your tutor?"

"No," replied Tzu Fang; "he is merely a neighbour. He discourses admirably upon Tao. That is why I praise him."

"Have you then no tutor?" enquired the Prince.

"I have," replied Tzu Fang.

"And who may he be?" said Prince Wen.

"Tung Kuo Shun Tzu," answered Tzu Fang.

"Then how is it you do not praise him?" asked the Prince.

"He is perfect," replied Tzu Fang. "In appearance, a man; in reality, God. Unconditioned himself, he falls in with the conditioned, to his own greater glory. Pure himself, he can still tolerate others. If men are without Tao, by a mere look he calls them to a sense of error, and causes their intentions to melt away. How could I praise him?"

Thereupon Tzu Fang took his leave, and the Prince remained for the rest of the day absorbed in silence. At length he called an officer in waiting and said, "How far beyond us is the man of perfect virtue! Hitherto I have regarded the discussion of holiness and wisdom, and the practice of charity and duty to one's neighbour, as the utmost point attainable. But now that I have heard of Tzu Fang's tutor, my body is relaxed and desires not movement, my mouth is closed and desires not speech. All I have learnt, verily it is mere undergrowth. And the kingdom of Wei is my bane."

When Wen Po Hsueh Tzu was on his way to Ch'i, he broke his journey in Lu. A certain man of Lu begged for an interview, but Wen Po Hsueh Tzu said, "No. I have heard that the gentlemen of the Middle Kingdom are experts in ceremonies and obligations, but wanting in knowledge of the human heart. I do not wish to see him."

So he went on to Ch'i; but once more at Lu, on his way home, the same man again begged to have an interview.

"When I was last here," cried Wen Po Hsueh Tzu, "he asked to see me, and now again he asks to see me. Surely he must have something to

入而嘆。明日見客，又入而嘆。其僕曰：「每見之客也，必入而嘆，何耶？」曰：「吾固告子矣：中國之民，明乎禮義而陋乎知人心。昔之見我者，進退一成規、一成矩，從容一若龍、一若虎。其諫我也似子，其道我也似父，是以嘆也。」仲尼見之而不言。子路曰：「吾子欲見溫伯雪子久矣。見之而不言，何邪？」仲尼曰：「若夫人者，目擊而道存矣，亦不可以容聲矣！」

顏淵問於仲尼曰：「夫子步亦步，夫子趨亦趨，夫子馳亦馳，夫子奔逸絕塵，而回瞠若乎後矣！」夫子曰：「回，何謂邪？」曰：「夫子步，亦步也，夫子言，亦言也；夫子趨，亦趨也，夫子辯，亦辯也；夫子馳，亦馳也，夫子言道，回亦言道也；及奔逸絕塵而回瞠若乎後者，夫子不言而信，不比而周，無器而民滔乎前，而不知所以然而已矣。」仲尼曰：「惡！可不察與！夫哀莫大於心死，而人死亦次之。日出東方而入於西極，萬物莫不比方，有首有趾者，待是而後成功。

communicate."

Whereupon he went and received the stranger, and on returning gave vent to sighs. Next day he received him again, and again after the interview gave vent to sighs. Then his servant asked him, saying, "How is it that whenever you receive this stranger, you always sigh afterwards?"

"I have already told you," replied Wen Po Hsueh Tzu, "that the people of the Middle Kingdom are experts in ceremonies and obligations but wanting in knowledge of the human heart. The man who visited me came in and went out as per compasses and square. His demeanour was now that of the dragon, now that of the tiger. He criticised me as though he had been my son. He admonished me as though he had been my father. Therefore I gave vent to sighs."

When Confucius saw Wen Po Hsueh Tzu, the former did not utter a word. Whereupon Tzu Lu said, "Master, you have long wished to see Wen Po Hsueh Tzu. How is it that when you do see him you do not speak?"

"With such men as these," replied Confucius, you have only to look, and Tao abides. There is no room for speech."

Yen Yuan asked Confucius, saying, "Master, when you go at a walk, I go at a walk. When you trot, I trot. When you gallop, I gallop. But when you dash beyond the bounds of mortality, I can only stand staring behind. How is this?"

"Explain yourself," said Confucius.

"I mean," continued Yen Yuan, "that as you speak, I speak. As you argue, I argue. As you preach Tao, so I preach Tao. And by 'when you dash beyond the bounds of mortality I can only stand staring behind,' I mean that without speaking you make people believe you, without striving you make people love you, without factitious attractions you gather people around you. I cannot understand how this is so."

"What is there to prevent you from finding out?" replied Confucius. "There is no sorrow to be compared with the death of the mind. The death of the body is of but secondary importance.

"The sun rises in the east and sets in the west.

There is no place which he does not illuminate; and those who have eyes and feet depend upon him to use them with success. When he comes forth, that is existence; when he disappears, that is non-existence.

"And every human being has that upon which he depends for death or

是出則存，是入則亡。萬物亦然，有待也而死，有待也而生。吾一受其成形，而不化以待盡。效物而動，日夜無隙，而不知其所終。薰然其成形，知命不能規乎其前。丘以是日徂。吾終身與汝交一臂而失之，可不哀與？女殆著乎吾所以著也。彼已盡矣，而女求之以為有，是求馬於唐肆也。吾服，女也甚忘；女服，吾也甚忘。雖然，女奚患焉！雖忘乎故吾，吾有不忘者存。」

孔子見老聃，老聃新沐，方將被髮而乾，慹然似非人。孔子便而待之。少焉見，曰：「丘也眩與？其信然與？向者先生形體掘若槁木，似遺物離人而立於獨也。」老聃曰：「吾游心於物之初。」孔子曰：「何謂邪？」曰：「心困焉而不能知，口辟焉而不能言。嘗為汝議乎其將：至陰肅肅，至陽赫赫。肅肅出乎天，赫赫發乎地。兩者交通成和而物生焉，或為之紀而莫見其形。消息滿虛，一晦一明，日改月化，日有所為，而莫見其功。生有所乎萌，死有所乎歸，始終相反乎無端，而莫知乎其所窮。非是也，且孰為之宗！」孔子曰：「請問游是。」老聃曰：「夫得是，至美

for life.

But if I, receiving this mind-informed body, pass without due modification to the end, day and night subject to ceaseless wear and tear like a mere thing, unknowing what the end will be, and in spite of this mind-informed body conscious only that fate cannot save me from the inevitable grave-yard,—then I am consuming life until at death it is as though you and I had but once linked arms to be finally parted for ever! Is not that indeed a cause for sorrow?

"Now you fix your attention upon something in me which, while you look, has already passed away. Yet you seek for it as though it must be still there,—like one who seeks for a horse in a market-place.

What I admire in you is transitory. Nevertheless, why should you grieve? Although my old self is constantly passing away, there remains that which does not pass away."

Confucius went to see Lao Tzu. The latter had just washed his head, and his hair was hanging down his back to dry. He looked like a lifeless body; so Confucius waited awhile, but at length approached and said, "Do my eyes deceive me, or is this really so? Your frame, Sir, seems like dry wood, as if it had been left without that which informs it with the life of man."

"I was wandering," replied Lao Tzu, "in the unborn."

"What does that mean?" asked Confucius.

"My mind is trammelled," replied Lao Tzu, "and I cannot know. My mouth is closed and I cannot speak. But I will try to tell you what is probably the truth.

"The perfect Negative principle is majestically passive. The perfect Positive principle is powerfully active. Passivity emanates from heaven above; activity proceeds from earth beneath. The interaction of the two results in that harmony by which all things are produced. There may be a First Cause, but we never see his form. His report fills space. There is darkness and light. Days come and months go. Work is being constantly performed, yet we never witness the performance. Life must bring us from somewhere, and death must carry us back. Beginning and end follow ceaselessly one upon the other, and we cannot say when the series will be exhausted. If this is not the work of a First Cause, what is it?"

"Kindly explain," said Confucius, "what is to be got by wandering as

至樂也。得至美而游乎至樂，謂之至人。」孔子曰：「願聞其方。」曰：「草食之獸，不疾易藪；水生之虫，不疾易水。行小變而不失其大常也，喜怒哀樂不入於胸次。夫天下也者，萬物之所一也。得其所一而同焉，則四支百體將為塵垢，而死生終始將為畫夜，而莫之能滑，而況得喪禍福之所介乎！棄隸者若棄泥塗，知身貴於隸也。貴在於我而不失於變。且萬化而未始有極也，夫孰足以患心！已為道者解乎此。」孔子曰：「夫子德配天地，而猶假至言以修心。古之君子，孰能脫焉！」老聃曰：「不然。夫水之於汋也，無為而才自然矣；至人之於德也，不修而物不能離焉。若天之自高，地之自厚，日月之自明，夫何脩焉！」孔子出，以告顏回曰：「丘之於道也，其猶醯雞與！微夫子之發吾覆也，吾不知天地之大全也。」

莊子見魯哀公，哀公曰：「魯多儒士，少為先生方者。」莊子曰：「魯少儒。」哀公曰：「舉魯國而儒服，何謂少乎？」莊子曰：「周聞之：儒

you said."

"The result," answered Lao Tzu, "is perfect goodness and perfect happiness. And he who has these is a perfect man."

"And by what means," enquired Confucius, "can this be attained?"

"Animals," said Lao Tzu, "that eat grass do not mind a change of pasture. Creatures that live in water do not mind a change of pond. A slight change may be effected so long as the essential is untouched.

"Joy, anger, sorrow, happiness, find no place in that man's breast; for to him all creation is One. And all things being thus united in One, his body and limbs are but as dust of the earth, and life and death, beginning and end, are but as night and day, and cannot destroy his peace. How much less such trifles as gain or loss, misfortune or good fortune?

"He rejects rank as so much mud. For he knows that if a man is of honourable rank, the honour is in himself, and cannot be lost by change of condition, nor exhausted by countless modifications of existence. Who then can grieve his heart? Those who practise Tao understand the secret of this."

"Master," said Confucius, "your virtue equals that of Heaven and Earth; yet you still employ perfect precepts in the cultivation of your heart. Who among the sages of old could have uttered such words?"

"Not so," answered Lao Tzu. "The fluidity of water is not the result of any effort on the part of the water, but is its natural property. And the virtue of the perfect man is such that even without cultivation there is nothing which can withdraw from his sway. Heaven is naturally high, the earth is naturally solid, the sun and moon are naturally bright. Do they cultivate these attributes?"

Confucius went forth and said to Yen Hui,

"In point of Tao, I am but as an animalcule in vinegar. Had not the Master opened my eyes, I should not have perceived the vastness of the universe."

When Chuang Tzu was at an interview with Duke Ai of Lu, the latter said, "We have many scholars, Sir, in Lu, but few of your school."

"In Lu," replied Chuang Tzu, "there are but few scholars."

"Look at the number who wear scholars' robes," said the Duke. "How can you say they are few?"

"Scholars who wear round hats," answered Chuang Tzu, "know the

者冠圜冠者，知天時，履句屨者，知地形，緩
佩玦者，事至而斷。君子有其道者，未必為其
服也；為其服者，未必知其道也。公固以為不
然，何不號於國中曰：「無此道而為此服者，其
罪死！」於是哀公號之五日，而魯國無敢儒服者。
獨有一丈夫儒服而立乎公門。公即召而問以國
事，千轉萬變而不窮。莊子曰：「以魯國而儒者
一人耳，可謂多乎？」

百里奚爵祿不入於心，故飯牛而牛肥，使秦
穆公忘其賤，與之政也。有虞氏死生不入於心，
故足以動人。宋元君將畫圖，眾史皆至，受揖
而立，舐筆和墨，在外者半。有一史後至者，
儃儃然不趨，受揖不立，因之舍。公使人視之，
則解衣槃礡臝。君曰：「可矣，是真畫者也。」

文王觀於臧，見一丈夫釣，而其釣莫釣。非
持其釣有釣者也，常釣也。文王欲舉而授之政，
而恐大臣父兄之弗安也；欲終而釋之，而不忍
百姓之無天也。於是旦而屬之大夫曰：「昔者寡
人夢見良人，黑色而髯，乘駁馬而偏朱蹄，號曰：
『寓而政於臧丈人，庶幾乎民有瘳乎！』」諸大

seasons of Heaven. Scholars who wear square shoes know the shape of Earth.

And scholars who loosely gird themselves are ready to decide whatever questions may arise. But scholars who have Tao do not necessarily wear robes; neither does the wearing of robes necessarily mean that a scholar has Tao. If your Highness does not think so, why not issue an order through the Middle Kingdom, making death the punishment for all who wear the robes without having the Tao?"

Thereupon Duke Ai circulated this mandate for five days, the result being that not a single man in Lu dared to don scholars' robes,—with the exception of one old man who, thus arrayed, took his stand at the Duke's gate.

The Duke summoned him to the presence, and asked him many questions on politics, trying to entangle him, but in vain. Then Chuang Tzu said,

"If there is only one scholar in Lu, surely that is not many."

Rank and power had no charms for Po Li Ch'i.

So he took to feeding cattle. His cattle were always fat, which caused Duke Mu of Ch'in to ignore his low condition and entrust him with the administration.

Shun cared nothing for life or death. He was therefore able to influence men's hearts.

Prince Yuan of Sung desiring to draw a map, the officials of that department presented themselves, and after making obeisance stood waiting for the order, more than half of them already licking their brushes and mixing their ink.

One of them arrived late. He sauntered in without hurrying himself; and when he had made obeisance, did not wait but went off home.

The Prince sent a man to see what he did. He took off his clothes and squatted down bare-backed.

"He will do," cried the Prince. "He is a true artist."

When Wen Wang was on a tour of inspection in Tsang, he saw an old man fishing. But his fishing was not real fishing, for he did not fish to catch fish, but to amuse himself.

So Wen Wang wished to employ him in the administration of government, but feared lest his own ministers, uncles, and brothers, might

夫蹴然曰：「先君王也。」文王曰：「然則卜之。」諸大夫曰：「先君之命，王其無它，又何卜焉。」遂迎臧丈人而授之政。典法無更，偏令無出。三年，文王觀於國，則列士壞植散群，長官者不成德，斔斛不敢入於四竟。列士壞植散群，則尚同也；長官者不成德，則同務也，斔斛不敢入於四竟，則諸侯無二心也。文王於是焉以為大師，北面而問曰：「政可以及天下乎？」臧丈人昧然而不應，泛然而辭，朝令而夜循，終身無聞。顏淵問於仲尼曰：「文王其猶未邪？又何以夢為乎？」仲尼曰：「默，汝無言！夫文王盡之也，而又何論刺焉！彼直以循斯須也。」

object. On the other hand, if he let the old man go, he could not bear to think of the people being deprived of such an influence.

Accordingly, that very morning he informed his ministers, saying, "I once dreamt that a Sage of a black colour and with a large beard, riding upon a parti-coloured horse with red stockings on one side, appeared and instructed me to place the administration in the hands of the old gentleman of Tsang, promising that the people would benefit greatly thereby."

The ministers at once said, "It is a command from your Highness' father."

"I think so," answered Wen Wang. "But let us try by divination."

"It is a command from your Highness' late father," said the ministers, "and may not be disobeyed. What need for divination?"

So the old man of Tsang was received and entrusted with the administration. He altered none of the existing statutes. He issued no unjust regulations. And when, after three years, Wen

Wang made another inspection, he found all dangerous organisations broken up, the officials doing their duty as a matter of course, while the use of measures of grain was unknown within the four boundaries of the State. There was thus unanimity in the public voice, singleness of official purpose, and identity of interests to all.

So Wen Wang appointed the old man Grand Tutor; and then, standing with his face to the north, asked him, saying, "Can such government be extended over the empire?"

The old man of Tsang was silent and made no reply. He then abruptly took leave, and by the evening of that same day had disappeared, never to be heard of again.

Yen Yuan said to Confucius, "If Wen Wang was unable to do this of himself, how was he able to do it by a dream?"

"Silence!" cried Confucius: "It is not for you to criticise Wen Wang who succeeded in fulfilling his mission. The dream was merely to satisfy the vulgar mind."

Lieh Yu K'ou instructed Po Hun Wu Jen in archery. Drawing the bow to its full, he placed a cup of water on his elbow and began to let fly. Hardly was one arrow out of sight ere another was on the string, the archer standing all the time like a statue.

"But this is shooting under ordinary conditions," cried Po Hun Wu

列御寇為伯昏無人射，引之盈貫，措杯水其肘上，發之，適矢復沓，方矢復寓。當是時，猶象人也。伯昏無人曰：「是射之射，非不射之射也。嘗與汝登高山，履危石，臨百仞之淵，若能射乎？」於是無人遂登高山，履危石，臨百仞之淵，背逡巡，足二分垂在外，揖御寇而進之。御寇伏地，汗流至踵。伯昏無人曰：「夫至人者，上窺青天，下潛黃泉，揮斥八極，神氣不變。今汝怵然有恂目之志，爾於中也殆矣夫！」

肩吾問於孫叔敖曰：「子三為令尹而不榮華，三去之而無憂色。吾始也疑子，今視子之鼻間栩栩然，子之用心獨奈何？」孫叔敖曰：「吾何以過人哉！吾以其來不可卻也，其去不可止也。吾以為得失之非我也，而無憂色而已矣。我何

Jen; "it is not shooting under extraordinary conditions. Now I will ascend a high mountain with you, and stand on the edge of a precipice a thousand feet in height, and see how you can shoot then."

Thereupon Wu Jen went with Lieh Tzu up a high mountain, and stood on the edge of a precipice a thousand feet in height, approaching it backwards until one-fifth of his feet overhung the chasm, when he beckoned to Lieh Tzu to come on. But the latter had fallen prostrate on the ground, with the sweat pouring down to his heels.

"The perfect man," said Wu Jen, "soars up to the blue sky, or dives down to the yellow springs, or flies to some extreme point of the compass, without change of countenance. But you are terrified, and your eyes are dazed. Your internal economy is defective."

Chien Wu said to Sun Shu Ao,

"Sir, you have been three times called to office without showing any elation, and you have been three times dismissed without displaying any chagrin. At first, I doubted you; but now I notice that your breathing is perfectly regular. How do you manage thus to control your emotions?"

"I am no better than other people," replied Sun Shu Ao. "I regard office when it comes as something which may not be declined; when it goes, as something which cannot be kept. To me both the getting and losing are outside my own self; and therefore I feel no chagrin. How am I better than other people?

"Besides, I am not conscious of office being either in the hands of others or in my own. If it is in the hands of others, my own personality disappears; if in mine, theirs. And amidst the cares of deliberation and investigation, what leisure has one for troubling about rank?"

When Confucius heard this, he said, "The perfect Sages of old!—cunning men could not defeat them; beautiful women could not seduce them; robbers could not steal from them;

Fu Hsi and the Yellow Emperor could not make friends of them. Life and death are great; yet these gave them no pang.

How much less then rank and power!

"The souls of such men pierced through huge mountains as though they had been nothing; descended into the abyss without getting wet; occupied lowly stations without chagrin. They filled the whole universe; and the more they gave to others, the more they had themselves."

以過人哉！且不知其在彼乎？其在我乎？其在彼邪，亡乎我，在我邪，亡乎彼。方將躊躇，方將四顧，何暇至乎人貴人賤哉！」仲尼聞之曰：「古之真人，知者不得說，美人不得濫，盜人不得劫，伏戲、黃帝不得友。死生亦大矣，而無變乎己，況爵祿乎！若然者，其神經乎大山而無介，入乎淵泉而不濡，處卑細而不憊，充滿天地，既以與人，己愈有。」

　　楚王與凡君坐，少焉，楚王左右曰凡亡者三。凡君曰：「凡之亡也，不足以喪吾存。夫凡之亡不足以喪吾存，則楚之存不足以存存。由是觀之，則凡未始亡而楚未始存也。

The Prince of Ch'u was sitting with the Prince of Fan. By and by, one of the officials of Ch'u said, "There were three indications of the destruction of the Fan State."

"The destruction of the Fan State," cried the Prince of Fan, "did not suffice to injure my existence.

And while the destruction of the Fan State did not suffice to injure my existence, the preservation of the Ch'u State will not be enough to preserve yours.

From this point of view it will be seen that while we Fans have not begun to be destroyed, you Ch'us have not begun to exist."

# 知北游第二十二

知北游於玄水之上，登隱弅之丘，而適遭無為謂焉。知謂無為謂曰：「予欲有問乎若：何思何慮則知道？何處何服則安道？何從何道則得道？」三問而無為謂不答也。非不答，不知答也。知不得問，反於白水之南，登狐闋之上，而睹狂屈焉。知以之言也問乎狂屈。狂屈曰：「唉！予知之，將語若。」中欲言而忘其所欲言。知不得問，反於帝宮，見黃帝而問焉。黃帝曰：「無思無慮始知道，無處無服始安道，無從無道始得道。」知問黃帝曰：「我與若知之，彼與彼不知也，其孰是邪？」黃帝曰：「彼無為謂真是也，狂屈似之，我與汝終不近也。夫知者不言，言者不知，故聖人行不言之教。道不可致，德不可至。仁可為也，義可虧也，禮相偽也。故曰：『失道而後德，失德而後仁，失仁而後義，失義而後禮。』禮者，道之華而亂之首也。故曰：『為道者日損，損之又損之，以至於無為。無為而無不為也。』今已為物也，欲復歸根，不亦難乎！其易也其唯大人乎！生也死之徙，死也生之始，

# CHAPTER XXII

## KNOWLEDGE TRAVELS NORTH

When Knowledge travelled north, across the Black Water, and over the Dark-Steep Mountain, he met Do-nothing Say-nothing and asked of him as follows:—

"Kindly tell me by what thoughts, by what cogitations, may Tao be known? By resting in what, by according in what, may Tao be approached? By following what, by pursuing what, may Tao be attained?"

To these three questions, Do-nothing Say-nothing returned no answer. Not that he would not answer, but that he could not. So when Knowledge got no reply, he turned round and went off to the south of the White Water and up the Ku-chueh Mountain, where he saw All-in-extremes, and to him he put the same questions.

"Ha!" cried All-in-extremes, "I know. I will tell you...."

But just as he was about to speak he forgot what he wanted to say. So when Knowledge got no reply, he went back to the palace and asked the Yellow Emperor. The latter said, "By no thoughts, by no cogitations, Tao may be known. By resting in nothing, by according in nothing, Tao may be approached. By following nothing, by pursuing nothing, Tao may be attained."

Then Knowledge said to the Yellow Emperor, "Now you and I know this, but those two know it not. Who is right?"

"Of those two," replied the Yellow Emperor, "Do-nothing Say-nothing is genuinely right, and All-in-extremes is near. You and I are wholly wrong. Those who understand it do not speak about it, those who speak about it do not understand it.

Therefore the Sage teaches a doctrine which does not find expression in words.

Tao cannot be made to come. Virtue cannot be reached.

Charity can be evoked. Duty to one's neighbour can be wrongly directed. Ceremonies are mere shams.

"Therefore it has been said, 'If Tao perishes, then Te will perish. If Te perishes, then charity will perish. If charity perishes, then duty to one's neighbour will perish. If duty to one's neighbour perishes, then ceremonies

孰知其紀！人之生，氣之聚也。聚則為生，散則為死。若死生為徒，吾又何患！故萬物一也。是其所美者為神奇，其所惡者為臭腐。臭腐復化為神奇，神奇復化為臭腐。故曰：『通天下一氣耳。』聖人故貴一。」知謂黃帝曰：「吾問無為謂，無為謂不應我，非不我應，不知應我也；吾問狂屈，狂屈中欲告我而不我告，非不我告，中欲告而忘之也；今予問乎若，若知之，奚故不近？」黃帝曰：「彼其真是也，以其不知也；此其似之也，以其忘之也；予與若終不近也，以其知之也。」狂屈聞之，以黃帝為知言。

天地有大美而不言，四時有明法而不議，萬物有成理而不說。聖人者，原天地之美而達萬物之理。是故至人無為，大聖不作，觀於天地之謂也。今彼神明至精，與彼百化。物已死生方圓，莫知其根也。扁然而萬物自古以固存。六合為巨，未離其內；秋豪為小，待之成體；天下莫不沉浮，終身不顧；陰陽四時運行，各得其序；惛然若亡而存；油然不形而神；萬物畜而不知：此之謂本根，可以觀於天矣！

will perish. Ceremonies are but a showy ornament of Tao, while oft-times the source of trouble.'

"Therefore it has been said, 'Those who practise Tao suffer daily loss. If that loss proceeds until inaction ensues, then by that very inaction there is nothing which cannot be done.'

"Now, we are already beings. And if we desire to revert to our original condition, how difficult that is! 'Tis a change to which only the greatest among us are equal.

"Life follows upon death. Death is the beginning of life. Who knows when the end is reached? The life of man results from convergence of the vital fluid. Its convergence is life; its dispersion, death. If then life and death are but consecutive states, what need have I to complain?

"Therefore all things are One. What we love is animation. What we hate is corruption. But corruption in its turn becomes animation, and animation once more becomes corruption.

"Therefore it has been said, The world is permeated by a single vital fluid, and Sages accordingly venerate One."

Then Knowledge said to the Yellow Emperor, "I asked Do-nothing Say-nothing, but he did not answer me. Not that he, would not; he could not. So I asked All-in-extremes. He was just going to tell me, but he did not tell me. Not that he would not; but just as he was going to do so, he forgot what he wanted to say. Now I ask you, and you tell me. How then are you wholly wrong?"

"Of those two," replied the Yellow Emperor, "the former was genuinely right, inasmuch as he did not know. The latter was near, inasmuch as he forgot. You and I are wholly wrong, inasmuch as we know."

When All-in-extremes heard of this, he considered that the Yellow Emperor had spoken well.

The universe is very beautiful, yet it says nothing. The four seasons abide by a fixed law, yet they are not heard. All creation is based upon absolute principles, yet nothing speaks.

And the true Sage, taking his stand upon the beauty of the universe, pierces the principles of created things. Hence the saying that the per fect man does nothing, the true Sage performs nothing, beyond gazing at the universe.

For man's intellect, however keen, face to face with the countless evo-

齧缺問道乎被衣，被衣曰：「若正汝形，一汝視，天和將至；攝汝知，一汝度，神將來舍。德將為汝美，道將為汝居。汝瞳焉如新生之犢而無求其故。」言未卒，齧缺睡寐。被衣大說，行歌而去之，曰：「形若槁骸，心若死灰，真其實知，不以故自持。媒媒晦晦，無心而不可與謀。彼何人哉！」

舜問乎丞，曰：「道可得而有乎？」曰：「汝身非汝有也，汝何得有夫道！」舜曰：「吾身非吾有也，孰有之哉？」曰：「是天地之委形也；生非汝有，是天地之委和也；性命非汝有，是天地之委順也；子孫非汝有，是天地之委蛻也。故行不知所往，處不知所持，食不知所味。天地之強陽氣也，又胡可得而有邪！」

孔子問於老聃曰：「今日晏閒，敢問至道。」老聃曰：「汝齊戒，疏瀹而心，澡雪而精神，掊擊而知。夫道，窅然難言哉！將為汝言其崖略。夫昭昭生於冥冥，有倫生於無形，精神生於道，形本生於精，而萬物以形相生。故九竅者胎生，八竅者卵生。其來無跡，其往無崖，無門無房，

lutions of things, their death and birth, their squareness and roundness,—can never reach the root. There creation is, and there it has ever been.

The six cardinal points, reaching into infinity, are ever included in Tao. An autumn spikelet, in all its minuteness, must carry Tao within itself. There is nothing on earth which does not rise and fall, but it never perishes altogether.

The Yin and the Yang, and the four seasons, keep to their proper order. Apparently destroyed, yet really existing; the material gone, the immaterial left;—such is the law of creation, which passeth all understanding. This is called the root, whence a glimpse may be obtained of God.

Yeh Ch'ueh enquired of P'i I about Tao.

The latter said, "Keep your body under proper control, your gaze concentrated upon One,—and the peace of God will descend upon you. Keep back your knowledge, and concentrate your thoughts upon One,—and the holy spirit shall abide within you. Virtue shall beautify you, Tao shall establish you, aimless as a new-born calf which recks not how it came into the world."

While P'i I was still speaking, Yeh Ch'ueh had gone off to sleep; at which the former rejoiced greatly, and departed singing,

> "Body like dry bone,
> Mind like dead ashes;
> This is true knowledge,
> Not to strive after knowing the whence.
> In darkness, in obscurity,
> The mindless cannot plan;—
> What manner of man is that?"

Shun asked Ch'eng, saying, "Can one get Tao so as to have it for one's own?"

"Your very body," replied Ch'eng, "is not your own. How should Tao be?"

"If my body," said Shun, "is not my own, pray whose is it?"

"It is the delegated image of God," replied Ch'eng. "Your life is not your own. It is the delegated harmony of God.

Your individuality is not your own. It is the delegated adaptability of God.

Your posterity is not your own. It is the delegated exuviae of God.

四達之皇皇也。邀於此者，四肢強，思慮恂達，耳目聰明。其用心不勞，其應物無方，天不得不高，地不得不廣，日月不得不行，萬物不得不昌，此其道與！且夫博之不必知，辯之不必慧，聖人以斷之矣！若夫益之而不加益，損之而不加損者，聖人之所保也。淵淵乎其若海，魏魏乎其若山，終則復始也。運量萬物而不匱。則君子之道，彼其外與！萬物皆往資焉而不匱。此其道與！「中國有人焉，非陰非陽，處於天地之間，直且為人，將反於宗。自本觀之，生者，暗醷物也。雖有壽夭，相去幾何？須臾之說也，奚足以為堯、桀之是非！果蓏有理，人倫雖難，所以相齒。聖人遭之而不違，過之而不守。調而應之，德也；偶而應之，道也。帝之所興，王之所起也。「人

You move, but know not how. You are at rest, but know not why. You taste, but know not the cause. These are the operation of God's laws. How then should you get Tao so as to have it for your own?"

Confucius said to Lao Tzu, "To-day you are at leisure. Pray tell me about perfect Tao."

"Purge your heart by fasting and discipline," answered Lao Tzu. "Wash your soul as white as snow. Discard your knowledge. Tao is abstruse and difficult of discussion. I will try, however, to speak to you of its outline.

"Light is born of darkness. Classification is born of formlessness. The soul is born of Tao. The body is born of the vital essence.

"Thus all things produce after their kind. Creatures with nine channels of communication are born from the womb. Creatures with eight are born from the egg.

"Of their coming there is no trace. In their departure there is no goal. No entrance gate, no dwelling house, they pass this way and that, as though at the meeting of cross-roads.

"Those who enter herein become strong of limb, subtle of thought, and clear of sight and hearing. They suffer no mental fatigue, nor meet with physical resistance.

"Heaven cannot but be high. Earth cannot but be broad. The sun and moon cannot but revolve. All creation cannot but flourish. To do so is their Tao.

"But it is not from extensive study that this may be known, nor by dialectic skill that this may be made clear. The true Sage will have none of these. It is in addition without gain, in diminution without loss, that the true Sage finds salvation.

"Unfathomable as the sea, wondrously ending only to begin again, informing all creation without being exhausted, the Tao of the perfect man is spontaneous in its operation. That all creation can be informed by it without exhaustion, is its Tao.

"In the Middle Kingdom there are men who recognise neither positive nor negative. They abide between heaven and earth. They act their part as mortals, and then return to the Cause.

"From that standpoint, life is but a concentration of the vital fluid, whose longest and shortest terms of existence vary by an inappreciable space,—hardly enough for the classification of Yao and Chieh.

生天地之間，若白駒之過隙，忽然而已。注然勃然，莫不出焉；油然漻然，莫不入焉。已化而生，又化而死。生物哀之，人類悲之。解其天弢，墮其天帙。紛乎宛乎，魂魄將往，乃身從之。乃大歸乎！不形之形，形之不形，是人之所同知也，非將至之所務也，此眾人之所同論也。彼至則不論，論則不至；明見無值，辯不若默；道不可聞，聞不若塞：此之謂大得。」

東郭子問於莊子曰：「所謂道，惡乎在？」莊子曰：「無所不在。」東郭子曰：「期而後可。」莊子曰：「在螻蟻。」曰：「何其下邪？」曰：「在稊稗。」曰：「何其愈下邪？」曰：「在瓦甓。」曰：「何其愈甚邪？」曰：「在屎溺。」東郭子不應。莊子曰：「夫子之問也，固不及質。正獲之問於監市履狶也，每下愈況。汝唯莫必，無乎逃物。至道若是，大言亦然。周遍咸三者，異名同實，其指一也。嘗相與游乎無有之宮，同合而論，無

"Tree-fruits and plant-fruits exhibit order in their varieties; and the relationships of man, though more difficult to be dealt with, may still be reduced to order.

The true Sage who meets with these, does not violate them. Neither does he continue to hold fast by them.

Adaptation by arrangement is Te. Spontaneous adaptation is Tao, by which sovereigns flourish and princes succeed.

"Man passes through this sublunary life as a white horse passes a crack. Here one moment, gone the next. Neither are there any not equally subject to the ingress and egress of mortality. One modification brings life; then another, and it is death. Living creatures cry out; human beings sorrow. The bow-sheath is slipped off; the clothes-bag is dropped; and in the confusion the soul wings its flight, and the body follows, on the great journey home!

"The reality of the formless, the unreality of that which has form,— this is known to all. Those who are on the road to attainment care not for these things, but the people at large discuss them. Attainment implies non-discussion: discussion implies non-attainment. Manifested, Tao has no objective value; hence silence is better than argument. It cannot be translated into speech; better then say nothing at all. This is called the great attainment."

Tung Kuo Tzu asked Chuang Tzu, saying, "What you call Tao,— where is it?"

"There is nowhere," replied Chuang Tzu, "where it is not."

"Tell me one place at any rate where it is," said Tung Kuo Tzu.

"It is in the ant," replied Chuang Tzu.

"Why go so low down?" asked Tung Kuo Tzu.

"It is in a tare," said Chuang Tzu.

"Still lower," objected Tung Kuo Tzu.

"It is in a potsherd," said Chuang Tzu.

"Worse still!" cried Tung Kuo Tzu.

"It is in ordure," said Chuang Tzu. And Tung Kuo Tzu made no reply.

"Sir," continued Chuang Tzu, "your question does not touch the essential. When Huo, inspector of markets, asked the managing director about the fatness of pigs, the test was always made in parts least likely to be fat. Do not therefore insist in any particular direction; for there is

所終窮乎！嘗相與無為乎！澹而靜乎！漠而清乎！調而閒乎！寥已吾志，無往焉而不知其所至，去而來而不知其所止，吾往焉而不知其所終，彷徨乎馮閎，大知入焉而不知其所窮。物物者與物無際，而物有際者，所謂物際者也。不際之際，際之不際者也。謂盈虛衰殺，彼為盈虛非盈虛，彼為衰殺非衰殺，彼為本末非本末，彼為積散非積散也。」

妸荷甘與神農學於老龍吉。神農隱几闔戶晝瞑。妸荷甘日中奓戶而入，曰：「老龍死矣！」神農擁杖而起，曝然放杖而笑，曰：「天知予僻陋謾訑，故棄予而死。已矣，夫子無所發予之狂言而死矣夫！」弇堈弔聞之，曰：「夫體道者，天下之君子所繫焉。今於道，秋豪之端萬分未得處一焉，而猶知藏其狂言而死，又況夫體道者乎！視之無形，聽之無聲，於人之論者，謂之冥冥，所以論道而非道也。」於是泰清問乎無窮，曰：「子知道乎？」無窮曰：「吾不知。」又問乎無為，無為曰：「吾知道。」曰：「子之知道，亦有數乎？」曰：「有。」曰：「其數若何？」無為曰：

nothing which escapes. Such is perfect Tao; and such also is ideal speech. Whole, entire, all, are three words which sound differently but mean the same. Their purport is One.

"Try to reach with me the palace of Nowhere, and there, amidst the identity of all things, carry your discussions into the infinite. Try to practise with me inaction, wherein you may rest motionless, without care, and be happy. For thus my mind becomes an abstraction. It wanders not, and yet is not conscious of being at rest. It goes and comes and is not conscious of stoppages. Backwards and forwards without being conscious of any goal. Up and down the realms of Infinity, wherein even the greatest intellect would fail to find an end.

"That which makes things the things they are, is not limited to such things. The limits of things are their own limits in so far as they are things. The limits of the limitless, the limitlessness of the limited,—these are called fulness and emptiness, renovation and decay. Tao causes fulness and emptiness, but it is not either. It causes renovation and decay, but it is not either. It causes beginning and end, but it is not either. It causes accumulation and dispersion, but it is not either."

O Ho Kan was studying with Shen Nung under Lao Lung Chi.

Shen Nung used to remain shut up, with his head on the table, absorbed in day-dreams. On one occasion, O Ho Kan knocked at the door, and entering said, "Lao Lung is dead!"

Thereupon Shen Nung, leaning on his staff, arose; and flinging down his staff with a bang, smiled and said, "O my Master, thou knewest me to be worthless and self-sufficient, and thou didst leave me and die. Now I, having no scope for my vain talk, I too will die."

When Yen Kang Tiao heard this, he said, "Those who exemplify Tao are sought after by all the best men in the empire. Now if one who has not attained to more Tao than the ten-thousandth part of the tip of an autumn spikelet, is still wise enough to withhold vain talk and die,—how much more those who exemplify Tao? To the eye it is formless, and to the ear it is noiseless. Those who discuss it, speak of it as 'the obscure.' But the mere fact of discussing Tao makes it not Tao."

At this the Empyrean asked Without-end, saying, "Do you know Tao?"

"I do not," replied Without-end; whereupon the Empyrean proceeded

「吾知道之可以貴、可以賤、可以約、可以散，此吾所以知道之數也。」泰清以之言也問乎無始，曰：「若是，則無窮之弗知與無為之知，孰是而孰非乎？」無始曰：「不知深矣，知之淺矣；弗知內矣，知之外矣。」於是泰清仰而嘆曰：「弗知乃知乎，知乃不知乎！孰知不知之知？」無始曰：「道不可聞，聞而非也；道不可見，見而非也；道不可言，言而非也！知形形之不形乎！道不當名。」無始曰：「有問道而應之者，不知道也；雖問道者，亦未聞道。道無問，問無應。無問問之，是問窮也；無應應之，是無內也。以無內待問窮，若是者，外不觀乎宇宙，內不知乎大初。是以不過乎昆侖，不游乎太虛。」

光曜問乎無有曰：「夫子有乎？其無有乎？」無有弗應也，光曜不得問而孰視其狀貌：窅然空然。終日視之而不見，聽之而不聞，搏之而不得也。光曜曰：「至矣，其孰能至此乎！予能有無矣，而未能無無也。及為無有矣，何從至此哉！」

to ask Inaction.

"I do know Tao," said Inaction.

"Is there any method," asked the Empyrean, "by which you know Tao?"

"There is," replied Inaction.

"What is it?" asked the Empyrean.

"I know," answered Inaction, "that Tao may honour and dishonour, bind and loose. That is the method by which I know Tao."

The Empyrean repeated these words to No-beginning, and asked him which was right, the ignorance of Without-end or the knowledge of Inaction.

"Not to know," replied No-beginning, "is profound. To know is shallow. Not to know is internal. To know is external."

Here the Empyrean broke in with a sigh, "Then ignorance is knowledge, and knowledge ignorance! But pray whose knowledge is the knowledge of not knowing?"

"Tao," said No-beginning, "cannot be heard. Heard, it is not Tao. It cannot be seen. Seen, it is not Tao. It cannot be spoken. Spoken, it is not Tao. That which imparts form to forms is itself formless; therefore Tao cannot have a name."

No-beginning continued, "He who replies to one asking about Tao, does not know Tao. Although one may hear about Tao, he does not really hear about Tao. There is no such thing as asking about Tao. There is no such thing as answering such questions. To ask a question which cannot be asked is vain. To answer a question which cannot be answered is unreal. And one who thus meets the vain with the unreal is one who has no physical perception of the universe, and no mental perception of the origin of existence,—unfit alike to roam over the K'un-lun peak or to soar into the Supreme Void."

Light asked Nothing, saying, "Do you, Sir, exist, or do you not exist?"

But getting no answer to his question, Light set to work to watch for the appearance of Nothing.

Hidden, vacuous,—all day long he looked but could not see it, listened but could not hear it, grasped at but could not seize it.

"Bravo!" cried Light. "Who can equal this? I can get to be nothing, but I cannot get as far as the absence of nothing. Assuming that Nothing

大馬之捶鉤者，年八十矣，而不失豪芒。大馬曰：「子巧與！有道與？」曰：「臣有守也。臣之年二十而好捶鉤，於物無視也，非鉤無察也。」是用之者，假不用者也，以長得其用，而況乎無不用者乎！物孰不資焉！

冉求問於仲尼曰：「未有天地可知邪？」仲尼曰：「可。古猶今也。」冉求失問而退。明日復見，曰：「昔者吾問『未有天地可知乎？』夫子曰：『可。古猶今也。』昔日吾昭然，今日吾昧然。敢問何謂也？」仲尼曰：「昔之昭然也，神者先受之；今之昧然也，且又為不神者求邪！無古無今，無始無終。未有子孫而有子孫可乎？」冉求未對。仲尼曰：「已矣，末應矣！不以生生死，不以死死生。死生有待邪？皆有所一體。有先天地生者物邪？物物者非物，物出不得先物也，猶其有物也。猶其有物也，無已！聖人之愛人也終無已者，亦乃取於是者也。」

顏淵問乎仲尼曰：「回嘗聞諸夫子曰：『無有所將，無有所迎。』回敢問其遊。」仲尼曰：「古之人，外化而內不化，今之人，內化而外不化。

has an objective existence, how can it reach this next stage?"

The man who forged swords for the Minister of War was eighty years of age. Yet he never made the slightest slip in his work.

The Minister of War said to him, "Is it your skill, Sir, or have you any method?"

"It is concentration," replied the man. "When twenty years old, I took to forging swords. I cared for nothing else. If a thing was not a sword, I did not notice it. I availed myself of whatever energy I did not use in other directions in order to secure greater efficiency in the direction required. Still more of that which is never without use;—

So that there was nothing which did not lend its aid.

Jen Ch'iu asked Confucius, saying, "Can we know about the time before the universe existed?"

"We can," replied Confucius. "Time was of old precisely what it is now."

At this rebuff, Jen Ch'iu withdrew. Next day he again visited Confucius and said, "Yesterday when I asked you that question and you answered me, I was quite clear about it. To-day I am confused. How is this?"

"Your clearness of yesterday," answered Confucius, "was because my answer appealed direct to your natural intelligence. Your confusion of to-day results from the intrusion of something other than the natural intelligence.

There is no past, no present, no beginning, no end.

To have posterity before one has posterity,—is that possible?"

Jen Ch'iu made no answer, and Confucius continued, "That will do. Do not reply. If life did not give birth to death, and if death did not put an end to life, surely life and death would be no longer correlates, but would each exist independently. What there was before the universe, was Tao. Tao makes things what they are, but is not itself a thing. Nothing can produce Tao; yet everything has Tao within it, and continues to produce it without end.

And the endless love of the Sage for his fellow-man is based upon the same principle."

Yen Yuan asked Confucius, saying, "Master, I have heard you declare that there may be no eagerness to conform, no effort to adapt. If so, pray how are we to get along?"

與物化者，一不化者也。安化安不化？安與之相靡？必與之莫多。狶韋氏之囿，黃帝之圃，有虞氏之宮，湯武之室。君子之人，若儒墨者師，故以是非相韲也，而況今之人乎！聖人處物不傷物。不傷物者，物亦不能傷也。唯無所傷者，為能與人相將迎。山林與，皋壤與，使我欣欣然而樂與！樂未畢也，哀又繼之。哀樂之來，吾不能御，其去弗能止。悲夫，世人直為物逆旅耳！夫知遇而不知所不遇，能能而不能所不能。無知無能者，固人之所不免也。夫務免乎人之所不免者，豈不亦悲哉！至言去言，至為去為。齊知之，所知則淺矣！」

"The men of old," replied Confucius, "practised physical, but not moral, modification.

The men of to-day practise moral, not physical modification.

Let your modification extend to the external only. Internally, be constant without modification.

"How shall you modify, and how shall you not modify? How reconcile the divergence?—By not admitting division.

"There was the garden of Hsi Wei, the park of the Yellow Emperor, the palace of Shun, the halls of T'ang and Wu.

These were perfect men; but had they been taught by Confucianists and Mihists, they would have hammered one another to pieces over scholastic quibbles. How much more then the men of to-day?

"The perfect Sage, in his relations with the external world, injures nothing. Neither does anything injure him. And only he who is thus exempt can be trusted to conform and to adapt.

"Mountain forests and loamy fields swell my heart with joy. But ere the joy be passed, sorrow is upon me again.

Joy and sorrow come and go, and over them I have no control.

"Alas! the life of man is but as a stoppage at an inn. He knows that which comes within the range of his experience. Otherwise, he knows not. He knows that he can do what he can do, and that he cannot do what he cannot do. But there is always that which he does not know and that which he cannot do; and to struggle that it shall not be so,—is not this a cause for grief?

"The best language is that which is not spoken, the best form of action is that which is without deeds.

Spread out your knowledge and it will be found to be shallow."

# 庚桑楚第二十三

　　老聃之役有庚桑楚者，偏得老聃之道，以北居畏壘之山。其臣之畫然知者去之，其妾之挈然仁者遠之。擁腫之與居，鞅掌之為使。居三年，畏壘大壤。畏壘之民相與言曰：「庚桑子之始來，吾洒然異之。今吾日計之而不足，歲計之而有余。庶幾其聖人乎！子胡不相與尸而祝之，社而稷之乎？」庚桑子聞之，南面而不釋然。弟子異之。庚桑子曰：「弟子何異於予？夫春氣發而百草生，正得秋而萬寶成。夫春與秋，豈無得而然哉？天道已行矣。吾聞至人，尸居環堵之室，而百姓猖狂，不知所如往。今以畏壘之細民，而竊竊焉欲俎豆予於賢人之間。我其杓之人邪！吾是以不釋於老聃之言。」弟子曰：「不然。夫尋常之溝，巨魚無所還其體，而鯢鰌為之制；步仞之丘陵，巨獸無所隱其軀，而孽狐為之祥。且夫尊賢授能，先善與利，自古堯、舜以然，而況畏壘之民乎！夫子亦聽矣！」庚桑子曰：「小子來！夫函車之獸，介而離山，則不免於罔罟之患；吞舟之魚，碭而失水，則蟻能苦之。故鳥獸不厭高，

# CHAPTER XXIII

## KENG SANG CH'U

Among the disciples of Lao Tzu was one named Keng Sang Ch'u. He alone had attained to the Tao of his Master. He lived up north, on the Wei-lei Mountains. Of his attendants, he dismissed those who were systematically clever or conventionally charitable. The useless remained with him; the incompetent served him. And in three years the district of Wei-lei was greatly benefited.

One of the inhabitants said in conversation, "When Mr. Keng Sang first came among us, we did not know what to make of him. Now, we could not say enough about him in a day, and even a year would leave something unsaid. Surely he must be a true Sage. Why not pray to him as to the spirits, and honour him as a tutelary god of the land?"

On hearing of this, Keng Sang Ch'u turned his face to the south in shame, at which his disciples were astonished. But Keng Sang said, "What cause have you for astonishment? The influence of spring quickens the life of plants, and autumn brings them to maturity. In the absence of any agent, how is this so? It is the operation of Tao.

"I have heard that the perfect man may be pent up like a corpse in a tomb, yet the people will become unartificial and without care.

But now these poor people of Wei-lei wish to exalt me among their wise and good. Surely then I am but a shallow vessel; and therefore I was shamed for the doctrine of Lao Tzu."

The disciples said, "Not so. In a sixteen-foot ditch a big fish has not room to turn round; but 'tis the very place for an eel. On a six or seven-foot hillock a large beast finds no shelter, while the uncanny fox gladly makes its lair therein. Besides, ever since the days of Yao and Shun it has always been customary to honour the virtuous, advance the able, give precedence to the good and useful. Why not then among the people of Wei-lei? Let them do it, Sir."

"Come here, my children," said Keng Sang Ch'u. "A beast big enough to swallow a cart, if it wanders alone from the hills, will not escape the sorrow of the snare. A fish big enough to gulp down a boat, if stranded on the dry shore will become a prey to ants. Therefore it is that birds and beasts

魚鱉不厭深。夫全其形生之人，藏其身也，不厭深眇而已矣！且夫二子者，又何足以稱揚哉！是其於辯也，將妄鑿垣牆而殖蓬蒿也。簡髮而櫛，數米而炊，竊竊乎又何足以濟世哉！舉賢則民相軋，任知則民相盜。之數物者，不足以厚民。民之於利甚勤，子有殺父，臣有殺君，正晝為盜，日中穴牆。吾語女：大亂之本，必生於堯、舜之間，其末存乎千世之後。千世之後，其必有人與人相食者也。」

南榮趎蹴然正坐曰：「若趎之年者已長矣，將惡乎託業以及此言邪？」庚桑子曰：「全汝形，抱汝生，無使汝思慮營營。若此三年，則可以及此言矣！」南榮趎曰：「目之與形，吾不知其異也，而盲者不能自見，耳之與形，吾不知其異也，而聾者不能自聞；心之與形，吾不知其異也，而狂者不能自得。形之與形亦辟矣，而物或間之邪？欲相求而不能相得。今謂趎曰：『全汝形，抱汝生，無使汝思慮營營。』趎勉聞道達耳矣！」庚桑子曰：「辭盡矣，奔蜂不能化藿蠋，越雞不能伏鵠卵，魯雞固能矣！雞之與雞，其德

love height, and fishes and turtles love depth. And the man who cares for himself hides his body. He loves the occult.

"As to Yao and Shun, what claim have they to praise? Their fine distinctions simply amounted to knocking a hole in a wall in order to stop it up with brambles; to combing each individual hair; to counting the grains for a rice pudding! How in the name of goodness did they profit their generation?

"If the virtuous are honoured, emulation will ensue. If knowledge be fostered, the result will be theft.

These things are of no use to make people good. The struggle for wealth is so severe. Sons murder their fathers; ministers their princes; men rob in broad daylight, and bore through walls at high noon. I tell you that the root of this great evil is from Yao and Shun, and that its branches will extend into a thousand ages to come. A thousand ages hence, man will be feeding upon man!"

Nan Yung Ch'u sadly straightened his seat and said, "But what is one of my age to do that he may attain to this?"

"Preserve your form complete," said Keng Sang, "your vitality secure. Let no anxious thoughts intrude. And then in three years' space you may attain to this."

"I do not know," said Nan Yung, "that there is any difference in the form of eyes; yet blind men cannot see. I do not know that there is any difference in the form of ears; yet deaf men cannot hear. I do not know that there is any difference in the form of hearts; yet fools cannot use theirs to any purpose. The forms are alike; yet there is something which differentiates them. One will succeed, and another will not. Yet you tell me to preserve my form complete, my vitality secure, and let no anxious thoughts intrude. But so far I only hear Tao with my ears."

"Well said!" cried Keng Sang; and then he added, "Small wasps cannot transform huge caterpillars.

Bantams cannot hatch the eggs of geese. The fowls of Lu can. Not that there is any difference in the hatching power of chickens. One can and another cannot, because one is naturally fitted for working on a large, the other on a small scale. My talents are of the latter order. I cannot transform you. Why not go south and see Lao Tzu?"

So Nan Yung took some provisions, and after a seven days' journey ar-

非不同也。有能與不能者，其才固有巨小也。今吾才小，小足以化子。子胡不南見老子！」南榮趎贏糧，七日七夜至老子之所。老子曰：「子自楚之所來乎？」南榮趎曰：「唯。」老子曰：「子何與人偕來之眾也？」南榮趎懼然顧其後。老子曰：「子不知吾所謂乎？」南榮趎俯而慚，仰而嘆曰：「今者吾忘吾答，因失吾問。」老子曰：「何謂也？」南榮趎曰：「不知乎？人謂我朱愚。知乎，反愁我軀。不仁則害人，仁則反愁我身；不義則傷彼，義則反愁我己。我安逃此而可？此三言者，趎之所患也。願因楚而問之。」老子曰：「向吾見若眉睫之間，吾因以得汝矣。今汝又言而信之。若規規然若喪父母，揭竿而求諸海也。汝亡人哉，惘惘乎！汝欲反汝情性而無由入，可憐哉！」南榮趎請入就舍，召其所好，去其所惡。十日自愁，復見老子。老子曰：「汝自洒濯，熟哉鬱鬱乎！然而其中津津乎猶有惡也。夫外韄者不可繁而捉，將內揵；內韄者不可繆而捉，將外揵。外內韄者，道德不能持，而況放道而行者乎！」南榮趎曰：「里人有病，里人問之，病者能言其病，

rived at the abode of Lao Tzu.

"Have you come from Keng Sang Ch'u?" said the latter.

"I have," replied Nan Yung.

"But why," said Lao Tzu, "bring all these people with you?"

Nan Yung looked back in alarm, and Lao Tzu continued, "Do you not understand what I say?"

Nan Yung bent his head abashed, and then looking up, said with a sigh, "I have now forgotten how to answer, in consequence of missing what I came to ask."

"What do you mean?" said Lao Tzu.

"If I do not know," replied Nan Yung, "men call me a fool. If I do know, I injure myself. If I am not charitable, I injure others. If I am, I injure myself. If I do not do my duty to my neighbour, I injure others. If I do it, I injure myself. My trouble lies in not seeing how to escape from these three dilemmas. On the strength of my connection with Keng Sang, I would venture to ask advice."

"When I saw you," said Lao Tzu, "I knew in the twinkling of an eye what was the matter with you. And now what you say confirms my view.

You are confused, as a child that has lost its parents. You would fathom the sea with a pole. You are astray. You are struggling to get back to your natural self, but cannot find the way. Alas! alas!"

Nan Yung begged to be allowed to remain, and set to work to cultivate the good and eliminate the evil within him. At the expiration of ten days, with sorrow in his heart, he again sought Lao Tzu.

"Have you thoroughly cleansed yourself?" said Lao Tzu. "But this grieved look.... There is some evil obstruction yet.

"If the disturbances are external, do not be always combating them, but close the channels to the mind. If the disturbances are internal, do not strive to oppose them, but close all entrance from without.

If the disturbances are both internal and external, then you will not even be able to hold fast to Tao, still less practise it."

"If a rustic is sick," said Nan Yung, "and another rustic goes to see him; and if the sick man can say what is the matter with him,—then he is not seriously ill. Yet my search after Tao is like swallowing drugs which only increase the malady.

I beg therefore merely to ask the art of preserving life."

然其病，病者猶未病也。 若趎之聞大道，譬猶飲藥以加病也。 趎願聞衛生之經而已矣。」老子曰：「衛生之經，能抱一乎！能勿失乎！能無卜筮而知吉凶乎！能止乎！能已乎！能舍諸人而求諸己乎！能翛然乎！能侗然乎！能兒子乎！兒子終日嗥而嗌不嗄，和之至也；終日握而手不掜，共其德也；終日視而目不瞬，偏不在外也。 行不知所之，居不知所為，與物委蛇，而同其波。 是衛生之經已。」南榮趎曰：「然則是至人之德已乎？」曰：「非也。 是乃所謂冰解凍釋者，能乎？夫至人者，相與交食乎地而交樂乎天，不以人物利害相攖，不相與為怪，不相與為謀，不相與為事，翛然而往，侗然而來。是謂衛生之經已。」曰：「然則是至乎？」曰：「未也。 吾固告汝曰：『能兒子乎！』兒子動不知所為，行不知所之，身若槁木之枝而心若死灰。 若是者，禍亦不至，福亦不來。 禍福無有，惡有人災也！」

宇泰定者，發乎天光。發乎天光者，人見其人。人有修者，乃今有恆。有恆者，人舍之，天助之。人之所舍，謂之天民；天之所助，謂之天子。

"The art of preserving life," replied Lao Tzu, "consists in being able to keep all in One, to lose nothing, to estimate good and evil without divination, to know when to stop, and how much is enough, to leave others alone and attend to oneself, to be without cares and without knowledge,—to be in fact as a child. A child will cry all day and not become hoarse, because of the perfection of its constitutional harmony.

It will keep its fist tightly closed all day and not open it, because of the concentration of its virtue. It will gaze all day without taking off its eyes, because its sight is not attracted by externals. In motion, it knows not whither it is bound; at rest, it is not conscious of doing anything; but unconsciously adapts itself to the exigencies of its environment. This is the art of preserving life."

"Is this then the virtue of the perfect man?" cried Nan Yung.

"Not so," said Lao Tzu. "I am, as it were, but breaking the ice.

"The perfect man shares the food of this earth, but the happiness of God. He does not incur trouble either from men or things. He does not join in censuring, in plotting, in toadying. Free from care he comes, and unconscious he goes;—this is the art of preserving life."

"This then is perfection?" inquired Nan Yung.

"Not yet," said Lao Tzu. "I specially asked if you could be as a child. A child acts without knowing what it does; moves without knowing whither. Its body is like a dry branch; its heart like dead ashes. Thus, good and evil fortune find no lodgment therein; and there where good and evil fortune are not, how can the troubles of mortality be?

"Those whose hearts are in a state of repose give forth a divine radiance, by the light of which they see themselves as they are. And only by cultivating such repose can man attain to the constant.

"Those who are constant are sought after by men and assisted by God. Those who are sought after by men are the people of God; those who are assisted by God are his chosen children.

"To study this is to study what cannot be learnt. To practise this is to practise what cannot be accomplished. To discuss this is to discuss what can never be proved. Let knowledge stop at the unknowable. That is perfection. And for those who do not follow this, God will destroy them!

"With such defences for the body, ever prepared for the unexpected, deferential to the rights of others,—if then calamities overtake you, these

　　學者，學其所不能學也；行者，行其所不能行也；辯者，辯其所不能辯也。知止乎其所不能知，至矣；若有不即是者，天鈞敗之。

　　備物以將形，藏不虞以生心，敬中以達彼。若是而萬惡至者，皆天也，而非人也，不足以滑成，不可內於靈臺。靈臺者有持，而不知其所持，而不可持者也。不見其誠己而發，每發而不當，業入而不舍，每更為失。為不善乎顯明之中者，人得而誅之；為不善乎幽閒之中者，鬼得而誅之。明乎人，明乎鬼者，然後能獨行。券內者，行乎無名；券外者，志乎期費。行乎無名者，唯庸有光；志乎期費者，唯賈人也。人見其跂，猶之魁然。與物窮者，物入焉；與物且者，其身之不能容，焉能容人！不能容人者無親，無親者盡人。兵莫憯於志，鏌邪為下；寇莫大於陰陽，無所逃於天地之間。非陰陽賊之，心則使之也。

　　道通，其分也，其成也毀也。所惡乎分者，其分也以備；所以惡乎備者，其有以備。故出而不反，見其鬼；出而得，是謂得死。滅而有

are from God, not from man. Let them not disturb what you have already achieved. Let them not penetrate into the soul's abode. For there resides the Will. And if the will knows not what to will, it will not be able to will.

"Whatsoever is not said in all sincerity, is wrongly said. And not to be able to rid oneself of this vice is only to sink deeper towards perdition.

"Those who do evil in the open light of day,—men will punish them. Those who do evil in secret,—God will punish them. Who fears both man and God, he is fit to walk alone.

Those who are devoted to the internal, in practice acquire no reputation. Those who are devoted to the external, strive for pre-eminence among their fellows. Practice without reputation throws a halo around the meanest. But he who strives for pre-eminence among his fellows, he is as a huckster whose weariness all perceive though he himself puts on an air of gaiety.

"He who is naturally in sympathy with man, to him all men come. But he who forcedly adapts, has no room even for himself, still less for others. And he who has no room for others, has no ties. It is all over with him.

"There is no weapon so deadly as man's will. Excalibur is second to it. There is no bandit so powerful as Nature.

In the whole universe there is no escape from it. Yet it is not Nature which does the injury. It is man's own heart.

"Tao informs its own subdivisions, their successes and their failures. What is feared in subdivision is separation.

What is feared in separation, is further separation.

Thus, to issue forth without return, this is development of the supernatural. To issue forth and attain the goal, this is called death. To be annihilated and yet to exist, this is convergence of the supernatural into One. To make things which have form appear to all intents and purposes formless,—this is the sum of all things.

"Birth is not a beginning; death is not an end. There is existence without limitation; there is continuity without a starting-point. Existence without limitation is Space. Continuity without a starting-point is Time. There is birth, there is death, there is issuing forth, there is entering in. That through which one passes in and out without seeing its form, that is the Portal of God.

"The Portal of God is Non-Existence. All things sprang from Non-Ex-

實，鬼之一也。以有形者象無形者而定矣！出無本，入無竅，有實而無乎處，有長而無乎本剽，有所出而無竅者有實。有實而無乎處者，宇也。有長而無本剽者，宙也。有乎生，有乎死，有乎出，有乎入。入出而無見其形，是謂天門。天門者，無有也，萬物出乎無有。有不能以有為有，必出乎無有，而無有一無有。聖人藏乎是。古之人，其知有所至矣。惡乎至？有以為未始有物者，至矣，盡矣，弗可以加矣！其次以為有物矣，物以生為喪也，以死為反也，是以分已。其次曰始無有，既而有生，生俄而死。以無有為首，以生為體，以死為尻；孰知有無死生之一守者，吾與之為友。是三者雖異，公族也。昭景也，著戴也，甲氏也，著封也，非一也。有生，黬

istence. Existence could not make existence existence. It must have proceeded from Non-Existence,

And Non-Existence and Nothing are One.

Herein is the abiding-place of the Sage.

"The knowledge of the ancients reached the highest point,—the time before anything existed.

This is the highest point. It is exhaustive. There is no adding to it.

"The second best was that of those who started from existence. Life was to them a misfortune. Death was a return home. There was already separation.

"The next in the scale said that at the beginning there was nothing. Then life came, to be quickly followed by death. They made Nothing the head, Life the trunk, and Death the tail of existence, claiming as friends whoever knew that existence and non-existence, and life and death were all One.

"These three classes, though different, were of the same clan; as were Chao Ching who inherited fame, and Chia who inherited territory.

"Man's life is as the soot on a kettle.

Yet men speak of the subjective point of view. But this subjective point of view will not bear the test. It is a point of knowledge we cannot reach.

"At the winter sacrifice, the tripe may be separated from the great toe; yet these cannot be separated.

He who looks at a house, visits the ancestral hall, and even the latrines. Thus every point is the subjective point of view.

"Let us try to formulate this subjective point of view. It originates with life, and, with knowledge as its tutor, drifts into the admission of right and wrong.

But one's own standard of right is the standard, and others have to adapt themselves to it. Men will die for this. Such people look upon the useful as appertaining to wisdom, the useless as appertaining to folly; upon success in life as honourable, upon failure as dishonourable.

The subjective point of view is that of the present generation, who like the cicada and the young dove see things only from their own standpoint.

"If a man treads upon a stranger's toe in the market-place, he apologises on the score of hurry. If an elder brother does this, he is quit with an exclamation of sympathy. And if a parent does so, nothing whatever is

也，披然日移是。嘗言移是，非所言也。雖然，不可知者也。臘者之有膍胲，可散而不可散也；觀室者周於寢廟，又適其偃焉，為是舉移是。請嘗言移是。是以生為本，以知為師，因以乘是非；果有名實，因以己為質；使人以為己節，因以死償節。若然者，以用為知，以不用為愚，以徹為名，以窮為辱。移是，今之人也，是蜩與學鳩同於同也。

蹍市人之足，則辭以放驁，兄則以嫗，大親則已矣。故日，至禮有不人，至義不物，至知不謀，至仁無親，至信辟金。

徹志之勃，解心之謬，去德之累，達道之塞。貴富顯嚴名利六者，勃志也。容動色理氣意六者，謬心也。惡欲喜怒哀樂六者，累德也。去就取與知能六者，塞道也。此四六者不蕩胸中則正，正則靜，靜則明，明則虛，虛則無為而無不為也。

done.

"Therefore it has been said, 'Perfect politeness is not artificial; perfect duty to one's neighbour is not a matter of calculation; perfect wisdom takes no thought; perfect charity recognises no ties; perfect trust requires no pledges.'

"Discard the stimuli of purpose. Free the mind from disturbances. Get rid of entanglements to virtue. Pierce the obstructions to Tao.

"Honours, wealth, distinction, power, fame, gain,—these six stimulate purpose.

"Mien, carriage, beauty, arguments, influence, opinions,—these six disturb the mind.

"Hate, ambition, joy, anger, sorrow, pleasure,—these six are entanglements to virtue.

"Rejecting, adopting, receiving, giving, knowledge, ability,—these six are obstructions to Tao.

"If these twenty-four be not allowed to run riot, then the mind will be duly ordered. And being duly ordered, it will be in repose. And being in repose, it will be clear of perception. And being clear of perception, it will be unconditioned. And being unconditioned, it will be in that state of in-action by which there is nothing which cannot be accomplished.

"Tao is the sovereign lord of Te.

Life is the glorifier of Te.

Nature is the substance of life.

The operation of that nature is action. The perversion of that action is error.

"People who know put forth physical power. People who know employ mental effort. But what people who know do not know is to be as the eye.

"Emotion which is spontaneous is called virtue passive. Emotion which is not evoked by the external is called virtue active. The names of these are antagonistic; but essentially they are in accord.

"Yi was skilled in hitting the bull's-eye; but stupid at preventing people from praising him for so doing.

The Sage devotes himself to the natural and neglects the artificial. For only the Perfect Man can devote himself profitably to the natural and arti-ficial alike. Insects influence insects; because insects are natural. When the Perfect Man hates the natural, it is the artificially natural which he hates.

　　道者，德之欽也；生者，德之胸也；性者，生之質也。性之動，謂之為；為之偽，謂之失。知者，接也；知者，謨也。知者之所不知，猶睨也。動以不得已之謂德，動無非我之謂治，名相反而實相順也。

　　羿工乎中微而拙乎使人無己譽。聖人工乎天而拙乎人。夫工乎天而俍乎人者，唯全人能之。雖蟲能蟲，雖蟲能天。全人惡天？惡人之天？而況吾天乎人乎！

　　一雀適羿，羿必得之，或也。以天下為之籠，則雀無所逃。是故湯以胞人籠伊尹，秦穆公以五羊之皮籠百里奚。是故非以其所好籠之而可得者，無有也。介者拸畫，外非譽也；胥靡登高而不懼，遺死生也。夫復謵不餽而忘人，忘人，因以為天人矣。故敬之而不喜，侮之而不怒者，唯同乎天和者為然。出怒不怒，則怒出於不怒矣；出為無為，則為出於無為矣。欲靜則平氣，欲神則順心。有為也，欲當則緣於不得已。不得已之類，聖人之道。

How much more man's alternate naturalness and artificiality?

"If a bird falls in with Yi, Yi will get it. Such is his skill. And if the world were made into a cage, birds would have no place of escape. So it was that by cookery T'ang got hold of I Yin, and by five rams' skins Duke Mu of Ch'in got Po Li Ch'i. But had these princes not been themselves successful at getting, they never would have got these men.

"A one-legged man discards ornament, his exterior not being open to commendation. Condemned criminals will go up to great heights without fear, for they no longer regard life and death from their former point of view. And those who pay no attention to their moral clothing and condition become oblivious of their own personality; and by thus becoming oblivious of their personality, they proceed to be the people of God.

"Wherefore, if men revere them, they rejoice not. If men insult them, they are not angered. But only those who have passed into the eternal harmony of God are capable of this.

"If your anger is external, not internal, it will be anger proceeding from not-anger. If your actions are external, not internal, they will be actions proceeding from inaction.

"If you would attain peace, level down your emotional nature. If you desire spirituality, cultivate adaptation of the intelligence. If you would have your actions in accordance with what is right, allow yourself to fall in with the dictates of necessity. For necessity is the Tao of the Sage."

# 徐無鬼第二十四

　　徐無鬼因女商見魏武侯，武侯勞之曰：「先生病矣，苦於山林之勞，故乃肯見於寡人。」徐無鬼曰：「我則勞於君，君有何勞於我！君將盈耆欲，長好惡，則性命之情病矣；君將黜耆欲，掔好惡，則耳目病矣。我將勞君，君有何勞於我！」武侯超然不對。少焉，徐無鬼曰：「嘗語君，吾相狗也。下之質執飽而止，是狸德也；中之質若視日；上之質若亡其一。吾相狗，又不若吾相馬也。吾相馬，直者中繩，曲者中鉤，方者中矩，圓者中規，是國馬也，而未若天下馬也。天下馬有成材，若卹若失，若喪其一，若是者，超軼絕塵，不知其所。」武侯大說而笑。徐無鬼出，女商曰：「先生獨何以說吾君乎？吾所以說吾君者，橫說之則以《詩》、《書》、《禮》、《樂》，從說之則以《金板》、《六弢》，奉事而大有功者不可為數，而吾君未嘗啟齒。今先生何以說吾君，

# CHAPTER XXIV

## Hsu Wu Kuei

Hsu Wu Kuei, introduced by Nu Shang, went to see Wu Hou of Wei.

The Prince greeted him sympathisingly, and said, "You are suffering, Sir. You must have endured great hardships in your mountain life that you should be willing to leave it and visit me."

"It is I who should sympathise with your Highness, not your Highness with me," answered Hsu Wu Kuei. "If your Highness gives free play to passion and yields to loves and hates, then the natural conditions of your existence will suffer.

And if your Highness puts aside passion and abjures loves and hates, then your senses of sight and hearing will suffer.

It is I who should sympathise with your Highness, not your Highness with me."

The Prince was too astonished to reply; and after a while Hsu Wu Kuei continued, "I will try to explain to your Highness how I judge of dogs. The lowest in the scale will eat their fill and then stop, like a cat. Those of the middle class are as though staring at the sun. The highest class are as though they had parted with their own individuality.

"But I do not judge of dogs as well as I judge of horses. I judge of horses as follows. Their straightness must be that of a line. Their curve must be that of an arc. Their squareness, that of the square. Their roundness, that of the compasses.

These are the horses of the State. They are not equal to the horses of the Empire. The horses of the Empire are splendid. They move as though anxious to get along, as though they had lost the way, as though they had parted with their own individuality. Thus, they outstrip all competitors, over the unstirred dust, out of sight!"

The Prince was greatly pleased and smiled. But when Hsu Wu Kuei went out, Nu Shang asked him, saying, "What can you have been saying to his Highness? Whenever I address him, it is either in a pacific sense, based upon the Canons of Poetry, History, Rites, and Music; or in a belligerent sense, based upon the Golden Roster or the Six Plans of Battle.

I have transacted with great success innumerable matters entrusted

使吾君說若此乎?」徐無鬼曰:「吾直告之吾相狗馬耳。」女商曰:「若是乎?」曰:「子不聞夫越之流人乎?去國數日,見其所知而喜;去國旬月,見所嘗見於國中者喜;及期年也,見似人者而喜矣;不亦去人滋久,思人滋深乎?夫逃虛空者,藜藋柱乎鼪鼬之徑,踉位其空,聞人足音跫然而喜矣,又況乎昆弟親戚之謦欬其側者乎!久矣夫莫以真人之言謦欬吾君之側乎!」

徐無鬼見武侯,武侯曰:「先生居山林,食芧栗,厭蔥韭,以賓寡人,久矣夫!今老邪?其欲干酒肉之味邪?其寡人亦有社稷之福邪?」徐無鬼曰:「無鬼生於貧賤,未嘗敢飲食君之酒肉,將來勞君也。」君曰:「何哉!奚勞寡人?」曰:「勞君之神與形。」武侯曰:「何謂邪?」徐無鬼曰:「天地之養也一,登高不可以為長,居下不可以為短。君獨為萬乘之主,以苦一國之民,以養耳目鼻口,夫神者不自許也。夫神者,好和而惡姦。夫姦,病也,故勞之。唯君所病之,何也?」武侯曰:「欲見先生久矣!吾欲愛民而為義偃兵,其可乎?」徐無鬼曰:「不可。愛民,害民之始也;為義偃兵,

to me, yet his Highness has never vouchsafed a smile. What can you have been saying to make him so pleased as all this?"

"I merely told him," replied Hsu Wu Kuei, "how I judged of dogs and horses."

"Was that all?" enquired Nu Shang, incredulously.

"Have you not heard," said Hsu Wu Kuei, "of the outlaw of Yueh? After several days' absence from his State, he was glad to meet any one he had known there. After a month, he was glad to meet any one he had even seen there. And after a year, he was glad to meet any one who was in any way like to his fellow-countrymen. Is not this a case of absence from one's kind increasing the desire to be with them?

"Thus a man who had fled into the wilderness, where bishop-wort chokes the path of the weasel and stoat, now advancing, now stopping,—how he would rejoice if the footfall of a fellow-creature broke upon his ear. And how much more were he to hear the sound of a brother's, of a relative's voice at his side. Long it is, I ween, since his Highness has heard the voice of a pure man at his side!"

Hsu Wu Kuei went to visit the Prince. The latter said, "Living, Sir, up in the hills, and feeding upon berries or satisfying yourself with leeks, you have long neglected me. Are you now growing old? Or do you hanker after flesh-pots and wine? Or is it that mine is such a well-governed State?"

"I am of lowly birth," replied Hsu Wu Kuei. "I could not venture to eat and drink your Highness' meat and wine. I came to sympathise with your Highness."

"What do you mean?" cried the Prince? "What is there to sympathise about?"

"About your Highness' soul and body," replied Hsu Wu Kuei.

"Pray explain," said the Prince.

"Nourishment is nourishment," said Hsu Wu Kuei.

"Being high up does not make one high, nor does being low make one low. Your Highness is the ruler of a large State, and you oppress the whole population thereof in order to satisfy your sensualities. But your soul is not a party to this. The soul loves harmony and hates disorder. For disorder is a disease. Therefore I came to sympathise. How is it that your Highness alone is suffering?"

"I have long desired to see you," answered the Prince. "I wish to love

造兵之本也。　君自此為之，　則殆不成。　凡成美，惡器也；君雖為仁義，　幾且偽哉！形固造形，　成固有伐，　變固外戰。　君亦必無盛鶴列於麗譙之間。　無徒驥於錙壇之宮，　無藏逆於得！無以巧勝人，　無以謀勝人，　無以戰勝人。　夫殺人之士民，兼人之土地，以養吾私與吾神者，其戰不知孰善？勝之惡乎在？君若勿已矣！修胸中之誠，　以應天地之情而勿攖。　夫民死已脫矣，　君將惡乎用夫偃兵哉！

　黃帝將見大隗乎具茨之山，　方明為御，　昌寓驂乘，　張若謵朋前馬，　昆閽滑稽後車；至於襄城之野，　七聖皆迷，　無所問塗。　適遇牧馬童子，問塗焉，　曰：「若知具茨之山乎？」曰：「然。」「若知大隗之所存乎？」曰：「然。」黃帝曰：「異哉小童！非徒知具茨之山，　又知大隗之所存。　請問為天下。」小童曰：「夫為天下者，　亦若此而已矣，

my people, and by cultivation of duty towards one's neighbour to put an end to war. Can this be done?"

"It cannot," replied Hsu Wu Kuei. "Love for the people is the root of all evil to the people.

Cultivation of duty towards one's neighbour in order to put an end to war is the origin of all fighting. If your Highness starts from this basis, the result can only be disastrous.

"Everything that is made good, turns out bad.

And although your Highness should make charity and duty to one's neighbour, I fear they would be spurious articles. For the inward intention would appear in the outward manifestation. The adoption of a fixed standard would lead to complications. And revolutions within lead to fighting without. Surely your Highness would not make a bower into a battlefield, nor a shrine of prayer into a scene of warfare!

"Have nothing within which is obstructive of virtue. Seek not to vanquish others in cunning, in plotting, in war. If I slay a whole nation and annex the territory in order to find nourishment for my passions and for my soul,—irrespective of military skill, wherein does the victory lie?

"If your Highness will only abstain, that will be enough. Cultivate the sincerity that is within your breast, so as to be responsive to the conditions of your environment, and be not aggressive. The people will thus escape death; and what need then to put an end to war?"

When the Yellow Emperor went to see Tao upon the Chu-tz'u Mountain, Fang Ming was his charioteer, Ch'ang Yu sat on his right, Chang Jo and Hsi P'eng were his outriders, and K'un Hun and Hua Chi brought up the rear.

On reaching the wilds of Hsiang-ch'eng, these seven Sages lost their way and there was no one of whom to ask the road. By and by, they fell in with a boy who was grazing horses, and asked him, saying, "Do you know the Chu-tz'u Mountain?"

"I do," replied the boy.

"And can you tell us," continued the Sages, "where Tao abides?"

"I can," replied the boy.

"This is a strange lad," cried the Yellow Emperor. "Not only does he know where the Chu-tz'u Mountain is, but also where Tao abides! Come tell me, pray, how would you govern the empire?"

又奚事焉！予少而自遊於六合之內，予適有瞀病，有長者教予曰：『若乘日之車而遊於襄城之野。』今予病少痊，予又且復遊於六合之外。夫為天下，亦若此而已。予又奚事焉！」黃帝曰：「夫為天下者，則誠非吾子之事，雖然，請問為天下。」小童辭。黃帝又問。小童曰：「夫為天下者，亦奚以異乎牧馬者哉！亦去其害馬者而已矣！」黃帝再拜稽首，稱天師而退。

知士無思慮之變則不樂，辯士無談說之序則不樂，察士無凌誶之事則不樂，皆囿於物者也。招世之士興朝，中民之士榮官。筋力之士矜難，勇敢之士奮患，兵革之士樂戰，枯槁之士宿名，法律之士廣治，禮樂之士敬容，仁義之士貴際。農夫無草萊之事則不比，商賈無市井之事則不比。庶人有旦暮之業則勸，百工有器械之巧則壯。錢財不積則貪者憂，權勢不尤則夸者悲，勢物之徒樂變，遭時有所用，不能無為也，此皆順比於歲，不物於易者也，馳其形性，潛之萬物，終身不反，悲夫！

"I should govern the empire," said the boy, "just the same as I look after my horses. What else should I do?

"When I was a little boy and used to live within the points of the compass, my eyes got dim of sight. An old man advised me to mount the chariot of the sun and visit the wilds of Hsiang-ch'eng. My sight is now much better, and I continue to dwell without the points of the compass. I should govern the empire in just the same way. What else should I do?"

"Of course," said the Yellow Emperor, "government is not your trade. Still I should be glad to hear what you would do."

The boy declined to answer, but on being again urged, cried out, "What difference is there between governing the empire and looking after horses? See that no harm comes to the horses, that is all!"

Thereupon the Emperor prostrated himself before the boy; and addressing him as Divine Teacher, took his leave.

If schemers have nothing to give them anxiety, they are not happy. If dialecticians have not their premises and conclusion, they are not happy. If critics have none on whom to vent their spleen, they are not happy. Such men are the slaves of objective existences.

Those who attract the sympathies of the world, start new dynasties. Those who win the people's hearts, take high official rank. Those who are strong undertake difficulties. Those who are brave encounter dangers. Men of arms delight in war. Men of peace think of nothing but reputation. Men of law strive to improve the administration. Professors of ceremony and music cultivate deportment. Moralists devote themselves to the obligations between man and man.

Take away agriculture from the husbandman, and his classification is gone. Take away trade from the merchant, and his classification is gone. Daily work is the stimulus of the labourer. The skill of the artisan is his pride. If money cannot be made, the avaricious man is sad. If his power meets with a check, the boaster will repine. Ambitious men love change.

Thus, men are always doing something; inaction is to them impossible. They observe in this the same regularity as the seasons, ever without change. They hurry to destruction, dissipating in all directions their vital forces, alas! never to return.

Chuang Tzu said, "If archers who aimed at nothing and hit something were accounted good shots, everybody in the world would be another Yi.

　莊子曰：「射者非前期而中，謂之善射，天下皆羿也，可乎？」惠子曰：「可。」莊子曰：「天下非有公是也，而各是其所是，天下皆堯也，可乎？」惠子曰：「可。」莊子曰：「然則儒墨楊秉四，與夫子為五，果孰是邪？或者若魯遽者邪？其弟子曰：『我得夫子之道矣，吾能冬爨鼎而夏造冰矣！』魯遽曰：『是直以陽召陽，以陰召陰，非吾所謂道也，吾示子乎吾道。』於是為之調瑟，廢一於堂，廢一於室，鼓宮宮動，鼓角角動，音律同矣。夫或改調一弦，於五音無當也，鼓之，二十五弦皆動，未始異於聲，而音之君已。且若是者邪？」惠子曰：「今乎儒墨楊秉，且方與我以辯，相拂以辭，相鎮以聲，而未始吾非也，則奚若矣？」莊子曰：「齊人蹢子於宋者，其命閽也不以完，其求鈃鐘也以束縛，其求唐子也而未始出域，有遺類矣！夫楚人寄而謫閽者，夜半於無人之時而與舟人鬥，未始離於岑而足以造於怨也。」

Could this be so?"

"It could," replied Hui Tzu.

"If there was no general standard of right in the world," continued Chuang Tzu, "but each man had his own, then everybody would be a Yao. Could this be so?"

"It could," replied Hui Tzu.

"Very well," said Chuang Tzu. "Now there are the Confucianists, the Mihists, the schools of Yang and Ping, making with your own five in all. Pray which of these is right?

"Possibly it is a similar case to that of Lu Chu?

"—A disciple said to him, 'Master, I have attained to your Tao. I can do without fire in winter: I can make ice in summer.'

"'You merely avail yourself of latent heat and latent cold,' replied Lu Chu. 'That is not what I call Tao. I will demonstrate to you what my Tao is.'

"Thereupon he tuned two lutes, and placed one in the hall and the other in the adjoining room.

And when he struck the Kung note on one, the Kung note on the other sounded; when he struck the chio note on one, the chio note on the other sounded. This because they were both tuned to the same pitch.

"But if he changed the interval of one string, so that it no longer kept its place in the octave, and then struck it, the result was that all the twenty-five strings jangled together. There was sound as before, but the influence of the key-note was gone. Is this your case?"

"The Confucianists, the Mihists, and the followers of Yang and Ping," replied Hui Tzu, "are just now engaged in discussing this matter with me. They try to overwhelm me with argument or howl me down with noise. Yet they have not proved me wrong. Why then should you?"

"A man of the Ch'i State," replied Chuang Tzu, "sent away his son into the Sung State, to be a door-keeper, with maimed body.

But a vase, which he valued highly, he kept carefully wrapped up.

"He who would seek for a stray child, but will not leave his home, is like to lose him.

"If a man of Ch'u, who was sent away to be a door-keeper, began, in the middle of the night, when no one was about, to fight with the boatman, I should say that before his boat left the shore he would already have

　　莊子送葬，過惠子之墓，顧謂從者曰：「郢人堊慢其鼻端若蠅翼，使匠人斲之。匠石運斤成風，聽而斲之，盡堊而鼻不傷，郢人立不失容。宋元君聞之，召匠石曰：『嘗試為寡人為之。』匠石曰：『臣則嘗能斲之。雖然，臣之質死久矣。』自夫子之死也，吾無以為質矣，吾無與言之矣！」

　　管仲有病，桓公問之，曰：「仲父之病病矣，可不謂，云至於大病，則寡人惡乎屬國而可？」管仲曰：「公誰欲與？」公曰：「鮑叔牙。」曰：「不可。其為人潔廉善士也。其於不己若者不比之。又一聞人之過，終身不忘。使之治國，上且鉤乎君，下且逆乎民。其得罪於君也，將弗久矣！」公曰：「然，則孰可？」對曰：「勿已，則隰朋可。其為人也，上忘而下畔，愧不若黃帝，而哀不己若者。以德分人謂之聖，以財分人謂之賢。以賢臨人，未有得人者也；以賢下人，未有不得人者也。其於國有不聞也，其於家有不見也。勿已，則隰朋可。」

got himself into considerable trouble."

Chuang Tzu was once attending a funeral, when he passed by the grave of Hui Tzu. Turning to his attendants, he said, "A man of Ying who had his nose covered with a hard scab, no thicker than a fly's wing, sent for a stone-mason to chip it off. The stone-mason plied his adze with great dexterity while the patient sat still and let him chip. When the scab was all off, the nose was found to be uninjured, the man of Ying never having moved a muscle.

"When Yuan, prince of Sung, heard of this, he summoned the stone-mason and said, 'Try to do the same for me.'

"'I used to be able to do it Sire,' replied the stone-mason, 'but my material has long since perished.'

"And I too, ever since he perished, have been without my material, having no one with whom I can speak."

Kuan Chung being at the point of death, Duke Huan went to see him.

"You are ill, venerable Sir," said the Duke, "really ill. You had better say to whom, in the event of your getting worse, I am to entrust the administration of the State."

"Whom does your Highness wish to choose?" enquired Kuan Chung.

"Will Pao Yu do?" asked the Duke.

"He will not," said Kuan Chung. "He is pure, incorruptible, and good. With those who are not like himself, he will not associate. And if he has once heard of a man's wrong-doing, he never forgets it. If you employ him in the administration of the empire, he will get to loggerheads with his prince and to sixes and sevens with the people. It would not be long before he and your Highness fell out."

"Whom then can we have?" asked the Duke.

"There is no alternative," replied Kuan Chung; "it must be Hsi P'eng. He is a man who forgets the authority of those above him, and makes those below him forget his. Ashamed that he is not the peer of the Yellow Emperor, he grieves over those who are not the peers of himself.

"To share one's virtue with others is called true wisdom. To share one's wealth with others is reckoned meritorious. To exhibit superior merit is not the way to win men's hearts. To exhibit inferior merit is the way. There are things in the State he does not hear; there are things in the family he does not see.

吳王浮於江，登乎狙之山，眾狙見之，恂然棄而走，逃於深蓁。有一狙焉，委蛇攫搔，見巧乎王。王射之，敏給搏捷矢。王命相者趨射之，狙執死。王顧謂其友顏不疑曰：「之狙也，伐其巧、恃其便，以敖予，以至此殛也。戒之哉！嗟乎，無以汝色驕人哉？」顏不疑歸而師董梧，以鋤其色，去樂辭顯，三年而國人稱之。

南伯子綦隱几而坐，仰天而噓。顏成子入見曰：「夫子，物之尤也，形固可使若槁骸，心固可使若死灰乎？」曰：「吾嘗居山穴之中矣。當是時也，田禾一睹我，而齊國之眾三賀之。我必先之，彼故知之；我必賣之，彼故鬻之。若我而不有之，彼惡得而知之？若我而不賣之，彼惡得而鬻之？嗟乎！我悲人之自喪者，吾又悲夫悲人者。吾又悲夫悲人之悲者，其後而日遠矣！」

仲尼之楚，楚王觴之。孫叔敖執爵而立。市南宜僚受酒而祭，曰：「古之人乎！於此言已。」曰：「丘也聞不言之言矣，未之嘗言，於此乎言之。市南宜僚弄丸而兩家之難解。孫叔敖甘寢秉羽而郢人投兵。丘願有喙三尺。」彼之謂不道之道，

There is no alternative; it must be Hsi P'eng."

The prince of Wu took a boat and went to the Monkey Mountain, which he ascended. When the monkeys saw him, they fled in terror and hid themselves in the thicket. One of them, however, disported himself carelessly, as though showing off its skill before the prince. The prince took a shot at it; but the monkey, with great rapidity, seized the flying arrow with its hand. Then the prince bade his guards try, the result being that the monkey was killed.

Thereupon the prince turned to his friend Yen Pu I, and said, "That monkey flaunted its skill and its dexterity in my face. Therefore it has come to this pass. Beware! Do not flaunt your superiority in the faces of others."

Yen Pu I went home, and put himself under the tuition of Tung Wu, with a view to get rid of such superiority. He put aside all that gave him pleasure and avoided gaining reputation. And in three years his praise was in everybody's mouth.

Tzu Chi of Nan-poh was sitting leaning on a table. He looked up to heaven and sighed, at which juncture Yen Ch'eng Tzu entered and said, "How, Sir, can such an important person as yourself be in body like dry wood, in mind like dead ashes?"

"I used to live in a cave on the hills," replied Tzu Chi. "At that time, T'ien Ho, because he once saw me, was thrice congratulated by the people of Ch'i. Now I must have given some indication by which he recognised me.

I must have sold for him to buy. For had I not manifested myself, how would he have recognised me? Had I not sold, how could he have bought?

"Alas! I grieve over man's self-destruction.

And then I grieve over one who grieves for another. And then I grieve over him who grieves over one who grieves for another! And so I get daily farther and farther away."

When Confucius went to Ch'u, the prince entertained him at a banquet. Sun Shu Ao stood up with a goblet of wine in his hand, and I Liao of Shih-nan poured a libation, saying, "On such occasions as this, the men of old were wont to make some utterance."

"Mine," replied Confucius, "is the doctrine of wordless utterances. Shall I who make no utterances, make utterance now?

此之謂不言之辯，故德總乎道之所一。而言休乎知之所不知，至矣。道之所一者，德不能同也；知之所不能知者，辯不能舉也；名若儒墨而凶矣。故海不辭東流，大之至也；聖人並包天地，澤及天下，而不知其誰氏。是故生無爵，死無謚，實不聚，名不立，此之謂大人。狗不以善吠為良，人不以善言為賢，而況為大乎！夫為大不足以為大，而況為德乎！夫大備矣，莫若天地；然奚求焉，而大備矣！知大備者，無求，無失，無棄，不以物易己也。反己而不窮，循古而不摩，大人之誠！

"I Liao of Shih-nan played with his ball, and the trouble of two houses was arranged.

Sun Shu Ao remained quietly in repose, and the men of Ying threw down their arms.

I should want a three-foot tongue indeed!

"Theirs was the Tao of inaction. His was the argument of silence. Wherefore, for Te to rest in undivided Tao, and for speech to stop at the unknowable,—this is perfection.

"With undivided Tao, Te cannot be coincident.

No argument can demonstrate the unknowable. Subdivision into Confucianists and Mihists only makes confusion worse confounded.

"The sea does not reject the streams which flow eastward into it. Therefore it is immeasurably great. The true Sage folds the universe in his bosom. His good influence benefits all throughout the empire, without respect to persons. Born without rank, he dies without titles. He does not take credit for realities.

He does not establish a name.

This is to be a great man.

"A dog is not considered a good dog because he is a good barker.

A man is not considered a good man because he is a good talker. How much less in the case of greatness? And if doing great things is not enough to secure greatness, how much less shall it secure virtue?

"In point of greatness, there is nothing to be compared with the universe. Yet what does the universe seek in order to be great?

"He who understands greatness in this sense, seeks nothing, loses nothing, rejects nothing, never suffers injury from without. He takes refuge in his own inexhaustibility. He finds safety in according with his nature. This is the essence of true greatness."

Tzu Chi had eight sons. He ranged them before him, and summoning Chiu Fang Yin, said to him, "Examine my sons physiognomically, and tell me which will be the fortunate one."

"K'un," replied Chiu Fang Yin, "will be the fortunate one."

"In what sense?" asked the father, beaming with delight.

"K'un," said Chiu Fang Yin, "will eat at the table of a prince, and so end his days."

Thereupon Tzu Chi burst into tears and said, "What has my son done

　　子綦有八子，陳諸前，召九方歅曰：「為我相吾子，孰為祥？」九方歅曰：「梱也為祥。」子綦瞿然喜曰：「奚若？」曰：「梱也將與國君同食以終其身。」子綦索然出涕曰：「吾子何為以至於是極也？」九方歅曰：「夫與國君同食，澤及三族，而況父母乎！今夫子聞之而泣，是禦福也。子則祥矣，父則不祥。」子綦曰：「歅，汝何足以識之。而梱祥邪？盡於酒肉，入於鼻口矣，而何足以知其所自來？吾未嘗為牧而牂生於奧，未嘗好田而鶉生於宎，若勿怪，何邪？吾所與吾子游者，游於天地。吾與之邀樂於天，吾與之邀食於地。吾不與之為事，不與之為謀，不與之為怪；吾與之乘天地之誠，而不以物與之相攖，吾與之一委蛇而不與之為事所宜，今也然，有世俗之償焉！凡有怪徵者，必有怪行，殆乎！非我與吾子之罪，幾天與之也！吾是以泣也。」無幾何而使梱之於燕，盜得之於道，全而鬻之則難，不若刖之則易。於是刖而鬻之於齊，適當渠公之街，然身食肉而終。

that this should be his fate?"

"Eating at the table of a prince," replied Chiu Fang Yin, "will benefit the family for three generations. How much more his father and mother! But for you, Sir, to go and weep is enough to turn back the luck from you. The son's fortune is good, but the father's bad."

"Yin," said Tzu Chi, "I should like to know what you mean by calling K'un fortunate. Wine and meat gratify the palate, but you do not say how these are to come.

"Supposing that to me, not being a shepherd, a lamb were born in the south-west corner of my hall; or that to me, not being a sportsman, quails were hatched in the north-east corner. If you did not call that uncanny, what would you call it?

"My sons and I do but roam through the universe. With them I seek the joys of heaven; with them I seek the fruits of earth. With them I engage in no business; with them I concoct no plots; with them I attempt nothing out-of-the-way. With them I mount upon the truth of the universe, and do not offer opposition to the exigencies of our environment. With them I accommodate myself naturally; but with them I do not become a slave to circumstances. Yet now the world is rewarding me!

"Every uncanny effect must be preceded by some uncanny cause. Alas! my sons and I have done nothing. It must be the will of God. Therefore I weep."

Shortly afterwards, when K'un was on his way to the Yen State, he was captured by brigands. To sell him as he was, would be no easy matter. To sell him without his feet would be easy enough. So they cut off his feet and sold him into the Ch'i State, where he became door-keeper to Duke Chu and had meat to his dinner for the rest of his life.

Yeh Ch'ueh meeting Hsu Yu, said to him, "Where are you going?"

"Away from Yao!" replied the latter.

"What do you mean?" asked Yeh Ch'ueh.

"Yao," said Hsu Yu, "thinks of nothing but charity. I fear he will become a laughing-stock to the world, and that in future ages men will eat one another.

"There is no difficulty in winning the people. Love them and they will draw near. Profit them and they will come up. Praise them and they will vie with one another. But introduce something they dislike, and they will

　　齧缺遇許由曰：「子將奚之？」曰：「將逃堯。」曰：「奚謂邪？」曰：「夫堯，畜畜然仁，吾恐其為天下笑。後世其人與人相食與！夫民，不難聚也；愛之則親，利之則至，譽之則勸，致其所惡則散。愛利出乎仁義，捐仁義者寡，利仁義者眾。夫仁義之行，唯且無誠，且假乎禽貪者器。是以一人之斷制利天下，譬之猶一覕也。夫堯知賢人之利天下也，而不知其賊天下也，夫唯外乎賢者知之矣。」

　　有暖姝者，有濡需者，有卷婁者。所謂暖姝者，學一先生之言，則暖暖姝姝而私自說也，自以為足矣，而未知未始有物也。是以謂暖姝者也。濡需者，豕蝨是也，擇疏鬣自以為廣宮大囿。奎蹄曲隈，乳間股腳，自以為安室利處。不知屠者之一旦鼓臂布草操煙火，而己與豕俱焦也。此以域進，此以域退，此其所謂濡需者也。卷婁者，舜也。羊肉不慕蟻，蟻慕羊肉，羊肉羶也。舜有羶行，百姓悅之，故三徙成都，至鄧之虛而十有萬家。堯聞舜之賢，舉之童土之地，曰：「冀

be gone.

"Love and profit are born of charity and duty to one's neighbour. Those who ignore charity and duty to one's neighbour are few; those who make capital out of them are many.

"For the operation of these virtues is not disinterested. It is like lending gear to a sportsman.

Wherefore, for one man to dogmatise for the good of the whole empire, is like splitting a thing at a single blow.

"Yao knows that good men benefit the empire. But he does not know that they injure it. Only those on a higher level than good men know this.

"There are nincompoops; there are parasites; there are enthusiasts.

"A man who learns from a single teacher, and then goes off exultant, satisfied with his acquirements though ignorant that there was a time when nothing existed,—such a one is a nincompoop.

"Parasites are like the lice on a pig's back. They choose bald patches, which are to them palaces and parks. The parts between the toes, the joints, the dugs, and the buttocks, are to them so many comfortable and convenient resting-places. They know not that one day the butcher will tuck up his sleeves and spread straw and apply fire, and that they will perish in the singeing of the pig. As they sow, so do they reap. This is to be a parasite.

"Of enthusiasts, Shun is an example. Mutton does not care for ants; it is the ants which care for the mutton. Mutton has a frowsy smell; and there is a frowsiness about Shun which attracts the people. Therefore it was that after three changes of residence, when he came to the Teng district, he had some hundred thousand families with him.

"Then Yao, hearing of his goodness, appointed him to a barren region, trusting, as he said, that Shun's arrival would enrich it. When Shun took up this appointment, he was already old, and his intellect was failing; yet he would not cease work and retire from office. He was, in fact, an enthusiast.

"So it is that the spiritual man dislikes a crowd. For where there is a crowd there is diversity, and where there is diversity advantage does not accrue. He is therefore neither very intimate, nor very distant. He clings to virtue and nourishes a spirit of harmony, in order to be in accord with his fellow-men. This is to be a divine man.

得其來之澤。」舜舉乎童土之地，年齒長矣，聰明衰矣，而不得休歸，所謂卷婁者也。是以神人惡眾至，眾至則不比，不比則不利也。故無所甚親，無所甚疏，抱德煬和，以順天下，此謂真人。於蟻棄知，於魚得計，於羊棄意。以目視目，以耳聽耳，以心復心。若然者，其平也繩，其變也循。古之真人！以天待人，不以人入天，古之真人！

得之也生，失之也死；得之也死，失之也生。藥也其實，菫也，桔梗也，雞癰也，豕零也，是為帝者也，何可勝言！句踐也以甲楯三千棲於會稽，唯種也能知亡之所以存，唯種也不知其身之所以愁。故日：鴟目有所適，鶴脛有所節，解之也悲。故日：風之過河也有損焉，日之過河也有損焉。請只風與日相與守河，而河以為未始其攖也，恃源而往者也。故水之守土也審，影之守人也審，物之守物也審。故目之於明也殆，耳之於聰也殆，心之於殉也殆，凡能其於府也殆，殆之成也不給改。禍之長也茲萃，其反也緣功，其果也待久。而人以為己寶，不亦悲乎！

"Leave wisdom to ants. Strive for what fishes desire.

"Leave attractiveness to mutton. Use your eyes to contemplate, your ears to listen to, your mind to consider, their own internal workings. For him who can do these things, his level will be that of a line, his modifications in due and proper season.

"Therefore, the divine man trusts to the natural development of events. He does not strive to introduce the artificial into the domain of the natural. Accordingly, life is a gain and death a loss, or death is a gain and life a loss.

"For instance, drugs. They are characteristically poisonous. Such are Chieh-Keng, Chi-Yung, and

Shih-Ling. Circumstances, however, make of each a sovereign remedy. The list is inexhaustible.

"When Kou Chien encamped with three thousand armed warriors at Kuei-ch'i, only Chung saw that defeat would be followed by a rally. Yet he could not foresee the evil that was to come upon himself. Wherefore it has been said, 'An owl's eyes are adapted to their use. A crane's leg is of the length required. 'Twould be disastrous to shorten it.'

"Thus it has been said, 'The wind blows and the river suffers. The sun shines and the river suffers.' But though wind and sun be both brought into relation with the river, it does not really suffer therefrom. Fed from its source, it still continues to flow on.

"The relation between water and earth is determinate. The relation between a man and his shadow is determinate. The relation between thing and thing is determinate.

"The relation between eye and vision is baneful.

The relation between ear and hearing is baneful. The relation between mind and object is baneful. The relation between all kinds of capacity and man's inner self is baneful. If such banefulness be not corrected, disasters will spring up on all sides. Retrogression is hard to achieve, and success long in coming. Yet alas! men regard such capacities as valuable possessions.

"The destruction of States and the ceaseless slaughter of human beings result from an inability to examine into this.

"The foot treads the ground in walking; nevertheless it is the ground not trodden on which makes up the good walk. A man's knowledge is lim-

故有亡國戮民無已，不知問是也。故足之於地也踐，雖踐，恃其所不蹍而後善博也；人之於知也少，雖少，恃其所不知而後知天之所謂也。知大一，知大陰，知大目，知大均，知大方，知大信，知大定，至矣！大一通之，大陰解之，大目視之，大均緣之，大方體之，大信稽之，大定持之。盡有天循，有照冥，有樞始，有彼則。其解之也，似不解之者；其知之也似不知之也，不知而後知之。其問之也，不可以有崖，而不可以無崖。頡滑有實，古今不代，而不可以虧，則可不謂有大揚搉乎！闔不亦問是已，奚惑然為！以不惑解惑，復於不惑，是尚大不惑。

ited; but it is upon what he does not know that he depends to extend his knowledge to the apprehension of God.

"Knowledge of the great One, of the great Negative, of the great Nomenclature, of the great Uniformity, of the great Space, of the great Truth, of the great Law,—this is perfection.

"The great One is omnipresent. The great Negative is omnipotent. The great Nomenclature is all-inclusive. The great Uniformity is all-assimilative. The great Space is all-receptive. The great Truth is all-exacting. The great Law is all-binding.

"The ultimate end is God. He is manifested in the laws of nature. He is the hidden spring. At the beginning, he was.

This, however, is inexplicable. It is unknowable. But from the unknowable we reach the known.

"Investigation must not be limited, nor must it be unlimited.

In this vague undefinedness there is an actuality. Time does not change it. It cannot suffer diminution. May we not then call it our great Guide?

"Why not bring our doubting hearts to investigation thereof? And then, using certainty to dispel doubt, revert to a state without doubt, in which doubt is doubly dead?"

# 則陽第二十五

　　則陽游於楚，夷節言之於王，王未之見。夷節歸。彭陽見王果曰：「夫子何不譚我於王？」王果曰：「我不若公閱休。」彭陽曰：「公閱休奚為者邪？」曰：「冬則擉鱉於江，夏則休乎山樊。有過而問者，曰：『此予宅也。』夫夷節已不能，而況我乎！吾又不若夷節。夫夷節之為人也，無德而有知，不自許，以之神其交，固，顛冥乎富貴之地。非相助以德，相助消也。夫凍者假衣於春，暍者反冬乎冷風。夫楚王之為人也，形尊而嚴。其於罪也，無赦如虎。非夫佞人正德，其孰能橈焉！故聖人，其窮也，使家人忘其貧；其達也，使王公忘爵祿而化卑。其於物也，與之為娛矣；其於人也，樂物之通而保己焉。故或不言而飲人以和，與人並立而使人化，父子之宜。彼其乎歸。居，而一間其所施。其於人心者，若是其遠也。故曰『待公閱休』。」

　　聖人達綢繆，周盡一體矣，而不知其然，性也。復命搖作而以天為師，人則從而命之也。憂乎知而所行恆無幾時，其有止也，若之何！生而美

348

# CHAPTER XXV

## TSE YANG

When Tse Yang visited the Ch'u State, I Chieh spoke of him to the prince; but the latter refused an audience.

Upon I Chieh's return, Tse Yang went to see Wang Kuo, and asked him to obtain an interview with the prince.

"I am not so fitted for that," replied Wang Kuo, "as Kung Yueh Hsiu."

"What sort of a man is he?" enquired Tse Yang.

"In winter," said Wang Kuo, "he catches turtles on the river. In summer, he reposes in some mountain copse. If any passers-by ask of him, he tells them, 'This is my home.' Where I Chieh could not succeed, still less should I. I am not equal even to him.

"He is a man without virtue, but possessed of knowledge. Were it not for an air of arrogance, he would be very popular with his superiors. But help without virtue is a hindrance. Shivering people borrowing clothes in the coming spring! Hot people thinking of last winter's icy blast!

"The prince of Ch'u is dignified and severe. In punishing, he is merciless as a tiger. Only a very practised or a very perfect man could influence him.

"The true Sage, when in obscurity, causes those around him to forget their poverty. When in power, he causes princes to forget ranks and emoluments, and to become as though of low estate. He rejoices exceedingly in all creation. He exults to see Tao diffused among his fellow-men, while suffering no loss himself.

"Thus, although silent, he can instil peace; and by his mere presence cause men to be to each other as father and son. From his very return to passivity comes this active influence for good. So widely does he differ in heart from ordinary men. Wherefore I said, 'Wait for Kung Yueh Hsiu.'

"The true Sage is free from all embarrassments. All things are to him as One. Yet he knows not that this is so. It is simply nature. In the midst of action he remains the same. He makes God his guide, and men make him theirs. He grieves that wisdom carries one but a short distance, and at times comes altogether to a deadlock.

"To a beauty, mankind is the mirror in which she sees herself. If no

者，人與之鑑，不告則不知其美於人也。 若知之，若不知之，若聞之，若不聞之，其可喜也終無已，人之好之亦無已， 性也。 聖人之愛人也， 人與之名，不告則不知其愛人也。 若知之，若不知之，若聞之， 若不聞之， 其愛人也終無已， 人之安之亦無已， 性也。 舊國舊都， 望之暢然。 雖使丘陵草木之緡入之者十九， 猶之暢然， 況見見聞聞者也， 以十仞之臺縣眾閒者也。

冉相氏得其環中以隨成， 與物無終無始， 無幾無時。 日與物化者， 一不化者也。 闔嘗舍之！夫師天而不得師天， 與物皆殉， 其以為事也，若之何？夫聖人未始有天， 未始有人， 未始有始， 未始有物， 與世偕行而不替， 所行之備而不洫， 其合之也， 若之何？湯得其司御門尹登恆為之傅之， 從師而不囿；得其隨成。 為之司其名；之名嬴法， 得其兩見。 仲尼之盡慮， 為之傅之。容成氏曰：「除日無歲， 無內無外。」

魏瑩與田侯牟約， 田侯牟背之， 魏瑩怒， 將使人刺之。 犀首公孫衍聞而恥之， 曰：「君為萬乘之君也， 而以匹夫從讎。 衍請受甲二十萬，

one tells her she is beautiful, she does not know that she is so. But whether she knows it or whether she does not know it, whether she hears it or whether she does not hear it, her joy will never cease, neither will mankind ever cease to take pleasure therein. It is nature.

"The love of a Sage for his fellows likewise finds expression among mankind. Were he not told so, he would not know that he loved his fellows. But whether he knows it or whether he does not know it, whether he hears it or whether he does not hear it, his love for his fellows is without end, and mankind cease not to repose therein.

"The old country, the old home, gladden a wanderer's eyes. Nay, though nine-tenths of it be a howling wilderness, still his eye will be glad. How much more to see sight and hear hearing, from a lofty dais suspended in their very midst!"

Jen Hsiang Shih reached the centre and attained.

He recognised no beginning, no end, no quantity, no time. Daily modified together with his environ ment, as part of One he knew no modification. Why not rest in this?

To strive to follow God and not to succeed is to display an activity fatal to itself. How can success ever be thus achieved?

The true Sage ignores God. He ignores man. He ignores a beginning. He ignores matter. He moves in harmony with his generation and suffers not. He takes things as they come and is not overwhelmed. How are we to become like him?

T'ang appointed his Equerry, Men Yin Teng Heng, to be his tutor, listening to his counsels but not being restricted by them. He got Tao for himself and a reputation for his tutor. But the reputation was a violation of principle, and landed him in the domain of alternatives.

As a tutor, Confucius pushed care and anxiety to an extreme limit.

Yung Ch'eng Shih said, "Take away days, and there would be no years. No inside, no outside."

Prince Hui of Wei had made a treaty with prince Wei of Ch'i, which the latter broke.

Thereupon prince Hui was wroth, and was about to send a man to assassinate him. But the Captain-General heard of this, and cried out in shame,

"Sire, you are ruler over a mighty State, yet you would seek the venge-

為君攻之，虜其人民，係其牛馬，使其君內熱發於背，然後拔其國。忌也出走，然後抶其背，折其脊。」季子聞而恥之，曰：「築十仞之城，城者既十仞矣，則又壞之，此胥靡之所苦也。今兵不起七年矣，此王之基也。衍亂人，不可聽也。」華子聞而醜之，曰：「善言伐齊者，亂人也；善言勿伐者，亦亂人也；謂『伐之與不伐亂人也』者，又亂人也。」君曰：「然則若何？」曰：「君求其道而已矣！」惠之聞之，而見戴晉人。戴晉人曰：「有所謂蝸者，君知之乎？」曰：「然。」「有國於蝸之左角者，曰觸氏；有國於蝸之右角者，曰蠻氏，時相與爭地而戰，伏尸數萬，逐北旬有五日而後反。」君曰：「噫！其虛言與？」曰：「臣請為君實之。君以意在四方上下，有窮乎？」君曰：

ance of a common man. Give me two hundred thousand warriors, and I will do the work for you. I will take his people prisoners, and carry off their oxen and horses. I will make the heat of the prince's mind break out on his back. Then I will seize his country, and he will flee. Then you can wring his neck as you please."

When Chi Tzu heard this, he cried out in shame and said, "If you are building a ten-perch wall, and when the wall is near completion, destroy it, you inflict great hardship on the workmen.

Now for seven years the troops have not been called out. That is, as it were, your Highness' foundation work. Listen not to the Captain-General. He is a mischievous fellow."

When Hua Tzu heard this, he was very indignant and said, "He who argued in favour of punishing the Ch'i State was a mischievous fellow. And he who argued against punishing the Ch'i State was a mischievous fellow. And he who says that either of the above is a mischievous fellow, is a mischievous fellow himself."

"Where then shall I find what to do?" enquired the prince.

"In Tao alone," said Hua Tzu.

When Hui Tzu heard this, he introduced Tai Chin Jen to the prince.

"There is a creature called a snail," said Tai Chin Jen. "Does your Highness know what I mean?"

"I do," replied the prince.

"There is a kingdom on its left horn," continued Tai Chin Jen, "ruled over by Aggression, and another on its right horn, ruled over by Violence. These two rulers are constantly fighting for territory. In such cases, corpses lie about by thousands, and one party will pursue the other for fifteen days before returning."

"Whew!" cried the prince. "Surely you are joking."

"Sire," replied Tai Chin Jen, "I beg you to regard it as fact. Does your Highness recognise any limit to space?"

"None," said the prince, "It is boundless."

"When, therefore," continued Tai Chin Jen, "the mind descends from the contemplation of boundless space to the contemplation of a kingdom with fixed boundaries, that kingdom must seem to be of dimensions infinitesimally small?"

"Of course," replied the prince.

「無窮。」曰：「知游心於無窮，而反在通達之國，若存若亡乎？」君曰：「然。」曰：「通達之中有魏，於魏中有梁，於梁中有王，王與蠻氏，有辯乎？」君曰：「無辯。」客出而君惝然若有亡也。客出，惠子見。君曰：「客，大人也，聖人不足以當之。」惠子曰：「夫吹筦也，猶有嗃也；吹劍首者，映而已矣。堯、舜，人之所譽也。道堯、舜於戴晉人之前，譬猶一映也。」

孔子之楚，舍於蟻丘之漿。其鄰有夫妻臣妾登極者，子路曰：「是稷稷何為者邪？」仲尼曰：「是聖人僕也。是自埋於民，自藏於畔。其聲銷，其志無窮，其口雖言，其心未嘗言。方且與世違而心不屑與之俱。是陸沉者也，是其市南宜僚邪？」子路請往召之。孔子曰：「已矣！彼知丘之著於己也，知丘之適楚也，以丘為必使楚王之召己也。彼且以丘為佞人也。夫若然者，其於佞人也羞聞其言，而況親見其身乎！而何以為存！」子路往視之，其室虛矣。

長梧封人問子牢曰：「君為政焉勿鹵莽，治民焉勿滅裂。昔予為禾，耕而鹵莽之，則其實

"Well then," said Tai Chin Jen, "in a kingdom with fixed boundaries there is the Wei State. In the Wei State there is the city of Liang. In the city of Liang there is a prince. In what does that prince differ from Violence?"

"There is no difference," said the prince.

Thereupon Tai Chin Jen took his leave, and the prince remained in a state of mental perturbation, as though he had lost something.

When Tai Chin Jen had gone, Hui Tzu presented himself, and the prince said, "Our friend is truly a great man. Sages are not his equal."

"If you blow through a tube," replied Hui Tzu, "the result will be a note. If you blow through the hole in a sword-hilt, the result will be simply whssh. Yao and Shun have been belauded by mankind; yet compared with Tai Chin Jen they are but whssh."

When Confucius went to Ch'u, he stopped at a restaurant on Mount I. The servant to a man and his wife who lived next door, got up on top of the house.

"Whatever is he doing up there?" asked Tzu Lu.

"He is a Sage," replied Confucius, "under the garb of a menial. He buries himself among the people.

He effaces himself at the wayside. Fame, he has none; but his perseverance is inexhaustible. Though his mouth speaks, his heart speaks not. He has turned his back upon mankind, not caring to abide amongst them. He has drowned himself on dry land. I think 'tis I Liao of Shih-nan."

Tzu Lu asked to be allowed to go and call him; but Confucius stopped him, saying, "No. He knows that I know what he is. He knows that I have come to Ch'u to recommend him to the prince. And he looks on me as a toady. Under the circumstances, as he would scorn to hear the words of a toady, how much more would he scorn to see him in the flesh! How could you keep him?"

Tzu Lu went to see, but the house was empty.

The border-warden of Ch'ang-wu said to Tzu Lao,

"A prince in his administrative details must not lack thoroughness; in his executive details he must not be inefficient. Formerly, in my ploughing I lacked thoroughness, and the results also lacked thoroughness. In my weeding I was inefficient, and the results were also inefficient. By and by, I changed my system. I ploughed deep, and weeded carefully, the result be-

亦鹵莽而報予；芸而滅裂之，其實亦滅裂而報予。予來年變齊，深其耕而熟耰之，其禾繁以滋，予終年厭飧。」莊子聞之曰：「今人之治其形，理其心，多有似封人之所謂，遁其天，離其性，滅其情，亡其神，以眾為。故鹵莽其性者，欲惡之孽，為性，萑葦蒹葭，始萌以扶吾形，尋擢吾性；並潰漏發，不擇所出，漂疽疥癰，內熱溲膏是也。」

　柏矩學於老聃，曰：「請之天下游。」老聃曰：「已矣！天下猶是也。」又請之，老聃曰：「汝將何始？」曰：「始於齊。」至齊，見辜人焉，推而強之，解朝服而幕之，號天而哭之，曰：「子乎！子乎！天下有大菑，子獨先離之。曰『莫為盜！莫為殺人！』榮辱立，然後睹所病；貨財聚，然後睹所爭。今立人之所病，聚人之所爭，窮

ing an excellent harvest, more than I could get through in a year."

Chuang Tzu, upon hearing this, observed, "The men of to-day in their self-regulation and their self-organisation are mostly as the Border-warden has described. They put their Godhead out of sight. They abandon their natural dispositions. They get rid of all feeling. They part with their souls, carried away by the fashion of the hour.

"Those who lack thoroughness in regard to their natural dispositions suffer an evil tribe to take the place thereof.

These grow up rank as reeds and rushes, at first of apparent value to the body, but afterwards to destroy the natural disposition. Then they break out, at random, like sores and ulcers carrying off pent-up humours."

Poh Chu was studying under Lao Tzu. "Let us go," said he, "and wander over the world."

"No," replied Lao Tzu, "the world is just as you see it here."

But as he again urged it, Lao Tzu said, "Where would you go to begin with?"

"I would begin," answered Poh Chu, "by going to the Ch'i State. There I would view the dead bodies of their malefactors. I would push them to make them rise. I would take off my robes and cover them. I would cry to God and bemoan their lot, as follows:—'O sirs, O sirs, there was trouble upon earth, and you were the first to fall into it!'

"I would say, 'Perhaps you were robbers, or perhaps murderers?' ... Honour and disgrace were set up, and evil followed. Wealth was accumulated, and contentions began. Now the evil which has been set up and the contentions which have accumulated, endlessly weary man's body and give him no rest. What escape is there from this?

"The rulers of old set off all success to the credit of their people, attributing all failure to themselves. All that was right went to the credit of their people, all that was wrong they attributed to themselves. Therefore, if any matter fell short of achievement, they turned and blamed themselves.

"Not so the rulers of to-day. They conceal a thing and blame those who cannot see it. They impose dangerous tasks and punish those who dare not undertake them. They inflict heavy burdens and chastise those who cannot bear them. They ordain long marches and slay those who cannot make them.

"And the people, feeling that their powers are inadequate, have re-

困人之身，使無休時，欲無至此，得乎！古之君人者，以得為在民，以失為在己；以正為在民，以枉為在己；故一形有失其形者，退而自責。今則不然，匿為物而愚不識，大為難而罪不敢，重為任而罰不勝，遠其塗而誅不至。民知力竭，則以偽繼之。日出多偽，士民安取不偽！夫力不足則偽，知不足則欺，財不足則盜。盜竊之行，於誰責而可乎？」

蘧伯玉行年六十而六十化，未嘗不始於是之，而卒詘之以非也。未知今之所謂是之非五十九非也。萬物有乎生而莫見其根，有乎出而莫見其門。人皆尊其知之所知，而莫知恃其知之所不知而後知，可不謂大疑乎！已乎！已乎！且無所逃。此則所謂然與，然乎？

仲尼問於大史大弢、伯常騫、狶韋曰：「夫衛靈公飲酒湛樂，不聽國家之政；田獵畢弋，不應諸侯之際；其所以為靈公者何邪？」大弢

course to fraud. For when there is so much fraud about, how can the people be otherwise than fraudulent? If their strength is insufficient, they will have recourse to fraud. If their knowledge is insufficient, they will have recourse to deceit. If their means are insufficient, they will steal. And for such robbery and theft, who is really responsible?"

When Chu Poh Yu reached his sixtieth year, he changed his opinions. What he had previously regarded as right, he now came to regard as wrong. But who shall say whether the right of to-day may not be as wrong as the wrong of the previous fifty-nine years?

Things are produced around us, but no one knows the whence. They issue forth, but no one sees the portal. Men one and all value that part of knowledge which is known. They do not know how to avail themselves of the unknown in order to reach knowledge. Is not this misguided?

Alas! alas! the impossibility of escaping from this state results in what is known as elective affinity.

Confucius asked the historiographers Ta T'ao, Poh Ch'ang Ch'ien, and Hsi Wei, saying, "Duke Ling was fond of wine and given up to pleasure, and neglected the administration of his State. He spent his time in hunting, and did not cultivate the goodwill of the other feudal princes. How was it he came to be called Ling?"

"For those very reasons," replied Ta T'ao.

"The Duke," said Poh Ch'ang Ch'ien, "had three wives. He was having a bath together with them when Shih Ch'in, summoned by his Highness, entered the apartment. Thereupon the Duke covered himself and the ladies. So outrageously did he behave on the one hand, and yet so respectful was he towards a virtuous man. Hence he was called Ling."

"When the Duke died," said Hsi Wei, "divination showed that it would be inauspicious to bury him in the old family burying-ground, but auspicious to bury him at Sha-ch'iu. And upon digging a grave there, several fathoms deep, a stone coffin was found, which, being cleaned, yielded the following inscription:—Posterity cannot be trusted. Duke Ling will seize this for his tomb.

"As a matter of fact, Duke Ling had been named Ling long before. What should these two persons know about it?"

Shao Chih asked T'ai Kung Tiao, saying, "What is meant by society?"

"Society," replied T'ai Kung Tiao, "is an agreement of a certain num-

曰：「是因是也。」伯常騫曰：「夫靈公有妻三人，同濫而浴。史鰌奉御而進所，搏幣而扶翼。其慢若彼之甚也，見賢人若此其肅也，是其所以為靈公也。」狶韋曰：「夫靈公也死，卜葬於故墓不吉，卜葬於沙丘而吉。掘之數仞，得石槨焉，洗而視之，有銘焉，曰：『不馮其子，靈公奪而里之。』夫靈公之為靈也久矣！之二人何足以識之！」

少知問於大公調曰：「何謂丘里之言？」大公調曰：「丘里者，合十姓百名而以為風俗也，合異以為同，散同以為異。今指馬之百體而不得馬，而馬係於前者，立其百體而謂之馬也。是故丘山積卑而為高，江河合水而為大，大人合并而為公。是以自外入者，有主而不執；由中出者，有正而不距。四時殊氣，天不賜，故歲成；五官殊職，君不私，故國治；文武大人不賜，故德備；萬物殊理，道不私，故無名。無名故無為，無為而無不為。時有終始，世有變化。禍福淳淳，至有所拂者而有所宜，自殉殊面；有所正者有所差，比於大澤，百材皆度；觀於大山，木石

ber of families and individuals to abide by certain customs. Discordant elements unite to form a harmonious whole. Take away this unity and each has a separate individuality.

"Point at any one of the many parts of a horse, and that is not a horse, although there is the horse before you. It is the combination of all which makes the horse.

"Similarly, a mountain is high because of its individual particles. A river is large because of its individual drops. And he is a just man who regards all parts from the point of view of the whole.

"Thus, in regard to the views of others, he holds his own opinion, but not obstinately. In regard to his own views, while conscious of their truth, he does not despise the opinions of others.

"The four seasons have different characteristics, but God shows no preference for either, and therefore we have the year complete.

The functions of the various classes of officials differ; but the sovereign shows no partiality, and therefore the empire is governed. There are the civil and the military; but the truly great man shows no preference for either, and therefore their efficacy is complete. All things are under the operation of varying laws; but Tao shows no partiality and therefore it cannot be identified.

Not being able to be identified, it consequently does nothing. And by doing nothing all things can be done.

"Seasons have their beginnings and their ends. Generations change and change. Good and evil fortune alternate, bringing sorrow here, happiness there.

He who obstinately views things from his own standpoint only, may be right in one case and wrong in another. Just as in a great jungle all kinds of shrubs are found together; or as on a mountain you see trees and stones indiscriminately mixed,—so is what we call society."

"Would it not do then," asked Shao Chih, "if we were to call this Tao?"

"It would not," replied T'ai Kung Tiao. "All creation is made up of more than ten thousand things. We speak of creation as the Ten Thousand Things merely because it is a convenient term by which to express a large number. In point of outward shape the universe is vast. In point of influence the Positive and Negative principles are mighty. Yet Tao folds

同壇。此之謂丘里之言。」少知曰：「然則謂之道，足乎？」大公調曰：「不然，今計物之數，不止於萬，而期曰萬物者，以數之多者號而讀之也。是故天地者，形之大者也；陰陽者，氣之大者也；道者為之公。因其大以號而讀之則可也，已有之矣，乃將得比哉！則若以斯辯，譬猶狗馬，其不及遠矣。」少知曰：「四方之內，六合之裡，萬物之所生惡起？」大公調曰：「陰陽相照相蓋相治，四時相代相生相殺。欲惡去就於是橋起，雌雄片合於是庸有。安危相易，禍福相生，緩急相摩，聚散以成。此名實之可紀，精微之可志也。隨序之相理，橋運之相使，窮則反，終則始，此物之所有。言之所盡，知之所至，極物而已。睹道之人，不隨其所廢，不原其所起，此議之所止。」少知曰：「季真之莫為，接子之或使。二家之議，孰正於其情，孰遍於其理？」大公調曰：「雞鳴狗吠，是人之所知；雖有大知，不能以言讀其所自化，又不能以意其所將為。斯而析之，精至於無倫，大至於不可圍。或之使，莫之為，未免於物而終以為過。或使則實，

them all in its embrace. For convenience' sake the bond of society is called great. But how can that which is thus conditioned be compared with Tao? There is as wide a difference between them as there is between a horse and a dog."

"Whence then," enquired Shao Chih, "comes the vitality of all things between the four points of the compass, between heaven above and earth beneath?"

"The Positive and Negative principles," answered T'ai Kung Tiao, "influence, act upon, and regulate each other. The four seasons alternate with, give birth to, and destroy one another. Hence, loves and hates, and courses rejected and courses adopted. Hence too, the intercourse of the sexes.

"States of peril and safety alternate. Good and evil fortune give birth to one another. Slowness and speed are mutually exclusive. Collection and dispersion are correlates. The actuality of these may be noted.

The essence of each can be verified. There is regular movement forward, modified by deflection into a curve. Exhaustion leads to renewal. The end introduces a new beginning. This is the law of material existences. The force of language, the reach of knowledge, cannot pass beyond the bounds of such material existences. The disciple of Tao refrains from prying into the states after or before. Human speculation stops short of this."

"Chi Chen," said Shao Chih, "taught Chance; Chieh Tzu taught Predestination.

In the speculations of these two schools, on which side did right lie?"

"The cock crows," replied T'ai Kung Tiao, "and the dog barks. So much we know. But the wisest of us could not say why one crows and the other barks, nor guess why they crow or bark at all.

"Let me explain. The infinitely small is inappreciable; the infinitely great is immeasurable. Chance and Predestination must refer to the conditioned. Consequently, both are wrong.

"Predestination involves a real existence.

Chance implies an absolute absence of any principle. To have a name and the embodiment thereof,—this is to have a material existence. To have no name and no embodiment,—of this one can speak and think; but the more one speaks the farther off one gets.

"The unborn creature cannot be kept from life.

莫為則虛。有名有實，是物之居；無名無實，在物之虛。可言可意，言而愈疏。未生不可忌，已死不可徂。死生非遠也，理不可睹。或之使，莫之為，疑之所假。吾觀之本，其往無窮；吾求之末，其來無止。無窮無止，言之無也，與物同理；或使莫為，言之本也。與物終始。道不可有，有不可無。道之為名，所假而行。或使莫為，在物一曲，夫胡為於大方？言而足，則終日言而盡道；言而不足，則終日言而盡物。道物之極，言默不足以載；非言非默，議有所極。」

The dead cannot be tracked. From birth to death is but a span; yet the secret cannot be known. Chance and Predestination are but a priori solutions.

"When I seek for a beginning, I find only time infinite. When I look forward to an end, I see only time infinite. Infinity of time past and to come implies no beginning and is in accordance with the laws of material existences. Predestination and Chance give us a beginning, but one which is compatible only with the existence of matter.

"Tao cannot be existent. If it were existent, it could not be non-existent. The very name of Tao is only adopted for convenience' sake. Predestination and Chance are limited to material existences. How can they bear upon the infinite?

"Were language adequate, it would take but a day to fully set forth Tao. Not being adequate, it takes that time to explain material existences. Tao is something beyond material existences. It cannot be conveyed either by words or by silence. In that state which is neither speech nor silence, its transcendental nature may be apprehended."

# 外物第二十六

外物不可必，故龍逢誅，比干戮，箕子狂，惡來死，桀、紂亡。人主莫不欲其臣之忠，而忠未必信，故伍員流於江，萇弘死於蜀，藏其血三年而化為碧。人親莫不欲其子之孝，而孝未必愛，故孝己憂而曾參悲。木與木相摩則然，金與火相守則流，陰陽錯行，則天地大駭，於是乎有雷有霆，水中有火，乃焚大槐。有甚憂兩陷而無所逃。螴蜳不得成，心若縣於天地之間，慰暋沈屯，利害相摩，生火甚多，眾人焚和，月固不勝火，於是乎有僓然而道盡。

莊周家貧，故往貸粟於監河侯。監河侯曰：「諾，我將得邑金，將貸子三百金，可乎？」莊

# CHAPTER XXVI

## CONTINGENCIES

Contingencies are uncertain. Hence the decapitation of Lung Feng, the disembowelment of Pi Kan, the enthusiasm of Chi Tzu, the death of Wu Lai, the flights of Chieh and Chou.

No sovereign but would have loyal ministers; yet loyalty does not necessarily inspire confidence. Hence Wu Yuan found a grave in the river; and Ch'ang Hung perished in Shu, his blood, after being preserved three years, turning into green jade.

No parent but would have filial sons; yet filial piety does not necessarily inspire love. Hence Hsiao Chi sorrowed, and Tseng Shen grieved.

Wood rubbed with wood produces fire. Metal exposed to fire will liquefy. If the Positive and Negative principles operate inharmoniously, heaven and earth are greatly disturbed. Thunder crashes, and with rain comes lightning, scorching up the tall locust-trees. One fears lest sky and land should collapse and leave no escape. Unable to lie perdu, the heart feels as though suspended between heaven and earth.

So in the struggle between peace and unrest, the friction between good and evil, much fire is evolved which consumes the inner harmony of man. But the mind is unable to resist fire. It is destroyed, and with it Tao comes to an end.

Chuang Tzu's family being poor, he went to borrow some corn from the prince of Chien-ho.

"Yes," said the prince. "I am just about collecting the revenue of my fief, and will then lend you three hundred ounces of silver. Will that do?"

At this Chuang Tzu flushed with anger and said, "Yesterday, as I was coming along, I heard a voice calling me. I looked round, and in the cart-rut I saw a stickleback.

"'And what do you want, stickleback?' said I.

"'I am a denizen of the eastern ocean,' replied the stickleback. 'Pray, Sir, a pint of water to save my life.'

"'Yes,' said I. 'I am just going south to visit the princes of Wu and Yueh. I will bring you some from the west river. Will that do?'

"At this the stickleback flushed with anger and said, 'I am out of my

周忿然作色曰：「周昨來，有中道而呼者。周顧視車轍中，有鮒魚焉。周問之曰：『鮒魚來！子何為者耶？』對曰：『我，東海之波臣也。君豈有斗升之水而活我哉？』周曰：『諾，我且南游吳越之王，激西江之水而迎子，可乎？』鮒魚忿然作色曰：『吾失我常與，我無所處。我得斗升之水然活耳。君乃言此，曾不如早索我於枯魚之肆！』」

任公子為大鉤巨緇，五十犗以為餌，蹲乎會稽，投竿東海，旦旦而釣，期年不得魚。已而大魚食之，牽巨鉤陷，沒而下，騖揚而奮鬐，白波若山，海水震蕩，聲侔鬼神，憚赫千里。任公子得若魚，離而腊之，自制河以東，蒼梧已北，莫不厭若魚者。已而後世輇才諷說之徒，皆驚而相告也。夫揭竿累，趣灌瀆，守鯢鮒，其於得大魚難矣，飾小說以干縣令，其於大達亦遠矣，是以未嘗聞任氏之風俗，其不可與經於世亦遠矣！

element. I have nowhere to go. A pint of water would save me. But to talk to me like this,—you might as well put me in a dried-fish shop at once.'"

Jen Kung Tzu got a huge hook on a big line, which he baited with fifty oxen. He squatted down at Kuei-chi, and cast into the eastern ocean. Every day he fished, but for a whole year he caught nothing. Then came a great fish which swallowed the bait, and dragging the huge hook dived down below. This way and that way it plunged about, erecting the dorsal fin. The white waves rolled mountain high. The great deep was shaken up. The noise was like that of so many devils, terrifying people for many miles around.

But when Jen Kung Tzu had secured his fish, he cut it up and salted it. And from Chih-ho eastwards, and from Ts'ang-wu northwards, there was none but ate his fill of that fish. Even among succeeding generations, gobemouches of the day recounted the marvellous tale.

To take a rod and line, and go to a pool, and catch small fry is a very different thing from catching big fish. And by means of a little show of ability to secure some small billet is a very different thing from really pushing one's way to the front. So that those who do not imitate the example of Jen Kung Tzu will be very far from becoming leaders in their generation.

When some Confucianists were opening a grave in accordance with their Canons of Poetry and Rites, the master shouted out, "Day is breaking. How are you getting on with the work?"

"Not got off the burial-clothes yet," answered an apprentice. "There is a pearl in the mouth."

Now the Canon of Poetry says—

> The greenest corn
> Grows over graves.
> In life, no charity;
> In death, no pearl.

So seizing the corpse's brow with one hand, and forcing down its chin with the other, these Confucianists proceed to tap its cheeks with a metal hammer, in order to make the jaws open gently and not injure the pearl!

A disciple of Lao Lai Tzu while out gathering fuel, chanced to meet Confucius. On his return, he said, "There is a man over there with a long body and short legs, round shoulders and drooping ears. He looks as

儒以《詩》、《禮》發冢。大儒臚傳曰：「東方作矣，事之何若？」小儒曰：「未解裙襦，口中有珠。」《詩》固有之曰：『青青之麥，生於陵陂。生不布施，死何含珠為？』接其鬢，壓其顪，儒以金椎控其頤，徐別其頰，無傷口中珠！」

老萊子之弟子出薪，遇仲尼，反以告，曰：「有人於彼，修上而趨下，末僂而後耳，視若營四海，不知其誰氏之子。」老萊子曰：「是丘也，召而來。」仲尼至。曰：「丘，去汝躬矜與汝容知，斯為君子矣。」仲尼揖而退，蹙然改容而問曰：「業可得進乎？」老萊子曰：「夫不忍一世之傷而驚萬世之患，抑固窶邪，亡其略弗及邪？惠以歡為驁，終身之醜，中民之行進焉耳，相引以名，相結以隱。與其譽堯而非桀，不如兩忘而閉其所譽。反無非傷也。動無非邪也。聖人躊躇以興事，以每成功。奈何哉其載焉終矜爾！」

宋元君夜半而夢人被髮闚阿門，曰：「予自宰路之淵，予為清江使河伯之所，漁者余且得予。」元君覺，使人占之，曰：「此神龜也。」君曰：「漁者有余且乎？」左右曰：「有。」君曰：「令

though he were sorrowing over mankind. I know not who he can be."

"It is Confucius!" cried Lao Lai Tzu. "Bid him come hither."

When Confucius arrived, Lao Lai Tzu addressed him as follows:—

"Ch'iu! Get rid of your dogmatism and your specious knowledge, and you will be really a superior man."

Confucius bowed and was about to retire, when suddenly his countenance changed and he enquired, "Shall I then be able to enter upon Tao?"

"The wounds of one generation being too much," answered Lao Lai Tzu, "you would take to yourself the sorrows of all time. Are you not weary? Is your strength equal to the task?

"To employ goodness as a passport to influence through the gratification of others, is an everlasting shame. Yet this is the common way of all, to lure people by fame, to bind them by ties of gratification.

"Better than extolling Yao and cursing Chieh is oblivion of both, keeping one's praises to oneself. These things react injuriously on self; the agitation of movement results in deflection.

"The true Sage is a passive agent. If he succeeds, he simply feels that he was provided by no effort of his own with the energy necessary to success."

Prince Yuan of Sung dreamed one night that a man with dishevelled hair peeped through a side door and said, "I have come from the waters of Tsai-lu. I am a marine messenger attached to the staff of the River God. A fisherman, named Yu Ch'ieh, has caught me."

When the prince awaked, he referred his dream to the soothsayers, who said, "This is a divine tortoise."

"Is there any fisherman," asked the prince, "whose name is Yu Ch'ieh?"

Being told there was, the prince gave orders for his appearance at court; and the next day Yu Ch'ieh had an audience.

"Fisherman," said the prince, "what have you caught?"

"I have netted a white tortoise," replied the fisherman, "five feet in semi-circumference."

"Bring your tortoise," said the prince. But when it came, the prince could not make up his mind whether to kill it or keep it alive. Thus in doubt, he had recourse to divination, and received the following response:—

Slay the tortoise for purposes of divination and good fortune will re-

余且會朝。」明日，余且朝。君曰：「漁何得？」對曰：「且之網得白龜焉，箕圓五尺。」君曰：「獻若之龜。」龜至，君再欲殺之，再欲活之，心疑，卜之，曰：「殺龜以卜吉。」乃刳龜，七十二鑽而無遺筴。仲尼曰：「神龜能見夢於元君，而不能避余且之網；知能七十二鑽而無遺筴，不能避刳腸之患。如是，則知有所困，神有所不及也。雖有至知，萬人謀之。魚不畏網而畏鵜鶘。去小知而大知明，去善而自善矣。嬰兒生無石師而能言，與能言者處也。」

惠子謂莊子曰：「子言無用。」莊子曰：「知無用而始可與言用矣。天地非不廣且大也，人之所用容足耳，然則廁足而墊之致黃泉，人尚有用乎？」惠子曰：「無用。」莊子曰：「然則無用之為用也亦明矣。」

sult.

So the tortoise was despatched. After which, out of seventy-two omens taken, not a single one proved false.

"A divine tortoise," said Confucius, "can appear to prince Yuan in a dream, yet it cannot escape the net of Yu Ch'ieh. Its wisdom can yield seventy-two faultless omens, yet it cannot escape the misery of being cut to pieces. Truly wisdom has its limits; spirituality, that which it cannot reach.

"In spite of the highest wisdom, there are countless snares to be avoided; If a fish has not to fear nets, there are always pelicans. Get rid of small wisdom, and great wisdom will shine upon you. Put away goodness and you will be naturally good. A child does not learn to speak because taught by professors of the art, but because it lives among people who can themselves speak."

Hui Tzu said to Chuang Tzu, "Your theme, Sir, is the useless."

"You must understand the useless," replied Chuang Tzu, "before you can discuss the useful.

"For instance, the earth is of huge proportions, yet man uses of it only as much as is covered by the sole of his foot. By and by, he turns up his toes and goes beneath it to the Yellow Spring. Has he any further use for it?"

"He has none," replied Hui Tzu.

"And in like manner," replied Chuang Tzu, "may be demonstrated the use of the useless.

"Could a man transcend the limits of the human," said Chuang Tzu, "would he not do so? Unable to do so, how should he succeed?

"The determination to retire, to renounce the world,—such alas! is not the fruit of perfect wisdom or immaculate virtue. From cataclysms ahead, these do not turn back; nor do they heed the approach of devouring flame. Although there are class distinctions of high and low, these are but for a time, and under the changed conditions of a new sphere are unknown.

"Wherefore it has been said, 'The perfect man leaves no trace behind.'

"For instance, to glorify the past and to condemn the present has always been the way of the scholar.

Yet if Hsi Wei Shih and individuals of that class were caused to re-appear in the present day, which of them but would accommodate himself to

莊子曰：「人有能遊，且得不游乎？人而不能遊，且得遊乎？夫流遁之志，決絕之行，噫，其非至知厚德之任與！覆墜而不反，火馳而不顧。雖相與為君臣，時也，易世而無以相賤。故曰：至人不留行焉。夫尊古而卑今，學者之流也。且以狶韋氏之流觀今之世，夫孰能不波，唯至人乃能遊於世而不僻，順人而不失己。彼教不學，承意不彼。

目徹為明，耳徹為聰，鼻徹為顫，口徹為甘，心徹為知，知徹為德。凡道不欲壅，壅則哽，哽而不止則跈，跈則眾害生。物之有知者恃息，其不殷，非天之罪。天之穿之，日夜無降，人則顧塞其竇。胞有重閬，心有天遊，室無空虛，則婦姑勃谿；心無天遊，則六鑿相攘。大林丘山之善於人也，亦神者不勝。德溢乎名，名溢乎暴，謀稽乎誸，知出乎爭，柴生乎守官，事果乎眾宜。春雨日時，草木怒生，銚鎒於是乎始修，草木之倒植者過半而不知其然。

靜默可以補病，眥搣可以休老，寧可以止遽。雖然，若是，勞者之務也，非佚者之所未嘗過

the age?

"Only the perfect man can transcend the limits of the human and yet not withdraw from the world, live in accord with mankind and yet suffer no injury himself. Of the world's teachings he learns nothing. He has that within which makes him independent of others.

"If the eye is unobstructed, the result is sight. If the ear is unobstructed the result is hearing. If the nose is unobstructed, the result is sense of smell. If the mouth is unobstructed, the result is sense of taste. If the mind is unobstructed, the result is wisdom. If wisdom is unobstructed, the result is Te.

"Tao may not be obstructed. To obstruct is to strangle. This affects the base, and all evils spring into life.

"All sentient beings depend upon breath. If this does not reach them in sufficient quantity, it is not the fault of God. God supplies it day and night without cease, but man stops the passage.

"Man has for himself a spacious domain. His mind may roam to heaven. If there is no room in the house, the wife and her mother-in-law run against one another. If the mind cannot roam to heaven, the faculties will be in a state of antagonism. Those who would benefit mankind from deep forests or lofty mountains are simply unequal to the strain upon their higher natures.

"Ill-regulated virtue ends in reputation. Ill-regulated reputation ends in notoriety. Scheming leads to confusion. Knowledge begets contentions. Obstinacy produces stupidity. Organised government is for the general good of all.

"Spring rains come in due season, and plants and shrubs burst up from the earth. Weeding and tending do not begin until such plants and shrubs have reached more than half their growth, and without being conscious of the fact.

"Repose gives health to the sick. Rubbing the eyelids removes the wrinkles of old age. Quiet will dispel anxieties. These remedies however are the resource only of those who need them. Others who are free from such ills pay no attention thereto.

"That which the true Sage marvels at in the empire, claims not the attention of the Divine man. That which the truly virtuous man marvels at in his own sphere, claims not the attention of the true Sage. That which

而問焉。聖人之所以駴天下，神人未嘗過而問焉；賢人所以駴世，聖人未嘗過而問焉；君子所以駴國，賢人未嘗過而問焉；小人所以合時，君子未嘗過而問焉。演門有親死者，以善毀爵為官師，其黨人毀而死者半。堯與許由天下，許由逃之；湯與務光，務光怒之；紀他聞之，帥弟子而踆於窾水，諸侯吊之。三年，申徒狄因以踣河。

荃者所以在魚，得魚而忘荃；蹄者所以在兔，得兔而忘蹄；言者所以在意，得意而忘言。吾安得夫忘言之人而與之言哉！」

the superior man marvels at in his State, claims not the attention of the truly virtuous man. How the mean man adapts himself to his age, claims not the attention of the superior man.

"The keeper of the Yen gate, having maltreated himself severely in consequence of the death of his parents, received a high official post.

His relatives thereupon maltreated themselves, and some half of them died.

"Yao offered the empire to Hsu Yu, but Hsu Yu fled. T'ang offered it to Wu Kuang, but Wu Kuang declined with anger.

"When Chi T'o heard of Hsu Yu's flight, he took all his disciples with him and jumped into the river K'uan; upon which the various feudal princes mourned for three years, and Shen T'u Ti had the river filled up.

"The raison d'etre of a fish-trap is the fish. When the fish is caught, the trap may be ignored. The raison d'etre of a rabbit-snare is the rabbit. When the rabbit is caught the snare may be ignored. The raison d'etre of language is an idea to be expressed. When the idea is expressed, the language may be ignored. But where shall I find a man to ignore language, with whom I may be able to converse?"

# 寓言第二十七

　　寓言十九，重言十七，巵言日出，和以天倪。寓言十九，藉外論之。親父不為其子媒。親父譽之，不若非其父者也；非吾罪也，人之罪也。與己同則應，不與己同則反；同於己為是之，異於己為非之。重言十七，所以己言也。是為耆艾，年先矣，而無經緯本末以期年耆者，是非先也。人而無以先人，無人道也；人而無人道，是之謂陳人。巵言日出，和以天倪，因以曼衍，所以窮年。不言則齊，齊與言不齊，言與齊不齊也。故日：「無言。」言無言，終身言，未嘗不言；終身不言，未嘗不言。有自也而可，有自也而不可；有自也而然，有自也而不然。惡乎然？然於然；惡乎不然？不然於不然。惡乎可？可於可；惡乎不可？不可於不可。物固有所然，物固有所可。無物不然，無物不可。非巵言日出，和以天倪，孰得其久！萬物皆種也，以不同形相禪，始卒若環，莫得其倫，是謂天均。天均者，

# CHAPTER XXVII

## LANGUAGE

Of language put into other people's mouths, nine tenths will succeed. Of language based upon weighty authority, seven tenths. But language which flows constantly over, as from a full goblet, is in accord with God.

When language is put into other people's mouths, outside support is sought. Just as a father does not negotiate his son's marriage; for any praise he could bestow would not have the same value as praise by an outsider. Thus, the fault is not mine, but that of others.

To that which agrees with our own opinions we assent; from that which does not we dissent. We regard that which agrees with our own opinion as right. We regard that which differs from our opinion as wrong. Language based on weighty authority is used to bar further argument. The authorities are our superiors, our elders in years. But if they lack the requisite knowledge and experience, being our superiors only in the sense of age, then they are not our superiors. And if men are not the superiors of their fellows, no one troubles about them. And those about whom no one troubles are merely stale.

Language which flows constantly over, as from a full goblet, is in accord with God.

Because it spreads out on all sides, it endures for all time. Without language, contraries are identical. The identity is not identical with its expression: the expression is not identical with its identity. Therefore it has been said, Language not expressed in language is not language. Constantly spoken, it is as though not spoken. Constantly unspoken, it is not as though not spoken.

From the subjective point of view, there are possibilities and impossibilities, there are suitabilities and unsuitabilities. This results from the natural affinity of things for what they are and their natural antagonism to what they are not. For all things have their own particular constitutions and potentialities. Nothing can exist without these.

But for language that constantly flows over, as from a full goblet, and is in accord with God, how should the permanent be attained?

All things spring from germs. Under many diverse forms these things

天倪也。莊子謂惠子曰：「孔子行年六十而六十化。始時所是，卒而非之，未知今之所謂是之非五十九非也。」惠子曰：「孔子勤志服知也。」莊子曰：「孔子謝之矣，而其未之嘗言。孔子云：『夫受才乎大本，復靈以生。鳴而當律，言而當法。利義陳乎前，而好惡是非直服人之口而已矣。使人乃以心服，而不敢蘁，立定天下之定。已乎，已乎！吾且不得及彼乎！』」

曾子再仕而心再化，曰：「吾及親仕，三釜而心樂；後仕，三千鍾不洎，吾心悲。」弟子問於仲尼曰：「若參者，可謂無所縣其罪乎？」曰：「既已縣矣！夫無所縣者，可以有哀乎？彼視三釜、三千鍾，如觀雀蚊虻相過乎前也。」

顏成子游謂東郭子綦曰：「自吾聞子之言，一年而野，二年而從，三年而通，四年而物，五年而來，六年而鬼入，七年而天成，八年而不知死、不知生，九年而大妙。

are ever being reproduced. Round and round, like a wheel, no part of which is more the starting-point than any other. This is called the equilibrium of God. And he who holds the scales is God.

Chuang Tzu said to Hui Tzu, "When Confucius reached his sixtieth year he changed his opinions. What he had previously regarded as right, he ultimately came to regard as wrong. But who shall say whether the right of to-day may not be as wrong as the wrong of the previous fifty-nine years?"

"He was a persevering worker," replied Hui Tzu, "and his wisdom increased day by day."

"Confucius," replied Chuang Tzu, "discarded both perseverance and wisdom, but did not attempt to formulate the doctrine in words. He said, 'Man has received his talents from God, together with a soul to give them life. He should speak in accordance with established laws. His words should be in harmony with fixed order. Personal advantage and duty to one's neighbour lie open before us. Likes and dislikes, rights and wrongs, are but as men choose to call them. But to bring submission into men's hearts, so that they shall not be stiff-necked, and thus fix firmly the foundations of the empire,—to that, alas! I have not attained.'"

Tseng Tzu held office twice. His emotions varied in each case.

"As long as my parents were alive," said he, "I was happy on a small salary. When I had a large salary, but my parents were no more, I was sad."

A disciple said to Confucius, "Can we call Tseng Tzu a man without cares to trouble him?"

"He had cares to trouble him," replied Confucius. "Can a man who has no cares to trouble him feel grief? His small salary and his large salary were to him like a heron or a mosquito flying past."

Yen Ch'eng Tzu Yu said to Tung Kuo Tzu Chi,

"One year after receiving your instructions I became naturally simple. After two years, I could adapt myself as required. After three years, I understood. After four years, my intelligence developed. After five years, it was complete. After six years, the spirit entered into me. After seven, I knew God. After eight, life and death existed for me no more. After nine, perfection.

"Life has its distinctions; but in death we are all made equal. That death should have an origin, but that life should have no origin,—can this

生有為，死也虧。公以其死也，有自也；而生陽也，無自也。而果然乎？惡乎其所適？惡乎其所不適？天有歷數，地有人據，吾惡乎求之？莫知其所終，若之何其無命也？莫知其所始，若之何其有命也？有以相應也，若之何其無鬼邪？無以相應也，若之何其有鬼邪？」

眾罔兩問於景曰：「若向也俯而今也仰，向也括而今也被髮；向也坐而今也起，向也行而今也止，何也？」景曰：「搜搜也，奚稍問也！予有而不知其所以。予，蜩甲也，蛇蛻也，似之而非也。火與日，吾屯也；陰與夜，吾代也。彼吾所以有待邪？而況乎以有待者乎！彼來則我與之來，彼往則我與之往，彼強陽則我與之強陽。強陽者，又何以有問乎！」

陽子居南之沛，老聃西遊於秦，邀於郊，至於梁而遇老子。老子中道仰天而嘆曰：「始以汝

be so? What determines its presence in one place, its absence in another?

"Heaven has its fixed order.

Earth has yielded up its secrets to man. But where to seek whence am I?

"Not knowing the hereafter, how can we deny the operation of Destiny? Not knowing what preceded birth, how can we assert the operation of Destiny? When things turn out as they ought, who shall say that the agency is not supernatural? When things turn out otherwise, who shall say that it is?"

The various Penumbrae said to the Umbra, "Before you were looking down, now you are looking up. Before you had your hair tied up, now it is all loosed. Before you were sitting, now you have got up. Before you were moving, now you are stopping still. How is this?"

"Gentlemen," replied the Umbra, "the question is hardly worth asking.

I do these things, but I do not know why. I am like the scaly back of the cicada, the shell of the locust,—apparently independent, but not really so. By firelight or in daylight I am seen: in darkness or by night I am gone. And if I am dependent on these, how much more are they dependent on something else? When they come, I come with them. When they go, I go with them. When they live, I live with them. But who it is that gives the life, how shall we seek to know?"

Yang Tzu Chu went southwards to P'ei, and when Lao Tzu was travelling westwards to Ch'in, hastened to receive him outside the city. Arriving at the bridge, he met Lao Tzu; and the latter standing in the middle of the road, looked up to heaven and said with a sigh, "At first, I thought you could be taught. I think so no more."

Yang Tzu Chu made no reply, but when they reached the inn, handed Lao Tzu water for washing and rinsing, and a towel and comb. He then removed his own boots outside the door, and crawling on his knees into the Master's presence, said, "I have been wishing to ask for instruction, Sir, but as you were travelling and not at leisure, I did not venture. You are now, Sir, at leisure. May I enquire the reason of what you said?"

為可教，今不可也。」陽子居不答。至舍，進盥漱巾櫛，脫屨戶外，膝行而前，曰：「向者弟子欲請夫子，夫子行不閒，是以不敢。今閒矣，請問其故。」老子曰：「而睢睢盱盱，而誰與居？大白若辱，盛德若不足。」陽子居蹴然變容曰：「敬聞命矣！」其往也，舍者迎將，其家公執席，妻執巾櫛，舍者避席，煬者避灶。其反也，舍者與之爭席矣！

"You have an overbearing look," said Lao Tzu. "Who would live with such a man? He who is truly pure behaves as though he were sullied. He who has virtue in abundance behaves as though it were not enough."

Yang Tzu Chu changed countenance at this, and replied, "I hear and obey."

Now when Yang Tzu Chu first went to the inn, the visitors there had come out to receive him. Mine host had arranged his mat, while the landlady held towel and comb. The visitors had given him up the best seats, and those who were cooking had left the stove free for him. But when he went back, the other visitors struggled to get the best seats for themselves.

# 讓王第二十八

堯以天下讓許由，許由不受。又讓於子州支父，子州之父曰：「以我為天子，猶之可也。雖然，我適有幽憂之病，方且治之，未暇治天下也。」夫天下至重也，而不以害其生，又況他物乎！唯無以天下為者，可以托天下也。

舜讓天下於子州之伯，子州之伯曰：「予適有幽憂之病，方且治之，未暇治天下也。」故天下大器也，而不以易生。此有道者之所以異乎俗者也。

舜以天下讓善卷，善卷曰：「余立於宇宙之中，冬日衣皮毛，夏日衣葛絺；春耕種，形足以勞動；秋收斂，身足以休食；日出而作，日入而息，逍遙於天地之間而心意自得。吾何以天下為哉！悲夫，子之不知余也。」遂不受。於是去而入深山，莫知其處。

舜以天下讓其友石戶之農。石戶之農曰：「捲捲乎，后之為人，葆力之士也。」以舜之德為未至也。於是夫負妻戴，攜子以入於海，終身不反也。

# CHAPTER XXVIII

## ON DECLINING POWER

Yao offered to resign the empire to Hsu Yu, but the latter declined.

He then offered it to Tzu Chou Chih Fu, who said, "There is no objection to making me emperor. But just now I am suffering from a troublesome disease, and am engaged in trying to cure it. I have no leisure to look after the empire."

Now the empire is of paramount importance. Yet here was a man who would not allow it to injure his chance of life. How much less then would he let other things do so? Yet it is only he who would do nothing in the way of government who is fit to be trusted with the empire.

Shun offered to resign the empire to Tzu Chou Chih Poh. The latter said, "Just now I am suffering from a troublesome disease, and am engaged in trying to cure it. I have no leisure to look after the empire."

Now the empire is a great trust; but not to sacrifice one's life for it is precisely where the man of Tao differs from the man of the world.

Shun offered to resign the empire to Shan Chuan. Shan Chuan said, "I am a unit in the sum of the universe. In winter I wear fur clothes. In summer I wear grass-cloth. In spring I plough and sow, toiling with my body. In autumn I gather in the harvest, and devote myself to rest and enjoyment. At dawn I go to work; at sunset I leave off. Contented with my lot I pass through life with a light heart. Why then should I trouble myself with the empire? Ah, Sir, you do not know me."

So he declined, and subsequently hid himself among the mountains, nobody knew where.

Shun offered the empire to a friend, a labourer of Shih Hu.

"Sire," said the latter, "you exert yourself too much. The chief thing is to husband one's strength;"—meaning that in point of real virtue Shun had not attained.

Then, husband and wife, bearing away their household gods and taking their children with them, went off to the sea and never came back.

When T'ai Wang Shan Fu was occupying Pin, he was attacked by savages. He offered them skins and silk, but they declined these. He offered them dogs and horses, but they declined these also.

大王亶父居邠，狄人攻之。事之以皮帛而不受，事之以犬馬而不受，事之以珠玉而不受。狄人之所求者土地也。大王亶父曰：「與人之兄居而殺其弟，與人之父居而殺其子，吾不忍也。子皆勉居矣！為吾臣與為狄人臣奚以異！且吾聞之，不以所用養害所養。」因杖筴而去之。民相連而從之。遂成國於岐山之下。夫大王亶父，可謂能尊生矣。能尊生者，雖貴富不以養傷身，雖貧賤不以利累形。今世之人居高官尊爵者，皆重失之。見利輕亡其身，豈不惑哉！

越人三世弒其君，王子搜患之，逃乎丹穴。而越國無君，求王子搜不得，從之丹穴。王子搜不肯出，越人薰之以艾。乘以王輿。王子搜援綏登車，仰天而呼曰：「君乎！君乎！獨不可以舍我乎！」王子搜非惡為君也，惡為君之患也。若王子搜者，可謂不以國傷生矣，此固越人之所欲得為君也。

韓魏相與爭侵地。子華子見昭僖侯，昭僖侯有憂色。子華子曰：「今使天下書銘於君之前，

He then offered them pearls and jade, but these too they declined. What they wanted was the territory.

"To live with a man's elder brother," said T'ai Wang Shan Fu,

"and slay his younger brother; to live with a man's father and slay his son,—this I could not bear to do. Make shift to remain here. To be my subjects or the subjects of these savages, where is the difference? Besides I have heard say that we ought not to let that which is intended to nourish life become injurious to life."

Thereupon he took his staff and went off. His people all followed him, and they founded a new State at the foot of Mount Ch'i.

Now T'ai Wang Shan Fu undoubtedly had a proper respect for life. And those who have a proper respect for life, if rich and powerful, do not let that which should nourish injure the body. If poor and lowly, they do not allow gain to involve them in physical wear and tear.

But the men of the present generation who occupy positions of power and influence, are all afraid of losing what they have got. Directly they see a chance of gain, away goes all care for their bodies. Is not that a cause for confusion?

In three successive cases the people of Yueh had put their prince to death. Accordingly, Shou, the son of the last prince, was much alarmed, and fled to Tan Hsueh, leaving the State of Yueh without a ruler.

Shou was at first nowhere to be found, but at length he was traced to Tan Hsueh. He was, however, unwilling to come forth, so they smoked him out with moxa. They had a royal carriage ready for him; and as Shou seized the cord to mount the chariot, he looked up to heaven and cried, "Oh! ruling, ruling, could I not have been spared this?"

It was not that Shou objected to be a prince. He objected to the dangers associated with such positions. Such a one was incapable of sacrificing life to the State, and for that very reason the people of Yueh wanted to get him.

The States of Han and Wei were struggling to annex each other's territory when Tzu Hua Tzu went to see prince Chao Hsi. Finding the latter very downcast, Tzu Hua Tzu said, "Now suppose the representatives of the various States were to sign an agreement before your Highness, to the effect that although cutting off the left hand would involve loss of the right, while cutting off the right would involve loss of the left, nevertheless

書之言曰：『左手攫之則右手廢，右手攫之則左手廢。然而攫之者必有天下。』君能攫之乎？」昭僖侯曰：「寡人不攫也。」子華子曰：「甚善！自是觀之，兩臂重於天下也，身亦重於兩臂。韓之輕於天下亦遠矣，今之所爭者，其輕於韓又遠。君固愁身傷生以憂戚不得也！」僖侯曰：「善哉！教寡人者眾矣，未嘗得聞此言也。」子華子可謂知輕重矣。

　　魯君聞顏闔得道之人也，使人以幣先焉。顏闔守陋閭，苴布之衣而自飯牛。魯君之使者至，顏闔自對之。使者曰：「此顏闔之家與？」顏闔對曰：「此闔之家也。」使者致幣，顏闔曰：「恐聽者謬而遺使者罪，不若審之。」使者還，反審之，復來求之，則不得已。故若顏闔者，真惡富貴也。

that whosoever would cut off either should be emperor over all,—would your Highness cut?"

"I would not," replied the prince.

"Very good," said Tzu Hua Tzu. "It is clear therefore that one's two arms are worth more than the empire. And one's body is worth more than one's arms, while the State of Han is infinitely less important than the empire. Further, what you are struggling over is of infinitely less importance than the State of Han. Yet your Highness is wearing out body and soul alike in fear and anxiety lest you should not get it."

"Good indeed!" cried the prince. "Many have counselled me, but I have never heard the like of this."

From which we may infer that Tzu Hua Tzu knew the difference between what was of importance and what was not.

The prince of Lu, hearing that Yen Ho had attained to Tao, despatched messengers with presents to open communications.

Yen Ho lived in a hovel. He wore clothes of coarse grass, and occupied himself in tending oxen.

When the messengers arrived, Yen Ho went out to meet them; whereupon they enquired, "Is this where Yen Ho lives?"

"This is Yen Ho's house," replied the latter.

The messengers then produced the presents; but Yen Ho said, "I fear you have made a mistake. And as you might get into trouble, it would be as well to go back and make sure."

This the messengers accordingly did. When however they returned, there was no trace to be found of Yen Ho. Thus it is that men like Yen Ho hate wealth and power.

Wherefore it has been said that the best part of Tao is for self-culture, the surplus for governing a State, and the dregs for governing the empire. From which we may infer that the great deeds of kings and princes are but the leavings of the Sage. For preserving the body and nourishing vitality, they are of no avail. Yet the superior men of to-day endanger their bodies and throw away their lives in their greed for the things of this world. Is not this pitiable?

The true Sage in all his actions considers the why and the wherefore. But there are those now-a-days who use the pearl of the prince of Sui to shoot a bird a thousand yards off.

　　故曰：道之真以治身，其緒餘以為國家，其土苴以治天下。由此觀之，帝王之功，聖人之餘事也，非所以完身養生也。今世俗之君子，多危身棄生以殉物，豈不悲哉！凡聖人之動作也，必察其所以之與其所以為。今且有人於此，以隨侯之珠，彈千仞之雀，世必笑之。是何也？則其所用者重而所要者輕也。夫生者，豈特隨侯之重哉！

　　子列子窮，容貌有飢色。客有言之於鄭子陽者，曰：「列御寇，蓋有道之士也，居君之國而窮，君無乃為不好士乎？」鄭子陽即令官遺之粟。子列子見使者，再拜而辭。使者去，子列子入，其妻望之而拊心曰：「妾聞為有道者之妻子，皆得佚樂，今有飢色。君過而遺先生食，先生不受，豈不命邪。」子列子笑，謂之曰：「君非自知我也。以人之言而遺我粟，至其罪我也，又且以人之言，此吾所以不受也。」其卒，民果作難而殺子陽。

　　楚昭王失國，屠羊說走而從於昭王。昭王反國，將賞從者。及屠羊說。屠羊說曰：「大王失國，說失屠羊；大王反國，說亦反屠羊。臣之爵祿

And the world of course laughs at them. Why? Because they sacrifice the greater to get the less. But surely life is of more importance even than the prince's pearl!

Lieh Tzu was poor. His face wore a hungry look.

A visitor one day mentioned this to Tzu Yang of Cheng, saying, "Lieh Tzu is a scholar who has attained to Tao. He lives in your Excellency's State, and yet he is poor. Can it be said that your Excellency does not love scholars?"

Thereupon Tzu Yang gave orders that Lieh

Tzu should be supplied with food. But when Lieh Tzu saw the messengers, he bowed twice and declined.

When the messengers had gone, and Lieh Tzu went within, his wife gazed at him, and beating her breast said, "I have heard that the wife and children of a man of Tao are happy and joyful. But see how hungry I am. His Excellency sent you food, and you would not take it. Is not this flying in the face of Providence?"

"His Excellency did not know me personally," answered Lieh Tzu with a smile. "It was because of what others said about me that he sent me the food. If then men were to speak ill of me, he would also act upon it. For that reason I refused the food."

Subsequently, there was trouble among the people of Cheng, and Tzu Yang was slain.

When Prince Chao of the Ch'u State lost his kingdom, he was followed into exile by his butcher, named Yueh.

On his restoration, as he was distributing rewards to those who had remained faithful to him, he came to the name of Yueh.

Yueh, however, said, "When the prince lost his kingdom, I lost my butchery. Now that the prince has got back his kingdom, I have got back my butchery. I have recovered my office and salary. What need for further reward?"

On hearing this, the prince gave orders that he should be made to take his reward.

"It was not through my fault," argued Yueh, "that the prince lost his kingdom, and I should not have taken the punishment. Neither was it through me that he got it back, and I cannot therefore accept the reward."

When the prince heard this answer, he commanded Yueh to be

已復矣，又何賞之有！」王曰：「強之！」屠羊說曰：「大王失國，非臣之罪，故不敢伏其誅；大王反國，非臣之功，故不敢當其賞。」王曰：「見之。」屠羊說曰：「楚國之法，必有重賞大功而後得見。今臣之知不足以存國，而勇不足以死寇。吳軍入郢，說畏難而避寇，非故隨大王也。今大王欲廢法毀約而見說，此非臣之所以聞於天下也。」王謂司馬子綦曰：「屠羊說居處卑賤而陳義甚高，子綦為我延之以三旌之位。」屠羊說曰：「夫三旌之位，吾知其貴於屠羊之肆也；萬鍾之祿，吾知其富於屠羊之利也；然豈可以貪爵祿而使吾君有妄施之名乎！說不敢當，願復反吾屠羊之肆。」遂不受也。

brought before him. But Yueh said, "The laws of the Ch'u State require that a subject shall have deserved exceptionally well of his prince before being admitted to an audience. Now my wisdom was insufficient to preserve this kingdom, and my courage insufficient to destroy the invaders. When the Wu soldiers entered Ying, I feared for my life and fled. That was why I followed the prince. And if now the prince wishes to set law and custom aside and summon me to an audience, this is not my idea of proper behaviour on the part of the prince."

"Yueh," said the prince to Tzu Chi, his master of the horse, "occupies a lowly position; yet his principles are of the most lofty. Go, make him a San Ching."

"I am aware," replied Yueh to the master of the horse, "that the post of San Ching is more honourable than that of butcher. And I am aware that the emolument is larger than what I now receive. Still, because I want preferment and salary, I cannot let my prince earn the reputation of being injudicious in his patronage. I must beg to decline. Let me go back to my butchery."

And he adhered to his refusal.

Yuan Hsien dwelt in Lu,—in a mud hut, with a grass-grown roof, an apology for a door, and two mulberry-trees for door-posts. The windows which lighted his two rooms were no bigger than the mouth of a jar, and were closed by a wad of old clothes. The hut leaked from above and was damp under foot; yet Yuan Hsien sat gravely there playing on the guitar.

Tzu Kung came driving up in a fine chariot, in a white robe lined with purple; but the hood of the chariot was too big for the street.

When he went to see Yuan Hsien, the latter came to the door in a flowery cap, with his shoes down at heel, and leaning on a stalk.

"Good gracious!" cried Tzu Kung, "whatever is the matter with you?"

"I have heard," replied Yuan Hsien, "that he who is without wealth is called poor, and that he who learns without being able to practise is said to have something the matter with him. Now I am merely poor; I have nothing the matter with me."

Tzu Kung was much abashed at this reply; upon which Yuan Hsien smiling continued, "To try to thrust myself forward among men; to seek friendship in mutual flattery; to learn for the sake of others; to teach for my own sake; to use benevolence and duty to one's neighbour for evil ends;

原憲居魯，環堵之室，茨以生草；蓬戶不完，桑以為樞；而甕牖二室，褐以為塞；上漏下濕，匡坐而弦。子貢乘大馬，中紺而表素，軒車不容巷，往見原憲。原憲華冠縰履，杖藜而應門。子貢曰：「嘻！先生何病？」原憲應之曰：「憲聞之，無財謂之貧，學而不能行謂之病。今憲，貧也，非病也。」子貢逡巡而有愧色。原憲笑曰：「夫希世而行，比周而友，學以為人，教以為己，仁義之慝，輿馬之飾，憲不忍為也。」

曾子居衛，縕袍無表，顏色腫噲，手足胼胝，三日不舉火，十年不製衣。正冠而纓絕，捉衿而肘見，納屨而踵決。曳縰而歌《商頌》，聲滿天地，若出金石。天子不得臣，諸侯不得友。故養志者忘形，養形者忘利，致道者忘心矣。

to make a great show with horses and carriages,—these things I cannot do."

Tseng Tzu lived in the Wei State. His wadded coat had no outside cloth. His face was bloated and rough. His hands and feet were horny hard. For three days he had had no fire; no new clothes for ten years. If he set his cap straight the tassel would come off. If he drew up his sleeve his elbow would poke through. If he pulled up his shoe, the heel would come off. Yet slipshod he sang the Sacrificial Odes of Shang, his voice filling the whole sky, as though it had been some instrument of metal or stone.

The Son of Heaven could not secure him as a minister. The feudal princes could not secure him as a friend. For he who nourishes his purpose becomes oblivious of his body. He who nourishes his body becomes oblivious of gain. And he who has attained Tao becomes oblivious of his mind.

"Come hither," said Confucius to Yen Hui. "Your family is poor, and your position lowly. Why not go into official life?"

"I do not wish to," replied Yen Hui. "I have fifty acres of land beyond the city walls, which are enough to supply me with food. Ten more within the walls provide me with clothes. My lute gives me all the amusement I want; and the study of your doctrines keeps me happy enough. I do not desire to go into official life."

"Bravo! well said!" cried Confucius with beaming countenance. "I have heard say that those who are contented do not entangle themselves in the pursuit of gain. That those who have really obtained do not fear the contingency of loss. That those who devote themselves to cultivation of the inner man, though occupying no position, feel no shame. Thus indeed I have long preached. Only now, that I have seen Yen Hui, am I conscious of the realisation of these words."

Prince Mou of Chung-shan said to Chan Tzu, "My body is in the country, but my heart is in town. What am I to do?"

"Make life of paramount importance," answered Chan Tzu, "and worldly advantage will cease to have weight."

"That I know," replied the Prince; "but I am not equal to the task."

"If you are not equal to this," said Chan Tzu, "then it were well for you to pursue your natural bent. Not to be equal to a task, and yet to force oneself to stick to it,—this is called adding one injury to another. And those who suffer such two-fold injury do not belong to the class of the

　　孔子謂顏回曰：「回，來！家貧居卑，胡不仕乎？」顏回對曰：「不願仕。回有郭外之田五十畝，足以給饘粥；郭內之田十畝，足以為絲麻；鼓琴足以自娛；所學夫子之道者足以自樂也。回不願仕。」孔子愀然變容，曰：「善哉，回之意！丘聞之，『知足者，不以利自累也；審自得者，失之而不懼；行修於內者，無位而不怍。』丘誦之久矣，今於回而後見之，是丘之得也。」

　　中山公子牟謂瞻子曰：「身在江海之上，心居乎魏闕之下，奈何？」瞻子曰：「重生。重生則利輕。」中山公子牟曰：「雖知之，未能自勝也。」瞻子曰：「不能自勝則從，神無惡乎？不能自勝而強不從者，此之謂重傷。重傷之人，無壽類矣！」魏牟，萬乘之公子也，其隱巖穴也，難為於布衣之士；雖未至乎道，可謂有其意矣。

　　孔子窮於陳蔡之間，七日不火食，藜羹不糝，顏色甚憊，而弦歌於室。顏回擇菜，子路、子貢相與言曰：「夫子再逐於魯，削跡於衛，伐樹於宋，窮於商周，圍於陳蔡。殺夫子者無罪，藉夫子者無禁。弦歌鼓琴，未嘗絕音，君子之

long-lived."

Prince Mou of Wei was heir to the throne of a large State. For him to become a hermit among the hills was more difficult than for an ordinary cotton-clothed scholar. And although he had not attained to Tao, he may be said to have been on the way thither.

When Confucius was caught between the Ch'ens and the Ts'ais, he went seven days without proper food. He ate soup of herbs, having no rice. He looked very much exhausted, yet he sat within playing his guitar and singing to it.

Yen Hui was picking over the herbs, while Tzu Lu and Tzu Kung were talking together. One of them said, "Our Master has twice been driven out of Lu. They will have none of him in Wei. His tree was cut down in Sung. He got into trouble in Shang and Chou. And now he is surrounded by the Ch'ens and the Ts'ais. Whoever kills him is to be held guiltless. Whoever takes him prisoner is not to be interfered with. Yet all the time he goes on playing and singing without cease. Is this the right thing for a superior man to do?"

Yen Hui said nothing, but went inside and told Confucius, who laid aside his guitar and said with a loud sigh, "Yu and Tzu are ignorant fellows.

Bid them come, and I will speak to them."

When they entered Tzu Lu said, "We seem to have made a thorough failure."

"What do you mean?" cried Confucius. "The superior man who succeeds in Tao, has success. If he fails in Tao, he makes a failure. Now I, holding fast to the Tao of charity and duty towards one's neighbour, have fallen among the troubles of a disordered age. What failure is there in that?

"Therefore it is that by cultivation of the inner man there is no failure in Tao, and when danger comes there is no loss of virtue. It is the chill winter weather, it is frost, it is snow, which bring out the luxuriance of the pine and the fir.

I regard it as a positive blessing to be thus situated as I am."

Thereupon he turned abruptly round and went on playing and singing.

At this Tzu Lu hastily seized a shield and began dancing to the music, while Tzu Kung said, "I had no idea of the height of heaven and of the depth of earth."

無恥也若此乎？」顏回無以應，入告孔子。孔子推琴，喟然而嘆曰：「由與賜，細人也。召而來，吾語之。」子路、子貢入。子路曰：「如此者，可謂窮矣！」孔子曰：「是何言也！君子通於道之謂通，窮於道之謂窮。今丘抱仁義之道以遭亂世之患，其何窮之為！故內省而不窮於道，臨難而不失其德。天寒既至，霜雪既降，吾是以知松柏之茂也。陳蔡之隘，於丘其幸乎。」孔子削然反琴而弦歌，子路扢然執干而舞。子貢曰：「吾不知天之高也，地之下也。」古之得道者，窮亦樂，通亦樂，所樂非窮通也。道德於此，則窮通為寒暑風雨之序矣。故許由虞於穎陽，而共伯得乎共首。

舜以天下讓其友北人無擇，北人無擇曰：「異哉，后之為人也，居於畎畝之中，而遊堯之門！不若是而已，又欲以其辱行漫我，吾羞見之。」因自投清泠之淵。

湯將伐桀，因卞隨而謀，卞隨曰：「非吾事也。」湯曰：「孰可？」曰：「吾不知也。」湯又因瞀光而謀，瞀光曰：「非吾事也。」湯曰：「孰

The ancients who attained Tao were equally happy under success and failure. Their happiness had nothing to do with their failure or their success. Tao once attained, failure and success became mere links in a chain, like cold, heat, wind, and rain. Thus Hsu Yu enjoyed himself at Ying-yang, and Kung Poh found happiness on the hill-top.

Shun offered to resign the empire to his friend Pei Jen Wu Tse.

"What a strange manner of man you are!" cried the latter. "Living in the furrowed fields, you exchanged such a life for the throne of Yao. And as if that was not enough, you now try to heap indignity upon me. I am ashamed of you."

Thereupon he drowned himself in the waters of Ch'ing-ling.

When T'ang was about to attack Chieh, he went to consult with Pien Sui.

"It is not a matter in which I can help you," said the latter.

"Who can?" asked T'ang.

"I do not know," replied Pien Sui.

T'ang then went to consult with Wu Kuang.

"It is not a matter in which I can help you," said the latter.

"Who can?" asked T'ang.

"I do not know," replied Wu Kuang.

"What do you think of I Yin?" asked T'ang.

"He forces himself," said Wu Kuang, "to put up with obloquy. Beyond this I know nothing of him."

So T'ang took I Yin into his counsels. They attacked Chieh, and vanquished him.

Then T'ang offered to resign the empire in favour of Pien Sui. But Pien Sui declined, saying, "When your Majesty consulted with me about attacking Chieh, you evidently looked on me as a robber.

Now that you have vanquished him, and you offer to resign in my favour, you evidently regard me as covetous. I was born indeed in a disordered age. But for a man without Tao to thus insult me twice, is more than I can endure."

So he drowned himself in the river Chou.

Then T'ang offered to resign in favour of Wu Kuang, saying, "The wise plan, the brave execute, the good rest therein,—such was the Tao of the ancients. Why, Sir, should not you occupy the throne?"

可?」曰:「吾不知也。」湯曰:「伊尹何如?」曰:「強力忍垢,吾不知其他也。」湯遂與伊尹謀伐桀,克之,以讓卞隨。卞隨辭曰:「后之伐桀也謀乎我,必以我為賊也;勝桀而讓我,必以我為貪也。吾生乎亂世,而無道之人再來漫我以其辱行,吾不忍數聞也!」乃自投椆水而死。湯又讓瞀光,曰:「知者謀之,武者遂之,仁者居之,古之道也。吾子胡不立乎?」瞀光辭曰:「廢上,非義也;殺民,非仁也;人犯其難,我享其利,非廉也。吾聞之曰:『非其義者,不受其祿;無道之世,不踐其土。』況尊我乎!吾不忍久見也。」乃負石而自沈於廬水。

　　昔周之興,有士二人處於孤竹,曰伯夷、叔齊。二人相謂曰:「吾聞西方有人,似有道者,試往觀焉。」至於岐陽,武王聞之,使叔旦往見之。與之盟曰:「加富二等,就官一列。」血牲而埋之。二人相視而笑,曰:「嘻,異哉!此非吾所謂道也。昔者神農之有天下也,時祀盡敬而不祈喜;其於人也,忠信盡治而無求焉。樂與政為政,樂與治為治。不以人之壞自成也,不以人之卑自

But Wu Kuang declined, saying, "To depose a ruler is not to do one's duty to one's neighbour. To slay the people is not charity. For others to suffer these wrongs, while I enjoy the profits, is not honest. I have heard say that one should not accept a wage unless earned in accordance with right; and that if the world is without Tao, one should not put foot upon its soil, still less rule over it! I can bear this no longer."

Thereupon he took a stone on his back and jumped into the river Lu.

At the rise of the Chou dynasty there were two scholars, named Po I and Shu Ch'i, who lived in Ku-tu.

One of these said to the other, "I have heard that in the west there are men who are apparently in possession of Tao. Let us go and see them."

When they arrived at Ch'i-yang, Wu Wang heard of their arrival and sent Shu Tan to enter into a treaty with them. They were to receive emoluments of the second degree and rank of the first degree. The treaty was to be sealed with blood and buried.

At this the two looked at each other and smiled. "Ah!" said one of them, "this is strange indeed. It is not what we call Tao.

"When Shen Nung ruled the empire, he worshipped God without asking for any reward. Sometimes it was the law he put in force; sometimes it was his personal influence he brought to bear. He was loyal and faithful to his people without seeking any return. He did not build his success upon another's ruin, nor mount high by means of another's fall, nor seize opportunities to secure his own advantage.

"But now that the Chous, beholding the iniquities of the Yins, have taken upon themselves to govern, we have intrigues above and bribes below. Troops are mobilised to protect prestige. Victims are slaughtered to give good faith to a treaty. A show of virtue is made to amuse the masses. Fighting and slaughter are made the means of gain. Confusion has simply been exchanged for disorder.

高也，不以遭時自利也。今周見殷之亂而遽為政，上謀而下行貨，阻兵而保威，割牲而盟以為信，湯行以說眾，殺伐以要利。是推亂以易暴也。吾聞古之士，遭治世不避其任，遇亂世不為苟存。今天下闇，周德衰，其並乎周以塗吾身也，不如避之，以潔吾行。」二子北至於首陽之山，遂餓而死焉。若伯夷、叔齊者，其於富貴也，苟可得已，則必不賴。高節戾行，獨樂其志，不事於世。此二士之節也。

"I have heard tell that the men of old, living in quiet times, never shirked their duties; but lighting upon troublous times, nothing could make them stay. The empire is now in darkness. The virtue of the Chous has faded. For the empire to be united under the Chous would be a disgrace to us. Better flee away and keep our actions pure."

Accordingly, these two philosophers went north to Mount Shou-yang, where they subsequently starved themselves to death.

Men like Poh I and Shu Ch'i, if wealth and honour came to them so that they could properly accept, would assuredly not have recourse to such heroic measures, nor would they be content to follow their own bent, without giving their services to their generation. Such was the purity of these two scholars.

# 盜跖第二十九

　　孔子與柳下季為友，柳下季之弟，名曰盜跖。盜跖從卒九千人，橫行天下，侵暴諸侯。穴室樞戶，驅人牛馬，取人婦女。貪得忘親，不顧父母兄弟，不祭先祖。所過之邑，大國守城，小國入保，萬民苦之。孔子謂柳下季曰：「夫為人父者，必能詔其子；為人兄者，必能教其弟。若父不能詔其子，兄不能教其弟，則無貴父子兄弟之親矣。今先生，世之才士也，弟為盜跖，為天下害，而弗能教也，丘竊為先生羞之。丘請為先生往說之。」柳下季曰：「先生言為人父者必能詔其子，為人兄者必能教其弟，若子不聽父之詔，弟不受兄之教，雖今先生之辯，將奈之何哉！且跖之為人也，心如涌泉，意如飄風，強足以距敵，辯足以飾非。順其心則喜，逆其心則怒，易辱人以言。先生必無往。」孔子不聽，顏回為馭，子貢為右，往見盜跖。盜跖乃方休卒徒大山之陽，膾人肝而餔之。孔子下車而前，見謁者曰：「魯人孔丘，聞將軍高義，敬再拜謁

# CHAPTER XXIX

## ROBBER CHE

Confucius was on terms of friendship with Liu Hsia Chi, whose younger brother was known as "Robber Che."

Robber Che had a band of followers nine thousand strong. He ravaged the whole empire, plundering the various nobles and breaking into people's houses. He drove off oxen and horses. He stole men's wives and daughters. Family ties put no limit to his greed. He had no respect for parents nor for brothers. He neglected the worship of his ancestors. Wherever he passed, the greater States flew to arms, the smaller ones to places of safety. All the people were sore distressed.

"A father," said Confucius to Liu Hsia Chi, "should surely be able to admonish his son; an elder brother to teach his younger brother. If this be not so, there is an end of the value attached to these relationships.

"Now you, Sir, are one of the scholars of the age, while your younger brother is the Robber Che, the scourge of the empire. You are unable to teach him, and I blush for you. Let me go and have a talk with him on your behalf."

"As to what you say, Sir, about fathers and elder brothers," answered Liu Hsia Chi, "if the son will not listen to his father, nor the younger brother to his elder brother, what becomes of your arguments then?

"Besides, Che's passions are like a bubbling spring. His thoughts are like a whirlwind. He is strong enough to defy all foes. He can argue until wrong becomes right. If you follow his inclinations, he is pleased. If you oppose them he is angry. He is free with the language of abuse. Do not go near him."

Confucius paid no attention to this advice; but with Yen Hui as charioteer and Tzu Kung on his right, went off to see Robber Che.

The latter had just encamped to the south of T'ai-shan, and was engaged in devouring a dish of minced human liver. Confucius alighted from his chariot, and advancing addressed the doorkeeper as follows:—

"I am Confucius of the Lu State. I have heard of the high character of your captain."

He then twice respectfully saluted the doorkeeper, who went in to an-

者。」謁者入通。盜跖聞之大怒，目如明星，髮上指冠，曰：「此夫魯國之巧偽人孔丘非邪？為我告之：『爾作言造語，妄稱文、武，冠枝木之冠，帶死牛之脅，多辭繆說，不耕而食，不織而衣，搖唇鼓舌，擅生是非，以迷天下之主，使天下學士不反其本，妄作孝弟，而徼倖於封侯富貴者也。子之罪大極重，疾走歸！不然，我將以子肝益晝餔之膳。』

孔子復通曰：「丘得幸於季，愿望履幕下。」謁者復通。盜跖曰：使來前！」孔子趨而進，避席反走，再拜盜跖。盜跖大怒，兩展其足，案劍瞋目，聲如乳虎，曰：「丘來前！若所言，順吾意則生，逆吾心則死。」

孔子曰：「丘聞之，凡天下有三德：生而長大，美好無雙，少長貴賤見而皆說之，此上德也；知維天地，能辯諸物，此中德也；勇悍果敢，聚眾率兵，此下德也。凡人有此一德者，足以

nounce his arrival.

When Robber Che heard who it was, he was furious. His eyes glared like stars. His hair raised his cap from his head as he cried out, "What! that crafty scoundrel Confucius of Lu? Go, tell him from me that he is a mere word-mongerer. That he talks nonsense about Wen Wang and Wu Wang. That he wears an extravagant cap, with a thong from the side of a dead ox. That what he says is mostly rhodomontade. That he consumes where he does not sow, and wears clothes he does not weave. That his lips patter and his tongue wags. That his rights and wrongs are of his own coining, whereby he throws dust in the eyes of rulers and prevents the scholars of the empire from reverting to the original source of all things.

That he makes a great stir about filial piety and brotherly love, glad enough himself to secure some fat fief or post of power. Tell him that he deserves the worst, and that if he does not take himself off his liver shall be in my morning stew."

But Confucius sent in again, saying, "I am a friend of Liu Hsia Chi. I am anxious to set eyes upon your captain's shoe-strings."

When the doorkeeper gave this second message, Robber Che said, "Bring him before me!" Thereupon Confucius hurried in, and avoiding the place of honour stepped back and made two obeisances.

Robber Che, flaming with anger, straddled out his two legs, and laying his hand upon his sword glared at Confucius and roaring like a tigress with young, said, "Ch'iu! come here. If what you say suits my ideas, you will live. Otherwise you will die."

"I have heard," replied Confucius, "that the world contains three classes of virtue. To grow up tall, of a beauty without compare, and thus to be the idol of young and old, of noble and lowly alike,—this is the highest class. To be possessed of wisdom which embraces the universe and can explain all things,—this is the middle class. To be possessed of courage which will stand test and gather followers around,—this is the lowest class.

"Now any man whose virtue belongs to either of these classes is fit to occupy the place and title of ruler. But you, Captain, unite all three in yourself. You are eight feet two in height. Your expression is very bright. Your lips are like vermilion. Your teeth like a row of shells. Your voice is like a beautiful bell;—yet you are known as Robber Che. Captain, I blush

南面稱孤矣。今將軍兼此三者，身長八尺二寸，面目有光，脣如激丹，齒如齊貝，音中黃鐘，而名曰盜跖，丘竊為將軍恥不取焉。將軍有意聽臣，臣請南使吳越，北使齊魯，東使宋衛，西使晉楚，使為將軍造大城數百里，立數十萬戶之邑，尊將軍為諸侯，與天下更始，罷兵休卒，收養昆弟，共祭先祖。此聖人才士之行，而天下之願也。」

盜跖大怒曰：「丘來前！夫可規以利而可諫以言者，皆愚陋恆民之謂耳。今長大美好，人見而說之者，此吾父母之遺德也。丘雖不吾譽，吾獨不自知邪？且吾聞之，好面譽人者，亦好背而毀之。今丘告我以大城眾民，是欲規我以利而恆民畜我也，安可久長也！城之大者，莫大乎天下矣。堯、舜有天下，子孫無置錐之地；湯、武立為天子，而後世絕滅；非以其利大故邪？且吾聞之，古者禽獸多而人少，於是民皆巢居以避之。晝拾橡栗，暮栖木上，故命之曰『有巢氏之民』。古者民不知衣服，夏多積薪，冬則煬之，故命之曰『知生之民』。神農之世，臥則居居，

for you.

"Captain, if you will hearken to me I will go south for you to Wu and Yueh, north to Ch'i and Lu, east to Sung and Wei, and west to Chin and Ch'u. I will have a great wall built for you of many li in extent, enclosing hamlets of many hundreds of thousands of inhabitants, over which State you shall be ruler. Your relations with the empire will enter upon a new phase. You will disband your men. You will gather your brothers around you. You will join in worship of your ancestors. Such is the behaviour of the true Sage and the man of parts, and such is what the world desires."

"Ch'iu! come here," cried Robber Che in a great rage. "Those who are squared by offers and corrected by words are the stupid vulgar masses. The height and the beauty which you praise in me are legacies from my parents. Even though you did not praise them, do you think I should be ignorant of their existence? Besides, those who flatter to the face speak evil behind the back. Now all you have been saying about the great State and its numerous population simply means squaring me by offers as though one of the common herd. And of course it would not last.

"There is no State bigger than the empire. Yao and Shun both got this, yet their descendants have not territory enough to insert an awl's point. T'ang and Wu Wang both sat upon the Imperial throne, yet their posterity has been obliterated from the face of the earth.

Was not this because of the very magnitude of the prize?

"I have also heard that in olden times the birds and animals outnumbered man, and that the latter was obliged to seek his safety by building his domicile in trees. By day he picked up acorns and chestnuts. At night he slept upon a branch. Hence the name Nest-builders.

"Of old, the people did not know how to make clothes. In summer they collected quantities of fuel, and in winter warmed themselves by fire. Hence the name Provident.

"In the days of Shen Nung, they lay down without caring where they were and got up without caring whither they might go. A man knew his mother but not his father. He lived among the wild deer. He tilled the ground for food. He wove cloth to cover his body. He harboured no thought of injury to others. These were the glorious results of an age of perfect virtue.

"The Yellow Emperor, however, could not attain to this virtue. He

起則于于。民知其母，不知其父，與麋鹿共處，耕而食，織而衣，無有相害之心。此至德之隆也。然而黃帝不能致德，與蚩尤戰於涿鹿之野，流血百里。堯、舜作，立群臣；湯放其主，武王殺紂。自是之後，以強陵弱，以眾暴寡。湯、武以來，皆亂人之徒也。今子修文、武之道，掌天下之辯，以教後世。縫衣淺帶，矯言偽行，以迷惑天下之主，而欲求富貴焉，盜莫大於子。天下何故不謂子為盜丘，而乃謂我為盜跖？子以甘辭說子路而使從之，使子路去其危冠，解其長劍，而受教於子，天下皆曰：『孔丘能止暴禁非。』其卒之也，子路欲殺衛君而事不成，身菹於衛東門之上，是子教之不至也。子自謂才士聖人邪？則再逐於魯，削跡於衛，窮於齊，圍於陳蔡，不容身於天下。子教子路菹此患，上無以為身，下無以為人，子之道豈足貴邪？世之所高，莫若黃帝，黃帝尚不能全德，而戰於涿鹿之野，流血百里。堯不慈，舜不孝，禹偏枯，湯放其主，武王伐紂，文王拘羑里。此六子者，世之所高也。孰論之，皆以利惑其真而強反其

fought with Ch'ih Yu at Cho-lu, and blood flowed for a hundred li. Then came Yao and Shun with their crowd of ministers. Then T'ang who deposed his sovereign, and Wu Wang who slew Chou. After which time the strong took to oppressing the weak, the many to coercing the few. In fact, ever since T'ang and Wu Wang we have had none other than disturbers of the peace.

"And now you come forward preaching the old dogmas of Wen Wang and palming off sophistries without end, in order to teach future generations. You wear patched clothes and a narrow girdle, you talk big and act falsely, in order to deceive the rulers of the land, while all the time you yourself are aiming at wealth and power! You are the biggest thief I know of; and if the world calls me Robber Che, it most certainly ought to call you Robber Ch'iu.

"By fair words you enticed Tzu Lu to follow you. You made him doff his martial cap, and ungird his long sword, and sit a disciple at your feet. And all the world cried out that Confucius could stop violence and prevent wrong-doing. By and by, when Tzu Lu wished to slay the prince of Wei, but failed, and was himself hacked to pieces and exposed over the eastern gate of Wei,—that was because you had not properly instructed him.

"You call yourself a man of talent and a Sage forsooth! Twice you have been driven out of Lu. You were tabooed in Wei. You were a failure in Ch'i. You were surrounded by the Ch'ens and the Ts'ais. In fact, the empire won't have you anywhere. It was your teaching which brought Tzu Lu to his tragical end. You cannot take care, in the first place, of yourself, nor, in the second place, of others. Of what value can your doctrine be?

"There is none to whom mankind has accorded a higher place than to the Yellow Emperor. Yet his virtue was not complete. He fought at Cho-lu, and blood ran for a hundred li. Yao was not paternal.

Shun was not filial.

The great Yu was deficient in one respect.

T'ang deposed his sovereign. Wu Wang vanquished Chou. Wen Wang was imprisoned at Yin Li.

"Now these six worthies enjoy a high reputation among men. Yet a fuller investigation shows that in each case a desire for advantage disturbed their original purity and forced it into a contrary direction. Hence the shamelessness of their deeds.

情性，其行乃甚可羞也。世之所謂賢士：伯夷、叔齊。伯夷、叔齊辭孤竹之君，而餓死於首陽之山，骨肉不葬。鮑焦飾行非世，抱木而死。申徒狄諫而不聽，負石自投於河，為魚鱉所食。介子推至忠也，自割其股以食文公，文公後背之，子推怒而去，抱木而燔死。尾生與女子期於梁下，女子不來，水至不去，抱梁柱而死。此六子者，無異於磔犬流豕、操瓢而乞者，皆離名輕死，不念本養壽命者也。世之所謂忠臣者，莫若王子比干、伍子胥。子胥沉江，比干剖心，此二子者，世謂忠臣也，然卒為天下笑。自上觀之，至於子胥、比干，皆不足貴也。丘之所以說我者，若告我以鬼事，則我不能知也；若告我以人事者，不過此矣，皆吾所聞知也。今吾告子以人之情，目欲視色，耳欲聽聲，口欲察味，

"Among those whom the world calls virtuous were Poh I and Shu Ch'i. They declined the sovereignty of Ku-chu and died of starvation on Mount Shou-yang, their corpses deprived of burial.

"Pao Chiao made a great show of virtue and abused the world in general. He grasped a tree and died.

"Shen T'u Ti, when no heed was paid to his counsels, jumped into the river with a stone on his back and became food for fishes.

"Chieh Tzu T'ui was truly loyal. He cut a slice from his thigh to feed Wen Wang. Afterwards, when Wen Wang turned his back upon him, he retired in anger, and grasping a tree, was burnt to death.

"Wei Sheng made an assignation with a girl beneath a bridge. The girl did not come, and the water rose. But Wei Sheng would not leave. He grasped a buttress and died.

"These four differed in no way from dogs and pigs going about begging to be slaughtered. They all exaggerated reputation and disregarded death. They did not reflect upon their original nature and seek to preserve life into the old age allotted.

"Among ministers whom the world calls loyal, none can compare with Wang Tzu, Pi Kan, and Wu Tzu Hsu. The last-mentioned drowned himself. Pi Kan was disembowelled. These two worthies are what men call loyal ministers; yet, as a matter of fact, all the world laughs at them!

"Thus, from the most ancient times down to Tzu Hsu and Pi Kan, there have been none deserving of honour. And as to the sermon you, Ch'iu, propose to preach to me,—if it is on ghostly subjects, I shan't understand them, and if it is on human affairs, why there is nothing more to be said. I know it all already.

"I will now tell you a few things. The lust of the eye is for beauty. The lust of the ear is for music. The lust of the palate is for flavour. The lust of ambition is for gratification. Man's greatest age is one hundred years. A medium old age is eighty years. The lowest estimate is sixty years. Take away from this the hours of sickness, disease, death, mourning, sorrow, and trouble, and there will not remain more than four or five days a month upon which a man may open his mouth to laugh. Heaven and Earth are everlasting. Sooner or later every man has to die. That which thus has a limit, as compared with that which is everlasting, is a mere flash, like the passage of some swift steed seen through a crack. And those who cannot

志氣欲盈。人上壽百歲，中壽八十，下壽六十，除病瘦死喪憂患，其中開口而笑者，一月之中不過四五日而已矣。天與地無窮，人死者有時，操有時之具，而托於無窮之間，忽然無異騏驥之馳過隙也。不能說其志意、養其壽命者，皆非通道者也。丘之所言，皆吾之所棄也，亟去走歸，無復言之！子之道，狂狂汲汲，詐巧虛偽事也，非可以全真也，奚足論哉！」

孔子再拜趨走，出門上車，執轡三失，目芒然無見，色若死灰，據軾低頭，不能出氣。

歸到魯東門外，適遇柳下季。柳下季曰：「今者闕然，數日不見，車馬有行色，得微往見跖邪？」孔子仰天而嘆曰：「然！」柳下季曰：「跖得無逆汝意若前乎？」孔子曰：「然。丘所謂無病而自灸也。疾走料虎頭，編虎須，幾不免虎口哉！」

子張問於滿苟得曰：「盍不為行？無行則不信，不信則不任，不任則不利。故觀之名，計之利，而義真是也。若棄名利，反之於心，則夫士之為行，不可一日不為乎！」滿苟得曰：「無恥者富，多信者顯。夫名利之大者，幾在無恥

gratify their ambition and live through their allotted span, are men who have not attained to Tao.

"Ch'iu! all your teachings are nothing to me. Begone! Go home! Say no more! Your doctrine is a random jargon, full of falsity and deceit. It can never preserve the original purity of man. Why discuss it further?"

Confucius made two obeisances and hurriedly took his leave. On mounting his chariot, he three times missed hold of the reins. His eyes were so dazed that he could see nothing. His face was ashy pale. With down-cast head he grasped the bar of his chariot, unable to find vent for his feelings.

Arriving outside the eastern gate of Lu, he met Liu Hsia Chi, who said, "I have not seen you for some days. From the look of your equipage I should say you had been travelling. I guess now you have been to see Che."

Confucius looked up to heaven, and replied with a sigh, "I have."

"And did he not rebuff you," asked Liu Hsia Chi, "as I said he would?"

"He did," said Confucius. "I am a man who has cauterized himself without being ill. I hurried away to smooth the tiger's head and comb out his beard. And I very nearly got into the tiger's mouth."

Tzu Chang asked Man Kou Te, saying, "Why do you not practise virtue? Otherwise, it is impossible to inspire confidence. And without confidence, no place. And without place, no wealth. Thus, with a view to reputation or to wealth, duty towards one's neighbour is the true key.

If you were to discard all thoughts of reputation and wealth and attend to the cultivation of the heart, surely you would not pass one day without practising the higher virtues."

"Those who have no shame," replied Man Kou Te,

"grow rich. Those who inspire confidence make themselves conspicuous.

Reputation and wealth are mostly to be got out of shamelessness and confidence inspired. Thus, with a view to reputation or to wealth, the confidence of others is the true key.

If you were to discard all thoughts of reputation and wealth, surely the virtuous man would then have no scope beyond himself?"

"Of old," said Tzu Chang, "Chieh and Chou sat upon the Imperial throne, and the whole empire was theirs. Yet if you were now to tell any common thief that his moral qualities resembled theirs, he would resent it

而信。故觀之名，計之利，而信真是也。若棄名利，反之於心，則夫士之為行，抱其天乎！」子張曰：「昔者桀、紂貴為天子，富有天下。今謂臧聚曰：『汝行如桀、紂。』則有怍色，有不服之心者，小人所賤也。仲尼、墨翟，窮為匹夫，今謂宰相曰『子行如仲尼、墨翟。』則變容易色，稱不足者，士誠貴也。故勢為天子，未必貴也；窮為匹夫，未必賤也；貴賤之分，在行之美惡。」滿苟得曰：「小盜者拘，大盜者為諸侯，諸侯之門，仁義存焉。昔者桓公小白殺兄入嫂，而管仲為臣；田成子常殺君竊國，而孔子受幣。論則賤之，行則下之，則是言行之情悖戰於胸中也，不亦拂乎！故《書》曰：『孰惡孰美？成者為首，不成者為尾。』」子張曰：「子不為行，即將疏戚無倫，貴賤無義，長幼無序；五紀六位，將何以為別乎？」滿苟得曰：「堯殺長子，舜流母弟，疏戚有倫乎？湯放桀，武王殺紂，貴賤有義乎？王季為適，周公殺兄，長幼有序乎？儒者偽辭，墨子兼愛，五紀六位，將有別乎？且子正為名，我正為利。名利之實，不順於理，不監於道。吾日與子訟於

as an insult. By such miserable creatures are they despised."

"Confucius and Mih Tzu, on the other hand, were poor and simple enough. Yet if you were to tell any Prime Minister of to-day that his moral qualities resembled theirs, he would flush with pride and declare you were paying him too high a compliment. So truly honourable is the man of learning.

"Thus, the power of a monarch does not necessarily make him worthy; nor do poverty and a low station necessarily make a man unworthy. The worthy and the unworthy are differentiated by the worthiness and unworthiness of their acts."

"A petty thief," replied Man Kou Te, "is put in gaol. A great brigand becomes ruler of a State.

And among the retainers of the latter, men of virtue will be found.

"Of old, Duke Huan, named Hsiao Poh, slew his elder brother and took his sister-in-law to wife. Yet Kuan Chung became his minister.

"T'ien Ch'eng Tzu killed his prince and seized the kingdom. Yet Confucius accepted his pay.

"To condemn a man in words, yet actually to take service under him,—does not this show us practice and precept directly opposed to one another?

"Therefore it was written, 'Who is bad? Who is good? He who succeeds is the head. He who does not succeed is the tail.'"

"But if you do not practise virtue," said Tzu Chang, "and make no distinction between kith and kin, assign no duties to the worthy and to the unworthy, no precedence to young and old, how then are the Five Bonds and the Six Ranks to be distinguished?"

"Yao slew his eldest son," answered Man Kou Te. "Shun banished his mother's brother. Was there kith and kin in that?

"T'ang deposed Chieh. Wu Wang slew Chou.

Was that the duty of the worthy towards the unworthy?

"Wang Chi was the legitimate heir, but Chow Kung slew his elder brother. Was that precedence of young and old?

"The false principles of the Confucianists, the universal love of the Mihists,—do these help to distinguish the Five Bonds and the Six Ranks?

"You, Sir, are all for reputation. I am all for wealth. As to which pursuit is not in accordance with principle nor in harmony with right, let us

無約，曰『小人殉財，君子殉名，其所以變其精、易其性，則異矣；乃至於棄其所為而殉其所不為，則一也。』故曰：無為小人，反殉而天；無為君子，從天之理。若枉若直，相而天極；面觀四方，與時消息。若是若非，執而圓機；獨成而意，與道徘徊。無轉而行，無成而義，將失而所為。無赴而富，無徇而成，將棄而天。比干剖心，子胥抉眼，忠之禍也；直躬證父，尾生溺死，信之患也；鮑子立乾，申子不自理，廉之害也；孔子不見母，匡子不見父，義之失也。此上世之所傳、下世之所語，以為士者正其言，必其行，故服其殃，離其患也。」

refer to the arbitration of Wu Yoh."

"The mean man," said Wu Yoh, "devotes himself to wealth. The superior man devotes himself to reputation. The moral results are different in each case. But if both would set aside their activities and devote themselves to doing nothing, the results would be the same.

"Wherefore it has been said, 'Be not a mean man. Revert to your natural self. Be not a superior man. Abide by the laws of heaven.'

"As to the straight and the crooked, view them from the standpoint of the infinite.

Gaze around you on all sides, until time withdraws you from the scene.

"As to the right and the wrong, hold fast to your magic circle, and with independent mind walk ever in the way of Tao.

"Do not swerve from the path of virtue; do not bring about your own good deeds,—lest your labour be lost. Do not make for wealth; do not aim at success,—lest you cast away that which links you to God.

"Pi Kan was disembowelled. Tzu Hsu had his eyes gouged out.

Such was the fate of loyalty.

"Chih Kung bore witness against his father. Wei Sheng was drowned. Such are the misfortunes of the faithful.

"Pao Chiao dried up where he stood. Shen Tzu would not justify himself.

Such are the evils of honesty.

"Confucius did not visit his mother.

K'uang Tzu did not visit his father.

Such are the trials which come upon the upright.

"The above instances have been handed down to us from antiquity and are discussed in modern times. They show that men of learning emphasized their precepts by carrying them out in practice; and that consequently they paid the penalty and fell into these calamities."

Discontent asked Complacency, saying, "There is really no one who does not either aim at reputation or make for wealth. If a man is rich, others flock around him. These necessarily take a subordinate position, and consequently pay him court. And it would seem that such subordination and respect constitute a royal road to long life, comfort, and general happiness. How is it then that you, Sir, have no mind for these things? Is it that you are wanting in wit? Or is it that you are physically unable to compete,

　　無足問於知和曰：「人卒未有不興名就利者。彼富則人歸之，歸則下之，下則貴之。夫見下貴者，所以長生安體樂意之道也。今子獨無意焉，知不足邪，意知而力不能行邪，故推正不妄邪？」知和曰：「今夫此人，以為與己同時而生，同鄉而處者，以為夫絕俗過世之士焉；是專無主正，所以覽古今之時，是非之分也，與俗化世，去至重，棄至尊，以為其所為也。此其所以論長生安體樂意之道，不亦遠乎！慘怛之疾，恬愉之安，不監於體；怵惕之恐，欣懽之喜，不監於心；知為為而不知所以為，是以貴為天子，富有天下，而不免於患也。」無足曰：「夫富之於人，無所不利，窮美究勢，至人之所不得逮，賢人之所不能及，俠人之勇力而以為威強，秉人之知謀以為明察，因人之德以為賢良，非享國而嚴若君父。且夫聲色滋味權勢之於人，心不待學而樂之，體不待象而安之。夫欲惡避就，固不待師，此人之性也。天下雖非我，孰能辭之！」知和曰：「知者之為，故動以百姓，不違其度，是以足而不爭，無以為故不求。不足故求之，爭四處

and therefore go in for being virtuous, though all the time unable to forget?"

"You and your friends," replied Complacency, "regard all men as alike because they happen to be born at the same time and in the same place as yourselves. You look on us as scholars who have separated from humanity and cast off the world, and who have no guiding principle beyond poring over the records of the past and present, or indulging in the logomachy of this and that.

"Were we to lead the mundane lives you do, it would be at the sacrifice of the very conditions of existence. And surely thus we should be wandering far from the royal road to long life, comfort, and general happiness. The discomfort of wretch edness, the comfort of well-being, you do not refer to the body.

The abjectness of terror, the elation of joy, you do not refer to the mind itself. You know that such things are so, but you do not know how they are so. Wherefore, though equalling the Son of Heaven in power, and with all the empire as your personal property, you would not be free from care."

"Wealth," replied Discontent, "is of the greatest service to a man. It enables him to do good, and to exert power, to an extent which the perfect man or the true Sage could never reach. He can borrow the courage and strength of others to make himself formidable. He can employ the wisdom and counsels of others to add clearness to his own deliberations. He can avail himself of the virtue of others and cause it to appear as his own. Without being in possession of a throne, he can wield the authority of a prince.

"Besides, the pleasures of music, beauty, rich food, and power, do not require to be studied before they can be appreciated by the mind; nor does the body need the example of others before it can enjoy them. We need no teacher to tell us what to like or dislike, to follow or to avoid. Such knowledge is instinctive in man. The world may condemn this view, but which of us is free from the taint?"

"The wise man," answered Complacency, "acts for the common weal, in pursuit of which he does not overstep due limits. Wherefore, if there is a sufficiency, he does not strive for more. He has no use for more, and accordingly does not seek it. But if there is not a sufficiency, then he seeks

而不自以為貪；有餘故辭之，棄天下而不自以
為廉。廉貪之實，非以迫外也，反監之度。勢
為天子，而不以貴驕人；富有天下，而不以財
戲人。計其患，慮其反，以為害於性，故辭而
不受也，非以要名譽也。堯、舜為帝而雍，非
仁天下也，不以美害生；善卷、許由得帝而不受，
非虛辭讓也，不以事害己。此皆就其利、辭其害，
而天下稱賢焉，則可以有之，彼非以興名譽也。」
無足曰：「必持其名，苦體絕甘，約養以持生，
則亦久病長阨而不死者也。」知和曰：「平為福，
有餘為害者，物莫不然，而財其甚者也。今富
人，耳營鐘鼓筦籥之聲，口嗛於芻豢醪醴之味，
以感其意，遺忘其業，可謂亂矣；侅溺於馮氣，
若負重行而上阪，可謂苦矣；貪財而取慰，貪
權而取竭，靜居則溺，體澤則馮，可謂疾矣；

for more. He strives in all directions, yet does not account it greed. If there is a surplus, he declines it. Even though he refused the whole empire, he would not account it honesty. To him, honesty and greed are not conditions into which we are forced by outward circumstances, but characteristics innate in the individual. He may wield the power of the Son of Heaven, but will not employ it for the degradation of others. He may own the whole empire, yet will not use his wealth to take advantage of his fellows. But a calculation of the troubles and the anxieties inseparable therefrom, cause him to reject these as injurious to his nature, not from a desire for reputation.

"When Yao and Shun occupied the throne, there was peace. They did not try to be beneficent rulers. They did not inflict injury by doing good.

"Shan Chuan and Hsu Yu both declined the proffered throne. Theirs was no empty refusal. They would not cause injury to themselves.

"In all these cases, each individual adopted the profitable course in preference to the injurious course. And the world calls them virtuous, whereby they acquire a reputation at which they never aimed."

"It is necessary," argued Discontent, "to cling to reputation. If all pleasures are to be denied to the body and one's energies to be concentrated upon health with a view to the prolongation of life, such life would be itself nothing more than the prolonged illness of a confirmed invalid."

"Happiness," said Complacency, "is to be found in contentment. Too much is always a curse, most of all in wealth.

"The ears of the wealthy man ring with sounds of sweet music. His palate is cloyed with rich meats and wine. In the pursuit of pleasure, business is forgotten. This is confusion.

"He eats and drinks to excess, until his breathing is that of one carrying a heavy load up a hill. This is misery.

"He covets money to surround himself with comforts. He covets power to vanquish rivals. But his quiet hours are darkened by diabetes and dropsy. This is disease.

"Even when, in his desire for wealth, he has piled up an enormous fortune, he still goes on and cannot desist. This is shame.

"Having no use for the money he has collected, he still hugs it to him and cannot bear to part with it. His heart is inflamed, and he ever seeks to add more to the pile. This is unhappiness.

為欲富就利，故滿若堵耳而不知避，且馮而不舍，可謂辱矣；財積而無用，服膺而不舍，滿心戚醮，求益而不止，可謂憂矣；內則疑劫請之賊，外則畏寇盜之害，內周樓疏，外不敢獨行，可謂畏矣。此六者，天下之至害也，皆遺忘而不知察，及其患至，求盡性竭財，單以反一日之無故而不可得也。故觀之名則不見，求之利則不得。繚意絕體而爭此，不亦惑乎！」

"At home, he dreads the pest of the pilfering thief. Abroad, the danger of bandit and highwayman. So he keeps strict guard within, while never venturing alone without. This is fear.

"These six are the greatest of the world's curses. Yet such a man never bestows a thought upon them, until the hour of misfortune is at hand. Then, with his ambitions gratified, his natural powers exhausted, and nothing but wealth remaining, he would gladly obtain one day's peace, but cannot do so.

"Wherefore, if reputation is not to be enjoyed and wealth is not to be secured, how pitiable it is that men should harass their minds and wear out their bodies in such pursuits!"

# 說劍第三十

　　昔趙文王喜劍，劍士夾門而客三千餘人，日夜相擊於前，死傷者歲百餘人，好之不厭。如是三年，國衰，諸侯謀之。太子悝患之，募左右曰：「孰能說王之意止劍士者，賜之千金。」左右曰：「莊子當能。」太子乃使人以千金奉莊子。莊子弗受，與使者俱，往見太子，曰：「太子何以教周，賜周千金？」太子曰：「聞夫子明聖，謹奉千金以幣從者。夫子弗受，悝尚何敢言！」莊子曰：「聞太子所欲用周者，欲絕王之喜好也。使臣上說大王而逆王意，下不當太子，則身刑而死，周尚安所事金乎？使臣上說大王，下當太子，趙國何求而不得也！」太子曰：「然。吾王所見，唯劍士也。」莊子曰：「諾。周善為劍。」太子曰：「然吾王所見劍士，皆蓬頭突鬢，垂冠，曼胡之纓，短後之衣，瞋目而語難，王乃說之。今夫子必儒服而見王，事必大逆。」莊子曰：「請治劍服。」治劍服三日，乃見太子。太子乃與見王，王脫白刃待之。莊子入殿門不趨，見王不拜。王曰：「子欲何以教寡人，使太子先？」曰：「臣

# CHAPTER XXX

## ON SWORDS

Of old, Wen Wang of Chao loved sword-play. Swordsmen thronged his halls, to the number of three thousand and more. Day and night they had bouts before the prince. In the course of a year, a hundred or so would be killed or wounded. Yet the prince was never satisfied.

Within three years, the State had begun to go to rack and ruin, and other princes to form designs upon it. Thereupon the Heir Apparent, Li, became troubled in mind; and said to the officers of his household, "Whosoever shall persuade the prince to do away with these swordsmen, to him I will give a thousand ounces of silver."

To this his officers replied, "Chuang Tzu is the man."

Thereupon the Heir Apparent sent messengers to Chuang Tzu with a thousand ounces of silver, which he would not accept, but accompanied the messengers back to their master.

"What does your Highness require of me,"

asked Chuang Tzu, "that you should bestow upon me a thousand ounces?"

"I had heard," replied the young prince, "that you were a famous Sage, and I ventured to send this money as a present to your servants.

But as you would not receive it, what more can I say?"

"I understand," answered Chuang Tzu, "that your Highness would have me cure the prince of his peculiar weakness. Now suppose that I do not succeed with the prince, and consequently with your Highness, the punishment of death is what I have to expect. What good would the thousand ounces be to me then?"

"On the other hand, if I succeed with the prince, and consequently with your Highness, the whole State of Chao contains nothing I could not have for the asking."

"You must know, however," said the young prince, "that my father will only receive swordsmen."

"Well," replied Chuang Tzu, "I am a good swordsman myself."

"Besides which," added the Heir Apparent, "the swordsmen he is accustomed to see have all dishevelled hair hanging over their temples. They

聞大王喜劍，故以劍見王。」王曰：「子之劍何能禁制？」曰：「臣之劍，十步一人，千里不留行。」王大說，曰：「天下無敵矣！」莊子曰：「夫為劍者，示之以虛，開之以利，後之以發，先之以至。願得試之。」王曰：「夫子休，就舍待命，令設戲請夫子。」王乃校劍士七日，死傷者六十餘人，得五六人，使奉劍於殿下，乃召莊子。王曰：「今日試使士敦劍。」莊子曰：「望之久矣！」王曰：「夫子所御杖，長短何如？」曰：「臣之所奉皆可。然臣有三劍，唯王所用，請先言而後試。」

wear slouching caps with coarse tangled tassels, and short-tailed coats. They glare with their eyes and talk in a fierce tone. This is what my father likes. But if you go to him dressed in your ordinary scholar's dress, the result is sure to be disastrous."

"I will accustom myself to the dress," replied Chuang Tzu; and after practising for three days, he went again to see the young prince, who accompanied him into his father's presence.

The latter drew a sharp sword and awaited Chuang Tzu's approach. But Chuang Tzu, when he entered the door of the audience chamber, did not hurry forward, neither did he prostrate himself before the prince.

"What have you to say to me," cried the prince, "that you have obtained your introduction through the Heir Apparent?"

"I have heard," replied Chuang Tzu, "that your Highness loves sword-play. Therefore I have come to exhibit my skill."

"What can you do in that line?" asked the prince.

"Were I to meet an opponent," said Chuang Tzu, "at every ten paces, I could go on for a thousand li without being stopped."

"Bravo!" cried the prince. "There is not your match in the empire."

"When I fight," continued Chuang Tzu, "I make a show of being weak but push a vigorous attack. The last to start, I am the first to arrive. I should like your Highness to make trial of me."

"Rest awhile," replied the prince. "Stay here and await orders. I will arrange a day for you."

Thereupon the prince spent seven days in trying his swordsmen. Some sixty of them were either killed or wounded, but at length he selected five or six and bade them attend in the audience-chamber with their swords. He then summoned Chuang Tzu and said, "Now I will see what your swordsmanship is worth."

"I have been longing for this," replied Chuang Tzu.

"Does it matter to you," asked the prince, "of what length your weapon may be?"

"Not at all," replied Chuang Tzu. "I have three swords, of which I will ask your Highness to choose one. We will then proceed to the trial."

"Which are your three swords?" enquired the prince.

"There is the sword of the Son of Heaven," said Chuang Tzu, "the sword of the Princes, and the sword of the People."

　王曰：「願聞三劍。」曰：「有天子劍，有諸侯劍，有庶人劍。」王曰：「天子之劍何如？」曰：「天子之劍，以燕谿石城為鋒，齊岱為鍔，晉衛為脊，周宋為鐔，韓魏為夾；包以四夷，裹以四時；繞以渤海，帶以常山；制以五行，論以刑德；開以陰陽，持以春夏，行以秋冬。此劍，直之無前，舉之無上，案之無下，運之無旁，上決浮雲，下絕地紀。此劍一用，匡諸侯，天下服矣。此天子之劍也。　」文王芒然自失，曰：「諸侯之劍何如？」曰：「諸侯之劍，以知勇士為鋒，以清廉士為鍔，以賢良士為脊，以忠聖士為鐔，以豪傑士為夾。此劍，直之亦無前，舉之亦無上，案之亦無下，運之亦無旁；上法圓天，以順三光，下法方地，以順四時，中和民意，以安四鄉。此劍一用，如雷霆之震也，四封之內，無不賓服而聽從君命者矣。此諸侯之劍也。」王曰：「庶

"What is the sword of the Son of Heaven?" asked the prince.

"The stone wall of Yen-ch'i is its point," replied Chuang Tzu.

"The mountains of Ch'i are its edge. Chin and Wei are its back. Chou and Sung are its hilt. Han and Wei are its sheath. It is enclosed in the four hordes of barbarians, wrapped in the four seasons, surrounded by the great ocean. It is made of the five elements. It is the arbiter of punishment and reward. It operates under the influence of the Yin and the Yang. In spring and summer it is at rest. In autumn and winter it moves abroad. Push it, it does not advance. Raise it, it does not go up. Lower it, it does not go down. Whirl it around, it does not change position. Above, it cleaves the floating clouds; below, it cuts through the density of earth. One flash of this blade, and the princes of the empire submit. Such is the sword of the Son of Heaven."

At this the prince seemed absorbed in his reflections. Then he enquired, saying, "And what is the sword of the Princes?"

"The Wise and brave," replied Chuang Tzu, "are its point. The incorruptible are its edge. The virtuous are its back. The loyal are its hilt. The heroic are its sheath. You may push this sword too, it will not advance. Raise it, it will not go up. Lower it, it will not go down. Whirl it around, it will not change position. Above, it models itself upon the round heaven, in order to keep in harmony with the sun, moon, and stars. Below, it models itself upon the square earth, in order to keep in harmony with the four seasons. It adapts itself to the wishes of the people, in order to diffuse peace on all sides. One flash of this blade is like a roaring clap of thunder. Between the boundaries of the State there is not left one but who yields and obeys the command of his prince. Such is the sword of the Princes."

"And the sword of the People?" enquired the prince.

"The sword of the People," replied Chuang Tzu, "has dishevelled hair hanging over its temples. It wears a slouching cap with coarse tangled tassel, and a short-tailed coat. It glares with its eyes and talks in a fierce tone. When it engages in conflict, above, it cuts off head and neck; below, it smites liver and lungs. Such is the sword of the People. It is like a game-cock. One day, its life is cut short, and it is of no more use to the State.

"Now you, great prince, wield sovereign power, and yet you devote yourself to this sword of the People. I am truly ashamed of it."

Thereupon the prince drew Chuang Tzu up on to the dais, and the at-

人之劍何如？」曰：「庶人之劍，蓬頭突鬢，垂冠，曼胡之纓，短後之衣，瞋目而語難，相擊於前，上斬頸領，下決肝肺。此庶人之劍，無異於鬥雞，一旦命已絕矣，無所用於國事。今大王有天子之位而好庶人之劍，臣竊為大王薄之。」王乃牽而上殿。宰人上食，王三環之。莊子曰：「大王安坐定氣，劍事已畢奏矣！」於是文王不出宮三月，劍士皆服斃其處也。

tendants served food, the king three times assisting with his own hand.

"Be seated, great prince," said Chuang Tzu, "and compose your mind. I have said all I have to say on swords."

After this the prince did not quit his palace for three months, while the swordsmen, submitting to the new order of things, died in their own homes.

# 漁父第三十一

　　孔子遊乎緇帷之林，休坐乎杏壇之上。弟子讀書，孔子弦歌鼓琴。奏曲未半。有漁父者，下船而來，須眉交白，被髮揄袂，行原以上，距陸而止，左手據膝，右手持頤以聽。曲終而招子貢、子路，二人俱對。客指孔子曰：「彼何為者也？」子路對曰：「魯之君子也。」客問其族。子路對曰：「族孔氏。」客曰：「孔氏者何治也？」子路未應，子貢對曰：「孔氏者，性服忠信，身行仁義，飾禮樂，選人倫，上以忠於世主，下以化於齊民，將以利天下。此孔氏之所治也。」又問曰：「有土之君與？」子貢曰：「非也。」「侯王之佐與？」子貢曰：「非也。」客乃笑而還，行言曰：「仁則仁矣，恐不免其身；苦心勞形以危其真。嗚呼！遠哉，其分於道也！」

　　子貢還，報孔子。孔子推琴而起，曰：「其聖人與！」乃下求之，至於澤畔，方將杖拏而引其船，顧見孔子，還鄉而立。孔子反走，再拜而進。客曰：「子將何求？」孔子曰：「曩者先生有緒言而去，丘不肖，未知所謂，竊待於下

# CHAPTER XXXI

## THE OLD FISHERMAN

Confucius, travelling in the Black Forest, rested awhile at Apricot Altar. His disciples sat down to their books, and he himself played upon the
lute and sang.

Half way through the song, an old fisherman stepped out of a boat and
advanced towards them. His beard and eyebrows were snowy white. His
hair hung loose, and he flapped his long sleeves as he walked over the fore-
shore. Reaching firm ground, he stood still, and with left hand on his knee
and right hand to his ear, listened.

When the song was finished, he beckoned to Tzu Kung and Tzu Lu,
both of whom went to him. Then pointing with his finger, he enquired,
saying, "What is that man doing here?"

"He is the Sage of Lu," replied Tzu Lu.

"Of what clan?" asked the old man.

"Of the K'ung family," replied Tzu Lu.

"And what is his occupation?" said the old man.

"He devotes himself," replied Tzu Lu, "to loyalty and truth. He practises charity and duty towards his neighbour. He regulates ceremonies and
music. He distinguishes the relationships of man. He is loyal to his prince
above, a reformer of the masses below. Thus he will be of great service to
the whole empire. Such is his occupation."

"Is he a ruler of a State?" asked the old man.

"He is not," said Tzu Kung.

"A minister?" said the old man.

"No," said Tzu Kung.

Then the old man laughed and walked away, saying, "Charity is charity, yet I fear he will not escape the wear of mind and tear of body which
imperil the original purity of man. How far, alas, has he wandered from
the true path!"

Tzu Kung went back and told Confucius, who, laying aside his lute,
arose and said, "This man is a Sage!"

Thereupon he followed the old man down the shore, catching him up
just as he was drawing in his boat with his staff. Perceiving Confucius, the

風，幸聞咳唾之音，以卒相丘也！」客曰：「嘻！甚矣，子之好學也！」孔子再拜而起，曰：「丘少而修學，以至於今，六十九歲矣，無所得聞至教，敢不虛心！」客曰：「同類相從，同聲相應，固天之理也。吾請釋吾之所有而經子之所以。子之所以者，人事也。天子諸侯大夫庶人，此四者自正，治之美也；四者離位而亂莫大焉。官治其職，人憂其事，乃無所陵。故田荒室露，衣食不足，征賦不屬，妻妾不和，長少無序，庶人之憂也；能不勝任，官事不治，行不清白，群下荒怠，功美不有，爵祿不持，大夫之憂也；廷無忠臣，國家昏亂，工技不巧，貢職不美，春秋後倫，不順天子，諸侯之憂也；陰陽不和，寒暑不時，以傷庶物，諸侯暴亂，擅相攘伐，以殘民人，禮樂不節，財用窮匱，人倫不飭，百姓淫亂，天子有司之憂也。今子既上無君侯有司之勢，而下無大臣職事之官，而擅飾禮樂，選人倫，以化齊民，不泰多事乎？且人有八疵，事有四患，不可不察也。非其事而事之，謂之摠；莫之顧而進之，謂之佞；希意道言，謂之諂；

old man turned round to receive him, at which Confucius stepped back and prostrated himself twice before advancing.

"What do you want, Sir?" asked the fisherman.

"Just now, venerable Sir," replied Confucius, "you left without finishing your remarks. In my stupidity I cannot make out what you mean.

Therefore I have come in the humble hope of hearing any words with which you may deign to help me."

"Well," said the old man, "you are certainly anxious to learn."

At this Confucius prostrated himself twice, and when he got up said, "Yes, I have been a student from my youth upwards until now, the sixty-ninth year of my age. Yet I have never heard the true doctrine, which I am now ready to receive without bias."

"Like species follow like," answered the old man. "Like sounds respond to like.

This is a law of nature. I will now with your leave apply what I know to what you occupy yourself with,—the affairs of men.

"The Son of Heaven, the princes, the ministers, and the people,—if these four fulfil their proper functions, the result is good government. If they quit their proper places, the result is unutterable confusion. When the officials mind their duties and the people their business, neither is injured by the other.

"Barren land, leaky roofs, want of food and clothing, inability to meet taxation, quarrels of wives and concubines, no precedence between young and old,—such are the sorrows of the people.

"Capacity unequal to one's duties, and inability to carry on routine work, absence of clean-handed ness, and carelessness among subordinates, lack of distinction and want of preferment,—such are the sorrows of ministers.

"The Court without loyal ministers and the State in rebellion, the artisan unskilful and the tribute unsatisfactory, the periodical levees unattended and the Son of Heaven displeased,—such are the sorrows of the princes.

"The two great principles of nature working inharmoniously, heat and cold coming at irregular seasons so that men and things suffer, the princes rebellious and fighting among themselves so that the people perish, music and ceremonies ill regulated, wealth dissipated, the relationships of man

不擇是非而言，謂之諛；好言人之惡，謂之讒；析交離親，謂之賊；稱譽詐偽以敗惡人，謂之慝；不擇善否，兩容頰適，偷拔其所欲，謂之險。此八疵者，外以亂人，內以傷身，君子不友，明君不臣。所謂四患者：好經大事，變更易常，以挂功名，謂之叨；專知擅事，侵人自用，謂之貪；見過不更，聞諫愈甚，謂之很；人同於己則可，不同於己，雖善不善，謂之矜。此四患也。能去八疵，無行四患，而始可教已。

disregarded, the masses sunk in immorality,—such are the sorrows which fall to the share of the Son of Heaven.

"But now you, Sir, occupying neither the more exalted position of ruler nor performing the subordinate functions of minister, nevertheless take upon yourself to regulate music and ceremonies and to distinguish the relationships of man, in order to reform the masses. Are you not travelling out of your own sphere?

"Further, men have eight blemishes, and there are four things which obstruct business. These should be investigated.

"Meddling with matters which do not matter to you, is prying.

"To push one's way in, regardless of neglect, is to be forward.

"To adapt one's thoughts and arrange one's words, is sycophancy.

"To applaud a person, right or wrong, is flattery.

"To love speaking evil of others, is slander.

"To sever friendships and break ties, is mischievousness.

"To praise people falsely with a view to injure them, is malice.

"To give ready assent with a view to worm out the wishes of others, good and bad alike, is to be a hypocrite.

"These eight blemishes cause a man to throw others into confusion and bring injury upon himself. The superior man will not have him for a friend; the enlightened prince will not employ him as his minister.

"To love the conduct of great affairs, and to introduce change into established order with a view to gain reputation,—this is ambition.

"To strive to get all into one's own hands, and to usurp what should be at the disposal of others,—this is greed.

"To know one's faults but not to correct them, to receive admonition but only to plunge deeper,—this is obstinacy.

"To suffer those who are like oneself, but as for those unlike not to credit them with the virtues they really possess,—this is bigotry.

"Such are the four things which obstruct business. And only he who can put aside the above eight and abstain from the above four is fit for instruction."

At this Confucius heaved a sigh of distress. Then having twice prostrated himself, he arose and said, "Twice was I driven from Lu. I was tabooed in Wei. My tree was cut down in Sung. I was surrounded by the Ch'ens and the Ts'ais. I know not what my fault is that I should have suf-

孔子愀然而嘆，再拜而起，曰：「丘再逐於魯，削跡於衛，伐樹於宋，圍於陳蔡。丘不知所失，而離此四謗者何也？」客淒然變容曰：「甚矣，子之難悟也！人有畏影惡跡而去之走者，舉足愈數而跡愈多，走愈疾而影不離身，自以為尚遲，疾走不休，絕力而死。不知處陰以休影，處靜以息跡，愚亦甚矣！子審仁義之間，察同異之際，觀動靜之變，適受與之度，理好惡之情，和喜怒之節，而幾於不免矣。謹修而身，慎守其真，還以物與人，則無所累矣。今不修身而求之人，不亦外乎！」

孔子愀然曰：「請問何謂真？」客曰：「真者，精誠之至也。不精不誠，不能動人。故強哭者雖悲不哀，強怒者雖嚴不威，強親者雖笑不和。真悲無聲而哀，真怒未發而威，真親未笑而和。真在內者，神動於外，是所以貴真也。其用於人理也，事親則慈孝，事君則忠貞，飲酒則歡

fered these four persecutions."

"Dear me!" said the old man in a vexed tone, "How slow of perception you are.

"There was once a man who was so afraid of his shadow and so disliked his own footsteps that he determined to run away from them. But the oftener he raised his feet the more footsteps he made, and though he ran very hard his shadow never left him. From this he inferred that he went too slowly, and ran as hard as he could without resting, the consequence being that his strength broke down and he died. He was not aware that by going into the shade he would have got rid of his shadow, and that by keeping still he would have put an end to his footsteps. Fool that he was!

"Now you occupy yourself with charity and duty to one's neighbour. You examine into the distinction of like and unlike, the changes of motion and rest, the canons of giving and receiving, the emotions of love and hate, and the restraint of joy and anger. Yet you cannot avoid the calamities you speak of.

"Reverently care for your body. Carefully pre serve your natural purity. Leave externals to others. Then you will not be involved. But as it is, instead of improving yourself you are trying to improve other people. Surely this is dealing with the external."

"Then may I enquire," said Confucius in a tone of distress, "what is the original purity?"

"Our original purity," replied the fisherman, "is the perfection of truth unalloyed. Without this, we cannot influence others. Hence, those who weep to order, though they mourn, do not grieve. Those who assume anger, though violent, do not inspire awe. Those who affect friendship, though they smile, are not in unison."

"Real mourning grieves in silence. Real anger awes without expression. Real friendship is unison without the aid of smiles. Our emotions are dependent upon the original purity within; and accordingly we hold the latter in esteem.

"If applied to human affairs, then in serving our parents we are filial, in serving our prince we are loyal, in the banquet hour we are merry, in the hour of mourning we are sad.

"The object of loyalty is successful service; of a banquet, mirth; of

樂，處喪則悲哀。忠貞以功為主，飲酒以樂為主，處喪以哀為主，事親以適為主。功成之美，無一其跡矣；事親以適，不論所以矣；飲酒以樂，不選其具矣；處喪以哀，無問其禮矣。禮者，世俗之所為也；真者，所以受於天也，自然不可易也。故聖人法天貴真，不拘於俗。愚者反此。不能法天而恤於人，不知貴真，祿祿而受變於俗，故不足。惜哉，子之蚤湛於人偽而晚聞大道也！」

孔子再拜而起曰：「今者丘得遇也，若天幸然。先生不羞而比之服役，而身教之。敢問舍所在，請因受業而卒學大道。」客曰：「吾聞之，可與往者與之，至於妙道，不可與往者，不知其道，慎勿與之，身乃無咎。子勉之！吾去子矣，吾去子矣！」乃刺船而去，延緣葦閒。

顏淵還車，子路授綏，孔子不顧，待水波定，不聞拏音而後敢乘。子路旁車而問曰：「由得為役久矣，未嘗見夫子遇人如此其威也。萬乘之主，千乘之君，見夫子未嘗不分庭伉禮，夫子猶有倨敖之容。今漁父杖拏逆立，而夫子曲要磬折，言拜而應，得無太甚乎？門人皆怪夫子矣，漁

mourning, grief; of serving parents, gratifying their wishes. If the service is accomplished, it matters not that no trace remain.

If parents be gratified, it matters not how. If a banquet results in mirth, the accessories are of no importance. If there be real grief in mourning, it matters not what ceremonies may be employed.

"Ceremonial is the invention of man. Our original purity is given to us from God. It is as it is, and cannot be changed. Wherefore the true Sage models himself upon God, and holds his original purity in esteem. He is independent of human exigencies. Fools, however, reverse this. They cannot model themselves upon God, and have to fall back on man. They do not hold original purity in esteem. Consequently they are ever suffering the vicissitudes of mortality, and never reaching the goal. Alas! you, Sir, were early steeped in deceit, and are late in hearing the great doctrine."

Confucius, having again prostrated himself twice, arose and said,

"It has been a godsend to meet you, Sir, to-day. Pray allow me to follow you as your servant, that I may benefit by your teaching. I venture to ask where you live that I may enter upon my duties and learn the great doctrine."

"I have heard," replied the old man, "that if a man is a fit companion, one may travel with him into the uttermost depths of Tao. But that if he is not a fit companion, and does not know Tao, one must avoid his company, that no harm may befall. Excuse me, I must leave you." Thereupon he pushed off his boat, and disappeared among the reeds.

"Yen Yuan then brought up the chariot, and

Tzu Lu offered the hand-cord to Confucius. But the latter paid no attention. He waited until the ripples on the water had smoothed down and the sound of the punt-pole had died away, before he ventured to get up.

Tzu Lu, who was at the side of the chariot, enquired saying, "Master, I have been in your service now for a long time, yet never did I see you treat any man like this. In the presence of a ruler of ten thousand or a thousand chariots, I have never seen you treated other than with great respect, while you yourself would wear a haughty air. Yet before this old fisherman, leaning on his punt-pole, you cringe and bow and prostrate yourself twice before answering. Is not this too much? The disciples do not know what to make of it. Why this behaviour to an old fisherman?"

"Yu!" cried Confucius, resting on the bar of the chariot; "it is difficult

人何以得此乎 ？」孔子伏軾而嘆，曰：「甚矣，由之難化也！湛於禮義有間矣，而朴鄙之心至今未去。進，吾語汝：夫遇長不敬，失禮也；見賢不尊，不仁也。彼非至人，不能下人。下人不精，不得其真，故長傷身。惜哉！不仁之於人也，禍莫大焉，而由獨擅之。且道者，萬物之所由也，庶物失之者死，得之者生，為事逆之則敗，順之則成。故道之所在，聖人尊之。今之漁父之於道，可謂有矣，吾敢不敬乎！」

to make anything of you. You have long studied ceremonies and duty to your neighbour, yet you have not succeeded in getting rid of the old evil nature. Come here, and I will tell you.

"To meet an elder without respect is want of ceremony. To see a Sage and not to honour him, is not to be in charity with man. Unless you are in charity with man, you cannot humble yourself before a fellow-creature. And unless you can honestly do this, you can never attain to that state of original purity; but the body will constantly suffer. Alas! there is no greater evil than not to be in charity with man. Yet in such a plight, O Yu, are you.

"Further. Tao is the source of all creation. Men have it, and live. They lose it, and die. Affairs in antagonism thereto, fail; in accordance therewith, succeed. Therefore, wherever Tao abides, there is the reverence of the true Sage. And as this old fisherman may be said to possess Tao, could I venture not to respect him?"

# 列禦寇第三十二

列御寇之齊，中道而反，遇伯昏瞀人。伯昏瞀人曰：「奚方而反？」曰：「吾驚焉。」曰：「惡乎驚？」曰：「吾嘗食於十漿，而五漿先饋。」伯昏瞀人曰：「若是，則汝何為驚已？」曰：「夫內誠不解，形諜成光，以外鎮人心，使人輕乎貴老，而䪞其所患。夫漿人特為食羹之貨，無多餘之贏，其為利也薄，其為權也輕，而猶若是，而況於萬乘之主乎？身勞於國，而知盡於事，彼將任我以事，而效我以功。吾是以驚。」伯昏瞀人曰：「善哉觀乎！汝處已，人將保汝矣！」無幾何而往，則戶外之屨滿矣。伯昏瞀人北面而立，敦杖蹙之乎頤，立有間，不言而出。賓者以告列子，

# CHAPTER XXXII

## LIEH TZU

When Lieh Tzu went to Ch'i, half way there he turned round and came back. Falling in with Poh Hun Wu Jen, the latter said, "How is it you are so soon back again?"

"I was afraid," replied Lieh Tzu.

"Afraid of what?" asked Poh Hun Wu Jen.

"Out of ten restaurants at which I ate," said Lieh Tzu, "five would take no payment."

"And what is there to be afraid of in that?" enquired Poh Hun Wu Jen.

"The truth within not being duly assimilated," replied Lieh Tzu, "a certain brightness is visible externally. And to conquer men's hearts by force of the external is to induce in oneself a disregard for authority and age which is the precursor of trouble.

"A restaurant keeper is one who lives by retailing soup. When his returns are counted up, his profit is but small, and his influence is next to nothing. But if such a man could act thus, how much more the ruler of a large State? His bodily powers worn out in the duties of his position, his mental powers exhausted by details of administration, he would entrust me with the government and stimulate me by reward. That is what I was afraid of."

"Your inner lights are good," replied Poh Hun Wu Jen; "but if you remain stationary at this point, the world will still gather around you."

Shortly afterwards Poh Hun Wu Jen went to visit Lieh Tzu, and lo! his court-yard was filled with boots.

Poh Hun Wu Jen stood there awhile, facing the north, his cheek all wrinkled by resting it on his staff. Then, without a word, he departed.

Upon this being announced to Lieh Tzu, he seized his shoes and ran out barefoot.

When he reached the outer gate, he called aloud, "Master! now that you have come, will you not give me medicine?"

"It is all over!" cried Poh Hun Wu Jen. "I told you that the world would gather around you. It is not that you can make people gather around you. You cannot prevent them from doing so. Of what use would

列子提屨，跣而走，暨於門，曰：「先生既來，曾不發藥乎？」曰：「已矣，吾固告汝曰：人將保汝，果保汝矣！非汝能使人保汝，而汝不能使人無保汝也，而焉用之感豫出異也！必且有感，搖而本才，又無謂也。與汝游者，又莫汝告也。彼所小言，盡人毒也。莫覺莫悟，何相孰也！巧者勞而知者憂，無能者無所求，飽食而敖遊，汎若不繫之舟，虛而敖遊者也！」

鄭人緩也，呻吟裘氏之地。祇三年而緩為儒。河潤九里，澤及三族，使其弟墨。儒墨相與辯，其父助翟。十年而緩自殺。其父夢之曰：「使而子為墨者，予也，闔胡嘗視其良？既為秋柏之實矣？」夫造物者之報人也，不報其人而報其人之天，彼故使彼。夫人以己為有以異於人以賤其親，齊人之井飲者相捽也。故曰：今之世皆緩也。自是，有德者以不知也，而況有道者乎！古者謂之遁天之刑。聖人安其所安，不安其所不安；眾人安其所不安，不安其所安。

my instruction be? Exerting influence thus unduly over others, you are by them influenced in turn. You disturb your natural constitution, and are of no further account.

> None of your companions
> Warn you of this.
> Their paltry talk
> Is but poison to a man.
> They are not awake, not alive to the situation.
> How should one of these help you?

"The shrewd grow weary, the wise grieve. Those who are without abilities have no ambitions. With full bellies they roam happily about, like drifting boats, not caring whither they are bound."

There was a man of the Cheng State, named Huan. He pursued his studies at a place called Ch'iu-shih. After three years only, he had graduated as a Confucianist; and like a river which fertilises its banks to a distance of nine li, so did his good influence reach into three families.

He caused his younger brother to graduate as a Mihist. But inasmuch as in the question of Confucianism versus Mihism, the father took the side of the Mihist, at the end of ten years Huan committed suicide.

Then the father dreamed that Huan appeared to him and said, "It was I who caused your son to become a Mihist. Why give all the credit to him who is but as the fruit of an autumn pine?"

Verily God does not reward man for what he does, but for what he is.

And it was in this sense that the younger brother was caused to become a Mihist.

Whereas a man who should regard his distinctive abilities as of his own making, without reference to his parents, would be like the man of Ch'i who dug a well and then wanted to keep others away from it.

Hence the saying that the men of to-day are all Huans.

Wherefore it follows that men of true virtue are unconscious of its possession. How much more then the man of Tao? This is what the ancients called escaping the vengeance of God.

The true Sage rests in that which gives rest, and not in that which does not give rest. The world rests in that which does not give rest, and not in that which does give rest.

　莊子曰：「知道易，勿言難。知而不言，所以之天也；知而言之，所以之人也；古之人，天而不人。」

　朱泙漫學屠龍於支離益，單千金之家，三年技成而無所用其巧。

　聖人以必不必，故無兵；眾人以不必必之，故多兵。順於兵，故行有求。兵，恃之則亡。

　小夫之知，不離苞苴竿牘，敝精神乎蹇淺，而欲兼濟道物，太一形虛。若是者，迷惑於宇宙，形累不知太初。彼至人者，歸精神乎無始，而甘冥乎無何有之鄉。水流乎無形，發泄乎太清。悲哉乎！汝為知在毫毛，而不知大寧！

　宋人有曹商者，為宋王使秦。其往也，得車數乘；王說之，益車百乘。反於宋，見莊子，曰：「夫處窮閭阨巷，困窘織屨，槁項黃馘者，商之所短也；一悟萬乘之主而從車百乘者，商之所長也。」莊子曰：「秦王有病召醫，破癰潰痤者得車一乘，舐痔者得車五乘，所治愈下，得車愈多。子豈治其痔邪？何得車之多也？子行矣！」

Chuang Tzu said, "To know Tao is easy. The difficulty lies in the elimination of speech. To know Tao without speech appertains to the natural. To know Tao with speech appertains to the artificial. The men of old were natural, not artificial.

"Chu P'ing Man spent a large patrimony in learning under Chih Li I how to kill dragons.

By the end of three years he was perfect, but there was no direction in which he could show his skill.

"The true Sage regards certainties as uncertainties; therefore he is never up in arms.

Men in general regard uncertainties as certainties; therefore they are constantly up in arms. To accustom oneself to arms causes one to fly to arms on every provocation; and to trust to arms is to perish."

"The intelligence of the mean man does not rise beyond bribes and letters of recommendation. His mind is be-clouded with trivialities. Yet he would penetrate the mystery of Tao and of creation, and rise to participation in the One. The result is that he is confounded by time and space; and that trammelled by objective existences, he fails to reach apprehension of that age before anything was.

"But the perfect man,—he carries his mind back to the period before the beginning. Content to rest in the oblivion of nowhere, passing away like flowing water, he is merged in the clear depths of the infinite.

"Alas! man's knowledge reaches to the hair on a hair, but not to eternal peace."

A man of the Sung State, named Ts'ao Shang, acted as political agent for the prince of Sung at the court of the Ch'in State. When he went thither, he had a few carriages; but the prince of Ch'in was so pleased with him that he added one hundred more.

On his return to Sung, he visited Chuang Tzu and said, "As for living in poverty in a dirty hovel, earning a scanty subsistence by making sandals, with shrivelled face and yellow ears,—this I could not do. Interviewing a powerful ruler, with a retinue of a hundred carriages,—that is my forte."

"When the prince of Ch'in is sick," replied Chuang Tzu, "and he summons his physician to open a boil or cleanse an ulcer, the latter gets one carriage. The man who licks his piles gets five. The more degrading the work, the greater the number of carriages given. You, Sir, must have been

　　魯哀公問乎顏闔曰：「吾以仲尼為貞幹，國其有瘳乎？」曰：「殆哉圾乎仲尼！方且飾羽而畫，從事華辭，以支為旨，忍性以視民，而不知不信，受乎心，宰乎神，夫何足以上民！彼宜女與？予頤與？誤而可矣！今使民離實學偽，非所以視民也，為後世慮，不若休之。難治也！」

　　施於人而不忘，非天布也，商賈不齒，雖以事齒之，神者弗齒。

　　為外刑者，金與木也；為內刑者，動與過也。宵人之離外刑者，金木訊之；離內刑者，陰陽食之。夫免乎外內之刑者，唯真人能之。

　　孔子曰：「凡人心險於山川，難於知天。天猶有春秋冬夏旦暮之期，人者厚貌深情。故有貌愿而益，有長若不肖，有順懁而達，有堅而縵，有緩而釬。故其就義若渴者，其去義若熱。故君子遠使之而觀其忠，近使之而觀其敬，煩使之而觀其能，卒然問焉而觀其知，急與之期而觀其信，委之以財而觀其仁，告之以危而觀其節，醉之以酒而觀其側，雜之以處而觀其色。九徵至，不肖人得矣。」

attending to his piles to get so many carriages. Begone with you!"

Duke Ai of Lu asked Yen Ho, saying, "Were I to make Confucius a pillar of my realm, would the State be profited thereby?"

"It would be most perilous!" replied Yen Ho. "Confucius is a man of outward show and of specious words. He mistakes the branch for the root.

He seeks to impress the people by an overbearing demeanour, the hollowness of which he does not perceive. If he suits you, and you entrust him with the welfare of the State, it will only be by mistake that he will succeed.

"To cause the people to leave the true and study the false does not so much affect the people of to-day as those of coming generations. Wherefore it is better not to have Confucius.

"The difficulty of governing lies in the inability to practise self-effacement. Man does not govern as God does.

"Merchants and traders are altogether out of the pale.

Or if chance ever brings them within it, their rights are never freely admitted.

"External punishments are inflicted by metal and wood. Internal punishments are inflicted by anxiety and remorse. Fools who incur external punishment are treated with metal or wood. Those who incur internal punishment are devoured by the conflict of emotions. It is only the pure and perfect man who can succeed in avoiding both."

Confucius said, "The heart of man is more dangerous than mountains and rivers, more difficult to understand than Heaven itself. Heaven has its periods of spring, summer, autumn, winter, day time and night. Man has an impenetrable exterior, and his motives are inscrutable. Thus some men appear to be retiring when they are really forward. Others have abilities, yet appear to be worthless. Others are compliant, yet gain their ends. Others take a firm stand, yet yield the point. Others go slow, yet advance quickly.

"Those who fly to duty towards their neighbour as though thirsting after it, drop it as though something hot. Thus the loyalty of the superior man is tested by employing him at a distance, his respectfulness by employing him near at hand. His ability, by troublesome missions. His knowledge, by unexpected questions. His trustworthiness, by specification of time limits. His integrity by entrusting him with money. His fidelity, by

　　正考父一命而傴，再命而僂，三命而俯，循牆而走，孰敢不軌！如而夫者，一命而呂鉅，再命而於車上舞，三命而名諸父。孰協唐許！

　　賊莫大乎德有心而心有睫，及其有睫也而內視，內視而敗矣！

　　凶德有五，中德為首。何謂中德？中德也者，有以自好也而訾其所不為者也。

　　窮有八極，達有三必，形有六府。美、髯、長、大、壯、麗、勇、敢，八者俱過人也，因以是窮；緣循、偃仰、困畏不若人，三者俱通達。知慧外通，勇動多怨，仁義多責。達生之情者傀，達於知者肖；達大命者隨，達小命者遭。

　　人有見宋王者，錫車十乘。以其十乘驕稚莊子。莊子曰：「河上有家貧恃緯蕭而食者，其子沒於淵，得千金之珠。其父謂其子曰：『取石來鍛之！夫千金之珠，必在九重之淵而驪龍頷下，子能得珠者，必遭其睡也。使驪龍而寤，子尚奚微之有哉！』今宋國之深，非直九重之淵也；宋王之猛，非直驪龍也；子能得車者，必遭其睡也。使宋王而寤，子為齏粉夫。」

dangerous tasks. His decorum, by filling him with wine. His morality, by placing him in disreputable surroundings. Under the application of these nine tests, the inferior man stands revealed.

"Cheng K'ao Fu, on receiving his first appointment, bowed his head. On receiving his second appointment, he hunched his back. On receiving his third appointment, he fell upon his face, walking away at the side of the path.

Who would not try to be like him?

"Yet ordinary men, on their first appointment, become self-important. On their second, they give themselves airs in their chariots. On their third, they call their own fathers by their personal names.

Which of them can be compared with Hsu Yu of old?

"There is nothing more fatal than intentional virtue, when the mind looks outwards.

For by thus looking outwards, the power of introspection is destroyed.

"There are five sources of injury to virtue.

Of these, that which aims at virtue is the chief. What is it to aim at virtue? Why a man who aims at virtue practises what he approves and con-demns what he does not practise.

> Compounds for sins he feels inclined to
> By damning those he has no mind to.

"There are eight causes of failure, three certain elements of success. There are six sources of strength and weakness.

"Beauty, a long beard, size, height, robustness, grace, courage, dar-ing,—these eight, in which men surpass their fellows, are therefore pass-ports to failure.

"Modesty, compliance, humility,—these three are sure roads to suc-cess.

"Wisdom manifests itself in the external.

Courage makes itself many enemies. Charity and duty towards one's neighbour incur many reproaches.

"To him who can penetrate the mystery of life, all things are revealed. He who can estimate wisdom at its true value, is wise. He who compre-hends the Greater Destiny, becomes himself part of it.

He who comprehends the Lesser Destiny, resigns himself to the inevi-table."

　或聘於莊子，莊子應其使曰：「子見夫犧牛乎？衣以文繡，食以芻叔，及其牽而入於大廟，雖欲為孤犢，其可得乎！」

　莊子將死，弟子欲厚葬之。莊子曰：「吾以天地為棺槨，以日月為連璧，星辰為珠璣，萬物為齎送。吾葬具豈不備邪？何以加此！」弟子曰：「吾恐烏鳶之食夫子也。」莊子曰：「在上為烏鳶食，在下為螻蟻食，奪彼與此，何其偏也！」

　以不平平，其平也不平；以不徵徵，其徵也不徵。明者唯為之使，神者徵之。夫明之不勝神也久矣，而愚者恃其所見入於人，其功外也，不亦悲夫！

A man who had been to see the prince of Sung and had been presented with ten chariots, was putting on airs in the presence of Chuang Tzu.

"At Ho-Shang," said the latter, "there was a poor man who supported his family by plaiting rushes. One day his son dived into the river and got a pearl worth a thousand ounces of silver. The father bade him fetch a stone and smash it to pieces, explaining that he could only have got such a pearl very deep down from under the nose of the dragon, which must have been asleep. And he said he was afraid that when the dragon waked, the boy would have a poor chance.

"Now the State of Sung is deeper than a deep river, and the prince of Sung is fiercer than a dragon. To get these chariots, you must have caught him asleep. And when he wakes, you will be ground to powder."

Some prince having invited Chuang Tzu to enter his service, Chuang Tzu said in reply to the envoy, "Sir, have you ever noticed a sacrificial ox? It is bedecked with ribbons and fares sumptuously. But when it comes to be slaughtered for the temple, would it not gladly exchange places with some neglected calf?"

When Chuang Tzu was about to die, his disciples expressed a wish to give him a splendid funeral. But Chuang Tzu said, "With Heaven and Earth for my coffin and shell; with the sun, moon, and stars as my burial regalia; and with all creation to escort me to the grave,—are not my funeral paraphernalia ready to hand?"

"We fear," argued the disciples, "lest the carrion kite should eat the body of our Master"; to which Chuang Tzu replied, "Above ground I shall be food for kites; below I shall be food for mole-crickets and ants. Why rob one to feed the other?

"If you adopt, as absolute, a standard of evenness which is so only relatively, your results will not be absolutely even. If you adopt, as absolute, a criterion of right which is so only relatively, your results will not be absolutely right. Those who trust to their senses become slaves to objective existences. Those alone who are guided by their intuitions find the true standard. So far are the senses less reliable than the intuitions. Yet fools trust to their senses to know what is good for mankind, with alas! but external results."

# 天下第三十三

　　天下之治方術者多矣，皆以其有為不可加矣。古之所謂道術者，果惡乎在？曰：「無乎不在。」曰：「神何由降？明何由出？」「聖有所生，王有所成，皆原於一。」不離於宗，謂之天人；不離於精，謂之神人；不離於真，謂之至人。以天為宗，以德為本，以道為門，兆於變化，謂之聖人。以仁為恩，以義為理，以禮為行，以樂為和，薰然慈仁，謂之君子。以法為分，以名為表，以參為驗，以稽為決，其數一二三四是也，百官以此相齒，以事為常，以衣食為主，蕃息畜藏，老弱孤寡為意，皆有以養，民之理也。古之人其備乎！配神明，醇天地，育萬物，和天

# CHAPTER XXXIII

## THE EMPIRE

Systems of government are many. Each man thinks his own perfect. Where then does what the ancients called the system of Tao come in? There is nowhere where it does not come in.

It may be asked whence our spirituality, whence our intellectuality. The true Sage is born; the prince is made. Yet all proceed from an original One.

He who does not separate from the Source is one with God. He who does not separate from the essence is a spiritual man. He who does not separate from the reality is a perfect man. He who makes God the source, and Te the root, and Tao the portal, passively falling in with the modifications of his environment,—he is the true Sage.

He who practises charity as a kindness, duty to one's neighbour as a principle, ceremony as a convenience, music as a pacificator, and thus becomes compassionate and charitable,—he is a superior man.

He who regulates his conduct by law, who regards fame as an external adjunct, who verifies his hypotheses, who bases his judgment upon proof,—such men rank one, two, three, four, etc. It is thus that officials rank. In a strict sense of duty, in making food and raiment of paramount importance, in caring for and nourishing the old, the weak, the orphan, and the widow, they all exemplify the principle of true government.

Thus far-reaching was the extension of Tao among the ancients.

The companion of the gods, the purifier of the universe, it nourishes all creation, it unites the empire, it benefits the masses. Illuminating the fundamental, it is bound up with the accessory, reaching to all points of the compass and to the opposite extremes of magnitude. There is indeed nowhere where it is not!

How it enlightened the polity of past ages is evidenced in the records which historians have preserved to us. Its presence in the Canons of Poetry, History, Rites, and Music, has been made clear by many scholars of Chou and Lu. It in forms the Canon of Poetry with its vigour, the Canon of History with its usefulness, the Canon of Rites with its adaptability, the Canon of Music with its harmonising influence, the Canon of Chang-

下，澤及百姓，明於本數，係於末度，六通四辟，小大精粗，其運無乎不在。其明而在數度者，舊法、世傳之史尚多有之；其在於《詩》、《書》、《禮》、《樂》者，鄒魯之士、搢紳先生多能明之。《詩》以道志，《書》以道事，《禮》以道行，《樂》以道和，《易》以道陰陽，《春秋》以道名分。其數散於天下而設於中國者，百家之學時或稱而道之。

天下大亂，賢聖不明，道德不一。天下多得一察焉以自好。譬如耳目鼻口，皆有所明，不能相通。猶百家眾技也，皆有所長，時有所用。雖然，不該不遍，一曲之士也。判天地之美，析萬物之理，察古人之全，寡能備於天地之美，稱神明之容。是故內聖外王之道，闇而不明，鬱而不發，天下之人各為其所欲焉以自為方。悲夫！百家往而不反，必不合矣！後世之學者，不幸不見天地之純，古人之大體。道術將為天下裂。

不侈於後世，不靡於萬物，不暉於數度，以繩墨自矯，而備世之急。古之道術有在於是者。

es with its mysterious Principles, and the Spring and Autumn with its discriminations. Spread over the whole world, it is focussed in the Middle Kingdom, and the learning of all schools renders constant homage to its power.

But when the world is disorganised, true Sages do not manifest themselves, Tao ceases to exist as One, and the world becomes cognisant of the idiosyncrasies of the individual. These are like the senses of hearing, sight, smell, and taste,—not common to each organ. Or like the skill of various artisans,—each excellent of its kind and each useful in its turn, but not equally at the command of all.

Consequently, when a mere specialist comes forward and dogmatises on the beauty of the universe the principles which underlie all creation, the position occupied by the ancients in reference to the beauty of the universe, and the limits of the supernatural,—it follows that the Tao of inner wisdom and of outer strength is obscured and prevented from asserting itself. Every one alas! regards the course he prefers as the infallible course. The various schools diverge never to meet again; and posterity is debarred from viewing the original purity of the universe and the grandeur of the ancients. For the system of Tao is scattered in fragments over the face of the earth.

Not to covet posthumous fame, nor to aim at dazzling the world, nor to pose as a benefactor of mankind, but to be a strict self-disciplinarian while lenient to the faults of others,—herein lay the Tao of the ancients.

Mih Tzu and Ch'in Hua Li became enthusiastic followers of Tao, but they pushed the system too far, carrying their practice to excess. The former wrote an essay Against Music, and another which he entitled Economy.

There was to be no singing in life, no mourning after death. He taught universal love and beneficence towards one's fellow men, without contentions, without censure of others. He loved learning, but not in order to become different from others. Yet his views were not those of the ancient Sages, whose music and rites he set aside.

The Yellow Emperor gave us the Hsien-ch'ih. Yao gave us the Ta-chang. Shun, the Ta-shao. Yu, the Ta-hsia. T'ang, the Ta-hu. Wen Wang, the P'i-yung. Wu Wang and Chou Kung added the Wu.

The mourning ceremonial of old was according to the estate of each,

墨翟、禽滑厘聞其風而說之。為之大過，已之大順。作為《非樂》，命之曰《節用》；生不歌，死無服。墨子泛愛兼利而非鬥，其道不怒；又好學而博，不異，不與先王同，毀古之禮樂。黃帝有《咸池》，堯有《大章》，舜有《大韶》，禹有《大夏》，湯有《大濩》，文王有辟雍之樂，武王、周公作《武》。古之喪禮，貴賤有儀，上下有等，天子棺槨七重，諸侯五重，大夫三重，士再重。今墨子獨生不歌，死無服，桐棺三寸而無槨，以為法式。以此教人，恐不愛人；以此自行，固不愛己。未敗墨子道，雖然，歌而非歌，哭而非哭，樂而非樂，是果類乎？其生也勤，其死也薄，其道大觳；使人憂，使人悲，其行難為也。恐其不可以為聖人之道，反天下之心。天下不堪。墨子雖獨能任，奈天下何！離於天下，其去王也遠矣！墨子稱道曰：「昔者禹之湮洪水，決江河而通四夷九州也，名川三百，支川三千，小者無數。禹親自操橐耜而九雜天下之川；腓無胈，脛無毛，沐甚雨，櫛疾風，置萬國。禹大聖也，而形勞天下也如此。」使後世之墨者，

and determined in proportion to rank. Thus, the body of the Son of Heaven was enclosed in a seven-fold coffin. That of a feudal prince, in a five-fold coffin. That of a minister, in a three-fold coffin. That of a private individual, in a two-fold coffin. But now Mih Tzu would have no singing in life, no mourning after death, and a single coffin of only three inches in thickness as the rule for all alike!

Such doctrines do not illustrate his theory of universal love; neither does his practice of them establish the fact of his own personal self-respect. They may not suffice to destroy his system altogether; though it is unreasonable to prohibit singing, and weeping, and rejoicing in due season.

He would have men toil through life and hold death in contempt. But this teaching is altogether too unattractive. It would land mankind in sorrow and lamentation. It would be next to impossible as a practical system, and cannot, I fear, be regarded as the Tao of the true Sage. It would be diametrically opposed to human passions, and as such would not be tolerated by the world. Mih Tzu himself might be able to carry it out; but not the rest of the world. And when one separates from the rest of the world, his chances of developing an ideal State become small indeed.

Mih Tzu argued in favour of his system as follows:—Of old, the great Yu drained off the flood of waters, and caused rivers and streams to flow through the nine divisions of the empire and the parts adjacent thereto,— three hundred great rivers, three thousand branches, and streams without number. With his own hands he plied the bucket and dredger, in order to reduce confusion to uniformity, until his calves and shins had no hair left upon them. The wind bathed him, the rain combed him; but he marked out the nations of the world, and was in very truth a Sage. And because he thus sacrificed himself to the commonwealth, ages of Mihists to come would also wear short serge jackets and straw sandals, and toil day and night without stopping, making self-mortification their end and aim, and say to themselves, "If we cannot do this, we do not follow the Tao of Yu, and are unworthy to be called Mihists."

The disciples of Hsiang Li Ch'in, the followers of the five princes, Mihists of the south, such as K'u Huo, Chi Ch'ih, and Teng Ling,—all these studied the canon of Mih Tzu, but their disagreements and agreements were not identical. They called each other schismatics, and quarrelled over the "hard and white," the "like and unlike," and argued over questions of

多以裘褐為衣，以跂蹻為服，日夜不休，以自苦為極，曰：「不能如此，非禹之道也，不足謂墨。」相里勤之弟子，五侯之徒，南方之墨者若獲、已齒、鄧陵子之屬，俱誦《墨經》，而倍譎不同，相謂別墨；以堅白同異之辯相訾，以觭偶不仵之辭相應；以巨子為聖人。皆願為之尸，冀得為其後世，至今不決。墨翟、禽滑釐之意則是，其行則非也。將使後世之墨者，必以自苦腓無胈、脛無毛相進而已矣。亂之上也，治之下也。雖然，墨子真天下之好也。將求之不得也，雖枯槁不舍也，才士也夫！

不累於俗，不飾於物，不苟於人，不忮於眾，願天下之安寧以活民命，人我之養，畢足而止，以此白心。古之道術有在於是者。宋銒、尹文聞其風而說之。作為華山之冠以自表，接萬物以別宥為始；語心之容，命之曰「心之行」。以聏合歡，以調海內。請欲置之以為主。見侮不辱，救民之鬥，禁攻寢兵，救世之戰。以此周行天

"odd and even." Chu Tzu was their Sage, and they wanted to canonise him as a saint, that they might carry on his doctrines into after ages. Even now these differences are not settled.

Thus we see that Mih Tzu and Ch'in Hua Li, while right in theory, were wrong in practice. They would merely have taught mankind to vie with each other in working the hair off their calves and shins. The evil of that system would have predominated over the good. Nevertheless, Mih Tzu was undoubtedly a well-meaning man. In spite of failure, with all its withering influences, he stuck to his text. He may be called a man of genius.

Not to be involved in the mundane, not to indulge in the specious, not to be overreaching with the individual, nor antagonistic to the public; but to desire the tranquillity of the world in general with a view to the prolongation of life, to seek no more than sufficient for the requirements of oneself and others, and by such a course to purify the heart,—herein lay the Tao of the ancients.

Sung Hsing and Yin Wen became enthusiastic followers of Tao. They adopted a cap, shaped like the Hua Mountain, as a badge. They bore themselves with kindly discrimination towards all things. They spoke of the passive qualities of the heart as though they had been active; and declared that whosoever could bring joy among mankind and peace within the girdle of ocean should be made ruler over them.

They suffered obloquy without noticing the insult. They preserved the people from strife. They prohibited aggression and caused arms to lie unused. They saved their generation from wars, and carried their system over the whole empire, to the delight of the high and to the improvement of the lowly. Though the world would have none of them, yet they struggled on and would not give way. Hence it was said that when high and low became tired of seeing them, they intruded themselves by force. In spite of all this, they did too much for others, and too little for themselves.

"Give us," said they, "but five pints of rice, and it will be enough." The master could not thus eat his fill; but the disciples, although starving, did not forget the world's claims.

Day and night they toiled on, saying, "Must we necessarily live? Shall we ape the so-called saviours of mankind?"

"The superior man," they say, "is not a fault-finder. He does not ap-

下，上說下教。雖天下不取，強聒而不舍者也。故曰：上下見厭而強見也。雖然，其為人太多，其自為太少；曰：「請欲固置五升之飯足矣，先生恐不得飽，弟子雖飢，不忘天下。」日夜不休，曰：「我必得活哉！圖傲乎救世之士哉！」曰：「君子不為苛察，不以身假物。以為無益於天下者，明之不如已也。」以禁攻寢兵為外，以情欲寡淺為內。其小大精粗，其行適至是而止。

公而不黨，易而無私，決然無主，趣物而不兩，不顧於慮，不謀於知，於物無擇，與之俱往，古之道術有在於是者，彭蒙、田駢、慎到聞其風而說之。齊萬物以為首，曰：「天能覆之而不能載之，地能載之而不能覆之，大道能包之而不能辯之。」知萬物皆有所可，有所不可，故曰：「選則不遍，教則不至，道則無遺者矣。」是故慎到棄知去己，而緣不得已。泠汰於物，以為道理。曰：「知不知，將薄知而後鄰傷之者也。」謑髁無任，而笑天下之尚賢也；縱脫無行，而非天下之大聖；椎拍輐斷，與物宛轉；舍是與非，苟可以免。不師知慮，不知前後，魏然而已矣。

propriate the credit of others. He looks on one who does no good to the world as a worthless fellow. He regards prohibition of aggressive actions and causing arms to lie unused, as external; the diminution and restraint of our passions, as internal. In all matters, great or small, subtle or gross, such is the point to which he attains."

To be public-spirited and belong to no party, in one's dealings not to be all for self, to move without being bound to a given course, to take things as they come, to have no remorse for the past, no anxiety for the future, to have no partialities, but to be on good terms with all,—herein lay the Tao of the ancients.

P'eng Meng, T'ien P'ien, and Shen Tao, became enthusiastic followers of Tao. Their criterion was the identity of all things. "The sky," said they, "can cover but cannot support us. The earth can support but cannot cover us. Tao can embrace all things but cannot deal with particulars."

They knew that in creation all things had their possibilities and their impossibilities. Therefore they said, "Selection excludes universality. Training will not reach in all directions. But Tao is comprehensive."

Consequently, Shen Tao discarded all knowledge and self-interest and became a fatalist.

Passivity was his guiding principle. "For," said he, "we can only know that we know nothing, and a little knowledge is a dangerous thing.

"Take any worthless fellow who laughs at mankind for holding virtue in esteem, any unprincipled vagabond who reviles the great Sages of the world, and subject him to torture. In his agony he will sacrifice positive and negative alike. If he can but get free, he will trouble no more about knowledge and forethought. Past and future will cease to exist for him, in his then neutral condition.

"Move when pushed, come when dragged. Be like a whirling gale, like a feather in the wind, like a mill-stone going round. The mill-stone as an existence is perfectly harmless. In motion or at rest it does no more than is required, and cannot therefore incur blame.

"Why? Because it is simply an inanimate thing. It has no anxieties about itself. It is never entangled in the trammels of knowledge. In motion or at rest it is always governed by fixed laws, and therefore it never becomes open to praise. Hence it has been said, 'Be as though an inanimate thing, and there will be no use for Sages.'

推而後行，曳而後往，若飄風之還，若羽之旋，若磨石之隧，全而無非，動靜無過，未嘗有罪。是何故？夫無知之物，無建己之患，無用知之累，動靜不離於理，是以終身無譽。故曰：「至於若無知之物而已，無用賢聖，夫塊不失道。」豪傑相與笑之曰：「慎到之道，非生人之行，而至死人之理，適得怪焉。」田駢亦然，學於彭蒙，得不教焉。彭蒙之師曰：「古之道人，至於莫之是、莫之非而已矣。其風窢然，惡可而言？」常反人，不見觀，而不免於魭斷。其所謂道非道，而所言之韙不免於非。彭蒙、田駢、慎到不知道。雖然，概乎皆嘗有聞者也。

"For a clod cannot be without Tao,"—at which some full-blooded young buck covered the argument with ridicule by crying out, "Shen Tao's Tao is not for the living, but for the dead!"

It was the same with T'ien P'ien. He studied under P'eng Meng; with the result that he learnt nothing.

P'eng Meng's tutor said, "Those of old who knew Tao, reached the point where positive and negative ceased to exist. That was all."

Now the bent of these men is one of opposition, which it is difficult to discuss. They act in every way differently from other people, but cannot escape the imputation of purpose.

What they call Tao is not Tao; and what they predicate affirmatively cannot escape being negative. The fact is that P'eng Meng, T'ien P'ien, and Shen Tao, did not know Tao. Nevertheless they all had a certain acquaintance with it.

To make the root the essential, to regard objective existences as accidental, to look upon accumulation as deficiency, and to meekly accept the dispositions of Providence,—herein lay the Tao of the ancients.

Kuan Yin and Lao Tzu became enthusiastic followers of Tao.

They based their system upon nothingness, with One as their criterion. Their outward expression was gentleness and humility. Their inward belief was in unreality and avoidance of injury to all things.

Kuan Yin said, "Adopt no absolute position. Let externals take care of themselves. In motion, be like water. At rest, like a mirror.

Respond, like the echo.

Be subtle, as though non-existent. Be still, as though pure. Regard uniformity as peace. Look on gain as loss. Do not precede others. Follow them."

Lao Tzu said, "He who conscious of being strong, is content to be weak,—he shall be a cynosure of men.

"He who conscious of purity, puts up with disgrace,—he shall be the cynosure of mankind.

"He who when others strive to be first, contents himself with the lowest place, is said to accept the contumely of the world.

"He who when others strive for the substantial, contents himself with the unsubstantial, stores up nothing and therefore has abundance. There he is in the midst of his abundance which comes to him without effort on

以本為精，以物為粗，以有積為不足，淡然獨與神明居。古之道術有在於是者，關尹、老聃聞其風而說之，建之以常無有，主之以太一，以濡弱謙下為表，以空虛不毀萬物為實。關尹曰：「在己無居，形物自著。」其動若水，其靜若鏡，其應若響。芴乎若亡，寂乎若清。同焉者和，得焉者失。未嘗先人而常隨人。老聃曰：「知其雄，守其雌，為天下谿；知其白，守其辱，為天下谷。」人皆取先，己獨取後。曰：「受天下之垢」。人皆取實，己獨取虛，無藏也故有餘，巋然而有餘。其行身也，徐而不費，無為也而笑巧；人皆求福，己獨曲全，曰：「苟免於咎」。以深為根，以約為紀。曰：「堅則毀矣，銳則挫矣」。常寬容於物，不削於人，可謂至極。關尹、老聃乎！古之博大真人哉！

his part. He does nothing, and laughs at the artifices of others.

"He who when others strive for happiness is content with security, is said to aim at avoiding evil.

"He who makes depth of fundamental importance and moderation his rule of life, is said to crush that which is hard within him and temper that which is sharp.

"To be in liberal sympathy with all creation, and not to be aggressive towards one's fellow-men,—this may be called perfection."

O Kuan Yin! O Lao Tzu! verily ye were the true Sages of old.

Silence, formlessness, change, impermanence, now life, now death, heaven and earth blended in one, the soul departing, gone no one knows where: suddenly, no one knows whither, as all things go in turn, never to come back again;—herein lay the Tao of the ancients.

Chuang Tzu became an enthusiastic follower of Tao. In strange terms, in bold words, in far-reaching language, he gave free play to his thoughts, without following any particular school or committing himself to any particular line.

He looked on the world as so sunk in corruption that it was impossible to speak gravely. Therefore he employed "goblet words" which apply in various directions; he based his statements upon weighty authority in order to inspire confidence; and he put words in other people's mouths in order to secure breadth.

In accord with the spirit of the universe, he was at peace with all creation. He judged not the rights and wrongs of mankind, and thus lived quietly in his generation. Although his book is an extraordinary production, it is plausible and harmless enough. Although the style is most irregular, it is at the same time ingenious and attractive.

As a thinker, he is endlessly suggestive. Above, he roams with God. Below, he consorts with those who are beyond the pale of life and death, who deny a beginning and an end. In relation to the root, he speaks on a grand and extensive scale. In relation to Tao, he establishes a harmony between man and the higher powers. Nevertheless, he yields to the modifications of existence and responds to the exigencies of environment. His arguments are inexhaustible, and never illogical. He is far-reaching, mysterious, and not to be fully explored.

Hui Tzu was a man of many ideas. His works would fill five carts. But

芴漠無形，變化無常，死與生與？天地并與？神明往與？芒乎何之？忽乎何適？萬物畢羅，莫足以歸。古之道術有在於是者，莊周聞其風而悅之。以謬悠之說，荒唐之言，無端崖之辭，時恣縱而不儻，不以觭見之也。以天下為沈濁，不可與莊語。以卮言為曼衍，以重言為真，以寓言為廣。獨與天地精神往來，而不敖倪於萬物。不譴是非，以與世俗處。其書雖瑰瑋，而連犿無傷也。其辭雖參差，而諔詭可觀。彼其充實不可以已。上與造物者游，而下與外死生無終始者為友。其於本也，弘大而辟，深閎而肆；其於宗也，可謂稠適而上遂矣。雖然，其應於化而解於物也，其理不竭，其來不蛻，芒乎昧乎，未之盡者。

惠施多方，其書五車，其道舛駁，其言也不中。厤物之意，曰：「至大無外，謂之大一；至小無內，謂之小一。無厚，不可積也，其大千里。天與地卑，山與澤平。日方中方睨，物方生方死。大同而與小同異，此之謂‘小同異’；萬物畢同畢異，此之謂‘大同異’。南方無窮而有窮。今日適越

his doctrines are paradoxical, and his terms are used ambiguously.

He calls infinite greatness, beyond which there is nothing, the Greater One. He calls infinite smallness, within which there is nothing, the Lesser One.

He says that that which is without dimensions measures a thousand li.

That heaven and earth are equally low. That mountain and marsh are equally level.

That the sun at noon is the sun setting.

That when an animal is born, it dies.

That the likeness of things partly unlike is called the lesser likeness of unlikes. That the likeness of things altogether unlike is called the greater likeness of unlikes. That southwards there is no limit, and yet there is a limit. That one can reach Yueh to-day and yet be there before. That joined rings can be separated. That the middle of the world is north of Yen and south of Yueh.

That he loves all creation equally, just as heaven and earth are impartial to all.

Accordingly, Hui Tzu was regarded as a great philosopher and a very subtle dialectician; and became a favourite with the other dialecticians of the day.

He said that there were feathers in an egg.

That a fowl had three feet.

That Ying was the world.

That a dog could be a sheep. That a mare could lay eggs. That a nail has a tail.

That fire is not hot.

That mountains have mouths.

That wheels do not press down the ground.

That the eye does not see.

That the finger does not touch. That the uttermost extreme is not the end. That a tortoise is longer than a snake.

That a carpenter's square is not square.

That compasses will not make a circle.

That a round hole will not surround a square handle. That the shadow of a flying bird does not move. That there is a moment when a swiftly-flying arrow is neither moving nor at rest. That a dog is not a hound.

而昔來。連環可解也。我知天之中央，燕之北、越之南是也。泛愛萬物，天地一體也。」惠施以此為大，觀於天下而曉辯者，天下之辯者相與樂之。卵有毛，雞三足。郢有天下，犬可以為羊。馬有卵。丁子有尾。火不熱。山出口。輪不蹍地。目不見。指不至，至不絕。龜長於蛇。矩不方，規不可以為圓。鑿不圍枘。飛鳥之景未嘗動也。鏃矢之疾，而有不行不止之時。狗非犬。黃馬驪牛三。白狗黑。孤駒未嘗有母。一尺之捶，日取其半，萬世不竭。辯者以此與惠施相應，終身無窮。桓團、公孫龍辯者之徒，飾人之心，易人之意，能勝人之口，不能服人之心，辯者之囿也。惠施日以其知與之辯，特與天下之辯者為怪，此其柢也。然惠施之口談，自以為最賢，曰：「天地其壯乎，施存雄而無術。」南方有倚人焉曰黃繚，問天地所以不墜不陷，風雨雷霆之故。惠施不辭而應，不慮而對，遍為萬物說。

That a bay horse and a dun cow are three.

That a white dog is black.

That a motherless colt never had a mother.

That if you take a stick a foot long and every day cut it in half, you will never come to the end of it.

And such was the stuff which dialecticians used to argue about with Hui Tzu, also without ever getting to the end of it.

Huan T'uan and Kung Sun Lung were of this class. By specious premisses they imposed on people's minds and drove them into false conclusions. But though they won the battle in words, they did not carry conviction into their adversaries' hearts. Theirs were but the snares of the sophist.

Hui Tzu daily devoted his intelligence to such pursuits, purposely advancing some preposterous thesis upon which to dispute. That was his characteristic. He had besides a great opinion of his own wisdom, and used to say, "The universe does not hold my peer."

Hui Tzu makes a parade of his strength, but is devoid of any sound system. An eccentric fellow in the south, named Huang Liao, asked why the sky did not fall and the earth sink; also, whence came wind, rain, and thunder.

Hui Tzu was not backward in replying to these questions, which he answered unhesitatingly. He went into a long discussion on all creation, and talked away without end, though to himself he seemed to be saying very little. He supplemented this with most extraordinary statements, making it his chief object to contradict others, and being desirous of gaining fame by defeating all comers. Thus, he was never popular. Morally, he was weak; physically, he was violent. His was a dark and narrow way.

說而不休，多而無已，猶以為寡，益之以怪，以反人為實，而欲以勝人為名，是以與眾不適也。弱於德，強於物，其涂隩矣。由天地之道觀惠施之能，其猶一蚊一虻之勞者也。其於物也何庸！夫充一尚可，曰愈貴道，幾矣！惠施不能以此自寧，散於萬物而不厭，卒以善辯為名。惜乎！惠施之才，駘蕩而不得，逐萬物而不反，是窮響以聲，形與影競走也，悲夫！

Looked at from the point of view of the Tao of the universe, the value of Hui Tzu may be compared with the efforts of a mosquito or a gadfly. Of what use was he to the world? As a specialist, he might have succeeded. But to let him put himself forward as an exponent of Tao, would have been dangerous indeed.

He would not however be content to be a specialist. He must needs roam insatiably over all creation, though he only succeeded in securing the reputation of a sophist.

Alas for the talents of Hui Tzu! He is extravagantly energetic, and yet has no success. He investigates all creation, but does not conclude in Tao. He makes a noise to drown an echo. He is like a man running a race with his own shadow. Alas!

# DISCOVER MORE ANCIENT WISDOM

We invite you to discover another treasure of ancient Chinese wisdom:

"Tao Te Ching" by Lao Tzu

Ultimate Bilingual Edition (4-in-1)

Lao Tzu explores the fundamental nature of existence and living in accord with the Way. This special edition includes the complete text in:

- English
- Traditional Chinese
- Simplified Chinese
- Ancient Seal Script

This unique format lets you explore different translations and witness the evolution of Chinese writing. Whether you're interested in philosophy, language, or personal growth, Lao Tzu's timeless wisdom will speak to you just as powerfully as Sun Tzu's.

Join thousands of readers who have discovered the profound insights of the Tao Te Ching through this comprehensive edition.

Find your copy at major online bookstores.